PURITANS
AND YANKEES

THE WINTHROP DYNASTY
OF NEW ENGLAND

1630-1717

BY RICHARD S. DUNN

The Norton Library

W · W · NORTON & COMPANY · INC ·

NEW YORK

TO THE MEMORY OF W . P. D.

Preface

IN the tiny village of Groton, Suffolk, the curious visitor can find an ancient gray stone church, standing among tall grass and tombstones against the open, gently rolling fields. Groton Church is a characteristic East Anglian medieval parish church. Her stout pebble tower and walls have been gently weathered by 500 years of wind, rain, and occasional sun. Her interior blends perfect form with honest country workmanship. The stone arcades, plaster walls, and hammer-beam roof are chaste enough to suit a Puritan. Only the ugly Victorian stained glass East window obtrudes—a gift from America in 1875. This East window commemorates Groton's one famous man: John Winthrop, who left his Groton manor house in 1630 to go to New England as governor of the Massachusetts Bay Company. Winthrop's manor house has long since disappeared, and the village itself can scarcely be found on a modern road map. Groton Church remains, looking much as she did when John Winthrop was her patron, the proper starting point for a chronicle of the adventures of Winthrop and his children in the new world.

It is a long way from Groton, Suffolk, to Groton, Massachusetts, or Groton, Connecticut, but the Winthrops drew strength from the change of scene. Governor Winthrop consecrated his life to the task of carving a new society from the wilderness and founded a New England family dynasty which continued in active public life throughout the seventeenth century. From 1630 to 1717, four members of the family—John Winthrop, his gifted son John Winthrop, Jr., and his grandsons Fitz John and Wait Still Winthrop—served almost continuously as high public officers, and forty-five years as governors, of Massachusetts and Connecticut. By the third generation, the dynasty was in decay. Fitz John and Wait Still were conspicuously weaker men than their father and grandfather, pushed into political prominence by the revolutionary crisis which rocked New England at the close of the seventeenth century. With Wait Still's death in 1717, the dynasty abruptly ended. During the eighteenth century, the Winthrops suffered political and social eclipse; the only significant member of the family was Professor John Winthrop of Harvard. The first three generations make a natural unit, when the Winthrops were indisputably the first family of New England. Viewed collectively, the public careers of the four members of the dynasty—their programs, achievements, and failures—are our best index to New England's early development.[1]

There are two special attractions in studying this seventeenth-century Winthrop dynasty. First, the family epitomizes New England's gradual transformation from Puritan to Yankee. John Winthrop was a man of the Puritan Revolution, a singleminded crusader who established a Bible commonwealth in Massachusetts and battled every sinner and wayward saint who tried to challenge his plan. John Winthrop, Jr., was a man of the Restoration, cosmopolitan, tolerant, and worldly, charming and wily, an entrepreneur who practiced the new science and technology. Fitz John and Wait Still Winthrop were men of the Glorious Revolution, narrowly secular and parochial, half-humorous and half-ludicrous, uncertain of their values, and always chiefly absorbed with fashion, status and the accumulation of real estate. The deterioration from public to private interest is striking. The Winthrops lived in an increasingly complex, confused, materialistic, self-seeking society. Yet Fitz and Wait Winthrop inherited a strong pride in their local culture and became champions of New England's traditional religious and political system. No one family can mirror all aspects of a society in transition, but the seventeenth-century Winthrops do exemplify the most profound cultural development of their era, the secularization of the New England conscience.

A second reason for studying the dynasty is that all four

[1] For general discussion of social and family structure in seventeenth century New England, see Edmund S. Morgan, *The Puritan Family* (Boston, 1944), and Norman H. Dawes' unpublished dissertation, "Social Classes in Seventeenth-Century New England" (Harvard University, 1941). L. S. Mayo's sumptuous genealogical study, *The Winthrop Family in America* (Boston, 1948), contains pleasant and frankly eulogistic sketches of all the seventeenth-century Winthrops.

men were important in shaping New England's relations with the mother country. Throughout the seventeenth century, the Winthrops grappled with the problem of colonial dependency —how to preserve self-respect and individuality while taking orders from a distant source of power. The problem scarcely existed in the 1630's and 1640's, when John Winthrop, as governor of Massachusetts, was able to pursue a simple and consistent policy toward the home government. Armed with the royal charter of 1629, he defied regulation by either Charles I or Parliament, and achieved virtual independence from England. But in the 1660's and 1670's, as the English imperial system began to take shape, John Winthrop, Jr., adopted a much less belligerent attitude. He obtained a royal charter for Connecticut and accepted Charles II's regulation in order to preserve his colony's privileges. In the 1680's, Fitz John and Wait Still Winthrop betrayed their heritage by participating in James II's authoritarian Dominion of New England. Yet Wait Winthrop was a leader in the revolution of 1689 which overthrew the Dominion, while Fitz Winthrop saved the Connecticut charter in the 1690's, and as governor of the colony reverted to his grandfather's policy of resisting home supervision.

The purpose of this study is to explore the interaction of these two themes, to show how the Winthrops, as they changed from Puritan to Yankee, adjusted to the evolving problem of colonial dependency. Perhaps it is necessary to add that the purpose is *not* to provide a balanced family history or group biography. The first John Winthrop, the most important single member of the family, is treated more briefly than his son and grandsons. This is partly because the later Winthrops have received much less attention from previous historians, but mostly because the story gathers momentum generation by generation. John Winthrop presided over a small community shaped according to his strong and simple tastes, immune from outside interference. But John Winthrop, Jr., had to adjust to the increasing pettiness and provinciality of New England society and to the home government's active supervision. In the last years of the seventeenth century, the old Puritan verities and the old autonomy from England were both gone, and Fitz and

Preface

Wait Winthrop had to cope with unprecedented pressures. The era of the Glorious Revolution marked the gravest crisis for colonial New England society. There is a peculiar fascination to this dark time of troubles. Neither the Winthrop brothers nor any of the other third-generation New Englanders were heroic figures, and their behavior was generally petty and fumbling, yet in the end they achieved as much as the stronger men before them.

Many kind friends have helped me to write this book. Wesley Frank Craven of Princeton University not only supervised my doctoral dissertation on John Winthrop and John Winthrop, Jr., but has given invaluable advice on shaping the subject into its present form. My wife, Mary Maples Dunn of Bryn Mawr College, has worked closely on the final revision of the manuscript, to my very great benefit. Morton Keller of the University of Pennsylvania and Jacob M. Price of the University of Michigan have discussed numerous interpretive problems. Stephen Riley and Malcolm Freiberg of the Massachusetts Historical Society, and Miss R. Miriam Brokaw and Mrs. Gail M. Filion of the Princeton University Press, have likewise been extremely helpful. The Committee on the Advancement of Research at the University of Pennsylvania generously granted me research funds for this project. For my first and finest teacher, who accompanied and encouraged me at every stage but the last, I reserve a separate page.

Contents

Map p. viii: "Exact Mapp of New England and New York," from *Magnalia Christi americana: or, The ecclesiastical history of New-England, from its first planting in the year of Our Lord, 1698. By the Reverend and learned Cotton Mather* (London, Printed for T. Parkhurst, 1702).

The portraits of the Winthrops are based on drawings by the author.

BOOK ONE

❧

JOHN WINTHROP
1588-1649

1. *The Founder*

SEVERAL years after coming to America as the first governor of the Massachusetts Bay Colony, John Winthrop received a letter of encouragement from an old Suffolk neighbor, James Hopkins, vicar of Great Wenham. All plantations have hard beginnings, Hopkins wrote, yet "when thinges are come to some perfection, it delighteth people to looke backe to their founders, and they glorie in their worthie interprises . . . he that brake the ice never wantes his honour; soe shall it be with you, whoe could never have advanced your name by any worthy actions, as you are like to doe by this." Winthrop, he predicted, will become famous like Moses and Joshua for carrying God's people into a heathenish place and turning barren ground into "the fertilest land upon earth."[1] Hopkins' prophecy came true. All American schoolboys and many adults can identify John Winthrop as a Founding Father, the chief planter of early Massachusetts and the embodiment of first-generation New England Puritanism.

John Winthrop is very easy to caricature, yet not so easy to describe. Portraits show an austerely formidable man, with heavy jaw, wide forehead, long nose, and a masklike face stamped with bleak sobriety. Yet the full mouth and deep, brooding gaze express his strong passion and sensuality. Winthrop's manifold writings exhibit the same paradoxical range of qualities. He left a good many formal tracts on religious and political subjects, the work of a lawyer and amateur theologian, stilted, intricate, and crabbed. His private journals are packed with keen, disciplined observation, precise details, and staggering prejudices. In letters to his wife or dear friends, the man could speak in cadences of naked joy and rhapsody. He displayed admirable self-mastery, and a less attractive mastery

[1] Allyn B. Forbes, ed., *Winthrop Papers, 1498-1649* (5 vols.; Boston, 1929-1947), III, 105-106; hereafter referred to as *Winthrop Papers*. Abbreviations for all references are on p. 357.

over other people.[2] But the central point is plain enough: John Winthrop was the first American whose keen awareness of human inadequacy drove him to demand responsible action from himself and from all his fellow men. He was the first keeper of the New England conscience.

❧ VERY little in Winthrop's early life as a Suffolk squire pointed toward his emigration to America in 1630. He showed no interest in the sea or in travel and adventure. He did not invest in overseas trading or colonizing ventures. Rather, he pursued the conventional career of a young country gentleman. He was born in the Armada year of 1588. His father, Adam Winthrop, belonged to the newly risen Suffolk gentry; the family estate at Groton derived directly from Henry VIII's dissolution of the monasteries. Young Winthrop spent the requisite year or so at Trinity College, Cambridge, and married the requisite well-dowered bride. He studied the law at Gray's Inn, learned to manage his properties, and by 1618 succeeded his father as lord of Groton manor. He was appointed justice of the peace, and in 1627 secured a minor government place as attorney at the Court of Wards. Meanwhile, he was buffeted by domestic tragedy. His first wife died in 1615, after ten years of marriage. He soon remarried, but his second wife died after only a year. In 1618 he married a third time. Margaret Tyndal, a woman of very fine character, was to be his loving helpmate for nearly thirty years. By 1630 the Winthrops had a large family, seven sons and a daughter.

[2] Two recent books present radically opposed views of John Winthrop. According to Edmund S. Morgan's *The Puritan Dilemma: The Story of John Winthrop* (Boston, 1958), the key to Winthrop was his superb self-discipline and balance, the fruit of his intense religious experience, enabling him to embrace the sinful world in order to remake it (pp. 8-12, 31-32, 75-76). Anya Seton's *The Winthrop Woman* (Boston, 1958) makes him instead a self-righteous kill-joy, who crucified his rebellious little niece by publicly whipping her and making her kiss the whip, and then thirty years later on his deathbed, sentimentally acknowledged his error (pp. 30-31, 524). It is a sad commentary on the current taste for "history" that Morgan's compact and provocative biography has been vastly outsold by Seton's prolix and pretentious historical novel. *The Puritan Dilemma* is much the best introduction to Winthrop's life. R. C. Winthrop's *Life and Letters of John Winthrop* (2 vols.; Boston, 1864-1867), the only other serious biography, is an extensive but uncritical compilation of correspondence and extracts from the Governor's *Journal*.

The only exceptional aspect of Winthrop's early life was his Puritanism. Sometime in his youth he underwent a shattering conversion experience which enlisted him in service to the will of God. Even for that intensely religious age, Winthrop's zeal was notable: he poured his whole resources into scriptural study and prayer. His religion gave him a strong conviction of social responsibility. As Winthrop's latest biographer puts it, he had to learn to do right in a world that does wrong. At first he tried to gain spiritual comfort by fleeing all worldly temptation, but this was empty escapism. Hence he resolved in Miltonic fashion "that the life which is most exercised with tryalls and temptations is the sweetest, and will prove the safeste. For such tryalls as fall within compasse of our callinges, it is better to arme and withstande them than to avoide and shunne them."[3] Having taught himself to face corruption, he became a crusader, determined to remake the world as far as possible.

By the summer of 1629, when he was already more than forty years old, Winthrop's situation was unsatisfactory. He was in debt, his Groton estate was apparently not flourishing, he could not provide for his eldest sons, who were reaching their majority, and he either was dismissed or resigned from his post at the Court of Wards.[4] More important, he was becoming deeply dissatisfied with Charles I's religious and political policy. Some of the more vociferous Puritans in the House of Commons in the later 1620's were his close friends. Winthrop himself was considered for a seat in the 1626 Parliament. He lent moral support to his Suffolk friends who were imprisoned that year and the next for resisting the King's forced loan, and he anxiously watched Charles' final break with Parliament in 1629. "I am veryly perswaded," he wrote gloomily to his wife Margaret in May 1629, "God will bringe some heavye Affliction upon this lande, and that speedylye." He added significantly that if "the Lord seeth it wilbe good for us, he will provide a shelter and hidinge place for us and ours."[5]

---

[3] Morgan, *The Puritan Dilemma*, pp. 8-11.

[4] For Winthrop's references to his financial condition in 1628-1629, see *Winthrop Papers*, I, 379; II, 59-61, 67, 126. For the Court of Wards, see *ibid.*, II, 94, 99-100.

[5] *Ibid.*, I, 311, 317, 324-26, 336-37, 392; II, 75, 91-92.

John Winthrop

The Lord's hiding place was to be New England; His shelter was the royal charter of the Massachusetts Bay Company. Winthrop himself had no part in the genesis of this company. In 1628 a diversified group of merchants, gentry, and clergy had organized a company in order to plant a colony on the New England coast, to convert and trade with the Indians, and to explore other avenues of profit. In March 1629 they secured a royal charter which incorporated them as the Massachusetts Bay Company. This charter empowered the company members (or freemen) to meet in four annual General Courts, to pass laws, admit new members, and elect their officers, a governor, deputy governor, and eighteen assistants. The company could make laws and ordinances, settle necessary "formes and Ceremonies of Government and Magistracy," and "correct punishe pardon governe and rule" all inhabitants of the plantation, as long as nothing was done contrary to English laws.[6] The Massachusetts Bay Company was not specifically required to reside in England. Since about half of the charter members intended to emigrate to New England, Governor Matthew Craddock proposed to the company General Court in July 1629 that the colonists in Massachusetts should be self-governing and not subordinate to the company in England.

Only at this point did John Winthrop join the Massachusetts Bay Company. Within three months he was catapulted into the leadership of the organization. Probably in the late spring or early summer of 1629 he had drawn up several elaborate sets of reasons for and against emigrating to New England, to settle his own mind. These treatises were circulated in manuscript among fellow Puritan gentlemen such as John Hampden and Sir John Eliot. In one of them, "General Observations for the Plantation of New England," Winthrop told bluntly enough why he wanted to emigrate: "All other Churches of Europe are brought to desolation, and it cannot be, but the like Judgment is cominge upon us . . . .This lande growes wearye of her Inhabitantes, so as man which is the most pretious of all Creatures, is heere more vile and base, then the earth they

[6] M.H.S. *Proc.*, XII, 262, 268, 270.

treade upon. . . .We are growne to that height of Intemperance in all excesse of Ryot, as no mans estate all most will suffice to keep sayle with his equalls. . . .The fountains of learninge and Religion are so corrupted . . . that most Children even the best wittes and of fayrest hopes, are perverted corrupted and utterly overthrowne by the multitude of evill examples and the licentious government of those seminaryes."

If previous American plantations had mostly failed, Winthrop argued that it was because their design was "carnall and not religious," their colonists were "unfitt instrumentes," the scum of the land, and their style of government was inappropriate.[7] Winthrop's arguments evidently carried great weight. On August 29, 1629, he went to Cambridge and joined eleven others in pledging that he would move with his family to Massachusetts if the company government and charter were also transferred to America. This condition, more radical than Craddock's proposal, was accepted by the company three days later. Winthrop now actively participated in company business. On October 20 the freemen elected a new slate of officers to lead the projected migration and take the charter with them. Winthrop supplanted Craddock as governor of the Massachusetts Bay Company.[8] It was the major turning point of his life.

On the evening of that October election day, John Winthrop sat in his brother-in-law Emanuel Downing's house in Fleet Street, London, writing to his devoted Margaret back home in Suffolk. Only toward the end of the letter did he mention how the Lord has been pleased "to call me to a further trust in this business of the plantation, then either I expected or finde my selfe fitt for (beinge chosen by the Company to be their Governor) . . . . O: that he would give me an heart now to answer his goodness to me, and the expectation of his people! I never

[7] *Winthrop Papers*, II, 114-17.

[8] For a full discussion of the evolution of the Massachusetts Bay Company, compare C. M. Andrews, *The Colonial Period of American History* (4 vols.; New Haven, 1934-1938), I, 344-99; Frances Rose-Troup, *The Massachusetts Bay Company and Its Predecessors* (New York, 1930); Allen French, *Charles I and the Puritan Upheaval* (London, 1955), pp. 331-52. Rose-Troup contends that Winthrop and his fellow Puritans usurped control of the Company in 1629, an argument which Andrews softens and French rejects.

had more need of prayers, helpe me (deare wife) and lett us sett our heartes to seeke the Lorde, and cleave to him sincearly."

Winthrop's election *was* rather remarkable. Of the four men nominated for the governorship, he was neither the wealthiest nor socially the most prominent. He was the most recent member of the company. The freemen, however, were obviously more impressed by other considerations which made him the ideal man for the job: his grave, authoritative demeanor, his ability to grasp issues and formulate policy, his driving moral commitment. Indeed Winthrop himself tells us that "in all probabilitye, the wellfare of the plantation depends upon my assistance: for the maine pillers of it being gentlemen of highe qualitye, and eminent partes, bothe for wisdome and godlinesse, are determined to sitt still, if I deserte them."[9] Winthrop thus shouldered his task with full awareness of his responsibility to his fellow adventurers and of their indebtedness to him. He immediately proved the high quality of his leadership by the speed, energy, and efficiency with which men, supplies, and ships were assembled so that the Massachusetts Bay Company could move across the Atlantic in the spring of 1630.

Unquestionably, religion was the prime impetus for Winthrop's emigration to America. Worldly motives were strictly subordinate. To be sure, his estate in England was too narrow for his growing family. A severe agricultural depression, combined with the loss of his post at the Court of Wards, had cut his income in half. Yet the likelihood of his being able to recoup his fortune in America was small. For the middling yeoman or artisan who had little or no stake in England, there was valid economic incentive for emigrating to America, especially under the auspices of a large, strongly subsidized company. For the gentleman emigrant, however, who was subsidizing the company by selling his English property, it was a different story. Every Englishman who had so far invested heavily in American colonization had lost his money. Raleigh claimed to have sunk £40,000 in his Virginia voyages; Lord Baltimore had lost £30,000 on Avalon in Newfoundland; the

[9] *Winthrop Papers*, II, 125, 161.

8

members of the Virginia Company collectively lost about £100,-
000. By 1630, detached observers of English colonization could
not accept Hakluyt's earlier sense of exuberant Elizabethan
achievement. Samuel Purchas lamented: "povertie, sicknesse,
deaths, in so rich a Soyle, and healthfull a Climate; what should
I say? I can deplore, I doe not much admire, that we have had
so much in Virginia, and have so little."[10] Yet John Winthrop
put up for sale his chief English patrimony, the Groton estate
which he valued at £5,760, in order to help finance the fleet
of 1630. It was a terrible risk.

Glory was a stronger motive for Winthrop in 1630 than gold.
He could anticipate enjoying power in America, which he never
could have at home. And if Massachusetts succeeded, her governor would achieve a personal triumph. The central fact in
Winthrop's universe, however, was not his personal glory but
the sovereignty of God. Success in this world and salvation in
the next turned entirely upon God's regenerative grace. God's
covenant bound Winthrop to spend "the small remainder of
my tyme, to the best service of the Churche which I may." For
all his self-discipline and sober, shrewd realism, John Winthrop was first and foremost a fanatic. It was this devotion to
God's purpose which made him such a strong leader in 1630.

In years to come, the Puritan crusade would prove all too
successful; that was its tragedy in England and America alike.
It would destroy Charles I without creating a viable substitute.
It would establish in New England a new conformity which
narrowed and deadened the original Puritan ideal. The sense
of righteousness which possessed both Winthrop and Cromwell,
the belief that whatever strength they had was the Lord's
strength, would insensibly turn to self-righteousness as they
dared to forget the inscrutability of God's will. But in 1630
there was little enough room for self-righteousness. Puritanism
was on the attack, not on the defensive. Winthrop's rapturous

[10] Samuel Purchas, *Hakluytus Posthumus, or Purchas His Pilgrimes* (20 vols.;
Glasgow, 1905-1907), XIX, 171. For a fuller discussion of the English sense of
disappointment in America, see Richard S. Dunn, "Seventeenth-Century English
Historians of America," in J. M. Smith, ed., *Seventeenth-Century America: Essays on Colonial History* (Chapel Hill, 1959), pp. 206-208.

conviction that God was calling His chosen people to a new life made bearable the parting from family and friends. His farewell letters of 1630 achieved an exaltation which he never again recaptured:

"Now thou the hope of Israell, and the sure helpe of all that come to thee, knitt the heartes of thy servantes to thy selfe, in faith and puritye: . . . Carrye us into thy Garden, that we may eate and be filled with those pleasures, which the world knows not: let us heare that sweet voyce of thine, my love my dove, my undefiled . . . let us sleep in thine arms, and awake in thy kingdome: the soules of thy servantes, thus united to thee, make as one in the bonde of brotherly Affection: Let not distance weaken it, nor tyme waste it, nor change dissolve it, nor selfe love eate it out: but when all meanes of other Communion shall faile, let us delight to praye each for other: and so let thy unworthy servant prosper in the love of his friendes as he truly loves . . . and wishes true happiness to them and to all theirs. Amen."[11]

⟨R⟩ On Easter Monday 1630, as his ship stood off the Isle of Wight preparing to sail west, Winthrop began to keep a day-by-day *Journal*. It was a symbolic action. Being a crusader, he had no illusion that he could cleanse himself from sin by crossing from the old world to the new. Still, he did believe that God was giving him a second life, and the *Journal* is a record of his progress through this new life. Winthrop continued to keep his *Journal* until his final illness in 1649, explaining and justifying his conduct as leader of the new colony and doing battle with his rivals and critics. It remains the prime source for early Massachusetts history.

During the long and terrifying ocean crossing, Winthrop also composed a lay sermon, "A Modell of Christian Charity," in which he explained to his fellow passengers the nature of

---

[11] *Winthrop Papers*, II, 126, 206. Alan Simpson's *Puritanism in Old and New England* (Chicago, 1955) offers an attractive discussion of the evolution of the Puritan movement, on both sides of the Atlantic, from initial "holy violence under compression" to final bankruptcy.

their collective covenant with God. Winthrop pictured Massachusetts as a Company of Christ, bound together by love. Members of the company must bear one another's burdens and practice a conformity stricter and stronger than the external unity of the Church of England. Should the covenant be kept, "wee shall finde that the God of Israell is among us, when tenn of us shall be able to resist a thousand of our enemies, when hee shall make us a prayse and glory, that man shall say of succeeding plantacions: the lord make it like that of New England." If the covenant is not kept, what then? With a famous Biblical simile, Winthrop expressed his belief in the divine mission of Massachusetts: "we must Consider that wee shall be as a Citty upon a Hill, the eyes of all people are upon us; soe that if wee shall deale falsely with our god in this work wee have undertaken and so cause him to withdrawe his present help from us, wee shall be made a story and a by-word through the world."[12]

This image of a city upon a hill is often quoted; it epitomizes the cosmic scale of Winthrop's thinking and the militance of his temper in 1630. It dramatizes the manifold differences between the Massachusetts Puritans and the Pilgrims who had settled at Plymouth ten years before. The Pilgrims, openly separating from the English church, were a small, humble, and harmless band who wished to retreat to a remote corner where they could set up a true church undisturbed. The Puritans posed a direct challenge to the home government. They schemed to reform the English church from within; they had numbers, wealth and rank; and by colonizing America they were making no retreat. Rather, they were setting up a model of the kind of state they hoped to see soon in England. Charles I could scarcely avoid noticing this new rival, for a city upon a hill is a public place, conspicuous to all observers, godless as well as godly.

Winthrop was predisposed to believe that the Lord had especially selected New England for His plantation. Sailing along the Maine coast in June 1630, the Governor eagerly described

[12] *Winthrop Papers*, II, 293-95.

his first impression of the new land, his attitude doubtless colored by the fact that the company had spent more than seventy days on board ship. "We had now fair sunshine weather," he wrote, "and so pleasant a sweet air as did much refresh us, and there came a smell off the shore like the smell of a garden." Like a modern Noah he adds: "There came a wild pigeon into our ship, and another small land bird." The buoyant tone of enthusiasm continued in early letters back to his family still in England despite the personal catastrophe of his son Henry's drowning almost immediately after their landing. "The Country is exceeding good," he reported in July 1630, "and the climate verye like our owne." Differences did appear as he became more familiar with his surroundings. Repeated entries in the *Journal* tell of deep snow and bitter cold in the winter, violent heat in the summer, and storms in all seasons. To Winthrop this was all part of God's plan. His attitude was not governed by romance nor secular patriotism, but by evidences of providential favor to the Bay area. The Indians, for instance, for 300 miles around "are swept awaye by the small poxe, . . . So as God hathe hereby cleered our title to this place." Winthrop from the outset had no patience with people who complained about hardships or supposed that God really intended them to settle in a balmier climate like Virginia or the West Indies. In February 1631, as the ranks of the inadequately provisioned colonists were being decimated by the rigors of the first winter, he noted grimly in his *Journal*: "It hath been always observed here, that such as fell into discontent, and lingered after their former conditions in England, fell into the scurvy and died."[13]

Through the first four crucial years, from 1630 to 1634, Winthrop remained governor of the Massachusetts Bay Company. In these years he did his best work, getting the colony organized and operating. He found on arrival that the company's advance guard of colonists, sent over in 1628, were living at Salem, but a quick reconnaissance convinced him that the larger, protected harbor a few miles to the south would

[13] John Winthrop, *The History of New England from 1630 to 1649*, ed. James Savage (2 vols.; Boston, 1853), I, 27, 54; hereafter referred to as *Journal*. See also *Winthrop Papers*, II, 306-307, 320; III, 171-72.

make a far better headquarters. Accordingly, the 1,000 colonists who had come over with him in the great fleet of 1630 quickly grouped themselves into half a dozen little towns, ringing Boston harbor. The first winter killed many people. New arrivals soon replaced them, and year by year the colony grew. Winthrop himself lived at first in Charlestown, but within a few months he decided to build his town house in Boston, and Boston became the capital. Winthrop's servants meanwhile staked out his farm of 600 acres, called Ten Hills, on the Mystic River. In 1631 the Governor built a bark, *The Blessing of the Bay*, to promote coastal trading. Later he acquired Governor's Island in Boston harbor, and other tracts. Most of these holdings remained undeveloped, however, and Winthrop's living costs were higher than they had been in England. He certainly had not improved his private fortune by moving to America.

Under Winthrop's direction, the Massachusetts colonists quickly laid down the main lines of a church-state system completely at variance with the system they had left behind in England. Unfortunately, Winthrop had no leisure during the first year to record adequately what was done, let alone why or how it was done. We do know that the first question debated at the first meeting of company officers in Massachusetts was: how shall the clergy be maintained? Before Winthrop's arrival, the settlers at Salem had organized a church which was congregational in form, like the church of the separatist Pilgrims at Plymouth, and which baldly rejected the liturgy and external structure of the Church of England. Winthrop and his fellow immigrants of 1630 followed Salem's precedent. In each town, a select group of self-nominated settlers gathered themselves into a church and elected a minister. The Massachusetts colonists were divided into two classes, the church members and the non-church members. Winthrop and three other men formed the Charlestown church. They elected John Wilson as their minister, Winthrop explains, without "any intent that Mr. Wilson should renounce his ministry he received in England."[14]

[14] Perry Miller, *Orthodoxy in Massachusetts, 1630-1650* (Cambridge, Mass., 1933), p. 135; *Journal*, I, 36-39.

Nevertheless, the Massachusetts churches *were* renouncing, in substance if not in theory, the all-inclusive, episcopal, liturgical establishment in England.

Winthrop was particularly responsible for the political organization of Massachusetts. He managed to convert the institutions of a trading company into the institutions of a godly commonwealth. In London, he had been elected governor by the company freemen meeting in a General Court, but only a handful of these freemen accompanied him to America. Winthrop realized that the Massachusetts colonists would not submit willingly to perpetual rule by a dozen company members. To assure law and order in Massachusetts, some of the other colonists must be allowed to enter the company as freemen. Yet if Winthrop opened freemanship to any or all of the colonists, he faced the possibility that non-Puritans might seize control of the government. Winthrop's solution to this problem was to redefine the privileges of citizenship. In May 1631, 118 planters were admitted as freemen, but without the legislative power which the charter specified for freemen. The magistrates and freemen then voted that henceforth only church members would be accepted as freemen, thus barring a majority of the colonists from any share in government. From 1630 to 1634 the entire executive, legislative, and taxing authority was vested in Governor Winthrop and his board of assistants. The General Court met annually rather than four times a year, and the freemen's only function was to re-elect their officers. Certainly Winthrop was tampering very freely with the royal charter.[15]

To uphold the tight mutual covenant which he had preached in his "A Modell of Christian Charity," Governor Winthrop insisted upon the colonists' obedience to the authority of the Massachusetts Bay Company. Both freemen and non-freemen

[15] N. B. Shurtleff, ed., *Records of the Governor and Company of the Massachusetts Bay in New England, 1628-1686* (5 vols.; Boston, 1853-1854), I, 79, 87; hereafter referred to as *Mass. Rec.* Most historians would agree with Andrews (*Colonial Period*, I, 432-39) in censuring Winthrop for his restrictions on the rights and requirements of citizenship. Morgan emphasizes Winthrop's generosity in extending some measure of citizenship to persons who previously had had none at all (*Puritan Dilemma*, pp. 90-95), but his argument is not very convincing.

were required to swear an oath of loyalty to the Massachusetts government; the oath made no mention of allegiance to the King. Sinners and malcontents were treated unceremoniously. On his arrival, Winthrop discovered a prime sinner. Just south of Boston, Thomas Morton had established a bacchanalian headquarters (complete with maypole) at his plantation, Merrymount. In August 1630 Morton's revels were rudely ended. His house was burned down, and he was put in the stocks and shipped to England. In June 1631 Philip Ratcliffe was whipped and had both ears cut off for what Winthrop called his "most foule, scandalous invectives against our churches and government." At about the same time, Sir Christopher Gardiner was ordered banished on suspicion of two crimes, bigamy and Roman Catholicism. When Morton, Ratcliffe, and Gardiner carried their grievances to England, they raised a troublesome question. Could a disgruntled colonist appeal to the crown against a Massachusetts court decision? The charter made no such provision, and the Bay authorities plainly set forth their view of the matter in the colony records for April 3, 1632: "Thomas Knower was sett in the bilbowes for threatening the Court that, if hee should be punist, hee would have it tryed in England wither hee was lawfully punished or not."[16] As in its relationship with the English church, Winthrop's government was renouncing, in substance if not in theory, the authority of the King.

Once Massachusetts was safely launched, Winthrop's fellow magistrates grew jealous of his dominance, and the colonists grew restless under his continuous rule. In 1632 the deputy governor, Thomas Dudley, arranged a meeting with Winthrop and several of the clergy, where he charged the Governor with overstepping his authority. Winthrop tried to answer Dudley's complaints. He pointed out that he was making no profit from the governorship; on the contrary, he was disbursing all colony expenses out of personal funds. Yet friction continued between the two men. In 1634 the freemen complained. Becom-

---

[16] Andrews, *Colonial Period*, I, 435; *Journal*, I, 41-43, 65-68; *Mass. Rec.*, I, 94.

ing at last suspicious of their political rights, two freemen from each town met in an assembly and asked Governor Winthrop to show them the Massachusetts Bay Company charter. They found, of course, that the charter gave the freemen power to legislate in General Court. Winthrop tried to explain that the freemen were too numerous and inexperienced to sit as a legislature. He offered, instead, to let them revise old laws and to present grievances to the assistants. But the freemen would have none of this.

Winthrop himself recorded what happened when the General Court assembled on May 14, 1634: "At this court it was ordered, that four general courts should be kept every year, and that the whole body of the freemen should be present only at the court of election of magistrates, etc., and that, at the other three, every town should send their deputies, who should assist in making laws, disposing lands, etc." By introducing the principle of representative government, the freemen had completed the evolution of a trading company charter into a colony constitution. Naturally they resented Winthrop's manipulation of the charter; although John Cotton preached them a sermon against dismissing magistrates from office, they dismissed Governor Winthrop. Dudley was elected in his place, and Winthrop relegated to the board of assistants.[17] This defeat of 1634 marked another turning point in Winthrop's career. He subsequently returned to the governorship and remained the leading man in the colony until his death, but he never regained the uncontested power of his earliest years in Massachusetts.

❧ FROM 1634 to 1637, John Winthrop was in eclipse as leader of the Bay Colony. "He is indeed a man of men," one observer remarked, "but he is but a man: & some say they have idolized him, & do now confess their error." The freemen did not reject him: he was elected an assistant for two years and deputy-governor in 1636. But even this eclipse was unfortunate. During these years Massachusetts was growing rapidly in numbers and social complexity, and the three men who succeeded

[17] *Journal*, I, 98-103, 152-53, 157.

him as governor—Thomas Dudley, John Haynes, and Henry Vane—were in one way or another all greater extremists than Winthrop, without his shrewdness or responsibility. Had Winthrop remained governor, his disciplined stewardship might have prevented the banishment of Roger Williams in 1636 and blunted the Antinomian crisis of 1636-1637, which almost pitched the colony into civil war.[18]

The case of Roger Williams exposed two factors which would eventually crush the Puritan crusade on both sides of the Atlantic: the Puritan tendency to proliferate into mutually exclusive sects, and the dominant sect's tendency to ossify into a rigid new orthodoxy. Williams was an uncompromising purist, whose religious zeal took more extreme form than Winthrop's: tempestuous rebellion, intellectual arrogance, and overflowing love for his fellow men. As soon as he began preaching at Salem in 1631, he announced that the Massachusetts churches ought to separate entirely from the Church of England. By 1635 he was pursuing a more alarming course. He dared the Massachusetts magistrates or clergy to try punishing him for his teachings. He called for separation of church and state; civil magistrates have no authority over religious matters, and, within the church, there must be freedom for the Salem congregation to differ from the other Massachusetts congregations. At this, the Massachusetts magistrates and clergy united against Williams. They were genuinely reluctant to persecute one of themselves. They tried discussions, reprimands, and warnings. But since Williams only became more belligerent, they soon decided (January 1636) to ship him back to England. The Massachusetts leaders' method of fusing into a solid phalanx against Williams anticipated Milton's discovery that new presbyter was but old priest writ large.

Winthrop deplored Williams' teaching, but he was unwilling to punish the man so harshly. Had he been governor at this time he might have been able to patch up or postpone the crisis. As it was, he secretly warned Williams of the magistrates' plan by advising him to slip away immediately from Salem to

[18] M.H.S. *Proc.*, 1st ser., V, 141; Morgan, *Puritan Dilemma*, pp. 115-16.

the Narragansett wilderness. Years later, Williams recalled how "that ever honored Governor, Mr. Winthrop, privately wrote to me to steer my course to Narragansett Bay and Indians, for many high and heavenly and public ends, encouraging me, from the freeness of the place from any English claims or patents." Williams tracked south through midwinter snow. Established with a small following at Providence, outside of Massachusetts jurisdiction, he lived up to his criticism of the Bay leadership by separating church membership from civil administration, breaking all ties with the home church and state, and buying his land from the Indians. Having a charity toward other men unspoiled by his contempt for their ideas, he kept for several years a warm and copious correspondence with Winthrop. In 1637 the two men even arranged the joint purchase of Prudence Island, six miles long, in the center of Narragansett Bay.[19]

By this time, Winthrop was embroiled with another Puritan extremist, Mrs. Anne Hutchinson. This vigorous lady was an Antinomian, who found Winthrop's religion spiritually dead. Retaining the Calvinist contempt for the unregenerate, she anticipated the Quakers' belief in regeneration through inspired, mystical union with God. Whereas Winthrop believed that man must prepare himself for God's election, even though he cannot achieve salvation through his own good deeds, Mrs. Hutchinson contemptuously called this a covenant of works. She held that man could not prepare himself for election, and that God bestows grace on the elect through direct revelation. Antinomianism in practice was levelling and anti-intellectual, challenging both the religious and social discipline of the colony. The governor of Massachusetts in 1636, Henry Vane, was himself an ardent supporter of Mrs. Hutchinson.

The Antinomian crisis began within Boston church, of which Winthrop was a member. Speaking up for orthodoxy, Winthrop found himself battling not only Mrs. Hutchinson and her coterie, but Master John Cotton, Governor Vane, and nearly all the other Boston church members. By early 1637, Antino-

---

[19] *Publications* of the Narragansett Club (6 vols.; Providence, 1866-1874), VI, 335; *Journal*, I, 194, 204, 209-10; Perry Miller, *Roger Williams* (Indianapolis, 1953), pp. 22-32; *Winthrop Papers*, III, 502-503, 508, 511; IV, 41.

mian Boston was pitted against most of the other towns, Governor Vane against Deputy-Governor Winthrop, and as the contention increased, "it began to be as common here to distinguish between men, by being under a covenant of grace or a covenant of works, as in other countries between Protestants and Papists." The decisive moment came on May 17, 1637, when the annual colony election took place at a crowded outdoor assembly in Cambridge. "There was great danger of a tumult that day," Winthrop tells us, for the Antinomian faction "grew into fierce speeches, and some laid hands on others; but seeing themselves too weak, they grew quiet." The election was a great victory for orthodoxy. Winthrop was chosen governor, while Vane and the other Antinomian magistrates were "quite left out." Winthrop's eclipse was ended.[20]

Having regained leadership of the colony, Winthrop wanted to prevent the further influx of Antinomians from England. The General Court ordered that visitors staying more than three weeks in Massachusetts must be approved by the magistrates. Vane quickly sailed for England, and when the remaining Antinomians obdurately refused to confess their errors, though "clearly confuted and confounded" (or so Winthrop says) in a synod of all the ministers and magistrates, the General Court in November 1637 banished Mrs. Hutchinson, John Wheelwright, and other ringleaders from the colony, and disfranchised or disarmed seventy-five of their followers. Winthrop himself wrote an account of how the Antinomians had been extirpated, for publication in England so that "all our godly friends might not be discouraged from coming to us." Looking for evidence of God's will, he found it in the fact that Anne Hutchinson soon had a miscarriage, and one of her companions, Mary Dyer, produced a stillborn monster. Winthrop's deep emotional involvement in the Antinomian struggle is shown by the eagerness with which he pried into the details of both cases, examined witnesses, ordered Mrs. Dyer's monstrosity dug out of its grave, and entered every nasty detail

[20] *Journal,* I, 254-55, 261-62; Thomas Hutchinson, *History of the Colony and Province of Massachusetts-Bay,* ed. L. S. Mayo (3 vols.; Cambridge, Mass. 1936), I, 54.

John Winthrop

of both fetuses into his *Journal*. Descriptions were even sent home for propaganda purposes.[21]

The expulsion of Williams and the Antinomians left Massachusetts a safer but duller place. It distressed Governor Winthrop to find that Williams gave sanctuary to Mrs. Hutchinson in Narragansett Bay, and that the two of them were hatching new heretical doctrines; "it was apparent," he concluded, "that God had given them up to strange delusions."[22] Other Massachusetts colonists were voluntarily migrating to regions beyond Winthrop's jurisdiction. In 1636, Thomas Hooker and John Haynes founded Connecticut colony. In 1638, John Davenport and Theophilus Eaton founded New Haven colony. These settlements, though independent of Massachusetts, at least followed the Bay model in church and state organization. But north of the Massachusetts border outcasts and rebels were settling in New Hampshire. To Winthrop, this scattering away from his city on a hill was a personal affront and a token of God's displeasure.

For three years, 1637-1640, Winthrop continued as governor. His fellow members of Boston church gradually forgave him for standing out so sharply against their Antinomianism. But soon he fell into personal economic difficulties. Absorbed in public duties, he unwisely left the entire management of his estate in the hands of a steward, James Luxford, who proceeded to swindle him by contracting loans in his name with various people in New England and at home. In 1639 Winthrop discovered that he was £2,600 in debt, and that some of his grasping neighbors had struck hard bargains with Luxford behind his back. The wretched Luxford was sentenced by the General Court to have his ears cut off. Winthrop had to sell much of his property on both sides of the Atlantic between 1639 and 1643, including most of the Ten Hills farm and the house in Boston, to satisfy his creditors. Voluntary contributions of nearly £500 were collected for him in several towns, surely a sign of his public esteem, though he seems to have expected more. The

[21] *Mass. Rec.*, I, 196, 207-208, 211-12; *Journal*, I, 265-67, 292-98, 313-16, 326-28; *Cal. S. P. Col.*, *1574-1660*, p. 259.
[22] *Journal*, I, 338, 340-41, 352-53, 356-58; *Winthrop Papers*, IV, 25-26.

General Court granted 3,000 acres of land to his wife. Winthrop himself, however, was demoted from governor to assistant, 1640-1642, and a brash deputy proposed that "two of their ancientist magistrates" (Winthrop undoubtedly being one) should be retired altogether from office "because they were grown poor."[23] There was no honorable place in the Puritan ethic for failure.

By the time Winthrop returned to the governorship in 1642, the fresh exhilaration of the early days was gone. He had become custodian of Massachusetts orthodoxy, his righteousness insensibly turning into self-righteousness, his disciplined control turning into harsh aggression. In the 1630's he had been content to banish sinners and rebel saints from Massachusetts; now he tried to pursue them beyond the Bay jurisdiction. His new adversary was Samuel Gorton, a self-educated lay preacher and self-styled holy man. Gorton had been driven out of Massachusetts for what Winthrop called his "familistical and absurd opinions," but he certainly posed a less serious challenge to Winthrop's establishment than Williams or Hutchinson had. In 1641 Gorton and his disciples came to Pawtuxet on Narragansett Bay, just south of Providence, in spite of the Pawtuxet settlers' efforts to keep them out. Four Pawtuxet men appeared in Boston, in September 1642, and offered to submit to Massachusetts' jurisdiction, in return for her protection against Gorton. The General Court agreed to this, as Winthrop candidly explains, "partly to rescue these men from unjust violence, and partly to draw in the rest of those parts . . . who now lived under no government, but grew very offensive, and the place was likely to be of use to us . . . for an outlet into the Narragansett Bay." The Massachusetts General Court appointed the four Pawtuxet men as justices of the peace. One of them, Robert Cole, had been repeatedly punished for drunkenness and cast out of the church when a resident of Massachusetts in the 1630's.[24]

[23] *Ibid.*, III, 173; IV, 161-63, 250, 329, 413-14; *Mass. Rec.*, I, 295; *Journal*, II, 3-4, 67; M.H.S. *Proc.*, 2nd ser., VII, 127-43; XI, 185-86.

[24] *Journal*, II, 69, 71, 102; *Mass. Rec.*, II, 26-27; Samuel Gorton, *Simplicities Defence against Seven-Headed Policy* (R.I.H.S. *Coll.*), II, 50, 191-93. For Gorton's turbulent career, see Kenneth W. Porter, "Samuel Gorton, New England Firebrand," *N.E.Q.*, VII, 405-44.

John Winthrop

With Winthrop's government claiming jurisdiction over an area immediately south of Providence and twenty miles south of Massachusetts' chartered limits, Roger Williams might remember with some bitterness how Winthrop had advised him in 1636 to settle in Narragansett Bay because of its freedom from English claims. Now Williams quickly sailed for England, to try to get a patent for the Narragansett Bay area. Samuel Gorton also took alarm. He and his followers moved out of the Providence-Pawtuxet area to Shawomet, farther south along the western shore of Narragansett Bay. They composed a sprawling, ranting letter to the Massachusetts government, in which Gorton was compared to Christ and Winthrop to Pontius Pilate. In reply, the Massachusetts General Court (September 12, 1643) ordered Gorton and his company to appear immediately in Boston and answer a complaint that they had usurped their Shawomet territory from the Indians. Gorton naturally refused. One of his disciples, Randall Holden, sent an insulting diatribe to "the great and honored Idol General, now set up in the Massachusetts," with many references to Judas Iscariot and a generation of vipers.[25]

The Massachusetts General Court dispatched three commissioners and forty soldiers to arrest the Gortonists unless they satisfactorily answered the Indian charges. To Winthrop, the real issue was Gorton's "horrible and detestable blasphemies, against God, and all magistracy." On reaching Shawomet, the Massachusetts troop found the Gortonists barricaded and ready for battle. Gorton wrote a comic account of the scene. He described the Bay commander exhorting his troops to advance, while hiding behind a great white oak tree. Many shots were fired, but the epic contest ended before any blood was shed. The Gortonists, ten strong, surrendered and were marched back to Boston. When soldiers and prisoners drew up before the governor's house, Gorton says that Winthrop came out and welcomed each one of his returning heroes: "God bless you, and prosper you—God bless and prosper you."[26]

---

[25] Gorton, *Simplicities Defence*, pp. 53, 62, 69-71, 80, 95-96, 262-71; *Journal*, II, 144-48, 165; Ebenezer Hazard, ed., *Historical Collections* (2 vols.; Philadelphia, 1792-1794), II, 10.

[26] *Journal*, II, 165-69, 171; Gorton, *Simplicities Defence*, pp. 98-112, 114-19.

The Gortonists were brought to trial before the General Court. Principally they were charged with religious errors, which they could not be made to recant. Many of the magistrates favored executing Gorton, but it was decided to place him and six companions in irons and set them at hard labor, each in a separate town. Winthrop soon discovered that the convicts "did corrupt some of our people, especially the women, by their heresies." Not knowing what else to do, the General Court set the Gortonists loose in March 1644. Back they came to Narragansett Bay.[27] Winthrop's plan to impose his style of orthodoxy throughout New England had been checkmated.

Within his own colony, Winthrop faced strong political opposition. In 1644-1645 he was demoted to deputy-governor, and in these years the deputies of the freemen made a concerted effort to enlarge their role in the Massachusetts government. The deputies wanted to abolish the magistrates' negative voice or power to veto a majority decision in the General Court. Winthrop was appalled. As he argued in a treatise on the subject, without the negative voice the colony government would become a mere democracy, "the meanest and worst of all formes of Government." Massachusetts was not yet to sink so low. In March 1644 the magistrates and deputies divided into separate houses, preserving the magistrates' aristocratic identity. But the deputies immediately questioned the magistrates' right in judicial cases to determine punishments at their own discretion and their right to govern the plantation between sessions of the General Court without a special commission. Once more Winthrop composed a treatise to rebut the deputies. In government, he argued, the wisest men must be given discretionary power to follow God's law as they see it. When the deputies got a copy of this treatise, they attacked it "as a dangerous libel of some unknown author." One deputy daringly charged that it "was worse than Gorton's letters, that it should be burnt under the gallows, that if some other of the magistrates had written it, it would have cost him his ears, if not his head. . . ."[28]

[27] *Ibid.*, pp. 124-25, 153, 232; *Journal*, II, 172-79, 188-89; *Mass. Rec.*, II, 51-52, 57.
[28] *Winthrop Papers*, IV, 383, 468-88; *Journal*, II, 83-86, 139-44, 193, 204-206, 250-57, 283-85; Miller, *Orthodoxy in Massachusetts*, p. 281.

However, the magistrates called in the elders to vindicate their exercise of power, which silenced most of the deputies for the time being.

Not for long. The most serious attack on Winthrop came in May 1645, when the people of Hingham complained to the General Court that he had tried to make them accept a militia captain whom they did not want. The deputies wished to hear the case, and Winthrop himself welcomed the opportunity to expose the "mutinous and seditious practice" of the Hingham people and to vindicate himself and his fellow magistrates. As the case opened in the Boston meetinghouse, he dramatically chose to sit before the court as the defendant, his head uncovered. Both sides were heard, and the magistrates demanded that Winthrop be pronounced innocent and the Hingham petition be branded false and scandalous. A bare majority of the deputies voted in Winthrop's favor, and most of them thought him not altogether free from blame. After much pressure and prolonged discussion, the court judged him legally acquitted and levied small fines against the Hingham petitioners. Nevertheless, it had been a humiliating ordeal for Winthrop.

Still, victory had been won, and when the court's verdict was read (July 3, 1645) the Deputy-Governor took the opportunity to stand up in the meetinghouse and make his famous "little speech" on the authority of the magistrates and the liberty of the people, a summary of his political philosophy. First he told the people that they had no business agitating against the magistrates they had chosen, who have covenanted with them to govern according to God's law as well as they know how. Second he explained that man in society must obey authority, because he has "a liberty to that only which is good, just and honest. . . . This liberty is maintained and exercised in a way of subjection to authority, it is of the same kind of liberty wherewith Christ hath made us free. . . . If you stand for your natural corrupt liberties, and will do what is good in your own eyes, you will not endure the least weight of authority. . .; but if you will be satisfied to enjoy such civil and lawful liberties, such as Christ allows you, then will you quietly and cheerfully submit unto that authority which is set over you . . .

for your good."[29] Winthrop had the last word. The Massachusetts people accepted their small liberty and his large authority. They returned him to the governorship in 1646, and there he remained until his death in 1649.

John Winthrop's speech on liberty and authority was his testament. Clearly much had changed since 1630, when he had summoned his fellow colonists to build in Massachusetts a city on a hill. Then he had spoken as a prophet, with a cosmic scale of imagery, sounding a bold and buoyant call for greatness. Now he spoke as an embattled, somewhat weary chieftain, trying to keep the status quo. Perpetual struggle against critics of his system—Thomas Morton, Roger Williams, Anne Hutchinson, Samuel Gorton, and the mutinous deputies in General Court—had narrowed and hardened John Winthrop. Since 1630 he had run afoul of almost every newcomer with new ideas; by 1645 his social ideal, however pragmatic, had become incurably petty and local. Yet the man's central quality had not changed at all. In 1630 and in 1645 he preached the same strong and simple doctrine: New England's glory and salvation, he said, is her collective conscience, which keeps the people responsible to God and to each other. Winthrop was the first, but by no means the last, New Englander to define liberty as riding easy in harness. His Puritan code of disciplined self-government was his best legacy to his son and grandsons, who would carry it into a more complex and secular world.

[29] *Journal*, II, 271-82; *Mass. Rec.*, III, 19-26; Perry Miller, "The Marrow of Puritan Divinity," C.S.M. *Publ.*, XXXII, 290-91.

2. *Splendid Isolation*

THROUGHOUT the seventeenth century, the Winthrops were New England's leading champions of political autonomy from England. For three generations they worked to protect the colonists' chartered privileges of self-government. John Winthrop started this family tradition. From 1630 to 1649, he kept as independent from the mother country as possible. He resisted all attempts by King and Parliament to control New England, and launched Massachusetts on a policy of splendid isolation.[1]

Here we see another side to Winthrop's conception of self-government. If liberty meant submission to discipline within the Massachusetts community, it also meant freedom from outside interference. Winthrop's bulwark against such interference was the charter which Charles I had issued to the Massachusetts Bay Company in 1629. Reluctant as he was to permit the company freemen their full chartered rights, Winthrop did not hesitate to stretch the company's corporate powers to the uttermost in order to make Massachusetts a self-sufficient, autonomous commonwealth. When he transferred the charter and the whole company machinery to America in 1630, he brought with him a one-sided view of allegiance to England. Fleeing from the King's tyranny, he accepted the royal delegation of authority, and violated the terms of the King's gift with audacity. In short, Winthrop received large and distinct privileges without acknowledging reciprocal obligations. It was a view which the New England colonists cherished for the next 145 years.

❧ AT the time Winthrop quit England, the home government had no real colonial policy nor colonial administration.

---

[1] For the full details of Winthrop's relations with the home government, see Richard S. Dunn, "John Winthrop, John Winthrop, Jr., and the Problem of Colonial Dependency in New England, 1630-1676" (Ph.D. dissertation, Princeton University, 1955), pp. 1-208.

Charles I left colonization to private initiative, simply charter-
ing private individuals and corporations with vast overseas
tracts, to be managed as they saw fit. So far this casual attitude
had produced poor results. In 1630 the only significant English
colony in North America was Virginia, which had passed into
the King's hands, thanks to the bankruptcy and paralysis of the
Virginia Company, which founded it. Plantation problems were
considered sporadically at meetings of the Privy Council or by
occasional temporary commissions of councilors, amidst more
urgent matters. The separatist Pilgrims, anathema to Charles
I, had been left unmolested at Plymouth for a decade. The
Massachusetts Bay Company, a much larger group with an
obvious Puritan tinge, was treated by the government with care-
lessness. The royal charter of 1629 gave Winthrop and his
colleagues more freedom than the Virginia Company had ever
secured. The King's ministers showed no interest in the company's mass exodus of 1630.

All this soon changed, thanks largely to Winthrop. On the
eve of his departure, he moved circumspectly, to avoid trouble
with the government. His promotional treatises of 1629, attacking the English church and state, were kept half-secret.
And on April 7, 1630, the day before his fleet set sail, Winthrop joined in signing a public letter, the *Humble Request* of
the Governor and Company of Massachusetts Bay, which asked
their brethren, the Anglican clergy (including those who "cannot now conceive so well of our way as we could desire") to
pray for the success of the new plantation. The Massachusetts
emigrants "esteem it our honour, to call the Church of England, from whence wee rise, our deare Mother, and cannot
part from our native Country, where she specially resideth,
without much sadness of heart, and many teares in our eyes. . . ."
This tender appeal was quickly published in London.

Once Winthrop was safe in America, he made no further effort at appeasement. The congregational organization of the
new Massachusetts churches differed so radically from Winthrop's mother Church of England that correspondents at home
cautioned him to slow down. His harsh treatment of Thomas
Morton, Philip Ratcliffe, and Sir Christopher Gardiner stirred

complaints in England "against the severitie of your Governement especially . . . about cuttinge off the Lunatick mans [Ratcliffe's] ears."[2] Then in 1632, Massachusetts was brought to the attention of the King's ministers. This happened when Sir Ferdinando Gorges, a colonizing entrepreneur who had long hoped to plant his proprietary domain in New England, discovered that Winthrop's colony was occupying the best land. Gorges asked the Privy Council to recall the Massachusetts Bay Company's royal charter. He collected evidence, according to Winthrop, "accusing us to intend rebellion, to have cast off our allegiance, and to be wholly separate from the church and laws of England; that our ministers and people did continually rail against the state, church and bishops there, etc."[3] The standard charge against Massachusetts for the next sixty years was already fully formed.

Winthrop's friends in England rallied to meet Gorges' charge. When the Privy Council heard the case, December 19, 1632, there was "long debate of the whole carriage of the Plantations of that Countrey," and a committee was appointed to investigate the Massachusetts Bay Company further. Winthrop's brother-in-law, Emmanuel Downing, barraged the committee with reports of Massachusetts' supply of timber and naval stores, and her shipbuilding potential. Such testimony was for the moment more persuasive than complaints against the colony's religious and political system. The committee re-

[2] *Winthrop Papers*, II, 232, 333; III, 76.

[3] "Records of the Council for New England," A.A.S. *Proc., 1866-1867*, pp. 107, 111; *Journal*, I, 68, 119, 122. The background of Gorges' quarrel with the Massachusetts Bay Company is complex. In 1620, Gorges had secured a royal charter for his Council for New England, with sole title to the vast tract from present Philadelphia to northern Nova Scotia. In 1628, when Gorges had temporarily lost interest, this council issued a land patent to the New England Company. In 1629, the New England Company obtained a royal charter that reconstituted it as the Massachusetts Bay Company and gave it legal equality with its patron, the Council for New England. In 1632, Gorges tried to inspect the patent which his council had issued to the New England Company in 1628 and discovered that it had been taken to America, along with the royal charter of 1629. The Council for New England then ordered (November 6, 1632) that all previously granted patents should be called in for reconfirmation, and Gorges turned to the Privy Council for help. See A. L. Rowse, *The Elizabethans and America* (New York, 1959), ch. 5, and Richard A. Preston's biography, *Gorges of Plymouth Fort* (Toronto, 1953), pp. 276-90.

ported (January 19, 1633) that a full investigation would require further witnesses from New England, and the Privy Council decided to let the company alone as long as "things were carried as was pretended when the Patents were granted." Winthrop's correspondents told him that the King even said "he would have them severely punished, who did abuse his governour and the plantation." Such an unexpected "deliverance out of so desperate a danger," Winthrop said to Governor Bradford of Plymouth, "maks it evident to all, that the lord hath care of his people hear." But friends in England reemphasized the need for elementary precautions. "I know," wrote London merchant Francis Kirby, "I shall not need to advise you that the prayeinge for our kinge be not neglected in any of your publique meetings, and I desire that you differ no more from us in Church government, then you shall find that we differ from the prescript rule of gods word."[4]

Winthrop paid little heed to this. He was working out his own independent view of the Massachusetts Bay Company's charter privileges. "That which the King is pleased to bestow upon us," he argued, "and we have accepted, is truly our owne." The colonists ought to express their own desires, not the King's. Hence Winthrop told his English Puritan friend, Sir Simonds D'Ewes, that he could not thank him for advising Massachusetts' conformity to the Church of England. "What you may doe in England where things are otherwise established, I will not dispute, but our case heere is otherwise: being come to clearer light and more Libertye."

Within Massachusetts, Winthrop had to deal with Roger Williams' subversive argument that the charter was not only irrelevant but invalid. Williams contended that the King had no authority to grant the Massachusetts Bay Company land in America. Possibly the King had no right to this land, Winthrop answered, yet "our God hathe right to it, and if he be pleased to give it us, who shall controll him or his termes?" Furthermore, it was "strange boldnesse" for Williams to iden-

[4] M.H.S. *Coll.*, 3rd ser., VIII, 320-25; *Acts Privy Council, Colonial*, I, 183, 185; W. H. Whitmore and W. S. Appleton, eds., *The Hutchinson Papers* (2 vols.; Prince Society, Albany, 1865), I, 58-59; *Journal*, I, 122-23; *Winthrop Papers*, III, 111-20.

tify Charles I as the accomplice of the Beast in Revelation. St. Paul had never railed in such fashion against the Roman emperor, nor should Williams "have provoked our Kinge against us, and putt a sworde into his hande to destroy us."[5] Similarly, he censured Williams' "indiscreet zeale" in starting a controversy in 1634 over the design of the Massachusetts flag. Williams urged his Salem people to stop displaying the King's colors, a red ensign with the red St. George's cross on a white canton in the upper left-hand corner, because the St. George's cross was a popish symbol of antichrist. John Endecott, the magistrate at Salem, ripped out the popish cross. This caused a great uproar. Winthrop feared that the defacing would be interpreted in England as an act of rebellion, and admonished Williams and Endecott for their rash presumption. Actually, he agreed with Williams that the St. George's cross was unacceptable even as a civil emblem. In 1636 it was removed from all military ensigns, and until the fall of the charter government fifty years later, Massachusetts had her own special flag, a red ensign with a plain white canton.[6]

Meanwhile, in 1633 an uncompromising foe of Puritans, William Laud, had become Archbishop of Canterbury. The new archbishop threw the full weight of his office into a countercrusade against Puritanism, not only in England, but in Scotland, Ireland, and the overseas plantations. Laud's attention was immediately drawn to New England. Seven hundred persons emigrated there in 1633, double the total for 1631-1632, and among them were two potent Puritan divines, John Cotton and Thomas Hooker. A Privy Council committee, under Laud's chairmanship, held up twelve more boatloads of emigrants for a week in February 1634 before reluctantly letting them sail. More significant, Laud's committee ordered former governor Matthew Craddock to produce the Massachusetts Bay Company charter. He revealed that it was in Mr. Winthrop's hands. The committee ordered him to send for it. Craddock's unwelcome

[5] *Ibid.*, 148-49, 172, 465; *Journal*, I, 145, 147.
[6] W. G. Perrin, *British Flags* (Cambridge, 1922), pp. 62-63, 115-18, 129-31; *Winthrop Papers*, III, 175; *Journal*, I, 174-75, 179, 183, 189, 215; M.H.S. *Proc.*, 1st ser., V, 135, 141; H. M. Chapin, *Roger Williams and the King's Colors* (Providence, R.I., 1928), pp. 20-22.

message arrived in Massachusetts with the fleet of immigrants in June.[7]

To tackle the Massachusetts Bay Company, the government obviously needed more established colonial administrative machinery than Laud's temporary Privy Council committee. Accordingly, on April 28, 1634, the Archbishop's committee was reconstituted as the Commission for Regulating Plantations, a self-sufficient executive body of Privy Councilors, empowered to hear and determine colonial complaints, to remove disloyal colonial governors, and to recall and revoke colonial patents. The commission was clearly aimed against the New England Puritans. Archbishop Laud, according to Thomas Morton, called two English members of the Massachusetts Bay Company "a couple of imposterous knaves," while the maimed Ratcliffe "was comforted by their lordships with the cropping of Mr. Winthrop's ears: which shows what opinion is held amongst them of King Winthrop with all his inventions and his Amsterdam fantastical ordinances. . . ." Both Morton and Gorges supposed that the company charter was already voided, that the King "hath reassumed the whole business into his own hands" as with Virginia in 1624, and would next appoint a royal governor general for New England.[8]

Actually, the Laud Commission took no action against the Massachusetts Bay Company for another year. Then in May 1635 it directed the Attorney General to open suit in the Court of King's Bench for repeal of the Massachusetts charter. The twenty-four charter members of the company were to be served a writ of *quo warranto* requiring them to answer by what right they governed the colony. According to the Attorney General's indictment, the Massachusetts Bay Company was not charged with misuse of its chartered powers; rather, the chartered powers themselves were declared "without any warrant or royall grant." Possibly the crown intended by denying the existence of the charter to force the company to produce it in

[7] *Journal*, I, 130, 161; *Cal.S.P.Dom.*, *1633-1634*, pp. 251, 288, 450-51; *Acts Privy Council, Colonial*, I, 199-201; Hazard, *Historical Collections*, I, 432.

[8] William Bradford, *Of Plymouth Plantation, 1620-1647*, ed. Samuel Eliot Morison (New York, 1953), pp. 422-25; *Journal*, II, 233-34; *Cal.S.P.Col.*, *1574-1660*, p. 178.

court. But how was the company to be forced to answer the indictment at all? The *quo warranto* was never served on the six patentees who had moved to Massachusetts, and who were the only charter members still active in the management of the company.[9] The charter members still in England appeared in court as summoned, but they renounced all claim to the chartered privileges under attack. The court refused Matthew Craddock's disclaimer, holding him responsible as the charter governor in 1629, but did not sentence him for usurping the chartered privileges. No other company member was caught. In Easter Term 1637 the Court of King's Bench found the company guilty as charged, and ordered its franchise seized into the King's hands. On May 3 the Privy Council ordered the Attorney General to call in the Massachusetts charter, and on July 23 Charles I proclaimed that he was assuming management of New England. Sir Ferdinando Gorges was appointed the royal governor.[10] After four years of effort, Gorges and Laud seemed to have vanquished the Massachusetts Bay Company.

It was only a paper victory. The court's judgment against the company was specious because the company government had been neither summoned nor convicted. Moreover, the court's judgment could not be enforced. Governor Gorges expected the home government to support him with a sizable number of soldiers, but there was no money in the royal treasury for such a project. A ship was built to carry Gorges to Boston, but it capsized and split in two at its launching. Sir Ferdinando himself, now nearly seventy years old, was feeling his age. "I am growne a little doubtfull of the state of my owne bodie," he confided to Secretary of State Coke in February 1637, "not

[9] J. P. Baxter, ed., *Sir Ferdinando Gorges and His Province of Maine* (3 vols.; Prince Society, Boston, 1890), III, 272; M.H.S. *Coll.*, 2d ser., VIII, 97; *Winthrop Papers*, IV, 341; *New England Historical and Genealogical Register*, XXXVIII, 210-15; Charles Deane, "The Forms in Issuing Letters Patent by the Crown of England," M.H.S. *Proc.*, 1st ser., XI, 186-87.

[10] Frances Rose-Troup, *John White, The Founder of Massachusetts* (New York, 1930), pp. 294-304; *Hutchinson Papers*, I, 116-18; *Cal.S.P.Col.*, *1574-1660*, p. 256.

able to indure the Sea any long tyme."[11] Clearly the Laud Commission's New England policy, bold in general outline, was on closer inspection flimsy and ephemeral.

The Archbishop's attack only strengthened John Winthrop's devotion to his company's charter powers. When Craddock transmitted the Privy Council's order of February 1634 to return the charter, Winthrop and his colleagues wrote nothing to the Privy Council and told Craddock that the question must be postponed until the next General Court. They began, however, to fortify Castle Island at the entrance to Boston harbor. In September 1634 a copy of Laud's new commission arrived. English friends warned Winthrop that the commission was "intended specially for us, and that there were ships and soldiers provided, given out as for . . . Virginia, but suspected to be against us, to compel us, by force, to receive a new governor, and the discipline of the church of England, and the laws of the commissioners. . . ." Mere evasion of the council's orders was not enough. In General Court, as Winthrop tells us, the threat of armed intervention "occasioned the magistrates and deputies to hasten our fortifications, and to discover our minds each to other." The court established a program to raise defense funds. It called for a general levy of £600, larger than any previous one, of which £500 was earmarked for military purposes. Labor was drafted to complete the fortification of Castle Island and to build other forts at Charlestown, Dorchester, and Salem. An emergency committee of war was appointed. The militia began training intensively, and arms and ammunition were distributed among the towns.[12]

On January 19, 1635, the Massachusetts clergy gathered at Boston to propound the question: "What we ought to do, if a general governour should be sent out from England?" The decision was unanimous: "We ought not to accept him, but defend our lawful possessions, (if we were able;) otherwise to avoid

---

[11] Sir Simonds D'Ewes, *Autobiography and Correspondence*, ed. J. O. Halliwell (2 vols.; London, 1845), II, 118; Preston, *Gorges of Plymouth Fort*, pp. 300-308; Baxter, *Ferdinando Gorges*, III, 265, 273, 278; *Journal*, I, 192.

[12] *Ibid.*, I, 160-61, 163, 171, 183; *Mass. Rec.*, I, 123-25, 129.

or protract." Had a royal governor actually appeared, it is hard to doubt that Massachusetts would have tried to resist him. The first overt rebellion against Charles I might have taken place in Boston harbor instead of Edinburgh.

As the months passed without any sign of an expeditionary force from England, the tension eased for Winthrop. In April 1635, fishermen at Marblehead reported two large ships hovering suspiciously off Cape Ann, and an alarm was raised in all the towns before it was discovered that the two ships were small and harmless. In May 1636 the Bay magistrates imposed new regulations on incoming ships, in order to safeguard Boston harbor. All ships must anchor at Castle Island on arrival, all cargoes must be opened to possible proscription by the governor before they could be offered for public sale, and all sailors must stay on shipboard after sunset—a moral regulation rather than a military one. As a special concession to the ship masters, the Massachusetts magistrates agreed to fly the idolatrous St. George's flag at Castle Island. Even this token display of allegiance, the King's colors displayed on an island ten miles out in the harbor, was wrung most grudgingly from Winthrop. The next year, when a ship refused to halt at Castle Island, the fort opened fire and killed a passenger, "an honest man" (unlike a sailor), says Winthrop. The inquest found that the victim "came to his death by the providence of God."[13]

When English friends reported to Winthrop in 1637 that the Massachusetts charter had been condemned, he was not much dismayed. By now he felt sure that the home government would not send over a governor general. The flow of immigrants to New England was greater each year. Three thousand settlers arrived in the summer of 1638 alone, and by the close of the decade some 20,000 persons had joined the great migration. In 1638 the Laud Commission sent the Massachusetts Bay Company officers an unequivocal order to return their charter by the next ship. In case of further contempt, the commissioners warned that they "will move his Majesty to reassume into his hands the whole Plantation," surely no great

[13] *Journal*, I, 188, 222-25, 271; II, 421.

threat considering that the King had already announced his resumption of control in 1637. Still, the Laud Commission's order troubled Governor Winthrop. Either he must disobey the royal government's command, or he must appear willing "to receive such a governour and such orders as should be sent to us." Winthrop preferred the first alternative. On September 6, 1638, he wrote a petition to the Laud Commission, asking that his company be left alone. As for the *quo warranto*, "wee do assure your Lordships that wee were never called to make answer to it; and if wee had, Wee doubt not but Wee have a sufficient plea to put in." Should the patent be taken away, New England must collapse, and the colonists either return to England or "remove to some other place"—where they would presumably set up an independent state.[14]

In 1639 Winthrop received another order from the Laud Commission to return the Massachusetts charter. This order, however, was almost conciliatory. The commissioners acknowledged Winthrop's petition, explained that "they meant to continue our liberties," and gave the company officers "full power to go on in the government of the people until we had a new patent sent us." Evidently the commissioners had retreated a long way from their aims of 1634-1637. Abandoning plans for a royal governor, abandoning hope of enforcing conformity in church and state, they merely required that Massachusetts derive her legal authority from the Laud Commission. Even this demand was excessive, since it could only be supported by empty threats. The Massachusetts General Court coolly decided not to answer the order at all. In case of further trouble, the colony refurbished her military plant. The court expended £540 on saltpeter and match from Holland and £280 on the forts at Castle Island and Charlestown. Two regiments of militia were mustered at Boston, one thousand strong, "able men, and well armed and exercised."[15]

As he reviewed this force, large enough to put up a real fight against any likely invader, and more numerous than the

[14] *Ibid.*, I, 317-24; *Cal.S.P.Col.*, *1574-1660*, p. 266; Hazard, *Historical Collections*, I, 432-36.
[15] *Winthrop Papers*, IV, 113; *Journal*, I, 358-60, 367; *Mass. Rec.*, I, 250-51, 259-60, 263.

entire band of settlers which he had led across the ocean in 1630, commander-in-chief John Winthrop might well feel confident and proud. He received no further threatening letters from Whitehall. By 1640 correspondents were telling of the King's defeat in Scotland and the summoning of an English Parliament. Charles I's personal government was collapsing, Archbishop Laud would soon be imprisoned in the Tower, and his Commission for Regulating Plantations was in limbo. For the first time Winthrop felt in the proper mood to send a present home to the King. It was a New England otter, which during the voyage to London symbolically slipped overboard and drowned.

Winthrop had scored a very easy victory over Laud. The Archbishop could not regulate New England in the 1630's for several obvious reasons: he was preoccupied with more pressing business, his colleagues and subordinates at Whitehall were indifferent to the Puritan colonists,[16] and he lacked the men and money to enforce his will. Laud's orders and threats had provoked Winthrop into exercising the chief attributes of an independent sovereign: requiring the people of Massachusetts to obey his government, while denying that he need obey any external authority. Indeed, Winthrop's victory over Laud was too easy. It encouraged Massachusetts to adopt a studied insolence toward the outside world which was hardly appropriate to her real feebleness.

IN 1640, with Charles I forced to summon Parliament for the first time in eleven years, his Puritan subjects drew together in transatlantic comradeship, sensing that at last God was calling them to action in England as He had a decade earlier in New England. "Help, I beseech you, Sir," wrote Sir Nathaniel Barnardiston, representing Suffolk in the new Parliament, to his old friend John Winthrop, "with all the might and force you can make, this great work. . . . Now we see and feele how much we are weakned by the loss of those that are

---

[16] One member of the Laud Commission, Lord Cottington, saw no use in bothering about any of the English overseas colonists, who "plant tobacco and Puritanism only, like fools." *Cal.S.P.Col., 1574-1660*, p. 276.

gonn from us, who should have stood in the gapp, and have wrought and wrasled mightely in this great busines. . . . I could wish sume of you wear hear before it endeth." Many New Englanders, particularly the abler and more ambitious ones, did return home in the 1640's to help Parliament defeat the King. More than a third of the young men who graduated from Harvard College between 1642 and 1656 went to England. At least sixty New Englanders found English ecclesiastical preferment, others became officers in the rebel army, and several sat in the Long Parliament.[17] But John Winthrop, like the majority of Massachusetts colonists, declined Barnardiston's invitation. Indeed, the very success of the Roundheads at home accelerated his detachment from English Puritanism.

The opening of the revolutionary crisis in England was by no means as joyful to Winthrop as to his friends at home, for it immediately plunged New England into an economic crisis. As early as March 1640, an English nephew of Winthrop wrote, "I thinke that ther will be fewe passengers Come over this yeare," and he was correct. Incoming ships brought plenty of merchandise to Boston, but few immigrants, thanks to the hope of parliamentary reform. This punctured Massachusetts' artificial boom of the 1630's, whereby the colonists had been able to import heavily from home without exporting much in return because they had a large supply of specie constantly replenished by immigrants bringing their life savings with them. In 1640 the planters could no longer sell their surplus produce to the new immigrants, the imported English goods drained off much of the colony's money supply, and prices immediately dropped to less than half their previous level. "God taught us the vanity of all outward things," Winthrop said, but the depression also demonstrated Massachusetts' economic dependence on England.[18]

By the close of 1640 Winthrop was gloomily recording that some colonists wanted to return to England, while others "bent

---

[17] *Winthrop Papers*, IV, 218; William L. Sachse, "The Migration of New Englanders to England, 1640-1660," *A.H.R.*, LIII, 260-61, 264.

[18] *Winthrop Papers*, IV, 216; *Journal*, II, 8, 21, 25, 29; *Mass. Rec.*, I, 304; Marion H. Gottfried, "The First Depression in Massachusetts," *N.E.Q.*, IX, 655-58, 660-61.

their minds wholly to removal to the south parts, supposing they should find better means of subsistence there." Winthrop suspected all southern regions of lasciviousness and degeneracy (especially that fleshpot, Virginia). To abandon New England was to rebel against God. Winthrop was prepared if necessary to banish people from Massachusetts, but he was not willing to have them leave voluntarily. Thus he struggled in 1640-1641 to block a mass migration to Providence Island in the West Indies. He wrote to Lord Saye and Sele, one of the Providence Island promoters, telling him "how evident it was, that God had chosen this country to plant his people in" and recalling God's punishment of those who tried to discourage the Israelites from going into the land of Canaan. When a Bay magistrate, John Humfry, recruited settlers for Providence Island on the grounds that they could no longer subsist in New England, Winthrop (himself deeply in debt) felt cause "to fear, that the Lord was not with them in this way."[19]

In May 1641 two small ships set sail from Boston for Providence Island with forty-three passengers, but when they arrived off the island, the leader entering the harbor was suddenly fired upon. The Spanish had captured the place one month before. God had devised a drastic punishment for the would-be migrants, and they sheepishly came back to New England. "This brought some of them to see their error," Winthrop says, "and acknowledge it in the open congregation, but others were hardened." Humfry was certainly hardened. He left for England in October 1641, sailing in company with three ministers and a schoolmaster who spent the whole voyage reviling New England, Winthrop tells us, until they ran into two terrible winter storms off the English coast. "Then they humbled themselves before the Lord, and acknowledged God's hand to be justly out against them for speaking evil of this good land and the Lord's people here," and the ship was saved.[20]

[19] A. P. Newton, *The Colonizing Activities of the English Puritans* (New Haven, 1914), pp. 250, 292; *Winthrop Papers*, IV, 166-67, 263-67; *Journal*, I, 400-401; II, 15-16.

[20] *Ibid.*, II, 39-40, 103-104; *Cal.S.P.Col., 1574-1660*, pp. 317-20; *Mass. Rec.*, II, 12-13.

Winthrop's triumph over Humfry would be hollow indeed unless Massachusetts could revive her depressed economy. To foster self-sufficiency, the Bay leaders built seven ships for transatlantic trade between 1640 and 1642, cultivated hemp and flax for cloth, and began "to look out to the West Indies for a trade in cotton." Nevertheless, hard times continued, and as the colonists began flocking home to England, Winthrop grew bitter. "Ask thy conscience," he wrote in 1642, "if thou wouldst have plucked up thy stakes, and brought thy family 3000 miles if thou hadst expected that all, or most, would have forsaken thee there . . . for if one may go, another may, and so the greater part, and so church and commonwealth may be left destitute in a wilderness, exposed to misery and reproach." The only remedy was to beg for help from friends at home and from the Long Parliament. Winthrop was hardly anxious to encourage Parliament's intervention. "We must then be subject to all such laws as they should make, or at least such as they might impose upon us; in which course though they should intend our good, yet it might prove very prejudicial to us." Yet after much argument, the General Court decided (June 1641) to send two clergymen and a merchant, Hugh Peter, Thomas Weld, and William Hibbins, to England as the colony's agents. They were to solicit donations, pacify the colony's merchant creditors, and negotiate commercial concessions from Parliament.[21]

Actually, English Puritans both inside and outside Parliament were very generous to Massachusetts in the years 1641-1643. All the Laudian restrictions on New England shipping were quickly removed. The three agents, Peter, Weld, and Hibbins, collected private gifts totalling upwards of £2000 by the summer of 1642. The next year, their promotional tract, *New Englands First Fruits*, drew in another £400 for the betterment of Harvard College and the conversion of the Indians. In 1643 the House of Commons granted Weld and Peter permission to take a collection in all London parishes, to pay for shipping homeless, orphaned or impoverished children from Ire-

[21] *Journal*, II, 30-31, 37-38, 105, 113; *Winthrop Papers*, IV, 311-15, 326-27; *Mass. Rec.*, I, 332; R. P. Stearns, "The Weld-Peter Mission to England," C.S.M. *Publ.*, XXXII, 193.

land or the London slums to New England as bonded servants. £875 was raised in this fashion, though much of the money was squandered and few children were actually sent over. Perhaps this was just as well. One of the servant boys was so brutally treated by his Massachusetts master ("as hanging him in the chimney, etc.," Winthrop reports) that he died. Meanwhile, on March 10, 1643, the House of Commons exempted New England exports and imports from the standard 5 percent customs duty levied on all the plantation trade. Of course this order assumed Parliament's power to legislate for New England. Winthrop, however, was strangely unconcerned about the Commons' presumption, while the Massachusetts General Court entered the order verbatim into the company records as a perpetual reminder of Parliament's generosity.[22] Despite Winthrop's jealousy, Puritans in Boston and London were still brothers in arms.

When war between King and Parliament broke out in England in 1642, the Massachusetts government decided to drop all formal allegiance to Charles I. There arose, Governor Winthrop explains, "a scruple about the oath which the governour and the rest of the magistrates were to take, viz., about the first part of it: 'You shall bear true faith and allegiance to our sovereign Lord King Charles,' seeing he had violated the privileges of parliament, and made war upon them, and thereby had lost much of his kingdom and many of his subjects; whereupon it was thought fit to omit that part of it for the present." Needless to say, there was no substitute pledge of allegiance to Parliament. The General Court pronounced in 1644 that Parliament was fighting on behalf of the King, to suppress "malignant Papists & delinquents." Still, the colonists avoided wholehearted commitment to the parliamentary cause. The three great New England divines, John Cotton, Thomas Hooker, and John Davenport, declined an invitation to attend the Westminster Assembly of 1643 and help reform the Church of England. Massachusetts' wartime economic policy expressed

[22] Leo F. Stock, ed., *Proceedings and Debates of the British Parliaments respecting North America, 1542-1754* (5 vols.; Washington, 1924-1941), I, 105-109, 139-42, 185-86; *Journal*, II, 50, 118-19, 225-27; R. P. Stearns, *The Strenuous Puritan* (Urbana, 1954), pp. 163-65; *Mass. Rec.*, II, 34.

the same detachment. The Boston merchants, desperate for English goods, insisted on trading with all English ships, whether from parliamentary London or the royalist western ports.[23]

During the civil war years, 1642-1646, Winthrop and his fellow magistrates had to handle several awkward incidents involving parliamentary ships in Boston harbor. In 1643, eight sailors on a warship belonging to the parliamentary admiral, the Earl of Warwick, were killed in accidents which Winthrop attributed to their evil speech against Massachusetts. The General Court fined Warwick's captain £20 for drunken brawling. The following year, a parliamentary privateer commanded by one Captain Stagg seized a Bristol ship in Boston harbor. Irate Boston merchants, who had loaded the Bristol ship with fish, "began to gather company and raise a tumult." Deputy-Governor Winthrop stepped in, and called a meeting of magistrates and elders to decide if Stagg could keep his prize. Winthrop himself did not choose to contest the validity of Stagg's privateering commission, nor his right to the prize. "The king of England," he reasoned, "was enraged against us, and all [the royalist] party, and all the popish states in Europe; and if we should now, by opposing the parliament, cause them to forsake us, we . . . should lie open as a prey to all men." Captain Stagg was allowed to sail away with his prize. A few months later, another parliamentary privateer, Captain Richardson, sailed into Boston harbor and attacked a royalist merchantman. This time the Massachusetts government took the royalist ship under her protection. When Captain Richardson ignored a command to stay off his would-be prize, the Boston shore battery opened up with two warning shots and prepared to sink him. Forty Massachusetts soldiers secured the royalist vessel. Captain Richardson hastily apologized. It turned out that his commission for privateering was issued under the authority of Admiral Warwick rather than Parliament, and he was told not to meddle with any ship in Boston harbor, for the Lord Admiral had no jurisdiction over Massachusetts.[24]

[23] *Journal*, II, 91-92, 112, 121, 216; *Mass. Rec.*, II, 69; *Winthrop Papers*, IV, 418; Miller, *Orthodoxy in Massachusetts*, pp. 274-77.
[24] *Mass. Rec.*, II, 69, 79, 82; *Journal*, II, 179-81, 222-29, 235-40.

In 1645 the General Court declared that no ship could fight any other ship within a Massachusetts harbor without license from the Bay government. The Boston and Charlestown shore batteries were prepared to enforce the peace in Boston harbor. The court also composed an address to Parliament, asking that parliamentary ships be prohibited from raiding New England. Winthrop feared that now all English ships would stay away. But he was wrong. By the close of the war, New England commerce was recovering. Parliament lifted the wartime excise tax, and the Massachusetts court freed English ships from its own new customs levy of sixpence per ton. In 1646 there was free trade between old and New England.[25]

The war crisis brought Winthrop new problems and hardships, but it also gave him his greatest opportunity to act like an independent sovereign. With King and Parliament absorbed at home, the Massachusetts Bay Company pushed her territorial limits northward and, after considerable negotiation, annexed the Piscataqua River settlements of New Hampshire in 1641. The next year she expanded her limits southward to annex Pawtuxet on Narragansett Bay. In 1643 she expanded further south and forcibly annexed Samuel Gorton's settlement at Shawomet. And in order to solidify New England orthodoxy, Massachusetts invited the three smaller colonies of Connecticut, New Haven, and Plymouth to join her in forming the New England Confederation in May 1643. This famous Confederation was an obvious expression of Massachusetts' wartime autonomy. Commissioners from the four plantations met in Boston under the presidency of Governor Winthrop to agree that all future wars should be planned and fought jointly, and that disputes between members of the Confederation should be discussed at annual meetings of the commissioners. Massachusetts was the dominant partner. In case of war, Massachusetts was to supply 150 militia men for every 85 supplied by the other three colonies together. The preamble to their articles of confederation explained that the four colonies were uniting because they were dangerously "encompassed with people of several

[25] *Mass. Rec.*, II, 116, 121, 131-32; III, 12, 17; *Journal*, II, 289, 294, 300-303; Stock, *Proceedings of the British Parliaments*, I, 157, 170.

nations and strange languages"—Indians, French, and Dutch. But it was no accident that Roger Williams' Narragansett Bay plantation was excluded from the Confederation. To Winthrop, Williams also spoke a strange language, and Massachusetts, Plymouth, Connecticut, and New Haven jointly refused to recognize his government or to deal with his fellow colonists until they submitted to the jurisdiction of one of the Confederation governments.[26]

Winthrop was not satisfied with enlarging Massachusetts' authority within New England; in 1643-1644 he led his colony into active intervention in French Acadia or Nova Scotia. It was a strange episode. Two French adventurers named Charles D'Aulnay and Claude La Tour, each claiming to rule Acadia in the name of the French crown, maintained rival forts on the Bay of Fundy. La Tour, being the weaker, sent envoys to Massachusetts for help, though he himself had harried English traders along the Maine coast. In June 1643 he sailed down to Boston with 140 armed men to make a personal plea. Governor Winthrop was convinced of his piety, and the Boston merchants were willing to equip him in the hope of tapping the Acadian fur supply or at least plundering D'Aulnay. Winthrop persuaded the Boston magistrates and deputies to let La Tour hire four fully manned ships complete with arms, ammunition, and other provisions for a two-month expedition, at the rate of £520 per month payable in peltry. Winthrop did not give the expeditionary force a commission of war. Even so, his action raised a heavy storm of protest from the outlying Massachusetts towns. Why were these foreign papists being so warmly entertained? Seven leading men from Ipswich bluntly told Winthrop in a public letter that he had drawn Massachusetts into war against D'Aulnay and the French state. Winthrop answered at length, but his arguments all boiled down to the fact that he liked La Tour. Privately he admitted that he had acted too precipitously.[27]

[26] *Journal*, II, 24, 33-34, 45, 50-51, 71, 102-103, 119-27; Bradford, *Of Plymouth Plantation*, p. 330; Hazard, *Historical Collections*, II, 10, 20-21.

[27] *Journal*, I, 139, 184; II, 106-107, 129-39, 150-54; Hazard, *Historical Collections*, I, 499-502; *Winthrop Papers*, IV, 394-410. For the details of the D'Aulnay-La Tour rivalry, see Francis Parkman, *The Old Regime in Canada* (Boston,

Certainly the decision to back La Tour worked out poorly in practice. The expeditionary force of Massachusetts volunteers sailed north in July 1643 and came home five weeks later. They had put D'Aulnay to flight, killed some of his men, and pillaged a shipload of 800 moose and beaver pelts, to Winthrop's distress, though the Boston merchants were undoubtedly hoping for more sizable loot. Many people expected D'Aulnay to take revenge by raiding outlying New England plantations, and in fact he did commission his ships to seize any Massachusetts vessels they could. During the winter of 1643-1644, the Boston harbor fortifications at Castle Island, which had been given up as too expensive, were refurbished and garrisoned with twenty men. La Tour reappeared in Boston in 1644, looking again for help. Though Winthrop still favored him, the Bay magistrates overruled him and forbade anyone to assist La Tour or attack D'Aulnay. The New England Confederation commissioners also rebuffed Winthrop. "No Jurisdiction within this Confederacon," they agreed in 1644, "shall permitt any voluntaries to go forth in a warlike way against any people whatsoever" without the commissioners' orders. D'Aulnay sent down an agent to arrange a settlement with the Massachusetts government. The two parties drew up a treaty mutually pledging to keep the peace and guaranteeing Massachusetts ships the right to trade freely with either of the French rivals. Boston merchants continued to assist La Tour, but they could not prevent D'Aulnay from capturing his fort. When in the end La Tour turned perfidiously against his Boston supporters, Winthrop could only find solace in Scripture: "there is no confidence in an unfaithful or carnal man."[28]

1910), pp. 3-20; John Bartlet Brebner, *New England's Outpost, Acadia before the Conquest of Canada* (New York, 1927), pp. 23-30.

[28] *Journal*, II, 162-63, 184-88, 210, 214, 219-20, 232, 241-48, 325, 466; *Mass. Rec.*, II, 36, 57, 63-65; Hazard, *Historical Collections*, II, 19-21, 53-54; *Winthrop Papers*, VI, 412-13. Winthrop's backing of La Tour also led to trouble with England. In 1644, Madame La Tour sued a London ship captain in Boston court for refusing to take her to her husband's fort. The court awarded her £2,000 damages, and the Bay authorities seized the ship's cargo, valued at £1,100, most of which was spent by Madame La Tour in hiring three Boston ships to carry her to Acadia. The chief loser was William Berkeley, Alderman of London, who petitioned the House of Lords (May 1645) to review the case, claiming that he and his partners had been robbed of £4,500. Fortunately for Winthrop, the Lords

Winthrop's policy in the mid-1640's toward Parliament, toward his neighbor New England colonies, and toward French Acadia, was nothing if not bold. The revolutionary crisis at home, far from drawing Winthrop closer to English Puritanism, had accentuated his tendency toward splendid isolation. He had a keener sense of loyalty to his particular plantation than to the general Puritan cause. Why imitate parliamentary England? The civil war, to Winthrop, was God's punishment upon the land, which Massachusetts might hope to escape by practicing true Christian liberty. "England is a State of long standing," he wrote in 1644, "yet we have had more positive and more holesome Lawes enacted in our short tyme then they had in many hundred yeares." As the steward of godly Massachusetts, he felt smugly superior to the practices "of England and other states, who walk by politic principles only."[29]

◈ THE PURITANS in England overthrew Archbishop Laud's Commission for Regulating Plantations only to create a new colonial administration which gave Winthrop more trouble than Laud had ever done. On November 2, 1643, Parliament constituted the Earl of Warwick, admiral of the parliamentary fleet, as governor in chief of all English colonies and as head of a parliamentary commission of eighteen members vested with broad powers to inspect records and to nominate and remove governors.[30] Whereas the Laud Commission had been designed to regulate internal and colonial affairs, the Warwick Commission was merely supposed to keep the colonies, especially the valuable West Indies, externally loyal to Parliament. It seemed to pose no threat to Massachusetts. The Earl of Warwick had been the Massachusetts Bay Company's first patron, issuing its original land patent in 1628. Perhaps half of the other commissioners were personal friends of John Winthrop. Unfortunately for Winthrop, the Warwick Commissioners were also friendly to his chief victims and adver-

declined to contest Massachusetts' treatment of Berkeley's ship. Stock, *Proceedings of the British Parliaments*, I, 160-67.

[29] *Journal*, II, 257; *Winthrop Papers*, IV, 474.

[30] Stock, *Proceedings of the British Parliaments*, I, 145-49, 152-53; V. T. Harlow, *A History of Barbados, 1625-1685* (Oxford, 1926), pp. 28-29.

saries, New England rebels like Roger Williams and Samuel Gorton.

Roger Williams came to England in 1643, looking for parliamentary protection against the Massachusetts Bay Company's invasion of his sanctuary on Narragansett Bay. He applied to the Warwick Commission for a patent incorporating Providence, Portsmouth, and Newport into a single, self-governing colony. But Thomas Weld, agent for Massachusetts, presented a completely contrary proposal. He asked the Warwick Commission to grant the Massachusetts Bay Company a Narragansett patent, annexing Williams' territory to Massachusetts. Weld and Williams also took opposite sides in the great pamphlet debate of 1643-1644 between conservative English Puritans who wanted a presbyterian national church and the rapidly proliferating radical Puritans who wanted neither national church nor discipline. Naturally Weld sided with the conservatives. In January 1644, a London printer brought out an anonymous pamphlet, *Antinomians and Familists Condemned by the Synod of Elders in New England*, which told how Massachusetts in 1637 had exposed and punished errors similar to the ones currently being spread by English radical sectaries. Actually this tract had been written by John Winthrop six years before and left unpublished till now. Weld arranged a second edition (February 1644) with a more imposing title: *A Short Story of the Rise, reign and ruine of the Antinomians, Familists & Libertines, that infected the Churches of New England*. He added a new preface telling how Mrs. Hutchinson had been massacred by Indians in 1643 ("Gods hand is . . . seene herein"), and underlining the similarity between her delusions and those embraced by the London enthusiasts of 1644. Winthrop's *Short Story,* so oddly exhumed, was no literary masterpiece, but it was popular enough to warrant several reprintings.[31]

[31] C. F. Adams, ed., *Antinomianism in the Colony of Massachusetts Bay, 1636-1638* (Prince Society, Boston, 1894), XXI, 74-75, 93-94. Weld was evidently not responsible for the initial publication of this tract, since he says, in his preface to the second edition, that he came across the book "already in print without any act of his." The dates for the first and second edition are taken from the *Catalogue of the Thomason Tracts, 1640-1661* (2 vols.; British Museum, 1908), I, 305, 310.

In total contrast to Weld and Winthrop, Roger Williams found that there was also an English market for radical ideas. In February 1644 he published two pamphlets, extolling liberty of conscience and condemning the Massachusetts government's dogmatic and persecuting policies. He also produced his *Key into the Language of America,* proof to the English public (and to the Warwick Commission) that he, rather than his Massachusetts opponents, had taken an active interest in the language and beliefs of the heathen Indians. In London of 1643-1644 there was taking place the same revolt against orthodoxy, against prescribed religious discipline, which had rocked Massachusetts in 1636-1637. Only this time the rebels were not being crushed. On March 14, 1644, the Warwick Commission issued Williams a patent granting full powers of self-government to the colony of Rhode Island and Providence Plantations. Staying in London just long enough to publish his most celebrated tract, *The Bloudy Tenent of Persecution for cause of Conscience,* Roger Williams sailed back to New England with his patent.

On September 17, 1644, Williams landed at Boston where he still stood under sentence of banishment. His passport was a letter from twelve members of Parliament, an impressive group including the Earl of Northumberland and Oliver St. John, both war leaders; Isaac Pennington, Lord Mayor of London; and three members of the Warwick Commission. Williams' sponsors informed the Massachusetts government that because Mr. Roger Williams was a worthy man, persecuted by the bishops, and because "of his great industry and travail in his printed Indian labours in your parts, the like whereof we have not seen extant from any part of America," Parliament has granted him and his people a charter of government. The main purpose of the letter was to chide Massachusetts for squabbling with the Narragansett settlers at this time of crisis, when Puritans everywhere ought to rally together against the royalist enemy. Winthrop entered this document into his *Journal* without comment.[32] He and his colleagues could not well con-

[32] *R.I.Rec.,* I, 143-46; *Publications* of the Narragansett Club, VI, 306; *Journal,* II, 236-38.

test Parliament's right to grant Williams a patent which did not infringe on the privileges of the Massachusetts Bay Company. They allowed Williams free passage to Narragansett Bay. Nevertheless, it hurt Winthrop to find Parliament sanctioning the religious delusions and civil chaos of the Narragansett plantations and to be lectured for not joining in loving friendship with outcasts.

Thomas Weld resorted to skulduggery in his effort to cancel the Warwick Commission's grant to Williams. Having drafted a patent which awarded the contested Narragansett region to the Massachusetts Bay Company, Weld solicited the commissioners individually, instead of presenting his proposal at a regular meeting of the commission. He secured the signatures of eight commissioners, a bare majority. Five of them had also signed Williams' patent. Weld's Narragansett patent was not, however, properly enrolled, sealed or dated by the commission. Weld filled in a date, December 10, 1643, which being a Sunday was a palpable forgery. He did not send the Massachusetts government his handiwork until 1645. The General Court sent Williams a bullying letter, warning him to make good his claim to govern Narragansett Bay, for Massachusetts had a patent rivalling his. But the matter was carried no further. Williams says that he "returned what I believed righteous and waighty to the hands of my true friend, Mr. Winthrop, the first mover of my coming into these parts, and to that answer of mine I never received the least reply." Winthrop must have realized that Weld's patent was worthless.[33]

Worse was yet to come. Samuel Gorton followed Williams' example and went to England in 1645 to get the Warwick Commission's permission for his return to Shawomet, which the Massachusetts government had taken from him two years before. Arriving in England, he obtained the arrest of two Massachusetts men "for satisfaction of the wrongs don him by the Bay," and complained to the commissioners about his barbarous treatment. Gorton also published his story, *Simplicities Defence*

<hr />

[33] *New England Historical and Genealogical Register*, XI, 41-43; *R.I.Rec.*, II, 162; *Publications* of the Narragansett Club, VI, 341; *Mass. Rec.*, III, 48-49; M.H.S. *Coll.*, 1st ser., I, 278-79. For a full discussion of Weld's Narragansett patent, see M.H.S. *Proc.*, 1st ser., V, 400-406; VI, 41-77.

against Seven-Headed Policy. He was not so simple as to miss any chance for contrasting his own loyalty to "the State of Old England" with Massachusetts' usurpation of sovereignty. The Bay government supplied Weld with evidence to be presented against Gorton, but in May 1646 the Warwick Commission decided to protect the rascal. Randall Holden, the man who had addressed the Massachusetts General Court as a generation of vipers, sailed into Boston in September, bringing Governor Winthrop orders from the Warwick Commission to let the Gortonists resettle undisturbed at Shawomet, with free passage through Massachusetts jurisdiction. Though the commissioners could not "easily receive any evil impression concerning your proceedings," they pointed out to Winthrop that Shawomet "is wholly without the bounds of the Massachusetts patent granted by his majesty." Winthrop would not let Holden disembark without the other magistrates' permission; some wanted to jail him; but he was allowed to pass through unhindered.

Gorton himself passed through Boston in 1648 with a safe-conduct from the Earl of Warwick. The General Court refrained from seizing him by the margin of one vote. Gorton says that the Narragansett Indians marvelled to see him return safe and sound. Massachusetts men had convinced the Indians that Gorton and his crew were not true Englishmen, so the Indians thought of them as a special people called Gorton-oges, and concluded that the war which they heard of in England was between the Englishmen and the Gorton-oges. Gorton's return must mean that the Massachusetts English did not dare to hurt their enemies because the Gorton-oges were winning the war in England.[34] The Indians' theory of history was not altogether foolish. By the time Winthrop died, Gorton's settlement at Shawomet was firmly and finally incorporated into Williams' colony of Rhode Island and Providence Plantations.

By 1646 the Warwick Commission had checkmated Winthrop's plan to extend his orthodoxy throughout New England. The next question was whether the commission would try to

[34] Gorton, *Simplicities Defence*, pp. 152-53, 166-67; *Winthrop Papers*, V, 92, 95; *Journal*, II, 329, 332-34, 343-44, 392-93; Stock, *Proceedings of the British Parliaments*, I, 176.

interfere with Winthrop's orthodoxy inside Massachusetts. The victorious Roundheads in England were rejecting the Massachusetts model in reforming their church and state. The Presbyterians, who dominated Parliament, found Massachusetts Puritanism too independent from the national church, while the Independents who led the New Model Army found it too dogmatically intolerant. Sir Henry Vane, leader of the Parliament radicals and former governor of Massachusetts, wrote Winthrop that his colony ought to learn to get along with people of differing religious views, as English Independents have had to do. Within Massachusetts, a number of merchants petitioned the General Court to suspend its laws persecuting Anabaptists and Antinomians. The colony was flooded with books from England, says Winthrop, "some in defence of anabaptism and other errors, and for liberty of conscience as a shelter for their toleration, etc., others in maintenance of the Presbyterial government (agreed upon by the assembly of divines in England) against the congregational way, which was practised here." The General Court summoned a synod at Cambridge in 1646 to reassert the correct form of church government and discipline, but both the Hingham church, a Presbyterian stronghold, and the Boston and Salem churches, influenced by radical sectaries recently come from England, boycotted this gathering. Mutiny spread to Plymouth Colony in 1646, where a bill providing for full religious toleration almost passed the General Court. "You would have admired," Edward Winslow wrote to Winthrop, "to have seen how sweet this carrion relished to the pallates of most of the deputies!"[35]

This variegated criticism of New England orthodoxy reached its peak in 1646-1647 when the Remonstrants, a group of seven men headed by an able young scientist and entrepreneur named Dr. Robert Child, appealed to Parliament for protection against the Massachusetts government. The rebels are known as Remonstrants because of the lengthy "Remonstrance and humble Petition" which they presented to the Bay General Court in

[35] *Journal*, II, 212, 304-308, 312-13, 319-20, 324, 329-32; *Winthrop Papers*, V, 13, 23-25, 55-56; *Hutchinson Papers*, I, 153; *Mass. Rec.*, II, 85, 149; III, 51; G. L. Kittredge, "Dr. Robert Child the Remonstrant," C.S.M. *Publ.*, XXI, 25-26.

May 1646. They humbly demanded the abolition of religious qualifications for the suffrage, and religious liberty for Presbyterians. Some historians argue that the Remonstrants were trying to liberalize Massachusetts' institutions, that they wanted the same political and religious freedom which Englishmen now enjoyed at home.[36] Others contend that Dr. Child and his friends abhorred liberty of conscience and aimed at supplanting Massachusetts' congregationalism with a Presbyterian church equally narrow and rigid.[37] It is best, however, not to classify the Remonstrants too neatly. They were a very motley crew, "of a Linsiwolsie disposition," as their contemporary critic Edward Johnson wrote, "some for Prelacy, some for Presbytery, and some for Plebsbytery, but all joined together in the thing they would, which was to stir up the people to dislike of the present Government." Dr. Child was a Presbyterian; five of his colleagues were not. Their plea for civil institutions on the English model and freedom for Presbyterianism, which the Massachusetts government would obviously reject, was designed for the purpose of inviting Parliament to regulate the internal affairs of the Bay Colony.

The Remonstrants' petition of May 1646 deliberately provoked the Massachusetts General Court. Why, it asked rhetorically, has God turned against Massachusetts, while England is now so prosperous? The answer was that thousands of her inhabitants are deprived of "our due and naturall rights, as free-borne subjects of the English nation." The Remonstrants demanded the extension of full civil liberties to all freeborn men rather than just church members. They called on the Massachusetts churches to admit the colonists at present excluded from membership, or else "grant liberty to settle themselves here in a church way, according to the best reformations of England and Scotland [i.e., Presbyterianism], if not, we and they shall be necessitated to apply our humble desires to the honorable house of parliament, who we hope will take

---

[36] See Samuel Eliot Morison, *Builders of the Bay Colony*, pp. 244-68; also J. T. Adams, *The Founding of New England* (Boston, 1921), pp. 213-14.

[37] See Kittredge, "Dr. Child the Remonstrant," C.S.M. *Publ.*, XXI, 2-3, 69-74; also Miller, *Orthodoxy in Massachusetts*, pp. 298-306; and Morgan, *The Puritan Dilemma*, pp. 198-202.

our sad conditions into their serious considerations, to provide able ministers for us ... or else ... to transport us to some other place, where we may live like christians."[38] The Remonstrants were raising the most serious internal challenge since the Antinomians. It was potentially more serious, for the Antinomians had no hope of protection from Charles I, while the Remonstrants had a good chance of help from Parliament, the protector of Williams and Gorton from persecution by Massachusetts.

Governor Winthrop tried to dissuade the Remonstrants from appealing to Parliament. He even offered them the freedom to form their own Presbyterian churches. But he headed a four-man committee which prepared a "declaration of the General Court," dismissing the Remonstrants' demands and their threat of appeal, arguing "that though we owed allegiance and subjection to [Parliament] ... yet by our own charter we had absolute power of government." In November 1646, the Remonstrants were haled before the General Court. Winthrop describes how Dr. Child invoked English protection without bothering to hear the court's formal answer to his petition: "The Doctor said, they did beneath themselves in petitioning to us, etc., and in conclusion appealed to the [Warwick] commissioners in England. The governor [Winthrop] told them, he would admit no appeal, nor was it allowed by our charter, but by this it appeared what their aim was in their petition; they complained of fear of perpetual slavery, etc., but their intent was, to make us slaves to them ... by threatening us with [Parliament's] authority." Winthrop was sorely pricked by the Remonstrants' charge that godly men in England were speaking ill of the country, and more persons were leaving than joining the plantation: "what calling have these men to publish this to our reproach?" Dr. Child asserted that the Massachusetts Bay Company members had no more privileges than any mechanic belonging to an English craft guild, which stung the General Court into claiming a greater degree of autonomy for Massachusetts than it had ever done. Not only was the Bay

[38] Edward Johnson, *The Wonder-working Providence of Sions Saviour in New England*, ed. J. Franklin Jameson (New York, 1910), p. 240; *Hutchinson Papers*, I, 215-19, 221.

commonwealth above the rank of an ordinary English corporation, but she was beyond the reach of English law: "our allegiance binds us not to the laws of England any longer than
while we live in England, for the laws of the parliament of
England reach no further, nor do the King's writs under the
great seal go any further; what the orders of state may, belongs not in us to determine."[39]

Seeing that the Remonstrants were determined to appeal to
Parliament, Winthrop and his brethren sentenced them to stiff
fines totalling £200. They watched while Dr. Child hurriedly
got ready to sail for England, and on the eve of his departure
they seized him for slipping away without paying his fine.
Searching the documents he was taking with him, they discovered a petition to Parliament, asking for a governor general or
commissioners who would impose on Massachusetts an oath of
allegiance and whatever religious covenants Parliament might
choose. Winthrop says that Child managed to collect the signatures of only twenty-five disreputable non-freemen, "pretending to be in the name, and upon the sighs and tears of many
thousands." The Remonstrants were saddled with huge new
fines totalling £750, equivalent to the tax annually levied in
the whole colony, and imprisonment until the fines were paid.
The General Court was so concerned about the Remonstrants'
appeal to Parliament that it raised £100 to send Edward Winslow as Massachusetts' special agent to the Warwick Commission. The Bay leaders also prepared a petition to the Warwick
Commission which coupled Dr. Child with Samuel Gorton and
asked the home government not to protect either of them. The
commission's interference in the Gorton case, according to the
petition, had curtailed Massachusetts' liberty to manage her
own affairs. As for the Remonstrants' appeal to Parliament,
"it would be destructive to all government. . .if it should be
in the liberty of delinquents to evade the sentence of justice,
and force us, by appeal, to follow them into England."[40]

Arriving in London early in 1647, agent Winslow published

[39] *Journal*, II, 341-47, 351-52, 356-57; *Winthrop Papers*, V, 134-35; Edward
Winslow, *New Englands Salamander Discovered* (London, 1647), pp. 12-13;
Hutchinson Papers, I, 228-39, 243, 246.
[40] *Journal*, II, 358-67, 374; *Mass. Rec.*, III, 109-10, 113; *Winthrop Papers*,
V, 87, 102; Kittredge, "Dr. Child the Remonstrant," C.S.M. *Publ.*, XXI, 38-41.

two pamphlets, one entitled *Hypocrisie Unmasked*, in which he vilified Samuel Gorton, and the other, *New Englands Salamander Discovered*, in which he did the same to Dr. Child. He also appeared before the Warwick Commission. Gorton was still in London to confront him at the hearing, and Winslow was unable to satisfy the commissioners that Massachusetts had the right to invade Shawomet. But in the case of the Remonstrants, he was successful. With Dr. Child sitting in Boston jail, none of the chief Remonstrants were in London to counter Winslow's argument, and on May 25, 1647, the commissioners returned a favorable answer to Massachusetts' memorial. They deprecated the Remonstrants' pretensions to a "general liberty to appeal hither" and explained that in receiving Gorton's complaint, "we intended not thereby to encourage any appeals from your justice. . .but to leave you with all that freedom and latitude that may, in any respect, be duly claimed by you." When Dr. Child finally reached England later in the year and applied to the commissioners, he got nowhere.[41] The Warwick Commission's supervision of New England was modest after all. If Massachusetts was not allowed to persecute colonists like Williams and Gorton who lived beyond her territorial limits, she still had liberty to persecute those like Child who lived within her jurisdiction.

◄┫ DESPITE the home government's rejection of the Remonstrants' appeal, Governor Winthrop saw little reason in the closing months of his life to revise his opinion that the Puritan Revolution was turning out very badly in England. Transplanted New Englanders like Hugh Peter wrote back pressing him to learn religious toleration. Old English friends who had kept pace with the changing climate of ideas, like the Baptist divine Henry Jacie, were alienated by his persistent bigotry. There were others to tell him of the chaos and contention among English Puritans and to thank him for safeguarding Massachusetts against it.

"The newes out of England is very sadd," Winthrop told

[41] *Journal*, II, 387-392; *Winthrop Papers*, v, 142, 159-60, 169; Kittredge, "Dr. Child the Remonstrant," C.S.M. *Publ.*, XXI, 45-46.

his son John in September 1648, during the Second Civil War, when Cromwell's New Model Army was fighting and beating her recent Scottish allies. The saddest news, perhaps, was that Winthrop's own son Stephen, an officer in Cromwell's army, was mixing in radical army politics and espousing liberty of conscience. "I hope his heart is with the Lord," Winthrop said, "for he writes christianly." The Governor's last extant letter, written in February 1649 a few days before the beginning of his final illness, reported that Cromwell's army was supreme in England and calling for justice against the King. He never knew of Pride's Purge or Charles I's trial and execution.[42]

John Winthrop remained the governor and spokesman for his commonwealth until the very end of his life. In 1647 his beloved wife Margaret died, but he soon married for the fourth time, a Boston shipmaster's widow who bore him his sixteenth child. He was several times seriously ill, however, and the skimpy closing entries in the *Journal* show that he was gradually wearing down. On March 26, 1649, he died, sixty-one years old, after struggling six weeks with "a feverish distemper." He bequeathed a more modest estate than he had inherited. He also left a void in the Bay Colony which none of his fellow planters could fill. The diary of John Hull, a young Boston goldsmith, contains the following successive entries for 1649:

> "Jan. 30. Great Charles the First was beheaded upon Tuesday, about two O'clock,—a very solemn and strange act; and God alone can work good by so great a change, both to the nation and to the posterity of the king.
>
> "March 26, '48-9. Our honored Governor, Mr. John Winthrop, departed this life, a man of great humility and piety, an excellent statesman, well skilled in the law, and of a public spirit."[43]

[42] *Winthrop Papers*, v, 137-38, 144-47, 157-59, 174-75, 204-207, 216-18, 261, 265-66, 280-81, 311-12.

[43] *Journal*, II, 378-79; *Mass. Rec.*, II, 232-36; *Winthrop Papers*, v, 319, 325, 333-37; John Hull, "Diary," A.A.S. *Transactions*, III, 172-73.

John Winthrop

John Winthrop's death closed the heroic age of Puritan New England. It had been an age of black and white, of the Devil's torment and God's redeeming providence. An age of loving fellowship and inspired formulation of great principles, punctuated by ugly violence, imprisonments, banishments, and mutilations. Winthrop's continuous struggle against external control from England had paralleled his struggle against internal critics of the Massachusetts commonwealth. In the 1630's, as the architect of a new "Modell of Christian Charity," which was to inspire his brethren at home to join in the regeneration of English society, he defensively shielded Massachusetts from Archbishop Laud with the royal charter. Then in the 1640's, with his brethren at home repudiating the Massachusetts model, he turned his chartered company into an aggressive, autonomous state. He ended almost as hostile to the Puritan Parliament as to Archbishop Laud. Isolated and maligned, he chauvinistically insisted that his own little society was superior to any other. Love of New England and her chartered liberties: this was the strong and simple doctrine which he bade his children reassert in the less heroic age ahead.

BOOK TWO

&

JOHN WINTHROP, JR.
1606-1676

3. *The Sagamore of Agawam*

AMONG second-generation New Englanders, there was no
more attractive figure than John Winthrop, Jr.[1] Founder
of three towns, industrialist, scientist, doctor, governor, diplo-
mat, farmer, land speculator, he reflected almost every aspect
of his burgeoning society. Religion framed his life, but he did
not experience his father's crusading zeal. He was energetic
and public spirited, but preferred science to politics. Whereas
the elder Winthrop wrote didactic tracts and diaries of religious
meditations, the son kept medical and alchemical notebooks.
One finds fugitive opinions of all sorts, but no systematic religious or political philosophy. Portraits of the two men suggest
the difference: John, Jr., has his father's long and homely face,
the deep-set eyes, the full mouth, the unmistakable Winthrop
nose. But he lacks the parental air of a dour headmaster. Instead
he has a half-humorous, friendly look.

John Winthrop, Jr., was all things to all men, a highly re-
ceptive person, open to new ideas, adaptable to new situations.
He inspired respect and affection from nearly everyone who
came to know him. He was equally a friend to the unbending
orthodox Puritan John Davenport, to the zealous radical Puritan Roger Williams, and to the proselytizing Catholic, Sir
Kenelm Digby. John, Jr., was a much less masterful man than
the elder Winthrop, less purposeful, less disciplined, less open.
For all his warmth and charm, he could be devious, even dishonest. He stepped easily enough into the family role of public
service, but it took him many years to settle down in New England, and much pressure to make him accept his father's code
of social responsibility.

❧ THROUGH most of his life John Winthrop, Jr., was
highly peripatetic. Not until he was over fifty did he settle
down permanently in one place. This wanderlust was stimu-
lated by the circumstances of his education. He was the eldest

[1] He signed himself simply "John Winthrop," but I will follow the custom
of many of his correspondents, who addressed their letters to "John Winthrop,
Junior," to distinguish son from father.

child, born at Groton, Suffolk, in 1606 when his father was barely eighteen years old. When at age sixteen he had completed the local grammar school at Bury St. Edmunds, the boy was not sent to his father's Cambridge, but to faraway Trinity College, Dublin. Trinity was a new, small, and struggling foundation, presided over by a zealous Puritan, Sir William Temple. In John's time there, communion was never celebrated nor surplices worn in the college chapel. John's uncle Emmanuel Downing lived in Dublin and could help him from becoming "ensnared with the lustes of youthe, which," the elder Winthrop warned, "are commonly covered under the name of recreations."[2]

One catches a glimpse of the boy's life at Dublin through letters from his father and younger brothers, largely filled with affectionate exhortations to seek the blessing of the Almighty. He worked hard, enjoyed his studies, and wrote home for more books—a lifelong pursuit. Considering the narrowness of the Dublin curriculum, young Winthrop's command of chemistry, medicine, and modern languages probably owed little to his university training. The elder Winthrop was pleased with his son's frugality and industry, but by the second year he was complaining that John did not write home enough. "I expected," he said, "to have had many Latine Epistles." Though he wanted John to stay long enough to earn a degree, the boy tired of the place and after two years came back to England.[3]

During the next three years, 1624 to 1627, John generally divided his time between London in the winter and Groton in the summer. It would be well, the elder Winthrop said, "if I could heare that you were resolved upon any good Course for the imployment of your life and talentes." John was enrolled as a law student at the Inner Temple, an excuse for living in London, collecting books, and mixing with congenial people like young Edward Howes, who quickened his interest in science and alchemy. He was looking for a wife, and his father suggested a certain cousin. "It is a Religious and worshipfull

[2] *Winthrop Papers*, I, 276; Constantia Maxwell, *A History of Trinity College, Dublin, 1591-1892* (Dublin, 1946), pp. 21-62.
[3] *Winthrop Papers*, I, 271-73, 275-79, 282-84, 288-89, 313-14, 318-19.

familye," he said, "but how the woman will like you I knowe not for she is somewhat crooked." John decided to try elsewhere.[4] At the outbreak of war with France, family influence procured for him a sinecure as secretary to a ship's captain in the Duke of Buckingham's campaign of 1627 to relieve La Rochelle, the Huguenot rebel stronghold besieged by the French royal army. The elder Winthrop abhorred the swashbuckling Buckingham. Still, he borrowed a map of France to follow the Duke's progress. John, in high spirits, reported home that the English were trying to break through to La Rochelle by gaining control of a large island at the mouth of the town harbor, but it cannot have been much fun when the English were ignominiously beaten off the island. Less than half of them came home alive.[5]

No sooner was he safely back than John struck out again in the summer of 1628 to see more of the world. He thought of going to New England with John Endecott's advance party of colonists for the Massachusetts Bay Company.[6] Instead, he toured the Mediterranean on a Levant Company merchant ship. This excursion took fourteen months, punctuated by long stops in Leghorn, Constantinople, Venice, and the Netherlands. John fell in with good company and received kind entertainment, but if he had an interesting time his letters home do not show it. The voyages from port to port were tediously long; the living expenses were always too high; he missed a chance to visit Jerusalem; at Venice he was put into the lazaretto for a month to make sure he was not carrying the plague. He got back to London on August 13, 1629.[7]

Finding on arrival that his father had just determined on emigrating to New England, John readily offered to join. America would be the best adventure yet, though he knew that the elder Winthrop could never accept his company on such terms. Therefore, with the infinite world-weariness of a seasoned twenty-three year old, John wrote his father: "I have

[4] *Ibid.*, I, 318, 335-37. John remained a bachelor until 1631.
[5] *Ibid.*, 347-48, 350-53, 358-60, 365.
[6] *Ibid.*, 385, 387, 389.
[7] *Ibid.*, 402-403, 408-11, 417-18; II, 69-70, 72-77, 103-105, 149-50.

seene so much of the vanity of the world that I esteeme noe more of the diversities of Countries than as so many Innes, whereof the travailer, that hath lodged in the best, or in the worst findeth noe difference when he cometh to his Journies end, and I shall call that my Countrie where I may most glorifie God and enjoy the presence of my dearest freindes, therefore heerin I submit my selfe to Godes wil, and yours, and with your leave doe dedicate meselfe (laying by all desire of other imploymentes whatsoever) to the service of God and the [Massachusetts Bay] Company. . . ."[8] John's dedication to God's service was real enough, but his decision of 1629 was not infused with all of his father's high moral purpose. If the journey to New England was a pilgrimage in his father's eyes, it was an odyssey to John.

John proved his maturity during the next two years by his excellent work in helping to launch the Massachusetts migration. Because of his experience with the Buckingham expedition he was designated as the plantation's military expert to lay out defenses against Indians. He examined the fort at Harwich, making a copy of its plan as a model for the Massachusetts Bay fortifications. "Hee is a very ingenious Gent," one of the company leaders told the elder Winthrop, "and I am persuaded will be of speciall use to the Plantation." John's greatest service was to shoulder his father's personal affairs, enabling the Governor to prepare the fleet of 1630 and sail with it. John stayed behind with the women and young children in the family, to bring them over as soon as Groton manor was sold and his father had readied new quarters in Massachusetts. He also acted as English business agent for the emigrants, traveling to Bristol in October 1630 to supervise and pay for an emergency shipload of provisions, desperately needed if the colony was to survive the first winter. His father was very grateful. "The unexpected troubles and necessities which are fallen upon us," he wrote from America, "will bringe a great deale of business and Care upon thee, but be not discouraged, it is the Lorde who hath cast it upon thee, and he will upholde and deliver thee."[9]

[8] *Ibid.*, II, 151.   [9] *Ibid.*, 178-79, 193, 305, 316-18.

It was no easy matter to wind up the family's over-extended business affairs in England. The elder Winthrop thought Groton was worth £5,760, but John had great difficulty in getting £4,200. He generously surrendered his entailed title to his father's English estate, and reinvested £1,500 of the Groton sale money as a settlement for his stepmother Margaret Winthrop and her young children. Then he found that he must raise enough ready cash to meet the bills from New England totalling about £3,000, which were drawn in his father's name.

In February 1631, John married his first cousin Martha Fones, who had been his father's ward. There was difficulty in securing her marriage portion. Though Martha had actually turned twenty-one, the London Court of Aldermen, with jurisdiction over the Fones property, fined John five marks for marrying a minor without consent. John managed to get away for America in August 1631 with his new wife, his stepmother, several other women and children, and several hundred barrels of luggage. Aside from meal, beef, cheese, and butter, he brought at least two hogsheads of books, a large supply of chemical glassware, and seeds for a herbal and medicinal garden.[10]

John's party landed at Boston harbor on November 4, 1631. Salutes were fired, the militia formed an honor guard, and most of the colonists turned out with gifts of food for their governor's newly arrived family. It was a royal welcome to New England.

IF John had been indisposed to settle down as a young man in England, the same youthful enthusiasm carried him from project to project in America. Totally unlike his father, who immediately imposed a disciplined social system on New England and spent the rest of his life defending it, the son had a frankly exploratory attitude toward the wilderness. Between 1631 and 1645, he roamed restlessly from place to place in New England, and twice revisited the mother country.

[10] *Ibid.*, 180-81, 299-300, 325-26; III, 1-6, 27, 32-37, 41-49, 91.

John's parentage and his own abilities provided immediate entry into Massachusetts' ruling circle. He joined the Boston church and was admitted a freeman. At the General Court of May 1632, when all the chief officers of the colony were for the first time publicly chosen by the freemen, he was elected an assistant, beginning forty-three years of almost continuous service in the magistracy of Massachusetts and Connecticut. But in the 1630's John only attended about half the court sessions, and never figured conspicuously in the deliberations. William Coddington, driven to Rhode Island in the Antinomian crisis, reminded John years later of how "thou bare thy testimony aginest persecution" when they were fellow Massachusetts magistrates from 1632 to 1637. Actually, John stayed away from the court session of November 1637 in which the Antinomian leaders were sentenced to banishment.[11] If he sought to temper the rigor of the Bay regime, he did so unobtrusively. Undoubtedly he had no desire to clash with his father. Already he was becoming known as "gentle" Mr. Winthrop, as a "meek and modest" magistrate.

For the first year in Massachusetts John lived under the parental wing, but he soon got a chance to strike out for himself. In 1633 the colony leaders decided to set up an outpost against the menacing French plantation at Port Royal by starting a new town at Agawam, the fertile land above Cape Ann, the most northerly coastal area within the Massachusetts patent. John was put in charge, says his father, but allowed "no more out of the bay than twelve men; the rest to be supplied at the coming of the next ships." To join this party required a certain spirit of adventure. Agawam was twenty-five miles from Boston and ten from the nearest neighbors, peculiarly open to Indian or French attack. John set forth with his twelve men in March 1633. Some of them later recalled his promise "that if we would come hither with him he would not forsake us but

---

[11] *Journal*, I, 76-80, 90-91; *Mass. Rec.*, I, 95, 205, 367; M.H.S. *Coll.*, 4th ser., VII, 287. Between 1632 and 1641, John attended 45 of the 82 Massachusetts court sessions where attendance is recorded. He was once fined for his absence (*Mass. Rec.*, I, 230). He often lived inconveniently far from Boston, and for a year in 1634-1635 was away in England. His father did not miss a single meeting, so far as the records show.

live and die with us."[12] That summer he supervised the laying
out of a town, soon to be called Ipswich, which because of its
good farm land grew by the end of the decade to be second in
importance only to Boston. John had a two-storied house in
Ipswich ready for his wife by winter, with four sparsely furnished rooms, a "cabinett of Surgerie" in the parlor and a chemical laboratory in the storehouse. He began to clear a farm
outside the town, with the help of three or more servants, including an Indian named Ned.[13]

John's friends nicknamed him "the Sagamore of Agawam"
after the Indian chief of the region around Ipswich. He scarcely
earned the title. Barely a year after Ipswich was started, in
October 1634, John was sailing back to England. His chief
reason for deserting the new plantation so quickly was the
tragic death of his wife Martha and her infant child in the late
summer of 1634. This marriage may not have been very happy,
for Martha was subject to "pasions and weaknes," and fits of
melancholy.[14] Poor John had little choice but to go back to
England for a new wife if he wanted to raise a family in America. Besides, there was family business to be cleared up in England, and a need for someone to report to the colony's backers
at home and to buy further supplies. Certainly his departure
was a nasty shock to Ipswich, as Nathaniel Ward, the newly
installed minister, boldly told him. But this was merely the
first of many occasions in which John left others to carry on a
project he had started.[15]

He made the winter voyage in a small and frail ship bound
for the west of England, but carried by storms "through many
desperate dangers" to Galway on the west coast of Ireland.

[12] This claim was made in an Ipswich petition of 1637 against John's removal
from the town, but only three of the ten known men who came with him from
Boston in 1633 signed the petition. See T. F. Waters, *A Sketch of the Life of
John Winthrop the Younger* (Ipswich Historical Society *Publications*, VII), p.
22; *Journal*, I, 118, 120; *Mass. Rec.*, I, 103, 105.

[13] For Ipswich's rapid growth, as measured by her tax and militia quota, see
Mass. Rec., I, 225, 243, 260, 294; for John's property in Ipswich, see George
A. Schofield, ed., *The Ancient Records of the Town of Ipswich, 1634-1650* (Ips-
wich, 1899), pp. 3-4; Waters, *John Winthrop the Younger*, pp. 10-16, 65-67.

[14] *Ibid.*, 9, 65-66; *Winthrop Papers*, III, 23-24, 73, 81, 94, 141, 165.

[15] *Ibid.*, 129, 131-32, 175, 177-78, 216. For a contrary view, see Newton,
Colonizing Activities of the English Puritans, p. 176.

Travelling overland, he reached Dublin by December and headed north for Ulster. "Keepe sufficient privacy," urged Joshua Hoyle, his old teacher at Trinity College, for Ireland under Lord Deputy Wentworth was a much more dangerous place for Puritans than when John had lived there as a student ten years before. Nevertheless, as he passed in Puritan circles from northern Ireland to Scotland and on to London, he met everywhere upper-class people who were vastly discontented with Charles I's personal rule and eager to talk about emigrating to New England. In Ulster, for instance, Sir John Clotworthy plotted with John by coded letters how to ship over livestock and servants without rousing the Lord Deputy's attention. He also discussed emigration with John Livingstone, an eminent Scotch-Irish divine, whose American grandson would marry John's granddaughter in Connecticut some seventy years later.[16]

In the spring of 1635 John reached London, just when the government was most actively hostile to New England. The trial of the Massachusetts Bay Company charter by *quo warranto* was about to open in the Court of King's Bench. On March 25 Emmanuel Downing sent John, who was visiting in Suffolk, a warning: "this day my brother Kirby came to me to tell me that mr. Atwood the leather seller was with him, to give notice that you should walk warily and close because there be some that laye wayte to Attach you." In this atmosphere John married his second wife, an eighteen year old girl named Elizabeth Reade. Her brother Thomas was a business acquaintance. Her step-father Hugh Peter was minister of the English church at Rotterdam. Both men accompanied John when he returned to New England. John and Elizabeth were to be happily married for thirty-seven years.[17]

At the time of his marriage John also contracted with a group of the most prominent Puritan lords and gentlemen, including Lord Saye and Sele, Lord Brooke, Sir Arthur Hesilrige, John Pym, and John Hampden, to set up a plantation for them on his return to New England, in the expectation that they would

[16] *Journal*, I, 205-206; *Winthrop Papers*, III, 180, 187-96, 227, 247-48, 388-89.
[17] *Ibid.*, 176, 194-95; Stearns, *The Strenuous Puritan*, 31-33.

soon settle there. This was the Saybrook project. John's employers had a deed of conveyance (March 19, 1632) from the Earl of Warwick to the Connecticut area, which up to 1635 was unoccupied save by rival Dutch and English trading posts on the Connecticut River. They had already broached to the Massachusetts government in 1634 the possibility of moving to Connecticut. Knowing that the Dutch might soon take possession, and that Sir Ferdinando Gorges was asking the King in the spring of 1635 to partition New England into vast proprietary grants for himself and friends, Lord Saye and his associates resolved to make good their claim by sending over an expedition under John Winthrop, Jr.[18]

At the end of July 1635 John sailed for Boston with a commission as "governor of the river Connecticut" for one year upon arrival and with instructions to build a fort near the river mouth, with an adjoining 1,500 acres of farm land and houses for the proprietors, "such houses as may receive men of qualitie." John was a natural choice for the task. Accompanying him as ambassadors for the prospective emigrants were Hugh Peter and young Henry Vane. The Saybrook project was no chimera. John's employers paid him an unspecified salary and £2,000 for labor and supplies in New England, sent after him a twenty-five ton bark laden with such things as ironwork for a portcullis and drawbridges and twenty or more men, including an experienced military engineer named Lion Gardiner. They urged John to build houses quickly, for they were "in a way of selling off their estates with the greatest expedicion." Henry Lawrence, one of the associates, wrote John optimistically in September that "there ar like to come more over next Summer both to be wittnes of what you have done and to thanke you for it, then you ar yett aware of."[19]

Through no fault of John Winthrop, Jr., Saybrook was dropped by its sponsors. There were three good reasons for this move. In the first place, Charles I's government would

[18] Andrews, *Colonial Period*, II, 128, n.3; Benjamin Trumbull, *A Complete History of Connecticut* (2 vols.; New Haven, 1818), I, 495-97; *Journal*, I, 160-61; Charles J. Hoadly, *The Warwick Patent* (Hartford, 1902), pp. 8-10.

[19] *Winthrop Papers*, III, 198-206, 209-12; Andrews, *Colonial Period*, II, 76, n. 1; *Journal*, I, 202-203, 207-208; M.H.S. *Coll.*, 3rd ser., III, 136-37.

not willingly permit such prominent Puritans to skulk out of England, and they found it impossible to sell their estates without attracting attention. As early as September 1635 some of them "found the Countrie full of reports of their going" and dared not stir further. In the second place, John found on reaching Boston in October 1635 that settlers from the Massachusetts towns of Dorchester, Watertown, and Newtown, during his absence in England, had appropriated the best land in the Connecticut Valley outside the Massachusetts limits and within the bounds of his clients' Warwick deed. They were busily setting up the towns of Hartford, Windsor, and Wethersfield. Finally, John found that men such as his father disliked the prospect of high-ranking English newcomers moving in and taking over the leadership of New England. The Saybrook gentlemen offered to join the Massachusetts government if a hereditary class of gentlemen was established and suffrage based on property instead of church membership. But the Bay Colony, prizing godliness above blue blood, rejected their terms.[20]

In the face of these difficulties, John's work in starting Saybrook plantation at the mouth of the Connecticut was not one of his happier performances. He stayed the first winter in Boston and Ipswich with his new wife, but shipped down twenty men to begin work in early November 1635, just in time to prevent a Dutch sloop from taking possession of the place. Saybrook was to be primarily a fort, the strongest in New England, supported by agriculture and traffic with other plantations.[21] During the winter of 1635-1636, John joined Peter and Vane in trying to persuade the Connecticut Valley settlers to acknowledge the rights and authority of the Saybrook group and leave sufficient room for them. John's bargaining position was weak. The Connecticut Valley settlers were already in possession, and John had no instructions for laying out a system of government which would incorporate them, so he had to agree in March 1636 that the Valley towns should govern themselves for the

[20] *Winthrop Papers*, III, 211; Hutchinson, *History of Massachusetts-Bay*, I, 410-13; Newton, *Colonizing Activities of the English Puritans*, pp. 181-84.
[21] *Journal*, I, 207, 209; *Winthrop Papers*, III, 238, 246, 254, 286.

time being under joint commission from himself and the Massachusetts court. Unfortunately the gentlemen in England expected him to make the Valley settlers reserve large tracts of land for them, and this he could not do.[22]

John finally came down to Saybrook in April 1636, but five months at his new plantation proved to be enough. The fort needed more men and provisions, but little money was being collected in England for further supplies. "The gentlemen seeme to be discouraged in their design heere," wrote the elder Winthrop, and John could sense that Saybrook was becoming orphaned. His workmen complained of ill treatment; they wanted the services of a minister and they wanted to eat something besides pease porridge. The local Indians, the warlike Pequots, were hostile toward the white men's infiltration into Connecticut. Tension mounted as several Indian traders were murdered. John had a commission from the Massachusetts government to treat with the Pequot sachem and threaten war unless the Pequots gave satisfaction. His diplomatic negotiations failed. In the name of Massachusetts he broke off relations with the Pequots, and then went up to report to the September General Court and see his newborn daughter.[23]

John quit Saybrook several months before the end of his term as governor, and left Lion Gardiner in charge of the thinly manned outpost, to spend a miserable winter behind the palisade, beleaguered by Pequots. Gardiner said, "it seemes that wee have neather masters nor owners but are left like so many servaunts whose masters are willinge to be quitt of them." Saybrook continued its anomalous existence without further direction from John and eventually joined the other Connecticut River towns in 1644. Meanwhile, John's employers in England also thought he had let them down. Not until March 1638 did they agree to reimburse him for his expenses. Then was Downing able to announce to his nephew, "I have cleared your reputation and fidelity with them all."[24]

[22] *Journal*, I, 203, 477-78; *Mass. Rec.*, I, 170-71; *Winthrop Papers*, III, 218-19, 229-30, 243, 274.

[23] *Ibid.*, 262, 266-68, 270-72, 281-85, 289; M.H.S. *Coll.*, 3rd ser., III, 138-40; *Mass. Rec.*, I, 177.

[24] M.H.S. *Coll.*, 3rd ser., III, 139-44; *Winthrop Papers*, III, 319-21, 323, 381-82, 513; IV, 20.

Disenchanted with Saybrook, John moved fitfully from place to place between 1636 and 1641. The town of Ipswich tried very hard to tie him down. "I feare," Nathaniel Ward wrote him in 1636, "your tye or obligation to this state and in speciall to this towne is more than you did well consider when you ingaged your self another way. . . ." To prevent John's transferring to Boston in 1637 as captain of the fort on Castle Island, fifty-seven Ispwich men asked the Bay government not to deprive "our Church & Towne of one whose presence is so gratefull & usefull to us." Ipswich bribed him with an additional grant of land on Castle Hill, which had been set aside as the town common, if he would stay. Nevertheless, he soon moved ten miles south to Salem. He also staked out a claim to Fisher's Island, off the Connecticut coast at the entrance of Long Island Sound.[25] By 1641 he had a grander outlet for his talent and energy. The near collapse of New England's economy, occasioned by the struggle at home between King and Parliament, prompted him to launch a New England ironworks to help restore the colonists' prosperity. For this project he needed English capital and skilled manpower. When the three Massachusetts agents, Peter, Weld, and Hibbins, sailed for England in August 1641 in the hope of resuscitating the Bay economy, John went along with them.

This English visit lasted almost two years. The atmosphere had changed enormously since John's last visit in 1635. He landed at Bristol in late September 1641 after a rough passage in a little sixty-ton ship from Newfoundland, to find King and Parliament heading into civil war. John remained rather disengaged from the revolutionary crisis. His main occupation was the ironworks project, but he also helped Peter and Weld to solicit money and supplies for the Bay Colony. John says he assisted the two agents in all their negotiations for over a year, "with many expensive travailes therein," on condition that he be paid £50 out of the collected money for his services. Quite likely he had a hand in the anonymous promotional tract, *New*

[25] *Ibid.*, III, 216-17; IV, 5, 11-13, 339; V, 187; Waters, *John Winthrop the Younger*, pp. 20-22; *The Ancient Records of the Town of Ipswich, 1634-1650*, pp. 7, 26; *Mass. Rec.*, I, 304; J. H. Trumbull, ed., *Public Records of the Colony of Connecticut* (10 vols.; Hartford, 1850-1877), I, 64-65; hereafter referred to as *Conn. Rec.*

Englands First Fruits, issued in the spring of 1643, which offered a reassuring picture of Harvard College and of the expanding Bay economy. John refused, however, to join Peter in a discreditable buccaneering expedition of 1642 known as the Adventurers for Ireland, authorized by Parliament to exact vengeance for the Catholic natives' savage rebellion against their Protestant English overlords. John's former employers, Lords Saye and Brooke, and some of the London merchants interested in his ironworks were among the Adventurers, investing money in the hope of Irish land and booty. John Humfry, defeated rival of the elder Winthrop in Massachusetts, was one of the commanding officers. "Good deare loveing Sagamore," Humfry wrote John in July 1642, "let us have your companie if possible." And he closed the letter in a striking valediction: "With my love and my love over and over and through and through I rest Your most affectionate foolish faithful John Humfry."[26]

John went to the continent for several months in the summer and fall of 1642 to study medicine and visit German and Dutch scientific friends. At about the same time, the renowned Moravian teacher and scholar, Comenius, also left England for Holland and Germany, disappointed in his hope of opening a Universal College for the advancement of learning. John was acquainted with Comenius twenty years later; perhaps he knew him now. If so, this would explain Cotton Mather's statement that "Comenius was indeed agreed withall, by our Mr. Winthrop in his Travels through the Low Countries, to come over into New-England, and Illuminate this College and Country, in the Quality of a President." The Harvard board of overseers seems to have asked John to look for a suitable European scholar who would preside over the struggling new college and build up its prestige. In any case, Comenius was diverted from Harvard to Sweden by Chancellor Oxenstierna.[27] Otherwise,

---

[26] *Winthrop Papers*, IV, 352; V, 122; Stearns, "The Weld-Peter Mission," C.S.M. *Publ.*, XXXII, 210-14; Stearns, *The Strenuous Puritan*, pp. 187-91; Richard Bagwell, *Ireland under the Stuarts and during the Interregnum* (3 vols.; London, 1909), II, 36-42.

[27] Samuel Eliot Morison, *The Founding of Harvard College* (Cambridge, 1935), pp. 243-45; Albert Matthews, "Comenius and Harvard College," C.S.M. *Publ.*, XXI, 155, 165-68, 178. It is possible that John's invitation to Comenius

John Winthrop, Jr.

John's continental trip was highly eventful. He went to Hamburg and from there overland, through country ravaged by twenty-four years of international war, to Amsterdam. His chest of clothes and books, shipped from Hamburg by sea, was confiscated by Flemish pirates. Returning to England by the close of 1642, John completed arrangements for his ironworks and was ready to embark for New England in May 1643. Again he ran into trouble. His ship, the *Anne Cleeve*, was held up at Gravesend by a port officer. Trapped off the English coast by unfavorable winds, the ship took fourteen weeks to cross the Atlantic, double the normal time. It was about the first of September before he and his workmen reached Boston, all of them sick with fever.[28]

It was twelve years since John's first arrival at Boston. His life had been far more cosmopolitan and adventurous than his father's, far less channeled to a system of philosophy, far less committed to New England. Happily his range of interests never narrowed. But from this point on, John's energies would be increasingly dedicated to the little world of New England.

AFTER managing his ironworks project for a year, John in 1645 turned once again to Connecticut, this time permanently. He founded his third town in the region known as Pequot, between the Connecticut River and Narragansett Bay, the former headquarters of the Indians who had been all but exterminated in the Pequot War of 1637. Pequot was rocky country, without the meadowland of the Connecticut Valley, though the harbor at the mouth of the Pequot River fifteen miles east of Saybrook was unobstructed, large, and deep. John evidently planned to stake out a sort of proprietary colony at the east end of Long Island Sound. He was then nearly forty years old, with only scattered pieces of property, mostly undeveloped, to pass on to his growing family. Now he hoped to expand his holdings. He already had title to Fisher's Island,

---

came not in 1642 but in 1661, when the two men were both again in the Netherlands. In 1662 the Harvard overseers were looking in England for a replacement for President Chauncey. But by this time, Comenius was an old man, and John had less connection with the college.

[28] *Winthrop Papers*, IV, 356, 361-63, 424-25; *Mass. Rec.*, II, 41.

a few miles off shore from Pequot harbor. He claimed a large coastal area further west, around the present town of Niantic, on the basis of a verbal agreement with an Indian sachem in 1636, when he was governor of Saybrook. And he could hope to make good an even more shadowy title, which he bought in 1645, to land on Long Island across the sound from Pequot.[29]

John applied to the Massachusetts General Court in June 1644 for permission to start his new plantation. Pequot lay outside the limits of Massachusetts' charter, but this did not prevent the court from accepting John's application. Selling the last of his property in Ipswich, John came down in the early summer of 1645 to set up a farm on Fisher's Island and then made a second trip, this time travelling overland from Boston in the early winter, to choose a good site at the mouth of Pequot River on the mainland for the town. In 1646 the first settlers began building. That autumn John moved his family from Ten Hills to Fisher's Island until his town house was ready, a stone building set on the point of land called Winthrop's Neck which jutted out into the Pequot River.[30]

Saybrook and the Connecticut River towns, which by this time were joined into the single government of Connecticut, welcomed John's new plantation but contested Massachusetts' jurisdiction over it. John himself professed to be neutral on this question, but he certainly wanted to remain within the suzerainty of Massachusetts if only because the remote Bay government would interfere less in his plans. In 1647 he ventured to tell the New England Confederation commissioners that some of the Pequot planters would be very disappointed with any jurisdiction other than Massachusetts. Nevertheless, the commissioners awarded the plantation to Connecticut. The Hartford government soon set strict boundaries to Pequot plantation, discounted John's Indian deed to the land at Niantic as

[29] *Winthrop Papers*, IV, 416; V, 46-47, 59-60; Hazard, *Historical Collections*, II, 93-94; I. M. Calder, "The Earl of Stirling and the Colonization of Long Island," *Essays in Colonial History presented to Charles McLean Andrews by his Students* (New Haven, 1931), pp. 85-87.

[30] *Mass. Rec.*, II, 71; *Winthrop Papers*, V, 19-20, 30, 100, 121; William R. Carlton, ed., "Overland to Connecticut in 1645: A Travel Diary of John Winthrop, Jr.," *N.E.Q.*, XIII, 504-505; Frances M. Caulkins, *History of New London* (New London, 1895), pp. 45-47, 59, 90-91.

merely "a transient airy passage," and warned him that his Long Island claim "will be founde weake."[31] To make matters worse John and the Connecticut government disagreed sharply about how to handle the Pequot Indians. Hartford wanted them kept in vassalage to the Mohegan Indians, who had been Connecticut's allies in the Pequot War. John wanted to take the Pequots under his own protection. He kept appealing to the commissioners of the New England Confederation until the elder Winthrop on his deathbed in March 1649 implored his son "as if it wear [sic] his last requst, that you wold strive no more about the pequod Indians." John finally persuaded the commissioners to allot the Pequots their own planting ground near the English plantation.[32]

Understandably, relations between the Pequot plantation and the Connecticut government were for several years decidedly cool. John continued to accept his annual election as a Massachusetts magistrate until 1650 and shunned the Connecticut elections, despite the Hartford authorities' repeated efforts in 1647, 1648, and 1649 to install him as a Connecticut magistrate in order to have some properly qualified official resident at Pequot. Governor Haynes grew angry, but John did not bother to come to the court at Hartford and take the freeman's oath until May 1650. He was finally elected a magistrate in absentia the following year. Even the name of the new town caused trouble. John and his fellow planters wanted to call it London. Hugh Peter assured John that this name would not be considered presumptuous in England. In the Connecticut court's opinion, the people of Pequot "looke too high," and ought to be satisfied with the name of Fair Harbor instead. The town would not accept this paltry substitute. When John Winthrop, Jr., took office as governor of Connecticut ten years later, one of the first things that happened was that Pequot was officially renamed New London. Subsequently the Pequot River was renamed the Thames.[33]

[31] *Journal*, II, 325; Hazard, *Historical Collections*, II, 16-17, 87, 93-94; *Winthrop Papers*, V, 100; *Conn. Rec.*, I, 185.

[32] *Winthrop Papers*, V, 82-83, 101, 111-12, 124-25, 131, 161, 263, 276-77, 281-82, 319, 354; Hazard, *Historical Collections*, II, 64-66, 87-92, 101, 131-32.

[33] *Conn. Rec.*, I, 157, 164, 179, 186, 207, 218, 310, 313; *Winthrop Papers*, V, 189-90, 315-16, 320, 345; Caulkins, *History of New London*, 59, 119.

At Pequot, John began farming on a very large scale. He stocked pigs, rabbits, goats, sheep, and cattle on Fisher's Island and smaller neighboring islands, ideal for the purpose because they were free from wolves and Indians. He had two farms (and later a third) on the mainland for crops and meadowland, one of them stretching three miles along the shore opposite Fisher's Island. At a town meeting, September 1, 1650, he and his heirs were granted the "priviledge and Right of ordering and disposing all publick Buildings and affairs of this towne, now and for the future." He was given a stone quarry, the town ferry, the right to build dams or watermills in any of the local streams, the right to hunt, fish, and cut wood anywhere within the town limits, and all of his land was made tax free. He was encouraged to manufacture glass, for which purpose the town gave him the "great white sandy beach over against Bachelors Cove" and let him dig freely for clay. To manufacture saltpeter he was given Gull Island outside Pequot harbor. He built and operated the town gristmill as well as a sawmill outside the town, getting various timber rights for the latter. Finally, since the Pequot Indians threatened to run away unless they could have the personal protection of Mr. Winthrop and live on his land, the town also granted him a peninsula at the mouth of the Mystic River for the Indians to settle on.[34] In a society where land was all important, John was now almost a feudal baron, with a far finer estate to pass on to his children than the elder Winthrop had been able to accumulate.

For ten years John lived at Pequot, and the town grew rather rapidly in population and wealth. But he still chafed at this sort of life. As one of his admirers told him, it seemed a pity "that your worship. . .should live in such a place as pequid whom god hath mad fitt to be guid of a greater people." As early as 1649, when his father died, John spoke of returning to Massachusetts. Roger Williams hoped he would come instead to Narragansett Bay and intimated that the Rhode Islanders would elect him their chief magistrate. He was also urged to move to Long Island within Dutch jurisdiction by George Bax-

[34] *Ibid.*, 58, 61, 66-67, 90, 94; Winthrop Papers, Massachusetts Historical Society Library (hereafter referred to as Winthrop Mss.), v, 9; xiii, 20; R. C. Winthrop Collection, Connecticut State Library (hereafter referred to as Winthrop Collection), i, 79.

ter, the English secretary to Governor General Peter Stuyvesant. "I have often tymes heard our Governour saye you should be acceptablie welcome unto him," Baxter reported, "& for matter of privilidge or accomodation, for your selfe or any others that shall come along with you, you shall have them soe large and ample, as hee hath power to give."[35] There was still another possibility. In 1649 a number of colonists who felt boxed in at New Haven and Connecticut agreed to migrate to the Delaware River, already occupied by the Dutch and the Swedes, and they asked John to be their leader. They wanted him to visit England "and procure a pattent for the planting of dillerway [Delaware] the which we question not but your worship could easily doe we being previe to the great favour your worship have in parlament. . . ." John talked about going to England, but he did not go, and the whole Delaware project was laid aside.[36]

In the 1650's he was more ardently sought after than ever before by people from other towns, especially New Haven and Hartford. This was partly because of his growing reputation as a physician. When John Davenport, pastor of New Haven church and dominant figure in New Haven Colony, wanted to return to England for his health, Governor Eaton begged John to forestall this terrible loss by moving to New Haven and taking care of her pastor.[37] The chief reason for John's popularity was that, in both New Haven and Connecticut, the few men of parts, education, and wealth were dying off. By 1658 New Haven had lost Eaton and Goodyear, who had been respectively governor and deputy-governor ever since the colony was organized. Hartford had lost Haynes and Hopkins, who between them had almost monopolized the Connecticut governorship and deputy-governorship. Such leaders were hard to replace. In all the little towns along the Connecticut Valley and Long Island Sound there was left only one man who had

[35] *Winthrop Papers*, V, 289, 313, 347, 355-56, 361; M.H.S. *Coll.*, 5th ser., I, 369-70.

[36] *Winthrop Papers*, V, 357, 361; M.H.S. *Coll.*, 4th ser., VI, 76-77, 280.

[37] *Ibid.*, 3rd ser., IX, 294-95, 297-99; 4th ser., VII, 452-66, 469-71; Winthrop Mss., V, 11, 14; Charles J. Hoadly, ed., *Records of the Colony of New Haven, 1653-1665* (Hartford, 1858), p. 120; I. M. Calder, ed., *Letters of John Davenport* (New Haven, 1937), p. 96.

unusual ability, reputation and experience as a public officer—
John Winthrop, Jr.

John took up residence in New Haven in 1656, drawn largely
by the establishment of a new ironworks company there. He
accepted the offer of a fine house next door to Davenport's,
though he balked at taking it rent-free. Mrs. Davenport got
the place ready in November 1655, cleaning the well, hiring a
maidservant, laying in wood, wheat, and candles, even warming
the rooms. But John temporarily succumbed to the lamentations of the Pequot people and postponed moving to New
Haven until the following year. It is questionable whether he
ever intended to move permanently from Connecticut to New
Haven, the narrowest and most staunchly orthodox of all New
England Puritan settlements. Pressed hard by his new neighbors, he would not engage himself to remain with them, though
in 1657 he did buy his house from the town for £100 in goats
from Fisher's Island.[38] He did not join New Haven church,[39]
and consequently was not a freeman, let alone a magistrate.
Pequot was begging him to return. "Wee, & the whole Towne
& Church wantes you. We are as naked without you, yea, indeed
we are as a body without a head. . . ." John gave the impression
that he would move back to Pequot if the townspeople finished
the work on his new stone house. Then in May 1657 Connecticut made a supreme effort to outbid New Haven. The
General Court at Hartford elected him governor, and dispatched a letter "to acquaint him to what place the Country
hath chosen him, & to desire his present assistance as much as
may bee."[40]

It may seem odd that Connecticut should choose as her governor a man who had been indifferent if not hostile to the colony government in the past, and who was now living outside
her jurisdiction. John had been a Connecticut magistrate since
1651, but had only attended the Hartford court sessions each

[38] Franklin B. Dexter, ed., *New Haven Town Records, 1649-1662* (New
Haven, 1917), pp. 241, 305-306, 313-14, 319; M.H.S. *Coll.*, 3rd ser., x, 11-15;
4th ser., VII, 476-77.

[39] He is not included in the list of members, admittedly incomplete for this
period, compiled by Franklin B. Dexter, *Historical Catalogue of the Members
of the First Church of Christ in New Haven, Connecticut, 1639-1914* (New
Haven, 1914).

[40] M.H.S. *Coll.*, 4th ser., VII, 73, 81-82; *Conn. Rec.*, I, 297-98.

May for the annual election. Actually, the colony needed a new leader from outside. There was a divisive, bitter controversy within Hartford Church over reinterpreting the covenant: whether to keep church membership restricted to regenerate persons, or to open it to the uncovenanted majority. The General Court hoped not merely to bring John back to Connecticut but to install him in Hartford, the seat of government and of the religious controversy. He was offered the late Governor Haynes' house and lands. John hesitated through the summer of 1657 while the court sent him a second and third invitation.[41] In the end he took the governorship, very reluctantly. Among his papers is an undated statement, evidently prepared for the Connecticut court: "I accept the place only because there may be no trouble nor interruption in the . . . court and government and upon this condition that I may have liberty at any tymes to be absent about my necessary occasions without any blame, having much businesse in other parts of the country . . . and to be freed from attending the public affaires of this colony when . . . my necessary businesse call me any other way." John moved his family up to Hartford in November. He presided for the first time over the Hartford Quarter Court on December 3, 1657.[42]

For several years after coming to Hartford John remained doubtful about staying there, or at least he kept other people in doubt. Connecticut's Fundamental Orders of 1638 specified "that noe person be chosen Governor above once in two yeares." Since John held onto his New Haven house, Davenport was expecting him back in 1658 at the expiration of his term at Hartford. John stayed on as deputy-governor of Connecticut, however, and in 1659 was re-elected governor. He told Davenport of his extreme unwillingness to be separated from New Haven, which did not prevent him from renting out the New Haven house on a long lease. This arrangement displeased the New Havenites, afraid that the property would deteriorate, and they insisted on repurchasing the house despite Davenport's plea that John might yet come back.[43]

[41] *Ibid.*, 301, 306, 308; Trumbull, *History of Connecticut*, I, 297-301; Winthrop Mss., XII, 22.
[42] *Ibid.*, V, 208; C.H.S. *Coll.*, XXII, 183.
[43] M.H.S. *Coll.*, 3rd ser., X, 21-22, 24-25, 31-32; 4th ser., VII, 493-96; *New*

Meanwhile there was the problem of operating John's extensive farm at Pequot (now New London) without living there. In 1659 John sent down one John Tinker as his steward to make the New London house livable, to supervise the servants who tended his cattle, sheep, and goats on Fisher's Island, and to start up his sawmill. Judging by the stream of dolorous reports, Tinker found the estate hard to manage. Like Davenport, he anticipated John's return to New London, and was therefore doubly distressed to learn of Deputy-Governor Welles' death in January 1660, "feareing least his loss may allso occation or nessessitate your worshipps abode where you are." Tinker's fears were realized. The Connecticut people looked more than ever to John as their chief; in a referendum of May 1660 the freemen voted to delete the restrictive clause in their Fundamental Orders, and proceeded to re-elect Governor Winthrop.[44] John was subsequently re-elected governor every year until his death sixteen years later.

His entrance into the Connecticut governorship saddled him, however unwillingly, with the burden which his father had gladly taken up in 1630. The difference between the two men's response to New England was striking enough. The elder Winthrop had come as a fully mature leader, with the habit of command and a plan of action. He was at the peak of his creativity in 1630, and subsequent experience only confirmed, narrowed, and hardened his original attitude. John Winthrop, Jr., on the other hand, came as a youth, unseasoned, flexible, experimental. He had no system to establish. Indeed, during his first twenty-five years in New England he was running away from his father's system, and hence (despite strong family ties) he staked out his own isolated pioneer community in Connecticut. John kept learning and broadening himself all through his life, but his subtle talents were not altogether suited to the New England frontier. To be tied down to one place and one job was alien to his temper. Still, after 1657 he followed the parental pattern, spending his remaining days in harness to the public trust.

Haven Town Records, 1649-1662, pp. 412-13, 446; Winthrop Mss., XI, 10. [44] M.H.S. *Coll.*, 4th ser., VII, 235; *Conn. Rec.*, I, 22, 346-47.

4. *Physician and Industrialist*

ONE day in 1640, John Winthrop, Jr., opened a book from his library. According to his father's *Journal*, it was a volume "wherein the Greek testament, the psalms and the common prayer were bound together. He found the common prayer eaten with mice, every leaf of it, and not any of the two other touched, nor any other of his books, though there were above a thousand." The volume in question is now owned by the Massachusetts Historical Society. A skeptic can find that the puritanical mouse was actually not quite so discriminating, for less than half the leaves of the Common Prayer are nibbled. But the elder Winthrop probably did not exaggerate the extremely large size of John's library. Several hundred of his books are still extant, in eight languages, half of them in Latin. They attest to a wide-ranging taste, heavily weighted toward science.[1]

The emphasis on science is hardly surprising, for John Winthrop, Jr.'s pursuit of science was his chief distinguishing trait. Left in England, he might have been a virtuoso, or gentleman scholar, studying the wonders of nature as a game to exercise the intellect. Living in frontier New England, John applied his scientific knowledge and skills to immediate practical purposes. He tried his hand as a physician, a salt maker, a lead miner, and an iron manufacturer. Though he lacked his father's ambition to make New England a model for the regeneration of the world, he did try to use New England as an experimental laboratory and to improve his fellow colonists' crude material environment. He was the most notable physician and industrialist in seventeenth-century English America.

JOHN liked to call himself a student, especially a student of physic. Medicine as generally practiced in the seven-

[1] *Journal*, II, 24; Stewart Mitchell, "Two Winthrops and a Mouse, 1640," C.S.M. *Publ.*, XXXII, 387-94; Samuel Eliot Morison, *The Intellectual Life of Colonial New England* (New York, 1956), pp. 134-36.

teenth century was not a branch of science. It was dominated by barber-surgeons with their bloodletting and by old wives and clergymen with their time-honored herbal potions. John Winthrop the elder was this sort of amateur herb doctor, who medicated his family and neighbors. Among the rather few medical practitioners whose approach was scientific, who attempted to study systematically the functioning of the body in health and disease, some still clung to the ancient teachings of Galen, based on the dogma of the four elements. Galen's method of purgation was the intellectual justification for the bleedings of the barber-surgeons and the vegetable pharmacopoeia of the old wives. But a new style of chemical therapy had been evolving, using drugs compounded out of minerals. Much of the work of this school was bogus, chemistry intermingled with magic, but it was the embryo of modern medical practice. John Winthrop, Jr.'s science was chiefly chemical, as demonstrated by the extant books from his library and the character of his scientific experimentation. Hence, when he took up the practice of medicine, he followed the chemical school. He was a self-trained physician, who considered medicine always as a side line, and who made no reported contribution to medical progress. Still, his work as a doctor was his most successful application of learning and scientific skill for the benefit of New England.

John had a surgical cabinet in his Ipswich house which he must have brought over in 1631. Probably he began tending sick friends and neighbors as soon as he arrived in New England. His reputation had spread by the 1650's. Among his patients were John Davenport and his father's old nemesis Samuel Gorton. He also tended many hundreds of humbler people. Two crammed volumes of his medical records for the years 1657-1669 reveal an astonishingly active medical practice.[2]

When he lived in New Haven, and for the first year or so in Hartford, John examined from two to a dozen or more patients almost every day. Most were local people, but some came from as far as Rhode Island. A great many were children. There were not many surgical cases. Measles or the ague were

---

[2] Winthrop Mss., XXa (1657-1660); XXb (1660-1669). The following paragraphs are based on a general survey of these two volumes.

frequently John's diagnoses; the general complaint was of internal pains. John's prescriptions were relatively few and simple. He used some old fashioned herbal recipes such as wormwood and anise, and he tried other vegetable potions: rhubarb, jalap, horse-radish, amber, and powder of coral. His favorite drugs were mineral, especially niter and antimony. The sovereign Winthrop medicine for curing almost anything, which his son Wait continued to administer after John's death, was a reddish powder chiefly compounded of niter and antimony which he called *rubila*.

John's pharmacology appears to have been sound and constructive and alive to advanced practice among contemporary European physicians. His extensive correspondence with English and continental scientists all through his New England days shows a constant effort to get the latest books and keep up with current ideas despite his geographical isolation. His patients certainly had great faith in his curative powers. In 1653, for instance, a New Haven man, totally paralyzed, sent a pathetic letter three months before his death asking if there would be any use in his coming to Pequot for treatments. John occasionally indulged in such prescriptions as an electuary of sowbugs, but he avoided the quackery of his celebrated English friend Sir Kenelm Digby, who gave him the recipe in 1656 for a brew with a taste like flat beer which would cure ulcers and knit broken bones. Six spoonfuls a day, said Digby, "and you shall see a strange effect in a weeke or two."[3]

After 1657 John was not only governor but physician to the whole populace of Connecticut. By the 1660's he saw patients in Hartford only once or twice a week. But he now established a regular medical circuit through the other Connecticut towns, so as to cover a wider geographical area than before. Nearby places like Windsor or Wethersfield, which did not require an overnight trip, he visited often. Distant towns like Norwalk or Springfield, Massachusetts, or Southampton, Long Island, he visited less often and then stayed several days. Between

[3] Oliver Wendell Holmes, "The Medical Profession in Massachusetts," *Massachusetts and Its Early History* (Boston, 1869), pp. 273-76, 279-80, 296-97; M.H.S. *Coll.*, 3rd ser., IX, 296-97; X, 17.

1657 and 1660 John doctored patients from about 500 different families, and an equally large number between 1660 and 1669. Something like half of the inhabitants of Connecticut and New Haven colonies in these years came to him for help. No wonder he was uncommonly beloved by his people.

ᴀᴒ ANOTHER quite different aspect of John's science was his experimentation in technology. Even before he came to America, he devised a windmill whose horizontal rather than vertical motion permitted it to be built close to the ground. "If there may be made any use of it," he told his father, "I desire New England should reap the benefit for whose sake it was invented."[4] During the next twenty-five years, John spent much time and money exploring New England's natural resources. In particular, he applied his knowledge of chemistry and mineralogy to launch the first industrial projects in New England.

When he first reached Boston, the only local occupations were farming, fishing, and fur trading. John tried a fur-trading partnership with Emmanuel Downing and Francis Kirby in London. Downing and Kirby shipped over shoes, red cloth, coats, and blankets which he was to barter with the Indians for beaver pelts. John actually did no trading. In 1632 William Pynchon peddled the first shipment of English goods (worth £108) for him and returned John 220 pounds of beaver, which netted the partners a profit of £9 each. When John moved to Ipswich in 1633 he ordered another £100 of colored cloth from his English partners and got permission to set up a trucking house on the Merrimac River, where he hoped to tap a fresh supply of furs.[5] Again, in 1636, he brought down to Saybrook £300 worth of cloth and trinkets, only to find that the Pequot Indians refused to trade.[6]

John then began his experiments to diversify the New England economy. First he tried to manufacture salt by extracting it from sea water. In 1638 he set up a saltworks along the sea-

[4] *Winthrop Papers*, II, 193-94.
[5] *Ibid.*, III, 82-84, 98, 116, 150-52, 162-63, 170; *Mass. Rec.*, I, 108.
[6] *Winthrop Papers*, III, 254, 286; M.H.S. *Coll.*, 3rd ser., III, 139-40.

shore in what is now Beverly, Massachusetts. Because the colonists were forced to import salt from England in order to preserve their meat and pack their fish, they willingly granted John a free supply of wood for fuel. In hot, dry countries saltmakers evaporate the water by means of the sun in open terraced ponds. The New England climate forced John to work indoors, where he tried to induce evaporation artificially "by the way of boyleing." He built a "salthouse," in which he apparently pumped sea water into large wooden pans, then boiled it into a more and more concentrated brine until the impurities were separated and the water entirely boiled away. His furnace, fueled by seacoal or charcoal, was specially designed so that the substance to be boiled could be placed in a wooden vessel, an important point in New England, where all ironmongery had to be imported. Operations at Beverly were discontinued after only a year or so either because the novelty wore off or, more likely, because his method did not work.[7]

Ten years later, John returned to his old idea. He had some iron pans cast for a projected salthouse at Pequot, which suggests that his wooden pans had not worked satisfactorily. He contracted with the Massachusetts government to produce 100 tons of salt within three years, at 3s. per bushel.[8] Plans were laid aside, but the need for a saltworks remained great. By 1655 imported salt was so expensive and in such short supply that the Massachusetts General Court appointed a committee to contract with one or more merchants for the colony's provision. John now thought he had improved his system and in 1656 obtained a twenty-one-year patent from Massachusetts to make salt "after a new way, never before devised or practised."[9]

John's friend Richard Leader undertook to try the new formula in Barbados, where the tropical climate permitted evaporation by the sun. He pledged to forfeit John £20,000

[7] M.H.S. *Proc.*, 2nd ser., III, 193; *Winthrop Papers*, III, 134, 136-37, 369; IV, 141; Waters, *John Winthrop the Younger*, p. 25; William B. Weeden, *Economic and Social History of New England, 1620-1789* (2 vols.; Boston, 1899), I, 169. For a contrary view of John's saltmaking, see Morison, *Builders of the Bay Colony*, pp. 274-75.

[8] *Winthrop Papers*, V, 230, 273, 289; *Mass. Rec.*, II, 229, 241.

[9] *Ibid.*, IV, pt. I, 91, 224, 259; M.H.S. *Coll.*, 5th ser., I, 378-80; M.H.S. *Proc.*, 2nd ser., III, 193; Winthrop Mss., XI, 54.

if he did not keep his system secret. Leader spent £600 constructing a series of terraced ponds in Barbados for the brine to ripen in, but the rainy season spoiled his work and he gave up. As an old man John was still confident that his system, whatever it was, would succeed if he ever found opportunity to test it "by the experiment of a great works, well compleated." Since by that time he was living inland at Hartford, the experiment was never made.[10]

Another of John's persistent hopes was to unearth lucrative mineral deposits. Dr. Robert Child, the future Remonstrant and a fellow student of science and technology, wrote John offering to "helpe forward the digging of some good mine, if you have found any in the country." Ever since he had first come to New England, John had been prospecting. About 1640 he searched the country systematically and at great expense, or so he claimed. When he visited England in 1641 he reported to Dr. Child that his "good mine" had been discovered. He had found a deposit of black lead or graphite in a hill at Tantiusques, near present Sturbridge, Massachusetts.[11]

The only black lead deposit hitherto known was in northern England, in Cumberland, so Dr. Child and several other people became interested in John's mine. "The common uses of black-lead," Dr. Child tells us, "are first to make black-lead pens [lead pencils] for Mathematicians, &c. 2. For Painters and Limners. 3. For those that work in Copper to make their hammer go glib. And lastly, if any great pieces be found, which is rare in Cumberland Mine, to make Combes of them, because they discolor gray hairs, and make black hair of a Ravenlike, or glittering blacknesse, much desired in Italy, Spain, &c."[12]

The commercial possibilities of graphite were certainly limited, but John hoped to extract silver from it. The chief drawback of the black lead at Tantiusques, which was used by the Indians to paint themselves, was its inaccessibility. Tantiusques lay in one of the last areas to be settled in southern New Eng-

[10] M.H.S. *Proc.*, 2nd ser., III, 193-95; M.H.S. *Coll.*, 5th ser., VIII, 133-34.
[11] *Winthrop Papers*, IV, 334, 355, 395, 424.
[12] Robert Child, "A large Letter concerning the Defects and Remedies of English Husbandry written to Mr. Samuel Hartlib," (1651) quoted by Kittredge, "Dr. Child the Remonstrant," C.S.M. *Publ.*, XXI, 113.

land, some twenty-five miles east of Springfield, which was the closest plantation, and four days' overland travel by wilderness trail from Boston.

In the autumn of 1644 John sent Stephen Day, famous as the first printer in the English colonies, to reconnoiter the place and buy the land surrounding the black lead hill from the local Indian sachem. He obtained title to the hill from the Massachusetts General Court. Next he hired a man to start mining, instructing him to follow the vein of graphite into the side of the hill by cutting an inclined open trench which would allow water to drain. John would pay £2 per ton, "when he hath digged up twenty Tunnes of good marchantable blacklead, and put it into an house safe from the Indians."[13] Nothing like twenty tons was dug up, but John was at least able to send samples of ore to England, France, and the Low Countries for analysis. Though some experts said the black lead contained a high proportion of silver, Dr. Child found that it yielded only £12 or £15 worth of pure silver per ton. "I am unwilling," he said, "to beate you out of your great hopes; nay I hope I shall not discourage you from digging lustily. . . ." For over ten years John made no further attempt to mine at Tantiusques.[14]

His final effort to exploit the mine came in 1657, when he worked out a complicated partnership with Thomas Clarke and William Paine of Boston. Profits were to be split three ways between John (as owner), the miners, and Clarke and Paine, who would market the back lead in England. Unless the ore yielded a high percentage of silver the profits could not be great, since black lead per se brought £8 or less a ton in England. The Tantiusques mine was expected to produce twenty or thirty tons a year. It produced far less than this. The miners squabbled among themselves and quit one after another. The vein of black lead was cased in hard rock which could only be broken through by firing, and the miners had to spend most

[13] *Winthrop Papers*, IV, 495-98; *Mass. Rec.*, II, 82. For a fuller account of John's efforts to mine black lead, see George H. Haynes, "The Tale of Tantiusques," A.A.S. *Proc.*, N.S., XIV, 471-97.
[14] *Winthrop Papers*, V, 6, 11-13, 21, 29, 221, 248, 324; Kittredge, "Dr. Child the Remonstrant," C.S.M. *Publ.*, XXI, pp. 112-13.

of their time carting wood for fuel. There was also the problem of breaking a forty-mile path from the mine to the Connecticut River and bringing in wagons to transport the black lead. By 1658 John owed his partners at least £100, Paine thought he was neglecting the business, and John himself concluded that the digging was so expensive he would get no profit from it. Some black lead was probably shipped to England, but the mine was again abandoned after two or three years.[15]

In projecting his saltworks and especially his lead mine, John delegated most of the actual work to others. This was only one reason for his failure. Both experiments had been stymied by lack of capital, high labor costs, and wilderness conditions. Reflecting some years later on his ill success with mining, John said: "it may be God reserves such of his bounties to future generations. Plantations in their beginnings have worke ynough, & find difficulties sufficient to settle a comfortable way of subsistence, there beinge buildings, fencings, clearinge and breakinge up of ground, lands to be attended, orchards to be planted, highways & bridges & fortifications to be made, & all thinges to doe, as in the beginninge of the world. Its not to be wondered if there have not yet beene *itinera subterranea*."[16]

c❦ JOHN's biggest industrial project was a New England ironworks. It was his answer to the depression of 1640. The political crisis in England, which was wrecking commercial relations between colonies and mother country, laid bare the inadequacy of New England's undiversified, overwhelmingly agrarian economy. It was imperative that the colonists enlarge their fishing industry, shipbuilding, and overseas commerce, and even produce their own cloth in the interests of self-sufficiency. Obviously, a local metal industry would help make New England less dependent on English imports.

During his prospecting John had found bog iron ore in Braintree, about ten miles southeast of Boston. Here he proposed to erect an ambitious ironworks. Not satisfied with the

---

[15] A.A.S. *Proc.*, N.S., XIV, 477-80; M.H.S. *Coll.*, 4th ser., VII, 403-10, 496-97; 5th ser., VIII, 49-50; Winthrop Mss., XI, 166.
[16] M.H.S. *Coll.*, 5th ser., VIII, 133.

primitive technique of turning ore directly into wrought iron at a single bloomery or hearth, John wanted to try the more sophisticated and expensive indirect process which required both a blast furnace and a forge. In the blast furnace, the iron ore would be smelted with charcoal and formed into crude pig iron or cast into pots, skillets, and other iron articles. In the forge or foundry, the pig iron would be reworked into bar iron for the local blacksmiths. Such an operation necessitated an elaborate and carefully designed physical plant, with a water-driven bellows to fire the great stone furnace, and a massive water-driven hammer in the forge. A large and specialized labor force was also needed: miners and carters to supply the ore; wood cutters and colliers to prepare the charcoal; founders, fillers, and potters to work the furnace; and finers and chafers to work the forge. The Massachusetts court in 1641 offered anyone who discovered a mine the right to work it for twenty-one years, but there was not enough local capital or skilled labor to build and operate a furnace and forge. John went to England in 1641 principally to gather men and money in the mother country for his ironworks.[17]

Getting Englishmen in the Civil War crisis to invest in an American ironworks was slow and difficult work, but John did remarkably well. By the spring of 1643 a joint-stock company was formed with a dozen or more businessmen taking shares, among them the Stourbridge iron manufacturer Thomas Foley and the London ironmonger Joshua Foote. Most of the partners invested £50 or £100. John raised an additional £250 by selling his farm in Topsfield, Massachusetts to a London merchant. He was able to lay out several hundred pounds in equipment, hire experienced workmen, and still have £1000 to spend in New England. Even before sailing, however, three of the

[17] *Winthrop Papers*, IV, 425; *Mass. Rec.*, I, 327. E. N. Hartley's *Ironworks on the Saugus* (Norman, Oklahoma, 1957) is a very full study of John's ironworks, which renders superfluous any extended discussion here. Hartley is particularly good at reconstructing the physical operation of the Braintree and Lynn works. But he inflates the significance of the whole venture, while minimizing its overriding weakness: the transatlantic cross-purposes of the Massachusetts government and the English investors. On this last point, see Bernard Bailyn, *The New England Merchants in the Seventeenth Century* (Cambridge, 1955), pp. 61-71.

seven ironworkers he hired ran away. The fourteen-week voyage to New England wasted the whole summer. By the time John and his workmen had regained strength and had reconnoitered possible sites for the works, it was too late in the season to begin operations.[18]

There is an unhappy similarity between John's ironworks company of 1643 and his previous English sponsors, the Saybrook Company of 1635. In both cases the investors were absentee Englishmen whose plans were wrecked because they conflicted with the local self-interest of the Massachusetts government. In the case of the ironworks, the Bay leaders hoped that at least half the shares in the enterprise would be taken by local people. A few Massachusetts merchants did invest, but almost all the capital came from England. Business interests on the two sides of the Atlantic proved to be scarcely more harmonious than political interests. The colonists expected the ironworks to produce cheaper articles than imported ironware. The English owners expected a profit. Starting in March 1644, there were a series of negotiations between the company and the Massachusetts court. The company was granted a twenty-one year monopoly on iron manufacturing as well as allotments of waste land and tax exemptions, provided that within a stated time limit it could supply the colonists with bar iron at no more than £20 per ton.

John set up his works at Braintree, which had a central location and what seemed to be a ready ore supply. The disadvantage was that the land around the mine was already in private hands. He bought 200 acres, built a blast furnace on it in 1644, and persuaded the adjacent towns of Boston and Dorchester to grant the company 4,500 acres of waste land several miles distant, where timber could be cut for fuel. By the spring of 1645 some tons of crude or pig iron had been cast. But £1,500 had already been expended, and an equal sum was needed to build a forge if bar iron was to be turned out.[19]

Characteristically, after launching the ironworks and managing it for a year, John now wished to retire. This time the

---

[18] *Winthrop Papers*, IV, 355, 370-72, 375, 377-80, 424-25; *Journal*, II, 261.
[19] *Winthrop Papers*, IV, 425-27, 465, 498-99; V, 6-7, 359; *Mass. Rec.*, II, 61, 81, 103-104, 125-26.

project could not be simply dropped. Too many persons had sunk money into it. The English owners, who recapitalized and reorganized themselves in 1645 as the Company of Undertakers for an Iron Works in New England, thought that John had chosen a poor location and was throwing away their money. They would not accept his purchase of land at Braintree, and summarily replaced him as resident manager by hiring Richard Leader, an experienced metallurgist, on a seven-year contract at £100 per annum. Emmanuel Downing wrote John from England that he had not argued with the Undertakers, fearing to "have putt more Jeolosies into their heads of you. . . . I told them I was well assured, mr. Leder should be a welcome man unto you, . . . then mr. Leder told them that he would not medle . . . without your free Consent and Contentment. . . ." Downing thought that John could collect three years' salary at £150 per annum for his services since 1643.[20] As in the case of the Saybrook Company, John was quitting under a cloud.

The ironworks company did considerably better under its new management. Leader gave full credit to John for helping to handle the unruly workmen, but it was Leader who built the forge at Braintree and a new furnace and forge at Lynn along the Saugus River a few miles north of Boston, which proved a more favorable situation than Braintree. In 1647 he quit the Braintree works for lack of ore, while the Saugus works was turning out pots, stoves, and skillets by the ton. The following year production of good bar iron reached seven or eight tons a week, and the company was soon exporting a little ironmongery out of the country.[21]

At last one of John's projects was working well. Unfortunately, the cost of the Saugus works mounted faster than its rate of production. The iron was sold for barter, since the colonists had no ready money. The absentee Undertakers wanted cash, but the Bay court asked: what advantage is there for Massachusetts if all the profits are exported to England? It would be better to exchange fish and barrel staves for foreign iron

[20] *Winthrop Papers*, v, 6-7, 11, 27.
[21] *Ibid.*, 140, 160, 209, 246, 262; Hartley, *Ironworks on the Saugus*, pp. 107-11, 115, 121-28.

than to permit a local ironworks to despoil timber in the production of goods which the colonists are not able to buy. The Undertakers were the ones to suffer. They poured thousands of pounds into building up the Saugus works over a ten-year period, and even brought over some sixty prisoners of war from Cromwell's Scottish campaign of 1650 to serve as laborers. The cost of production was still too high, and the distance from England prevented close supervision. The Undertakers were dissatisfied with Richard Leader's management as they had been with Winthrop's, and his successor, John Gifford, ran the company into bankruptcy by 1653.

When the local courts held the company responsible for £1,366 in debts, the Undertakers protested: "wee will and doe Intend to make suite to the highest Authoritye heere [in England], . . . having discovered so much Corruption in that Countrye." The Undertakers sued Gifford for misappropriating £13,000 of their funds. After two years of haggling, the Bay General Court judged that Gifford owed the Undertakers £1,225, and after two more years Gifford managed to clear himself with his English employers. But by this time (1657) the company originally promoted by John Winthrop, Jr., was ruined. Though the Saugus works continued to operate into the 1660's, its twenty-one year monopoly was set aside by the Massachusetts government.[22]

Long before this debacle, John had moved to Pequot. Probably it was no accident that he left the Bay just in time to miss the climax of the battle over the Remonstrance. Dr. Child, who had invested £450 in the ironworks, came over to Massachusetts in 1645 to help Leader supervise it. "Dr. Child is come," Hugh Peter had written John, "that honest man who will bee of exeeding great use if the Country know how to improve him, indeed he is very very usefull. I pray let us not play tricks with such men by our jelousyes." Peter recognized that Child's opinions and manner would stir trouble; he was also quite right about the man's usefulness. It was thanks to

[22] *Mass. Rec.*, III, 91-93; IV, pt. 1, 217-20, 241-44, 252, 311; George F. Dow, ed., *Records and Files of the Quarterly Courts of Essex County, Massachusetts, 1636-1683* (8 vols.; Salem, 1911-1921), I, 400-401.

Child as much as to Leader that the Saugus ironworks was operating so effectively by 1647. Much of Dr. Child's quarrel with Massachusetts in 1646 stemmed from the clash of interests between the ironworks company and the Bay government. John shared all his scientific, medical, and technological interests with the doctor and had no more congenial friend. On moving to Pequot, he left behind one of his younger children to spend the winter in Child's family. In the spring of 1647 he asked Child to visit Pequot. "I should willingly have come along with your man," was the reply, "but your father (I thanke him) hath bin the especiall occasion of my stoppage here and imprisonment. . . ." John saw to it that Child never had to pay the final £50 of his £250 fine.[23] Actually the Remonstrants, in an extreme fashion, were fighting John's battle. He knew that his father's insistence on operating Massachusetts like a sovereign state, dissociated from Parliament as well as King, was harming New England's economic development.

The Braintree experience did not sour John's zeal for iron making. At Pequot he claimed to have "discovered some quantity of the best sort of Iron Ston that hath yet beene discovered lying convenient to be wrought in those parts. . . ." Beyond sending a sample of "metalline sand" to be tested for iron at Boston, however, he did not pursue the idea of setting up a Pequot ironworks. There was no chance of inducing a new group of English Undertakers to capitalize the venture. "Sir," Thomas Peter (Hugh's brother) wrote John from London in 1648, "there is no good to be done for Pequite by the Londoners, who for the major part are base and rotten. nothing to be don with the Parliament but matters of high Consequence." Still John volunteered in 1651 to search Connecticut for minerals as he had previously done in Massachusetts.[24] Traditional stories have come down of his prospecting in the Connecticut hills and bringing back gold. We do not hear, however, of a Connecticut gold rush.

John did find a new deposit of iron ore in New Haven colony

[23] *Winthrop Papers*, V, 30, 140-41; Kittredge, "Dr. Child the Remonstrant," C.S.M. *Publ.*, XXI, pp. 60-61; *Mass. Rec.*, II, 199.
[24] *Winthrop Papers*, IV, 465-66; V, 140, 160, 233; *Conn. Rec.*, I, 222-23.

between the towns of New Haven and Branford, and in the spring of 1655 he negotiated with the New Haven colony leaders about establishing a new ironworks company. This time he seemed to have the formula for success: a good site, strong local backing, and experienced management. The New Havenites were pathetically eager to start an ironworks. Most of the colony leaders had come from London in 1638 as well-to-do merchants expecting to make New Haven a commercial center, and had seen it become a backwater, hemmed in by Connecticut and New Netherland. An ironworks might pick up the whole economy. To avoid the transatlantic tension which had plagued John's first venture, the new company was to be locally owned. In the fall of 1655 it was announced that a furnace and forge would be built at Stony River between New Haven and Branford, and twenty men began damming the river. In February 1656 a company of undertakers was formally organized. Ownership was divided equally four ways between John Winthrop, Jr., Deputy-Governor Stephen Goodyear, and multiple subscribers from the two towns. Because John found the site and provided the workmen, he was excused from the cost of building the furnace and dam, or carting fuel. The company was granted land, timber and mining rights, tax exemptions and other privileges.[25]

The most ominous feature of the new company was its slender capitalization. John's principal partner, Deputy-Governor Stephen Goodyear, was a merchant already heavily encumbered with debts. Much of the working capital seems to have been supplied by three merchants, William Paine and Thomas Clarke of Boston, and Thomas Yale of New Haven, who together lent John £400.[26]

John came to New Haven in 1656 to manage the operation but made very slow progress. It was decided to build the blast furnace for making pig iron and to postpone building the forge for refining it. Stephen Goodyear bought a ship apparently to

[25] *New Haven Town Records, 1649-1662*, pp. 235, 260-61, 279; Winthrop Mss., XIII, 115; I. M. Calder, *The New Haven Colony* (New Haven, 1934), p. 157; Hartley, *Ironworks on the Saugus*, pp. 280-86.

[26] *New Haven Town Records, 1649-1662*, p. 376; M.H.S. *Coll.*, 4th ser., VII, 404; *New Haven Colony Records, 1653-1665*, pp. 285, 305-307.

carry the pig iron up to the Saugus foundry. Unhappily John could not even turn out pig iron because he was unable to find hearth stones to pave the base of his furnace which could withstand the high temperature of molten metal. A set of stones shipped over from England in 1658 proved to be no good, and it was the following summer before a new supply from a quarry near London arrived at New Haven.[27]

In 1657 the company lost both its leaders, Winthrop and Goodyear. The ironworks was running them both into debt, and they concluded that it would not succeed without more capital. Goodyear went off to England in search of additional financial backing either from private persons or from Cromwell's government. In April 1658 William Hooke, former New Haven minister, wrote to John from London: "I know not, yet, what Mr. Goodyeere will do; the ebbe is so low in the State, that he could not have come at a worse time, hardly, for help about your iron-works, or in reference to any other designe for the good of N.E., which will require any greate cost." Shortly after this, Goodyear died. John had already left for Hartford to accept the governorship of Connecticut and had leased his share in the company to two outsiders from Boston for seven years without asking New Haven's permission. The lessees were Thomas Clarke and William Paine, who were simultaneously trying to work John's Tantiusques lead mine. Paine had just bought half-title to the floundering Saugus ironworks and hoped to coordinate operations at Saugus, Braintree, and New Haven.[28]

The people of New Haven were properly annoyed. They were saddled with the disadvantages of an ironworks, particularly the influx of ruffianly workmen, while the hoped for trade and profits were to be drained off to Boston. Nevertheless, the colony government encouraged Clarke and Paine to proceed. Under their management the New Haven works operated certainly until 1669, but the yield seems to have been slight. In

[27] M.H.S. *Coll.*, 4th ser., VII, 402-404, 500, 502; *New Haven Town Records, 1649-1662*, p. 412; Calder, *The New Haven Colony*, p. 159; Winthrop Mss., XIII, 116.

[28] M.H.S. *Coll.*, 4th ser., VII, 403, 589; *New Haven Town Records, 1649-1662*, pp. 321-30.

1663 it appears that the first pig iron was only just produced. John was sensitive enough to criticism of his abandoning the management of the works that he offered to sell out completely. John Davenport counselled against this, hoping that he would come back to New Haven. "Here is no question made," he told John, "of your reall intendments for the good of the iron works, & of this place, nor suspicion of your seeking selfe-advantages thereby, to the hurt of this place." Davenport could not persuade him to resume an active role in the company. In 1661, after the death of William Paine, he made out a new arrangement with Captain Clarke and Paine's son, John, leasing them his share, this time for nine years, to make what profit they could out of it.[29]

John's efforts at iron manufacturing had worked somewhat better than the salt making and lead mining, but not well enough. The reasons for failure were always the same: John had too little perseverance and too little money to cope with frontier conditions. Only one of his projects, the Saugus ironworks, succeeded, and that was the achievement of Leader and Child, not Winthrop. Even the Saugus works had fallen victim to the conflict between its English owners and the Bay government. Plainly New England's industrial possibilities at this stage were severely limited. After 1657 John finally gave up. On taking the Connecticut governorship, he made no further attempts at applied science.

Notwithstanding the failure of John's technological projects, New England by the 1650's had progressed economically far beyond the pre-Civil War situation. Two native industries had blossomed forth: lumbering and fishing, both of which required less initial outlay and brought quicker returns than iron manufacturing. The New England merchants discovered that they could build seagoing ships, load them with local grain, lumber, and fish, and exchange these products for the wine, sugar, cotton, and tobacco of the West Indies and southern Europe which were needed at home and in England. New Englanders had in fact evolved a prosperous commercial economy,

[29] *Ibid.*, pp. 330-31, 349; *1662-1684*, p. 146; M.H.S. *Coll.*, 4th ser., VII, 406, 499-500, 524; Winthrop Mss., v, 29.

with the Boston merchant as the key figure. But since domestic manufacturing had proved to be inefficient, the prosperity of the colonists in general and of the Boston merchants in particular continued to depend on imported manufactured articles and luxury goods.

The psychological effect of John Winthrop, Jr.'s industrial experiments in New England was quite contrary to his father's religious and social experiment. The colonists could not achieve an economic self-sufficiency to match their intellectual self-sufficiency. When John himself became a colonial political leader, he knew from experience the benefits of close ties with England and discarded the elder Winthrop's intransigent attitude toward the home government. Absorbing the lessons of twenty-five years as an unsuccessful industrial promoter, John saw that the economic future lay in membership within the emerging English mercantile system.

5. *Splendid Isolation Reconsidered*

WHEN John Winthrop, Jr., took up the governorship of Connecticut in 1657, Oliver Cromwell's Puritan dictatorship was at its zenith. The shadow of this masterful man, the self-appointed lieutenant of God, stretched across the Atlantic. Cromwell was the first English statesman to conceive of the colonies as instruments of national policy, and he laid the groundwork for the English imperialism which took shape in the latter half of the seventeenth century. Hence, the progress of the Puritan revolution at home was whittling down the autonomy of the Puritan settlements overseas. Just as in the 1640's, when Parliament exerted larger influence over New England affairs than the King had done, so in the 1650's Cromwell intervened in New England with proportionately greater effect.

John found it necessary in the Cromwell era to reconsider his father's policy of splendid isolation. Not that he denied the ever-widening distinction between New and old England. Like most of his fellow colonists, John stood apart from Cromwell's imperialist plans. He did not visit his homeland during the 1650's. Nonetheless, he was sympathetic with much that the great Oliver was doing, especially Cromwell's policy of religious liberty, which the elder Winthrop would most have hated. At the same time John could see (as his father never would have) the essential tragedy of Cromwell's dictatorship: the bankruptcy of the Puritan crusade. With a keener sense than most of his New England neighbors, John knew that the heroic Puritan age was passing. Partly because of his detachment from English events, partly because of his disenchantment with Puritanism, John adopted a circumspect attitude toward Cromwell's government which prepared him for the startling change of 1660.

97

John Winthrop, Jr.

⟡ JOHN WINTHROP, JR., could easily have found employment in England with Cromwell's regime. Several of his close relatives held important posts in the Protectorate government. His cousin John Maidstone was steward of the Lord Protector's household. Another cousin, George Downing, was scoutmaster-general or chief intelligence officer of Cromwell's army in Scotland, and became the English ambassador at The Hague in 1657. His uncle Emmanuel Downing was clerk to the Scottish Council of State. His brother-in-law, Colonel Thomas Reade, was military governor of Stirling in Scotland.[1] His step-father-in-law, Hugh Peter, was installed in Archbishop Laud's chambers as a preacher at Whitehall and dashed off impulsive notes to John, urging him to come home and share the fruits of victory.[2] Most pertinent of all, his younger brother, Colonel Stephen Winthrop, was one of the Protector's most loyal adherents and sat in the Parliament of 1656-1658. "God hath done great things heare in England, Scotland & Irland," he wrote to John, "& not any persecuting spiritt either in nation or persons doth stand when discovered." Stephen's letters voiced disapproval of New England's continuing bigotry and persecution. "Youre brother flourisheth in good esteeme," Roger Williams reported to John in 1654, "and is eminent for maintaining the Freedome of the Conscience as to matters of Beliefe, Religion and Worship."[3]

Both Stephen Winthrop and George Downing took active parts in shaping English colonial policy during the 1650's. Winthrop was a member of the Protector's standing committee on the plantations. The chief colonial interest of Cromwell and his colleagues lay in the Caribbean sugar islands rather than New England, and they were naturally more indulgent

[1] M.H.S. *Coll.*, 4th ser., VI, 77-81, 84-85, 116; 5th ser., I, 41-42, 47; John Beresford, *The Godfather of Downing Street, Sir George Downing, 1623-1684* (London, 1925), pp. 53, 124; Sir Charles Firth and Godfrey Davies, *The Regimental History of Cromwell's Army* (2 vols.; Oxford, 1940), II, 563-66.

[2] Stearns, *The Strenuous Puritan*, pp. 334-35; M.H.S. *Coll.*, 4th ser., VI, 113-14; VII, 281.

[3] *Winthrop Papers*, V, 13, 102, 114, 320, 356; Firth and Davies, *Regimental History of Cromwell's Army*, I, 181-84, 191; M.H.S. *Coll.*, 3rd ser., X, 1-2; 5th ser., VIII, 213; C. H. Firth, ed., *The Clarke Papers* (4 vols.; Camden Society, N.S., nos. 49, 54, 61-62. 1891-1901), III, 11; Robert Vaughan, ed., *The Protectorate of Oliver Cromwell* (2 vols.; London, 1839), I, 87-88.

to their fellow Puritans than to the royalist planters of Virginia and the West Indies. Before Cromwell seized power, in the Commonwealth period of 1649-1653, Parliament had decreed her dominion over all English plantations, and the Council of State sent out punitive expeditions against the Chesapeake and Caribbean colonists who had proclaimed allegiance to Charles II and brought them to acknowledge the Commonwealth. The home government also began to legislate a protectionist commercial policy, to build the English empire into a self-contained, self-sufficient unit. In 1650 all foreign ships were banned from trading with any English colony without license from the Council of State. In 1651 Parliament passed the famous Navigation Act aimed specifically against Dutch traders, which declared that all colonial produce exported to England must be carried in English or colonial ships and that all European goods imported to the colonies must be carried directly from the port of first shipment in either native, English or colonial ships. In 1652 England went to war against the Dutch.

Despite this bellicose mercantilist policy, New England continued to receive economic favors from the Commonwealth government without surrendering much freedom of action. As in the 1640's New England shipping was exempted from customs payments. When the Dutch war cut off England's normal source of naval supplies from the Baltic, the Council of State in 1653 ordered pine masts from New England, 10,000 barrels of tar, and allocated £10,000 for the subsidization of production.[4] The English public also generously subsidized the Reverend John Eliot's efforts to Christianize the Massachusetts Indians. Stephen Winthrop wrote John that "the conversion of the Indians with you maks New England very Famous." Parliament incorporated the Society for the Propagation of the Gospel in New England to sponsor Eliot's work. In five years over £10,000 was raised, enough of which was invested

---

[4] Stock, *Proceedings of the British Parliaments*, I, 218-21; Hazard, *Historical Collections*, I, 636-38; *Cal.S.P.Col., 1574-1660*, pp. 344, 347, 392-94, 398-99; R. G. Albion, *Forests and Sea Power, The Timber Problem of the Royal Navy, 1652-1862* (Cambridge, Mass., 1926), 206-07, 213, 234-41.

in landed property so that by 1658 there was a safe annual income of £600 to be spent on the Indians.[5]

The only New England colony to pay explicit homage to the Commonwealth government was Rhode Island. Roger Williams in 1652 secured a confirmation of his 1644 patent from the Council of State. Recounting his English visit to John, he told how the "Secretarie of the Councell, (Mr. Milton) for my Dutch I read him, read me many more Languages." Connecticut and New Haven did not apply to the Commonwealth for new patents, though neither of these colonies had clear title to the land they occupied, to say nothing of a charter of government. Massachusetts still adhered to the independent policy of the elder Winthrop. In 1651 the General Court remonstrated to the Commonwealth government on hearing "that it is the parliaments pleasure that we should take a new patent from them, and keep our courts, and issue our warrants in their names, which we have not used either in the late Kinges time or since, not being able to discerne the need of such an injunction: These thinges make us doubt and fear what is intended towards us." There was no need to worry. The home government did not ask for further external signs of allegiance. In 1652 the Massachusetts General Court decreed that all inhabitants take an oath of fidelity "to the lawes of this jurisdiction" with no mention of England. Massachusetts' establishment of her own mint, also in 1652, was another gesture of independence. Her celebrated pine tree shillings were issued for more than thirty years thereafter, inscribed simply "Massachusetts in New England, A. D. 1652." Further, the Bay government felt free to annex the towns along the Maine coast. In 1653 the people of Kittery, York, Wells, and Saco acknowledged themselves subject to Massachusetts.[6]

[5] *Winthrop Papers*, v, 356; Hazard, *Historical Collections*, I, 635-36; II, 145-48, 311, 351-58, 389; Stock, *Proceedings of the British Parliaments*, I, 210; Hutchinson, *History of Massachusetts-Bay*, I, 137-41; George P. Winship, ed., *The New England Company of 1649 and John Eliot* (Prince Society, Boston, 1920), XXXVI, xxxv-xxxvi; Morison, *Builders of the Bay Colony*, pp. 299, 309-10.

[6] M.H.S. *Coll.*, 3rd ser., x, 4; Hutchinson, *History of Massachusetts-Bay*, I, 428; *Mass. Rec.*, IV, pt. 1, 79-80, 93, 109-10, 122-32, 157-65; Palfrey, *History of New England*, II, 404-405.

Splendid Isolation Reconsidered

Though Massachusetts reached her peak of autonomy in the early 1650's, she never claimed to be a sovereign state. Several historians have mistakenly reported that on October 29, 1652, the Bay government declared herself an independent commonwealth, with full sovereignty. This story has no confirmation in the colony records.[7] Royalist critics later charged that the Massachusetts Puritans "did solicit Cromwell by one Mr. Wensloe to be declared a Free State," but actually Massachusetts behaved more deferentially to Cromwell's Protectorate than to the Commonwealth. The elder Winthrop had long called Massachusetts a commonwealth and had kept legal relations with England as nebulous as possible. Winthrop's successors could not advance beyond his position without proclaiming independence in the manner of 1776, and this step they did not take. Indeed Massachusetts made one token display of allegiance to the Commonwealth. Deciding that the English flag used by the Commonwealth, with the hated St. George's cross, was "a necessary badge of distinction betwixt the English and other nations in all places of the world, till the state of England shall alter the same, which wee much desier," the General Court voted to fly this flag from the fort on Castle Island.[8]

Oliver Cromwell's assumption of military dictatorship in England and his bold foreign policy, 1653-1658, showed the New Englanders how feeble was their position in the game of international power politics. Governor Haynes of Connecticut relayed to John "newes from England of astonishing nature:. . .The Parliament of England & Councell of State are both disolved," and he described how on April 20, 1653, Cromwell told the members of the Rump that they had sat too long already and might now take their ease, while army officers hauled Speaker Lenthall out of his chair. Cromwell had previously written John Cotton of his readiness to serve New England. "I am a poore weak creature," he said, "and not worthy the name of a worme, yet accepted to serve the Lord and his

[7] I have not been able to trace the origin of this story. Viola Barnes, *The Dominion of New England* (New Haven, 1923), p. 6, states that Massachusetts declared independence; the *Encyclopedia of American History*, Richard B. Morris, ed. (New York, 1953), p. 36, repeats the allegation.

[8] *N.Y.Col.Doc.*, III, 112; *Mass. Rec.*, IV, pt. 1, 41.

people."[9] The gulf was deep, however, between the hidebound Cotton and the non-sectarian Cromwell, who shielded all the wild new religious sects emerging from the Civil War, even the Quakers with their repudiation of Puritan religious experience and their contempt for Puritan church organization. When Cromwell's Council asked the New England governments in March 1654 to proclaim him Lord Protector and issue warrants in his name, Rhode Island was again alone in complying. The Protector soon made it clear that New England was part of his system.

When Cromwell established his Protectorate, the Anglo-Dutch war was in progress, with one of the areas of conflict being the North Atlantic coast, New Netherland versus New England. The Commonwealth government had exhorted the New Englanders to "demean themselves against the Dutch as against those who are enemies to the Commonwealth." By the spring of 1653 New Haven and Connecticut spread the alarm that the Dutch were preparing to invade New England. The commissioners of the New England Confederation declared that if God called them to forestall this invasion by making war against the Dutch, 500 men must be raised from Massachusetts, Plymouth, Connecticut, and New Haven.[10] But Massachusetts, expected to contribute two-thirds of these troops, took a detached view of the crisis since the Dutch were not her immediate neighbors and refused to let the commissioners order out her men. Connecticut captured the Dutch trading post at Hartford, but it was now clear that help was required from England for more serious operations.[11]

New Englanders anxious to prosecute the Dutch attack applied in the fall of 1653 to Oliver Cromwell. William Hooke of New Haven asked Cromwell to command the Bay government to join the other colonists against the Dutch. Two Massachusetts men, John Leverett and Robert Sedgwick, disgusted

[9] M.H.S. *Coll.*, 4th ser., VII, 462-64; *Hutchinson Papers*, I, 266.

[10] *Cal.S.P.Col.*, *1574-1660*, pp. 386-87; Dixon Ryan Fox, *Yankees and Yorkers* (New York, 1940), pp. 90-97; Hazard, *Historical Collections*, II, 212-23, 231.

[11] Hutchinson, *History of Massachusetts-Bay*, I, 434-35; Hazard, *Historical Collections*, II, 250-56, 270-307; *Mass. Rec.*, IV, pt. 1, 140-44, 165-73; *Conn. Rec.*, I, 254.

with their government's pacifism, went to England in search of military aid. The fact that peace terms were being concluded with the Dutch did not stop the Lord Protector from giving them four ships, 200 men, and a commission to recruit additional New England forces for an attack on New Netherland. Roger Williams told John Winthrop, Jr., that it was "a most ingenuous and unchristian designe."[12]

Undoubtedly Cromwell intended that the appearance of this squadron in Boston harbor, the first English military expedition to be sent to New England, would impress upon Massachusetts colonists their duty to the Protectorate. The rumor circulated that Cromwell was appointing a governor-general for New England. John was told that the expedition of 1654 had a double aim, "to settle Government amongst the Colonyes" in addition to attacking New Netherland. Two of the ships reached Boston several weeks ahead of Leverett and Sedgwick, and some of the men got into a brawl with the local watch. When the constabulary "comanded them to goe before the Governour, they retorned that they weare Cromwells boyes, telling them that when the Governour was come on shoare they would."[13]

Despite this dismaying incident, Connecticut and New Haven convoked special assemblies which voted to join Leverett and Sedgwick's Dutch campaign. Plymouth was less cooperative, but even Massachusetts judged it politic to permit the enlistment of 500 volunteers. It was too late. On June 20, 1654, when a force of 800 to 900 men had been assured, word reached Boston of the peace treaty between England and the Netherlands. Cromwell's commissioners wanted to ignore the peace treaty, but the weathercock colonials immediately called off their war preparations and lifted their ban against Dutch trade.[14] Sedgwick sailed his fleet north and seized the French forts at Penobscot, St. John, and Port Royal. This was really

[12] Thomas Birch, ed., *A Collection of the State Papers of John Thurloe* (7 vols.; London, 1742), I, 564-65; M.H.S. *Coll.*, 3rd ser., X, 3.

[13] *Ibid.*, 4th ser., VI, 290; VII, 417.

[14] Birch, *Papers of John Thurloe*, II, 418-20, 425-26; Winthrop Mss., XIII, 66; *Conn. Rec.*, I, 259-61; *New Haven Colony Records, 1653-1665*, pp. 100-112; *Mass. Rec.*, IV, pt. 1, 195-97; *Hutchinson Papers*, I, 284-85.

piracy, since England was not at war with France, but it pleased the colonial merchants. The English held Acadia for the next thirteen years. The Lord Protector assumed title to the province and reimbursed Leverett and Sedgwick for their public service.[15]

Cromwell, as Roger Williams told John, looked on New England "only with an eye of pitie, as poore, cold and useles." His real colonial interest was disclosed at the end of 1654 when he sent a large expedition to seize one or more of the Spanish islands in the West Indies. Cromwell's Western Design was much more old-fashioned than the recent Dutch war, being an anti-Catholic stroke in an increasingly secular era, and an Elizabethan buccaneering raid against an empire which had lost its primacy. It stirred Williams into ecstatic hopes of "greater & greater Revolutions aproaching," and Stephen Winthrop wrote his brother: "it is not the maner of the Lord Protector to doe things by halves. He will tugg with Spaine for it, cost what will." Cromwell did not tug very effectively with Spain, though he spent perhaps a million pounds. His expedition managed to capture Jamaica, after being decimated by tropical disease and a three-year guerilla war.[16] The Protector wanted New Englanders to abandon their cold and barren settlements and plant in Jamaica, arguing that they had a clear call to better "their outward condition, God having promised his people should be the head and not the tail." He even appointed a Massachusetts magistrate, Daniel Gookin, to proselyte for Jamaica. Gookin traveled through New England in 1656, talking to the colony leaders and spreading in all the towns printed declarations of the liberal terms Cromwell offered. But he had to admit to Cromwell's foreign minister John Thurloe that the fruit of his labors was hardly worth the Protector's knowledge.[17] Only

[15] Birch, *Papers of John Thurloe*, II, 426, 583-84; M.H.S. *Coll.*, 4th ser., VI, 83; *Cal.S.P.Col.*, *1574-1660*, pp. 424, 444-45, 450, 453; Hutchinson, *History of Massachusetts-Bay*, I, 156.

[16] *Hutchinson Papers*, I, 306-308; M.H.S. *Coll.*, 4th ser., VI, 289-91; 5th ser., I, 380-81; VIII, 216.

[17] Birch, *Papers of John Thurloe*, IV, 440, 449; V, 6-7, 509-10; VI, 362; Hutchinson, *History of Massachussets-Bay*, I, 163-64; *Cal.S.P.Col.*, *1574-1660*, pp. 429-30; *New Haven Colony Records*, *1653-1665*, p. 180; A.A.S. *Transactions*, XII, pp. 97-99.

gradually could it be seen that the Western Design was not a failure, as Jamaica evolved into England's most valuable West Indies possession.

Cromwell had been unable to set in motion the Puritan apocalypse which Roger Williams was longing for. He had led his people toward a very different vision, of a far-flung English empire bound together in wealth and power.

It was against this background that John Winthrop, Jr., became governor of Connecticut in 1657. His colony was an agrarian community of about 5,000 inhabitants widely scattered among twelve small towns along the Connecticut river valley and both shores of Long Island Sound. The total population was only one quarter that of Massachusetts. Connecticut was expanding steadily, however, to the disadvantage of both New Haven colony and Dutch New Netherland. The towns of Fairfield, Stratford, Norwalk, Middletown, and Saybrook effectively restricted New Haven's jurisdictional limits, while Southampton and East Hampton were outposts on the east end of Long Island. John did a good deal to improve the affairs of his colony between 1657 and 1660, not by offering a new program but by the conciliatory spirit with which he administered the laws.

His first achievement was to patch over the ecclesiastical disputes which were splitting the Hartford, Wethersfield, and Middletown churches. The Hartford fracas was resolved in favor of the party which wanted to enlarge the church covenant, foreshadowing the Half-Way Covenant proposed by the Massachusetts clergy in 1662. While church membership was being broadened, political suffrage was being narrowed. The General Court introduced several regulations between 1657 and 1659 designed to bar unsavory persons from settling as "admitted inhabitants" in Connecticut and imposed a new property qualification of £30 for freemen or full citizens. Previously the only requirement for admission as a Connecticut freeman had been good behavior.[18] Considering the further

[18] *Conn. Rec.*, I, 21-23, 96, 290, 331, 351; David H. Fowler, "Connecticut's Freemen: The First Forty Years," *W.M.Q.*, 3rd ser., XV, 314-15.

franchise restrictions which John inserted in Connecticut's 1662 charter, it is clear that he approved of this anti-democratic trend. He was never, however, so explicitly critical of the *vox populi* as his father or his two sons.

John showed himself more consistently compassionate than Oliver Cromwell. He opposed the Protector's war policy, while sharing his toleration of radical religious sects. In contrast to the general Connecticut sentiment, he had complimented Peter Stuyvesant during the Anglo-Dutch war on his "christian-like" efforts to keep peace with New England, and said he hoped for "a speedy composure of those sadd differences betweene the 2 nations in Europe."[19] Again, in the finest expression of his conciliatory spirit, John stood out against the persecution of the Quakers. George Fox's movement was supplanting Puritanism in New and old England as the vital new spiritual force, crusading against the status quo, against steeplehouses and hireling priests, against external covenants and creeds. New England orthodoxy was miserably caught in the toils of its exclusion policy by the Quakers' eagerness for martyrdom. Certainly if John could have persuaded his fellow magistrates to ignore the would-be martyrs, the Quaker menace would never have amounted to much.

Trouble started in 1656, shortly before John became governor, when the first Quakers ventured into Boston. The Bay Colony leaders saw them as instruments of Satan, more dangerous than the Antinomians in the 1630's or the Gortonists in the 1640's. Each of the four orthodox New England Confederation governments quickly passed legislation to exclude them, but Rhode Island decided to tolerate them, much as Roger Williams loathed their religion. The Quakers continued to infiltrate from their Rhode Island base, and Massachusetts (followed at some distance by Plymouth and New Haven) met the crisis by jailing, fining, whipping, branding, and banishing. Connecticut's laws had been passed before Winthrop took office. According to the Quaker George Bishop's tract of 1661, *New-England Judged, by the Spirit of the Lord*, "as for

[19] M.H.S. *Coll.*, 4th ser., VI, 523.

Connecticote, there was little done, the Governour being a tender Man."[20]

In September 1658, urged on by Massachusetts, the commissioners of the New England Confederation recommended a drastic course of action: that any Quakers who reappeared after being twice punished and expelled should be executed. John, as commissioner for Connecticut, withheld his sanction from this proposal. Between 1659 and 1661 four undaunted believers proceeded to challenge Massachusetts' death decree, and the Bay government hanged them. John tried to stop this sorry business. All the Quaker apologists in England who broadcast the news of their comrades' colonial martyrdom singled him out as their defender. "Ye Cruel Murderers!" George Bishop shouted at the Bay government, "did not John Winthrope, the Governour of the Jurisdiction of Connecticote, labour with you, that ye would not put them to Death? And did he not say unto you, that he would beg it of you on his bare Knees, that ye would not do it?"[21] Connecticut was much less bothered than her neighbors by Quaker visitors. Eight of them were expelled between 1656 and 1660, but with a minimum of cruelty. John received congratulations from Roger Williams and the old Antinomian Captain, John Underhill, both victims of earlier Massachusetts persecution, for the publicity being given in England to "your prudent and moderate hand in these late (Quaker) trials amongst us."[22] This favorable English publicity would soon prove useful.

Another side of John's conduct in these years, his acquisition of real estate, was much less congenial to Roger Williams. Not satisfied with being the owner of Fisher's Island and the largest proprietor in New London, John now obtained further large properties in the great unsettled area between New London and Narragansett Bay. In this he typified the second gen-

[20] *Conn. Rec.*, I, 283-84, 303, 308; George Bishop, *New-England Judged, by the Spirit of the Lord* (London, 1703), p. 160.

[21] *Ibid.*, pp. 72, 157; Hazard, *Historical Collections*, II, 400; *Conn. Rec.*, I, 324; M.H.S. *Coll.*, 4th ser., VII, 287-88. For a fuller account of the Quaker martyrdom, see Rufus M. Jones, *The Quakers in the American Colonies* (London, 1911), pp. 26-110.

[22] Bishop, *New-England Judged*, pp. 226-27; M.H.S. *Coll.*, 3rd ser., X, 28; 4th ser., VII, 186.

eration's increasingly pronounced drive for property, which was supplanting the first settlers' religious impulse. Williams lamented the change. New England's Puritan society, he said, was being torn apart by "a depraved appetite after the great vanities, dreams and shadows of this vanishing life, great portions of land, land in this wilderness. . . ."[23] John's land claims would later enmesh his sons in lawsuits, and they precipitated an arid quarrel between Connecticut and Rhode Island over the Narragansett Country—the most confused, petty, and time-consuming boundary dispute in all New England history.

John's real estate ventures in the late 1650's were casually conceived. In 1659, for instance, several Indian sachems sold a vaguely defined tract north of New London, which was called Quinebaug, approximately thirty miles long and fifteen wide, to four of their English friends, Governor Endecott of Massachusetts, Governor Winthrop of Connecticut, and Joshua Huse and Amos Richardson of Boston. John's share of Quinebaug was thus over one hundred square miles. The Connecticut court confirmed his purchase, at least partially, by granting him 1,500 acres to plant a new town at Quinebaug. But the town was not started. The claim remained dormant until John's sons began developing Quinebaug in the 1690's.[24] In similar fashion he was given generous lots of land by the town of New London in the Pequot Country, east along the seacoast at Mystic and Pawcatuck Rivers. Massachusetts challenged Connecticut's jurisdiction over this area, and since Connecticut could not produce a copy of her alleged charter, the Warwick patent of 1632, to sustain her claim, the New England Confederation commissioners decided to award the town being started at Pawcatuck River to Massachusetts. As an interested party, John abstained from voting on this matter. He was learning the disadvantages of living in a colony without positive territorial rights.[25]

Much more crucial was John's interest further east, in the

[23] *Publications* of the Narragansett Club, VI, 342.

[24] Winthrop Collection, I, 110; *Conn. Rec.*, I, 337-38; Winthrop Mss., XVII, 104; Caulkins, *History of New London*, pp. 94-102.

[25] Clarence Winthrop Bowen, *The Boundary Disputes of Connecticut* (Boston, 1882), pp. 31-32; Hazard, *Historical Collections*, II, 395-97, 415-22.

Narragansett Country, a tract of roughly four hundred square miles which now comprises the southwestern third of the state of Rhode Island. Because of the Indians who lived there, and the rocky and marshy terrain, it was one of the last sections of the New England seaboard to be occupied by the English. The only really fruitful land lies in a strip along the western shore of Narragansett Bay and rises in a chain of low hills, from the ridge of which one has a handsome prospect of Conanicut Island just offshore. Here is Boston Neck, containing some of the choicest pasture in New England, the site of the great stock farms of the Narragansett planters in the eighteenth century. Up to the late 1650's this upland pasture had also been left to the Indians, save for Richard Smith's solitary trading house along the Pequot Path that led from Providence to New London. Connecticut, Massachusetts, and Rhode Island all held (or claimed to hold) English land patents embracing the Narragansett Country, all three issued under the seal of the same man, the Earl of Warwick! Connecticut claimed the Warwick patent of 1632. Massachusetts had the Narragansett patent of 1643. Rhode Island's patent, secured by Roger Williams in 1644, was more recent than the other two, but unlike them it was a regularly enrolled and authentic legal instrument. Nevertheless, the Narragansett Country was very nearly stolen away from Rhode Island by Roger Williams' good friend, John Winthrop, Jr.

John's connection with the Narragansett Country began back in 1648, when the Massachusetts General Court granted him three thousand acres at Pawcatuck River, on condition that he manufacture salt for the Bay Colony. Humphrey Atherton, captain in the Massachusetts militia and investor in real estate, wanted to know "whether there be any good place for a plentetion nere whare you had sum land granted the last Court: allso whather it would staind with your Convenience to have a plentetion nere you." John's title to the Pawcatuck land soon lapsed. Atherton, however, was determined to obtain land in this area. He offered to share with Roger Williams whatever lands he could get from the Indians if Williams would be his interpreter. Williams refused, since Atherton was invading

Rhode Island's jurisdictional limits and stirring up the Narragansetts. John joined Williams in 1650 in warning Atherton not to start a war with the Narragansetts.[26] Yet he showed no respect for Rhode Island's jurisdictional rights over the Narragansett Country. When Atherton arranged a private deal with the Indians in 1659 for the purchase of the choicest Narragansett land, John was one of his partners.

In June and July 1659, with several partners (mostly from Massachusetts) Atherton bought Boston Neck and a second, more northerly, tract along the Bay shore from the local Indian sachems. In this Atherton (or Narragansett) Company, John's name headed the list of partners. Enemies of Atherton charged that he kept one Indian sachem drunk for several days and carried him up to Boston before buying the land for a song.[27] John later said that he personally knew nothing of the land purchase at the time, and that his name was used without his knowledge or consent. Perhaps so, but a letter of July 9, 1659, from another of the Atherton partners, Amos Richardson, suggests that John was not altogether ignorant of the transaction: "Sir, you may remember, when I spoke with you last at New London, I gave you a hint of my intents concerning the Narragancet country, which business, as I conceive, is fully effected with the chief sachem. The quantity [of land purchased], as I judge, is twelve mile alongst in the Narragancet Bay. The trading-house being in the middle, it is judged to be the only place in the country for a plantation. There are at present seven purchasers besides yourself. The purchase hath cost six score pound. Many there is that would willingly join in it; but we shall do nothing before we speak with you, yourself being mentioned first in the purchase. . . .if this come once to be settled, it will make Quinnebawge of greater value."[28] Quinebaug, it may be remembered, was the district north of

[26] *Winthrop Papers*, V, 273, 279, 282-83; *Publications* of the Narragansett Club, VI, 342-43; M.H.S. *Coll.*, 3rd ser., IX, 289-91; 5th ser., VIII, 42.

[27] J. R. Bartlett, ed., *Records of the Colony of Rhode Island* (10 vols.; Providence, 1856-1865), I, 403-404, 464 (hereafter referred to as *R.I. Rec.*); M.H.S. *Coll.*, 5th ser., IX, 8-9; William D. Miller, "The Narragansett Planters," A.A.S. *Proc.*, N.S., XLIII, 57-59.

[28] N.Y.H.S. *Coll.*, II, 90-91; M.H.S. *Coll.*, 5th ser., IX, 7-8; Winthrop Mss., X, 123.

New London where Winthrop and Richardson had just joined in another vast Indian purchase.

John was clearly a passive partner in this Narragansett business. His name was being used to lend stature to the company. John paid for his share in the purchase, however, and he met with the other proprietors in November 1659 when they divided Boston Neck into eight equal farms. Furthermore, he exercised his authority as governor of Connecticut in the company's interest. When Rhode Island threatened to appeal to the home government if the company did not stop trespassing, he joined the other Narragansett partners in a conciliatory letter to the Rhode Island court. Roger Williams, ever magnanimous, replied to him in February 1660: "I have seene youre hand to a letter to this Colony (as to youre late purchase of some land at Nariganset:) The sight of youre hand hath quieted some jealousies amongst us that the Bay (by this purchase) designed some prejudice to the Libertie of Conscience amongst us:. . .my endeavoure shall be (with Gods helpe) to wellcome . . .youre interest in these parts."[29]

Meanwhile, with John's assistance, the Atherton partners were extorting the title to the whole Narragansett Country from the befuddled Indians. The Narragansetts had been creating disturbances in eastern Connecticut and Long Island, and in September 1660 the New England Confederation commissioners, John among them, issued an ultimatum. Unless the Narragansetts, in expiation for their crimes, paid 595 fathoms of wampum within four months to the governor of Connecticut, the Connecticut government would exact the sum by armed force. In case the Indians could not produce such a large supply of wampum, they were graciously permitted to mortgage the whole of the Narragansett Country to the New England Confederation. Captain Atherton, the honest broker, came to the Indians' rescue. He wrote John that he found the sachems "in a very sad condision not knowing how to discharge their engagement to the commissioners: & they intrated mee to heelpe

[29] M.H.S. *Coll.*, 3rd ser., X, 28; 5th ser., IX, 10-12; *R.I. Rec.*, I, 421-39; J. N. Arnold, ed., "The Fones Record," *Rhode Island Colonial Gleanings*, I, (1894), 4-5; Winthrop Mss., X, 83.

them. . .which upon sume condissions I have undertaken wherein your selfe is interested." Atherton's way of helping the Indians was to pay the necessary wampum to Governor Winthrop on condition that the mortgage on the Narragansett Country be transferred to his company. John balked, but Atherton swore there was "nothing but plaineness" in the scheme, and he persuaded John to accept his wampum. When the Indians failed to redeëm the mortgage within six months, it was foreclosed, and the company claimed ownership of the whole region. Naturally Rhode Island refused to recognize the validity of this transaction. It became more than ever in the proprietors' interest to have the Narragansett Country placed within the jurisdiction of a more sympathetic government, ·such as Connecticut.[30]

John's intervention in the Narragansett Country is difficult to reconcile with his protection of the Quakers. His father had been more consistent. When the elder Winthrop had moved into Rhode Island in 1643 it had been to purge New England of religious error. Indubitably New England was not what it used to be, but at least the tradition of persecuting Rhode Island was being carried on.

  By the mid 1650's, John's English correspondents were beginning to warn him that despite the external vigor of Cromwell's regime, the new Jerusalem was not yet securely built in England. Hugh Peter stopped urging him to come home. As Roger Williams pointed out, the godly party is "now in the sadle and at the helme, so high that *non datur descensus nisi cadendo*:" they cannot descend without falling. Letters from England were full of details on Cromwell's failure to find a constitutional basis for his power. John heard how the anguished Protector cried out to his 1654 Parliament "that he would wallow in his blood" before permitting restrictions on his power. In 1658 William Hooke, who had left New Haven church to become Cromwell's chaplain at Whitehall,

---

[30] *Ibid.*, X, 123; *Conn. Rec.*, I, 353, 355, 576-77; Hazard, *Historical Collections*, II, 432-34; *R.I. Rec.*, I, 465-66; M.H.S. *Proc.*, 2nd ser., II, 150-52; M.H.S. *Coll.*, 3rd ser., I, 213-17; 5th ser., IX, 12-13, 25-26.

described the Protector's fatal dilemma. His government was so desperately in need of money that another parliament would have to be summoned, but no parliament would accept Cromwell's arbitrary sword-power. "The land is full of discontents," Hooke concluded, "& the Cavaleerish party doth still expect a day, & nourish hopes of a Revolucion."[31] By the time of his death in 1658, Cromwell was as badly trapped as Charles I had been in 1640.

It was immediately clear to John's English friends that the new Protector was a poor replacement for his father. They found Richard Cromwell a much more ordinary person, "more soft & tender, & penetrable with easier cares by much," untrained for his job and unhappy in it. "I know not what will become of us," Hooke lamented to John, "we are eene at our witts end. . . . Neither are the feares of God's people (for ought I see) suitable to the appearance of danger; nor such a spirit of prayer stirring as sometimes there was."[32] After twenty years the crusade of the godly party in England was burning out.

The legatees of Puritanism who fought among themselves for the control of England, 1658-1660, were quite unable to pursue a colonial policy, let alone exert pressure on the New England governments. In February 1660 Roger Williams reported to John, "it is said that in the late Parliament yourselfe were one of the three in nomination for General Governour over New England, which how ever that designe ripend not yet youre name keepes up an high esteeme &c."[33] John may have been held in high esteem by Parliament, but he paid no more heed than the other New England officials to Parliament's navigation laws of 1650 and 1651.

In November 1659 an English privateer commanded by one Captain Penny took two Dutch vessels in Long Island Sound and claimed them as prizes under the terms of the Navigation Act. Penny's victims called this piracy, and since one of the seizures occurred within Connecticut waters, the question was

---

[31] *Ibid.*, 3rd ser., I, 181-84; X, 2-3; 4th ser., VI, 115, 292-95; VII, 204, 420, 472-73, 588-89.
[32] *Ibid.*, 3rd ser., I, 197; 4th ser., VII, 590-93; 6th ser., III, 426-427.
[33] *Ibid.*, 3rd ser., X, 28.

referred to John. Uncertain what to do, he asked his kinsman John Richards in Boston for a copy of the Navigation Act and for the advice of the Massachusetts authorities. Richards replied that the act did empower Penny to take Dutch ships importing non-Dutch cargo, but the Bay governor "tells me that they have refused the execution of it here and would soe doe still, it too much entrenching uppon us. I had hoped to have sent you the act. Captain Breedon had one, but cannot finde it at present." Indeed, no copy of the act could be found in New England. Suit was brought before both the New Haven and Connecticut courts, and it was found that both of the captured ships were English rather than Dutch. Captain Penny had to sail off without either of his prizes.[34]

The whole episode had disquieted the New Netherland merchants, and Governor Stuyvesant pointedly inquired from John whether there was any English "interdiction to prevent our people from freely trading in your Colonies just as New Englanders may trade here." If so, the Dutch would stay away. John soothingly said he presumed that the English and Dutch colonists shared in "that common benefit of corespondency according to the act of Parliament, as our principalls and their Subjects in Europe doe enjoy. We have not in our Colony any orders to the contrary."[35] Both he and Stuyvesant well knew that Parliament had declared commercial war on the Dutch, but in March of 1660 it was still practicable for New Englanders to pretend ignorance of the home government's regulations.

The halcyon days, however, by now were almost over. New Englanders generally registered shock and dismay as they followed, blow by blow, the sequence of events at home which culminated in Charles II's restoration (May 1660) and the final ruin of England's godly commonwealth. John Davenport sorrowfully wished that his English friends were safely in New England. Roger Williams was sickened to find that "the

[34] *Ibid.*, 5th ser., VIII, 56-57; Winthrop Mss., XVII, 82; Gardner Weld Allen, "The Case of Captain Penny," M.H.S. *Proc.*, LVIII, 117-30.

[35] *Ibid.*, LVIII, 124-25; G. L. Beer, *Origins of the British Colonial System, 1578-1660* (New York, 1908), pp. 398-99.

bloudie whore is not yet drunck enough with the bloud of the Saintes." Governor Leete in New Haven, Amos Richardson in Boston, and Richard Leader in Barbados all voiced similar sentiments. The only one of John's correspondents to rejoice at "Gods great worke in bringing the king againe into England" was his brother Samuel Winthrop, a sugar planter in St. Christophers, no doubt softened by the tropics.[36]

John did not share in this repugnance to the new order in England. When his cousin John Maidstone, former steward of the Lord Protector's household, wrote a long letter (March 24, 1660) reviewing the rise and fall of Cromwell's regime, his mood was one of defeat and disillusion. John replied on September 19, 1660, very grateful to Maidstone "for your great paines in so excellent & most elaborate epitome of those many strange actings and events" in England. It was much the best account he had read. But the burden of John's answer to Maidstone was to contrast New England, with its striking material progress during the past twenty years, with the mother country, racked by convulsions. The colonists now produced abundant meat and grain for export, and new settlers could cheaply hire or buy houses and farms little different from country habitations in England. On reading Maidstone's narrative, John said, he was awed by the stupendous events at home. But the net effect was "to make us thankfully acknowledge that peace we have injoyed heere in these poor colonies. . .who hath beene an hiding place to such unworthy ones when their precious bretheren have beene so long under the hurries, hazards, and sufferings by civill warres, the sense whereof. . .hath stirred up a spiritt of praier to seeke often to the throne of grace, that setled peace and prosperity may returne to our deare native country, in whose happinesse we shall exeedingly rejoyce."[37]

What John wanted for his native land, more than any particular republican or monarchical regime, was an end to twenty

[36] M.H.S. *Coll.*, 3rd ser., X, 31, 40-41; 4th ser., VII, 515, 543-44; 5th ser., VII, 249; M.H.S. *Proc.*, 2nd ser., III, 197; *New England Historical & Genealogical Register*, XXXII, 422.

[37] M.H.S. *Coll.*, 3rd ser., I, 193; 5th ser., VIII, 63-68.

years of turmoil. The elder Winthrop had also lamented the turmoil of the English Civil War, but John's craving for a return to settled peace and prosperity was different. It was the new common sense view which millions of his fellow Englishmen were coming more and more to take. By 1660 many men who had long followed the vision of Jerusalem felt the necessity for a firmly constituted government which England had not had since 1641 and which Charles II could more probably provide than anyone else. The enthusiasm with which the King was greeted on May 29 can be explained partly by traditional loyalty to the throne, partly by revulsion against army rule and Puritan blue laws, partly by the fickleness of the mob, but most of all by the longing for settled peace and prosperity. John had not abandoned his father's religious values, but he had come to feel that man cannot live by dogma alone. He was more willing than most of his New England neighbors to find merits in the Restoration.

6. *Winning the Connecticut Charter*

THE masterstroke of John Winthrop, Jr.'s career was his attainment in 1662 of the Connecticut charter from Charles II. He persuaded the home government to bestow upon his colony privileges and powers which sanctioned Connecticut's exceptional degree of self-governing autonomy throughout the colonial era, and which served as her constitution for over 150 years, until 1818. John's long labors in England, 1661-1663, mark the peak of his magnanimous public service. His charter negotiations, however, have presented historians with something of a puzzle. On the one hand, he seemingly treated New Haven Colony very shabbily, since he secured boundary limits for Connecticut which engulfed New Haven and enabled his colony to annex her protesting neighbor. On the other hand, he seemingly helped John Clarke get Rhode Island's parallel charter of 1663. "To Winthrop," concludes Charles M. Andrews, "even more than to Williams or Clarke who wrote the preliminary draft, is due" Rhode Island's chartered guarantee of liberty of conscience.[1] Was John working for the aggrandizement of Connecticut, or altruistically for the benefit of all New England?

When John's charter negotiations are closely examined, it becomes clear that his purpose was not at all altruistic. His agency was exclusively in the interests of Connecticut. He not only helped subvert New Haven Colony, he did his best to hinder and emasculate Clarke's Rhode Island charter. The central factor in John's trip to England was his bold effort, partly successful, to exploit the fluid situation of the early 1660's in order to enlarge the territorial limits of Connecticut at the expense of all her neighbors, New Haven, Rhode Island, and New Netherland.

[1] Andrews, *Colonial Period*, II, 46.

◔ WORD that Charles II had been proclaimed in England reached Boston on July 27, 1660. The only colony to consider open repudiation of the King was New Haven, and even stout Master Davenport resignedly accepted the Merry Monarch as God's instrument: "our comfort is," he told John, "that the Lord raigneth, and his counsels shall stand. In rightly obeying this King we shall become faithful to whatsoever powers [God] settles over us."[2] Back in 1634 Massachusetts could defy the threat of coercion from England in the reasonable certainty that the King had neither the will nor the resources to back up his paper orders. The military expeditions sent to America by the Commonwealth and Protectorate, however, taught the New Englanders that it was no longer safe to defy any stable home regime, particularly an unsympathetic one.

Furthermore, New Englanders were increasingly nervous about their neighbors on the Hudson and St. Lawrence. Things had changed since 1643, when the elder Winthrop had stepped into a feeble squabble between La Tour and D'Aulnay, two solitary adventurers. The colonists realized that if they now cut themselves loose from home support there was the likelihood of a well organized French or Dutch invasion fleet which they could no better resist than the military power of England. Nor was independence from the English government economically feasible in the face of the increasing mercantilist connection between commerce and politics. From 1660 on, New England governments would continue to strive for as much autonomy as possible, but within the framework of the British imperial system.

Each of the New England governments handled the question of how to deal with the restored monarchy in a somewhat individual fashion. None except Massachusetts had a royal charter, so their title to self-government was suspect in the eyes of royal officials. Naturally each colony wanted its existing frame of government endorsed by the new home regime. Rhode Island in particular needed royal protection against the New England Confederation, and she demonstrated her loyalty by proclaiming the King in October 1660, before any of

[2] M.H.S. *Coll.*, 4th ser., VII, 516.

her neighbors. Further action was delayed by lack of money. In August 1661 the Rhode Island Assembly ordered that £200 be raised, and instructed Dr. John Clarke, the colony's London agent, to secure royal confirmation of Williams' patent of 1644. Meanwhile Massachusetts had been postponing action in the vain hope that the monarchy would not last. Then John Leverett, the Bay's London agent for the past decade, reported that the royal government was being deluged with complaints against Massachusetts. "The generall vogue of people," Leverett said, "is that a governour will be sent over. . . ." Immediately the General Court composed suitably vague and unctuous addresses (December 19, 1660) to King and Parliament, and sent Leverett instructions on how to defend the colony. The King was not proclaimed in Massachusetts, however, until the following August.[3] Plymouth Colony proclaimed the King in June 1661, but could not afford to send an agent to England in quest of a royal charter.

In New Haven Colony, anti-monarchical sentiment continued stronger than in the other New England colonies. New Haven had no English patent; she had merely bought land from the Indians. In the spring of 1661 the colonists opened negotiations with Stuyvesant to move into the wilds of what is now New Jersey, where they might enjoy autonomy under Dutch suzerainty.[4] New Haven's reluctance to share the other New Englanders' new-found royalism is well illustrated by the story of Goffe and Whalley. These gentlemen had signed Charles I's death warrant and had served as major generals in Cromwell's army; they were among the several score of Englishmen who had risen to prominence in the 1640's and 1650's as Cromwellians or republicans and had fled abroad in 1660 to escape execution or imprisonment. Most of the exiles retreated to Holland, Germany, and Switzerland. Goffe and Whalley were almost alone in coming to New England. Evidently those men who were public enemies of the King in 1660 wanted to stay out of the reach of English law. Most of them fared rather

[3] *R.I. Rec.*, I, 433-34, 442-48; Hutchinson, *History of Massachusetts-Bay*, I, 179-81; *Hutchinson Papers*, II, 41-42; *Mass. Rec.*, IV, pt. 1, 449-56.
[4] Calder, *The New Haven Colony*, pp. 216-19.

miserably no matter what place of exile they chose. Certainly Goffe and Whalley found New England a most unsafe retreat and their only unswerving friends in New Haven.

The two regicides were treated as honored guests upon their arrival in Boston, July 1660, until it was rumored that a royal governor might be sent over. The question then became whether to detain the two visitors to be shipped back to England if called for or permit them to escape. Goffe and Whalley left for New Haven just before a royal proclamation arrived calling for their apprehension. Two months later in May 1661, Governor Endecott commissioned two young royalists, Thomas Kirke and Thomas Kellond, to arrest them. Kirke and Kellond went first to Hartford where they found Governor Winthrop exceedingly cooperative. He could afford to be, because he knew that the regicides had passed beyond Connecticut's jurisdiction. He made a great bustle about launching a search throughout the colony, gave Kirke and Kellond a Connecticut warrant, and packed them off for New Haven the very morning after their arrival. "They are very deserving gentlemen," John wrote Endecott, "for the great care, diligence, and activity in the vigorous and speedy prosecution of that design wherein you had employed them."[5] John may have been trying to throw the two hunters off their scent, because he gave them a false rumor that Goffe and Whalley were in New Amsterdam. Actually Kirke and Kellond suspected the truth, that their quarry was hidden in or near New Haven. Since the New Haven government would give them no help, they had to return to Boston empty-handed and the two refugees were allowed to live out their days in safe if dreary retirement on the New England frontier.

New Haven's resistance to the Restoration worked enormously to Connecticut's advantage. Connecticut's legal status in 1660 was almost as unsatisfactory as New Haven's. She claimed to have inherited the powers acquired by the Saybrook proprietors when they were planning to colonize on the Connect-

[5] N.Y.H.S. *Coll.*, II, 17; A.A.S. *Transactions*, III, 199; *Hutchinson Papers*, II, 55; Winthrop Mss., V, 28; Lemuel A. Welles, *The Regicides in Connecticut* (Hartford, 1935), pp. 3-4.

icut River. The Earl of Warwick, president of the Council for New England, had issued the Saybrook gentlemen a deed of conveyance (March 19, 1632) to a large tract incorporating the territories of both Connecticut and New Haven colonies. He had purportedly also issued them a patent, the Warwick patent of 1632, which had never since been seen and was probably a fiction. In 1644 George Fenwick, one of the Saybrook partners, promised to the Connecticut government "that all the lands from Narragansett River [Bay] to the fort of Saybrook, mentioned in a patent granted by the earl of Warwick to certain nobles and gentlemen, shall fall in under the jurisdiction of Connecticut, if it come into his power."[6] Even if the Warwick patent did exist, Fenwick was not legally qualified to convey it. He was only selling Connecticut the eastern half of the tract conveyed to the Saybrook proprietors by the Warwick deed, which was completely unacceptable, since almost all of Connecticut's towns lay west of Saybrook and the Connecticut River. In short, the Fenwick purchase was of little use. What Connecticut needed in 1660 was to have the King confirm the alleged Warwick patent in the name of Connecticut Colony or grant her a new royal charter. Since New Haven was a geographical enclave within Connecticut, either of these alternatives would almost inevitably embrace both colonies.

John Winthrop, Jr., was the pivotal figure in Connecticut's plans. In October 1660 he wrote his son Fitz, "I told you of some probabilities of my going over for England: the same thoughts are continued, and the occasions of this colony will require some to goe over. . . .but because it cannot be till summer there is no certaine conclusion about it." At the same time John requested his brother-in-law Colonel Reade to ask his commander, General Monck, the most powerful man in England in 1660, for his favor toward Connecticut.[7]

By March 1661 the Connecticut court reached the final decision to send Governor Winthrop to England as the colony agent. The court proclaimed its allegiance to the King. The

---

[6] Trumbull, *History of Connecticut*, I, 508. Trumbull prints Warwick's deed of conveyance, which he confuses with the alleged patent, in *ibid.*, 495-96.

[7] Winthrop Mss., V, 18-19; M.H.S. *Coll.*, 5th ser., 69-72.

necessary preparations for John's mission were completed by June so that he could sail that summer. An address and a petition to the King were drafted. Charles II was asked to believe that Connecticut had no patent because she had refused to make illegal engagements with any of the recent English regimes. The King was asked either to confirm the colony's privileges as contained in the Warwick patent or to grant a new charter as liberal as the Massachusetts charter of 1629. John was given £80 for current expenses and a letter of credit for £500 to cover whatever charges he would incur in London.[8]

The extent of Connecticut's territorial ambitions in 1661 is revealed by her instructions to agent Winthrop. He was to look for a copy of the Warwick patent in England to see if its terms were suitably generous. Otherwise he was to petition for a charter with boundaries stretching "eastward to Plimouth line, northward to the limits of the Massathusetts Collony, and westward to the Bay of Delloway, if it may bee."[9] The new Connecticut would incorporate not only New Haven, but the whole of Rhode Island and Dutch New Netherland.

John had personal reasons for wanting to take the Narragansett Country from Rhode Island, and Long Island from the Dutch. His Narragansett land purchase could best be protected by merging the Narragansett Country into Connecticut. Similarly, he held land on Long Island, now uneasily divided between the English and the Dutch. Since 1650 the eastern three-quarters of the island had been ceded to New England, with the dividing line at Oyster Bay. The Dutch exercised jurisdiction over ten villages adjoining Manhattan, while there were only six scattered villages along the edge of the Sound and on the eastern end to be administered by New Haven and Connecticut. However, the English colonists greatly outnumbered their Dutch neighbors, and were infiltrating into New Netherland jurisdiction to such an extent that five of the ten Dutch villages were predominantly English in composition. When John learned that the people of Setauket, Long Island, were

[8] *Conn. Rec.*, I, 361-62, 367-70, 582-83; C. A., Foreign Correspondence, II, 5; Trumbull, *History of Connecticut*, I, 511-12; C.H.S. *Coll.*, XXIV, 6-7; Albert C. Bates, *The Charter of Connecticut* (Hartford, 1932), pp. 11-12.
[9] *Conn. Rec.*, I, 580-81.

agitating to break their union with Connecticut, he warned them (June 1661) that Connecticut has "long since proclaymed the king our soveraigne lord. . . .you and wee are all under the supreme power of his majesty, and he may. . .imply displeasure if any particular persons shall endeavour to make. . .divitions amongst you."[10] Ostentatious loyalty to Charles II was to be the new cement for Connecticut colony.

John's relationship in 1661 with New Haven, where he had many dear friends, was deliberately equivocal. It has been supposed that he agreed to a cooperative plan proposed by Governor William Leete of New Haven whereby John was to procure a single patent for the two colonies, and that John had no intention of infringing on New Haven's liberties when he went to England.[11] The fact is that he evaded collaboration with Leete. Preparations for his trip were kept pretty well hidden. When Leete wrote John on April 11, 1661, he had not yet heard of the agency. As late as May 24, after the petition and address to the King, letters to high court officials, and instructions to the agent had been drawn up in almost final form, John wrote to Leete: "it is as you mention that I have some thoughts of a voyage into England but I expect to heare further by the next ships before having an absolute resolution but am in a way of preparation. . . .If I goe for England you may please to command me what your occasions require. . . ."[12]

It was a perfunctory offer, and John could figure that many New Havenites would refuse to beg the King's favor. Stubborn John Davenport, for instance, asked John (June 16) to "desist from your purposed voyage to England, at least, for this yeare." But while John was hastily arranging to sail for Europe from New Amsterdam,[13] Governor Leete decided that New Haven must come to terms with the King. He was prompted by a letter from the Connecticut government, reminding New Haven of "our own real and true right, to those parts of the Countrey where you are seated, both by conquest

---

[10] Winthrop Mss., v, 28.

[11] Calder, *The New Haven Colony*, pp. 220-21; Andrews, *Colonial Period*, II, 141.

[12] M.H.S. *Coll.*, 4th ser., VII, 546-48; Winthrop Mss., v, 28.

[13] M.H.S. *Coll.*, 4th ser., VII, 520; 5th ser., I, 391; VIII, 73.

purchase and possession. . . ."[14] Leete went up to Hartford
and proposed to John that New Haven be included within the
Connecticut patent as a separate and autonomous unit. John
appeared amenable, and Leete went back to New Haven and
drew up a petition for him to present to the King. John quickly
left for New Amsterdam, bypassing New Haven territory, so
that while poor Leete was waiting in Guilford with his petition
he had already gone by way of Saybrook. Before sailing, John
assured Davenport that he was not trying to annex New Haven,
and in case Connecticut's boundaries were drawn that broadly,
"Newhaven Colony should be at full liberty to join with them
or not."[15]

Clearly John was saying one thing to Leete and another to
Davenport. All that Leete could do was send a copy of his
petition to John in England and ask him to look out for New
Haven's interest. In August 1661 the New Haven court proclaimed the King. "I wish," Leete wrote to John, "that you
& wee could procure one Pattent, to reach beyond Delawar. . . ."
The Connecticut court had in fact given John instructions to
procure such a patent, but solely in the name of the Connecticut government.[16]

John embarked at New Amsterdam on a Dutch ship named
De Trouw in mid-July. He chose New Amsterdam rather than
Boston in order to avoid requests for assistance in England
from Massachusetts and Plymouth. Governor Prince of Plymouth found himself in much the same hapless position as
Leete. "We ar not a litell greved," he wrote on September 29,
1661, to John in England, "that we had not the hapynes to
know of your gowing for England, tell after your departur,
and so prevented of communicating our mind unto you. . .as
to our own Collony in pertekler." Prince, like Leete, asked
John to present his colony's petition to the King.[17] Winthrop's

[14] C.A., Foreign Correspondence, II, 4.

[15] *New Haven Colony Records, 1653-1665*, pp. 419-20, 521; *Cal.S.P.Col.,
1661-1668*, p. 125; *New Haven Town Records, 1662-1684*, p. 13.

[16] M.H.S. *Coll.*, 4th ser., VII, 548-50.

[17] E. B. O'Callaghan, ed., *Documents Relative to the Colonial History of the
State of New York* (14 vols.; Albany, 1856-1883), II, 460 (hereafter referred
to as *N.Y.Col.Doc.*); M.H.S. *Coll.*, 5th ser., I, 392-93.

agency, however, was being financed solely by Connecticut for Connecticut's sole advantage.

John did not wish to injure his New Haven friends, or Roger Williams, or even the Dutch, but he was hardly such an innocent as to overlook the implications of the instructions he carried. Being a practical businessman, he saw that the great agricultural, commercial, and industrial potentialities of Long Island Sound could be far better realized if the mainland towns along the Sound, the Connecticut river towns, the Long Island towns, and the unexploited Narragansett region were all joined in one economic and political unit. John knew, too, that the New Haven leaders were despondent and uncertain of their colony's future. Most of the New Havenites would readily pool their numbers, energies, wealth, and resources with the people of Connecticut if given a good reason for doing so. This was Winthrop's grand design in 1661.

AFTER a tedious Atlantic passage, John landed at Amsterdam on September 6, 1661. There he conferred with the directors of the Dutch West India Company, who operated New Netherland. In Amsterdam and Leyden he was visited by a number of old friends, scientists and scholars, among them perhaps Comenius, whom he had invited to Harvard twenty years before. He reached London on September 18 and took lodgings with a merchant named William Whiting, formerly of Hartford, in his house on Coleman Street, next door to the church where John Davenport had once been minister.[18]

When he had last visited his native land in 1641-1643, John had seen the English people harden into mutiny against their King. Now he found himself in the midst of a reverse process, the solidification of the royalist triumph of 1660. The very figure of the new monarch, the Black Boy, romantically tall, dark, and handsome, with his curling hair and proud, sensuous face, enraptured Englishmen surfeited with godliness. Some Tories have remained in ecstasy ever since.

John's relatives who had been enjoying the fruits of power in the 1650's made the leap from Cromwell to Charles II

[18] Winthrop Mss., V, 29; XI, 21; M.H.S. *Coll.*, 5th ser., I, 394.

with varying degrees of success. His cousin George Downing had been knighted in 1660 for betraying government secrets to Charles Stuart just before the Restoration, and remained the English ambassador at The Hague. John visited him there; the conversation may have been rather strained. It was at the time when Sir George was watching for English anti-monarchists who had fled to the continent. He caught three of the regicides in 1662 and sent them to their execution in England. John later visited his old aunt Lucy Downing at Sir George's Cambridge manor house. "You did me a great honour," Downing wrote, "to be pleased to goe so farre to a dirty hoole to see my mother," but he bristled at John's recommendation that the old lady be given a £100 annuity. Generosity to his mother was not one of Sir George's strongest points. Years later Mrs. Downing complained that though her son had paid out some £13,000 in real estate investments, he called her covetous when she expressed dissatisfaction with her annual allowance of £23.[19]

John's brother-in-law Thomas Reade had stayed in command of his regiment through 1659-1660 while his commander, General Monck, was using his army to secure the reestablishment of the monarchy. He lost his job when Charles II reduced the army; in October 1660 his regiment was disbanded.[20] Had John's brother Stephen, a more conspicuous Cromwellian than Reade, not died in 1658, he might have been in danger of death in 1660. Hugh Peter, John's stepfather-in-law, was one of the few men exempted from the King's general pardon because of his role in Charles I's execution. He was hanged and quartered in October 1660.[21] Another victim of the Restoration was Sir Henry Vane, who had worked with John on the Saybrook project. Vane was awaiting trial for treason, and would be executed in 1662.

In this atmosphere John's immediate task was to size up the new regime's colonial attitude. He found that merchants and

[19] *Ibid.*, 4th ser., VI, 524-25, 543-44; 5th ser., I, 53, 62; Beresford, *The Godfather of Downing Street*, pp. 115-21, 140-46.
[20] Firth and Davies, *Regimental History of Cromwell's Army*, II, 566-69; M.H.S. *Coll.*, 6th ser., III, 428-32.
[21] Winthrop Mss., V, 29a; XIII, 119; Stearns, *The Strenuous Puritan*, pp. 155-56, 181-82, 422.

bureaucrats on the one hand and courtiers on the other were working at cross-purposes over the question of how to manage and develop the plantations. The merchants and bureaucrats wanted to expand the imperial program which had been first blocked out during the Commonwealth era. Sir George Downing was the leading spokesman of this mercantilist school in the early 1660's. Parliament passed a new Navigation Act in 1660, elaborating the trade regulations of 1650 and 1651, with the additional specification that certain tropical commodities of particular value to the mother country were to be exported only to England.

In 1660 also, the King appointed a Council of Trade and a Council for Foreign Plantations, the membership of each council carefully balanced between Privy Councilors and lay experts. The Council for Foreign Plantations was designed to keep in touch with all the colony governments, to investigate colonial evasions of orders from home, and to recommend new colonial policies to the Privy Council. Counteracting the merchants' and bureaucrats' drive for imperial centralization, the courtiers still saw the overseas plantations as essentially a vehicle for the King's favor to his privileged subjects. Charles II, more fond of his personal role as fulcrum of the court aristocracy than of his impersonal role as English national leader, considered colonial grants to be his cheapest and most painless form of patronage. England's colonial expansion of the 1660's was undertaken by members of the court circle. The founding of Carolina was entrusted in 1663 to eight courtiers, and the following year Dutch New Netherland was generously given to the King's brother, the Duke of York. Naturally these aristocratic proprietors were jealous of their personal privileges and resisted administrative interference from Whitehall.

John could not hope to exploit the inchoate situation by writing pamphlets publicizing Connecticut's cause, as New England agents had done in the 1640's and 1650's. What was needed was money, entree to the court circle, and connections among the merchants and bureaucrats. John had all three. He had much more money than Rhode Island's agent Clarke. The Connecticut government had given him a letter of credit on which he raised £500 from three London merchants in 1662. This probably covered most of the charges in fees and tips for passing the Connecticut charter through the seals. The merchant creditors sent a ship to New London and received 2,000 bushels of wheat and 1,200 of pease in payment from the colony. But John spent far more than £500 on his agency. In February 1663 he borrowed another £1,500 from the merchant John Harwood, mortgaging Fisher's Island and the Tantiusques lead mine, which he estimated at 50,000 acres of land, together with 900 head of livestock, to Harwood in security. He also borrowed £484 from another merchant, Henry Ashurst. Some of this money John undoubtedly needed for purely personal expenses, but it is clear that much of it was spent in the service of Connecticut.[22] He wrestled with this enormous debt for the rest of his days. Harwood was finally paid off in 1677.

John had entree to the court circle through his old employer of 1635, Lord Saye and Sele, now Charles II's Lord Privy Seal. Though Lord Saye was a dying man living in retirement, he forwarded John's request for assistance to another old Puritan, the Earl of Manchester, who was Lord Chamberlain and a member of all the councils on plantation affairs. Manchester "loves those that are godly," Lord Saye wrote to John on December 14, 1661, "& he & I did joyne together that our godly friends of New England might injoy their just whrits & liberties."[23] Lord Saye was also one of the few people still alive who could tell John about the mysterious Warwick patent of 1632. Unfortunately he only deepened the mystery. John's kinsman John Richards visited the old nobleman to inquire about the patent. "My Lord is very ready to be any way Assistant to you," he reported to John on December 18, "but by reason of age; and infirmityes. . .he remembers little thereof. The partyes to whom the pattent was granted with himself (from his Majesty) as he remembers were My Lord of Warwicke, Lord Manchester, Lord Brooke, Mr Prinne, Nathaniel Rich, mr Fenwicke, which are all he remembers. . . .This is all (upon

[22] C.H.S. *Coll.*, I, 52-55; Winthrop Mss., Deeds, 48; X, 18; *Conn. Rec.*, II, 231.

[23] Trumbull, *History of Connecticut*, I, 513-14; *Conn. Rec.*, I, 584-85; M.H.S. *Coll.*, 5th ser., I, 394.

much discourse) we could any way gather from Him."

Lord Saye's recollection that Charles I had issued a royal charter to the Saybrook partners must certainly have been mistaken. John did unearth a copy of the deed of conveyance which Warwick had given to the Saybrook gentlemen in 1632, finding it among the papers of Edward Hopkins, a former governor of Connecticut who had died in England.[24] This deed marked off a tract running from Narragansett River (i.e., Narragansett Bay) 120 miles southwest along Long Island Sound to the New Netherland border. Since he could not find a copy of the patent itself, John had to petition the King for a new charter. At least the deed gave some basis for Connecticut's territorial claim.

John's strongest suit was his excellent connections among the lay experts who were agitating for a purposeful, centralized English colonial policy. He had good friends among the leading English scientists and technologists, men such as Samuel Hartlib, Sir Kenelm Digby, and Sir William Brereton, who were being sounded by the royal government as never before for advice on state policy. One of the first persons with whom John got in touch was Samuel Hartlib, an agriculturist best remembered today as the recipient of Milton's treatise on education. "I heare the Court are upon sending a Governor into New England," Hartlib told John on October 9, 1661, and strongly urged that he get acquainted with his physician friend, Dr. Benjamin Worsley, who "hath much the eare of the Lord Chauncellour [Clarendon], and I believe in reference to the Plantations Hee is Privy to most Transactions." In fact, Worsley introduced himself to John, sending him a copy of the King's instructions for the Council of Trade, "wherein I could be glad if we might be furthered with your Advice."[25] With the patronage of Saye and Manchester and the contact with Worsley, it is not surprising that John's case for Connecticut was quickly heard.

The best evidence of John's good standing in the Restoration milieu is his prompt admission three months after arriving

[24] Winthrop Mss., XIV, 94; XVII, 83.

[25] M.H.S. *Proc.*, XVI, 214-15; Winthrop Mss., XX, 110; Andrews, *Colonial Period*, II, 133; IV, 58-60.

in England to the newly formed Royal Society, designed to band together the foremost English practitioners of experimental knowledge. Possibly during his last visit to London in the early 1640's John had helped to instigate an informal scientific club, known as "the invisible college," which became the nucleus of the Royal Society.[26] The great chemist Robert Boyle, chief moving spirit behind the new society, arranged to meet with John on December 19, 1661, "to discourse of some of the Affaires, & Rarity's of Your Countrey." John was proposed for membership in the Royal Society by his old friend Sir William Brereton, the mathematician. He was admitted on January 1, 1662.[27]

The first colonial fellow of the Royal Society joined wholeheartedly in its work as long as he stayed in England. Indeed, the president of the society in 1733 asserted that Winthrop "did greatly contribute to the obtaining our charter," referring to Charles II's charter grant to the Royal Society six months after John became a member. John's special province was explaining the useful natural products of America. At Robert Boyle's request he delivered a report on how to cultivate and cook Indian corn. It is possible, he said, to brew corn beer which "wilbe of a very good browne Colour, and be a pleasant and wholesome drinke. . .without any windy Quality." True to the society's Baconian principles, he demonstrated the truth of this assertion by presenting several bottles of "a pale, well-tasted, middle beer" which he had brewed from corn bread. On another occasion John exhibited a more bizarre American

[26] In 1741, when the Royal Society dedicated volume 40 of its *Philosophical Transactions* to John's grandson, the dedicatory letter spoke of how John "was one of those, who first form'd the Plan of the *Royal Society*; and had not the Civil Wars happily ended as they did, Mr. *Boyle* and Dr. *Wilkins*, with several other learned Men, would have left *England*, and, out of Esteem for the most excellent and valuable Governor, JOHN WINTHROP the younger, would have retir'd to his newborn Colony, and there have establish'd that SOCIETY *for promoting Natural Knowledge*, which these Gentlemen had formed . . . in *Embryo* among themselves." This story sounds largely, if not entirely, the invention of John's grandiloquent grandson.

[27] Winthrop Mss., V, 30; XI, 35; *Record of the Royal Society of London* (4th ed. London, 1940), p. 377; *The Signatures in the First Journal-Book and the Charter-Book of the Royal Society* (London, 1912), xvi; T. E. James, "John Winthrop, Original Fellow of the Royal Society of London," *Discovery* (October 1925), pp. 390-92.

product, showing the society something puzzlingly referred to as "an earth, brought by him out of New England, which swam for about half an hour, and then sunk to the bottom."[28]

Since the bent of the society in its first few years was strongly utilitarian, it was fitting that John should propose to his fellow members a new system of credit banking, which he thought would promote the expansion of trade. He spoke repeatedly of New England's commercial and industrial potentialities, of his efforts to mine black lead, and how tar and pitch could be made from New England pitch-pine. He wanted the Royal Society to advise the navy commissioners to build some of their warships in New England. When a New England-built ship docked in London in January 1663, the society asked John to present a report on it. But on this topic he could have saved his breath. No royal warship was built in New England until 1696.[29]

John also found time, while in England, to advise the Society for the Propagation of the Gospel in New England, which had been founded in 1649 to sponsor Indian mission work and was reconstituted by the King in 1662. Robert Boyle was president of this organization. The society records do not indicate that John attended any of the board meetings, but he did give Boyle a plan for civilizing the Narragansett and Pequot Indians, teaching them trade and agriculture, converting them, and incidentally making them better customers for English produce. This plan admittedly required an initial investment of at least £5,000, and was evidently rejected as being too ambitious.[30] It was a typical Winthrop project, a mixture of business and idealism, shrewdness and humanity.

◄℞ DESPITE John's strong assets, the procurement of a charter for his colony proved to be a long and arduous task. This was because several fellow New Englanders in London

[28] *Journal*, I, 79; Fulmer Mood, "John Winthrop, Jr., on Indian Corn," *N.E.Q.*, X, 121-33; Thomas Birch, *History of the Royal Society of London* (4 vols.; London, 1756-1757), I, 198, 205, 206.

[29] M.H.S. *Coll.*, 5th ser., VIII, 86-87; Birch, *History of the Royal Society*, I, 99-102, 112-13, 178; Albion, *Forests and Sea Power*, p. 244.

[30] M.H.S. *Coll.*, 5th ser., IX, 45-47.

protested against his grand design for Connecticut. John had to deal simultaneously with three widely different antagonists. One was Dr. John Clarke, trying to get a charter for Rhode Island. Another was Captain John Scott, a rascally real estate speculator trying to get a proprietary patent for the whole of Long Island. Clarke and Scott naturally objected to John's territorial ambitions. The third adversary, Samuel Maverick, objected to the whole idea of a Connecticut charter, and wanted the King to impose a royal governor on disloyal New England.

Winthrop and Clarke do not seem to have met during John's first four months in London. Rhode Island had not yet sent Clarke any money to start the expensive business of suing for a charter. Clarke later wrote the Rhode Islanders a long and blistering letter, August 8, 1662, full of fascinating details on the Connecticut-Rhode Island charter negotiations. Clarke said he did not know whether to marvel more at "the cruell, deceit-full, Barbarous and traiterous dealings of a professing people," namely Connecticut, or at "the stupid senseless careless frame of those that governe in our Collony." If Rhode Island had properly supplied him, Clarke could have "procured you a Pattent either before Wintropp had come or should have bin so farr before hand with him in that respect that the greatest part of the trouble. . .had bin prevented but now it is to ad-miration that I can yet tell you that you are not yet wholey swallowed up."[31]

With Clarke at first immobilized, John's only obstacle was Samuel Maverick, who belonged, like Morton, Gorton, and Child before him, to the impressive line of rebel colonists who were harried out of Massachusetts and then tried to persuade the home government to punish the Bay Puritans for bigotry and treason. Maverick was less concerned about the rest of New England. "Conecticott and Newhaven," he told Lord Chan-cellor Clarendon, "have no Pattents that I know but govern by Combination amongst them selves, but in a strange confused way. . .and I conceive will be no otherwise untill his Majestie be pleased to call all againe in to his owne hands. . . ." Mav-

---

[31] Winthrop Mss., XI, 160. This copy of Clarke's letter in the Winthrop Papers is in John Winthrop, Jr.'s handwriting. It would be interesting to know when and how John got hold of this document, which paints him in such rich, black colors.

erick had always been personally cordial to John, however, and
wrote in complimentary terms about the industrial projects "of
that ingenious Gentleman Mr. John Winthrop." In England,
John actually kept up some sort of alliance with Maverick. In
an undated letter to Clarendon, Maverick concludes: "My good
Lord I beseech you pardon my presumption, Mr Winthrop
Capt. Breedon and my selfe, and another or two, are ready all
wayes to wait on your Lordship."[32] Captain Thomas Breedon
was another New Englander lobbying against the semi-autonomous Puritan governments. The Connecticut governor chose
to keep strange company.

Sometime between September 1661 and February 1662
John composed his colony's petition to the King. He asked that
Connecticut be bounded on the east by Narragansett Bay, on
the north by the Massachusetts line, on the west by the Pacific
Ocean, and on the south by the Atlantic Ocean, thus embracing
most of Rhode Island, all of New Haven, and much of New
Netherland, with a vast transcontinental belt of virgin land for
future expansion. He was requesting infinitely broader territorial limits than those he found in Warwick's deed of conveyance to the Saybrook proprietors. John claimed that he was
merely describing the bounds of the alleged Warwick patent,
"the Originall Pattent being lost in a Fatall Fire at Saybrook
fort. . .and the Duplicate being lost amonst those papers car-
ryed beyond the Seas by the Lord Keeper Finch" on the eve
of the Civil War. It is noticeable that he was not entirely following his instructions from the Connecticut court. For one
thing, he did not expressly ask for the whole territory of Rhode
Island up to the Plymouth line; obviously his intention was to
leave the four Rhode Island towns alone, while annexing the
Narragansett Country. Furthermore, in selecting fourteen persons as charter magistrates John deliberately left out five of
the current Connecticut magistrates and inserted several Long
Island planters in their places, emphasizing the charter's in-
clusion of Long Island.[33]

[32] N.Y.H.S. *Coll.*, II, 21, 37; *Cal.S.P.Col.*, *1661-1668*, pp. 17, 79; M.H.S.
Proc., 2nd ser., I, 244; M.H.S. *Coll.*, 5th ser., VIII, 72.
[33] C.H.S. *Annual Report* (1904), p. 23; *Cal.S.P.Col.*, *1661-1668*, p. 74; *Conn.
Rec.*, I, 580-81; Andrews, *Colonial Period*, II, 132.

Since Clarke had finally received £40 from Rhode Island, he and John each applied to the King for their respective charters at almost the same time. In early February 1662, Secretary of State Sir Edward Nicholas was considering both petitions. The Earl of Clarendon held a hearing in the council chamber and told Winthrop and Clarke he was willing to give charters to them both. Clarke reported that he offered to settle privately any neighborly differences over boundaries before their petitions were drafted in final form, but that John "turned away and refused the motion and grew strainger & strainger thereupon I grew jealous of him & plyed my busines with double dilligence." Clarke still felt assured that Rhode Island's petition would be granted and accordingly wrote home that everything was progressing smoothly except for his need of more money. The lack of money, however, was nearly ruinous. While Clarke's petition stood still, Winthrop's application was approved within a few weeks and the Connecticut charter was drawn up, dated April 23, and enrolled and sealed on May 10, 1662. "Such was his advantage by the helpe of a silver key," Clarke remarked bitterly, "that he could pass along by a private entrance way, that I could not in the leaste discover him nor what he was doeing untill he had got out his Pattent under the broade seale."[34]

A rather different picture was painted by an eighteenth-century Connecticut poet, Roger Wolcott, who composed a long epic celebrating John's achievement. According to Wolcott:

Ere long, great Charles was in his counsel sat,
With some choice nobles of his cabinet. . . .
Winthrop, brought in before his prince's feet,
Prostrates himself with reverence, the king to greet. . . .
'O may you pardon us while we entreat
'Your royal favour in the thing we want,
'T' incorporate us by your charter-grant.
'The land we've purchased, or subdued by fight,
'And bought of Fenwick what was Warwick's right,

[34] Winthrop Mss., XI, 160; *Cal.S.P.Col., 1661-1668*, pp. 4-5, 20, 71, 74-75, 79, 86-88; *R.I. Rec.*, I, 482.

'And all at the endeavour of our own,
'Without the least disbursement from the throne.'

Great Charles, who gave attention all the while,
Looking on Winthrop with a royal smile,
Until that of his father's woes he speaks,
Which drew the crystal rivers down his cheeks:
But seeing Winthrop his address had clos'd,
The King his mind and countenance compos'd,
And with as bright an air of majesty,
As Phoebus shews when he serenes the sky,
Made this resolve upon the agency:
'Be it so then, and WE OURSELF decree,
'CONNECTICUT shall be a COLONY;
'Enfranchis'd with such ample liberties
'As thou, their friend, shalt best for them devise:'[35]

There is also the story in Cotton Mather's *Magnalia Christi Americana* that when John had a private audience with the King, "he presented his majesty with a ring, which Charles I had upon some occasion given to his grandfather; and the King not only accepted his present, but also declared, that he accounted it one of his *richest jewels*."[36] When or why Charles I would have given a ring to Adam Winthrop, an obscure squire who died before Charles came to the throne, is hard to conceive. Yet Mather's story has figurative truth. John Winthrop, Jr., ought to have been well received by a sovereign who appreciated winning manners and a scientific taste.

On May 8 the triumphant agent wrote to Bristol, inquiring about ships sailing for New England. On May 13 he wrote to the Connecticut treasurer that the charter "hath now newly passed the great seale, and is as full and large for bounds and priviledges as could be desired, so as I hope all will be well satisfied about the charge that has been necessary for the af-

[35] Roger Wolcott, "A Brief Account of the Agency of the Honourable John Winthrop, Esq., in the Court of King Charles the Second, Anno Dom. 1662," M.H.S. *Coll.*, 1st ser., IV, 263-64, 296-97.

[36] Cotton Mather, *Magnalia Christi Americana* (2 vols.; Hartford, 1820), I, 144.

fecting and prosecuting a business of such consequence. . . ."

The bounds and privileges were certainly large. The colony was incorporated as an entirely self-governing body. The existing political structure was left intact, except that the franchise was now entirely restricted to freemen, whereas "admitted inhabitants" had previously been allowed to vote for deputies to the General Court. Also, all officers were now required to take the oath of supremacy. Connecticut must conform to English law, but as in the Massachusetts charter of 1629 there was no provision for enforcing conformity. The boundaries of the colony could be interpreted to be the same as in John's petition. They were loosely defined, incorporating "All that parte of our Dominions in Newe England" south of the Massachusetts line, from Narragansett Bay to the South Sea or Pacific Ocean.[37]

As soon as he heard that John's charter had passed the seals, Clarke rushed to Lord Chancellor Clarendon and persuaded him to call in the document, so that he could examine it. What he found confirmed his suspicions. On May 14 Clarke appealed to the King "according to your Royall word, for a speedy dispatch of a good & ample Charter for the Colonie of Rhode Island. . ., and that the Charter lately granted unto my neighbor Mr. Wintrup may againe be reviewed by your Majesty, for as much as therby he hath injuriously swallowed up the one half of our Colonie. . . ."[38] The Connecticut charter was held in restraint by Clarendon, and a fractious argument ensued between the two agents.

Far from admitting he had foiled Clarke's plans, John claimed it was just the other way around. Clarke was not seriously trying to get a charter; he was just trying to prevent Connecticut from getting one. "I never knew till Friday last," John told Clarendon on June 7, 1662, "that Mr Clerke was Agent for Road Iland; he then told me of it himselfe, and I heard not of it before." This was mere word play, since he admitted

---

[37] Winthrop Mss., XI, 24; C.H.S. *Coll.*, I, 52; A. C. Bates and C. M. Andrews, eds., *The Charter of Connecticut, 1662* (Hartford, 1933), pp. 20-21.

[38] Winthrop Mss., XI, 160; N.Y.H.S. *Coll.*, II, 44; *Cal.S.P.Col., 1677-1680*, p. 589.

to knowing that Clarke (agent or not) was looking after Rhode Island's interests in London. Winthrop's Narragansett partners had sent him express instructions "that we may not be given up to Rhod-Island for government, but affixed to the jurisdiction of Connectacut. This we earnestly choose; that we intensely dread; for Roade Island is (pardon necessity's word of truth) a *rodde* to those that love to live in order,—a road, refuge, asylum to evil livers." In a paper justifying his proceedings, John argued that Rhode Island only needed the Narragansett Bay islands and the territory immediately surrounding her two mainland towns, Providence and Warwick, because her population was so scanty. His basic hope was that the two governments would amalgamate. "I am sorry there should be any controversy between friends," he wrote to his Narragansett partners in September 1662, yet he went on to remark plaintively that if only Rhode Island "had desired to have joined with our Colony, I doubt not but they might have had all equal liberties with them [Connecticut]."[39]

The attempt to annex Rhode Island territory, whatever the motive, was a bad mistake. It contributed to the home government's intervention in New England's internal affairs, it gave Connecticut false pretensions which she did not abandon until more than fifty years after John's death, and it cost John an extra year in England. In June and July 1662 the two agents met several times in Clarendon's presence, with Robert Boyle fruitlessly trying to mediate between them. John would not consent to any alterations until Clarke first sued for a Rhode Island charter. Meanwhile, he not only wrote to his Narragansett partners asking to be supplied with additional complaints against Rhode Island, but drafted a petition to the King for them to sign, requesting that the Narragansett Country be included within Connecticut patent.[40] Though John himself could not yet go home, he did get Clarendon's permission to send his charter to Connecticut, stirring the hot-tempered Clarke into fresh paroxysms of rage. The duplicate was still

[39] M.H.S. *Coll.*, 5th ser., VIII, 75-76; IX, 27-30, 33-34; Winthrop Mss., XII, 25.
[40] *Conn. Rec.*, II, 542; C.A., Colonial Boundaries, I, 44.

in London, but John's shipment of the charter to Hartford (where it was publicly read on October 9, 1662) made it almost impossible to bind the people of Connecticut to any alterations in their new boundaries.[41]

At this point, John Scott joined the *dramatis personae*. Scott had been in London since 1660, vainly trying to confirm his claim to Long Island. He saw in the Connecticut-Rhode Island controversy a new chance for personal profit, at both agents' expense. In July 1662 Winthrop and Clarke agreed to submit their boundary dispute to the arbitration of Robert Boyle and Sir Thomas Temple, governor of Nova Scotia. When the agents and arbitrators met, Clarke brought Samuel Maverick as his counsel and found that Winthrop was accompanied by "Scot of Long Iland, a confident, bold fellow that can say anything . . .and Wait his sone as bold & as confidant as he." They discussed a compromise solution in which the boundary between the two colonies would be drawn through the center of the Narragansett Country, twelve miles west of the Bay, leaving Boston Neck in the hands of Rhode Island. According to Winthrop, Clarke rejected this proposal. According to Clarke, Scott and Wait Winthrop defeated it by making the affair appear so intricate that the arbitrators were unwilling to judge. Clarendon told Clarke that the dispute must be settled before he would issue Rhode Island a new charter. Still Clarke told the Rhode Islanders not to be "discouraged by the noise of Wintrops Pattent being got. It will be sent for againe."[42] Meanwhile Scott decided to pay New England a quick visit in the fall of 1662, in the hope of exploiting the unresolved quarrel.

On arrival, Scott addressed himself to three groups affected by Connecticut's new charter: the New Haven colonists, the Long Island colonists, and the Narragansett proprietors. He found that the Connecticut government, upon receipt of the charter, was trying to enforce her suzerainty over both New Haven and Long Island. The New Havenites were aroused by

[41] Winthrop Mss., V, 196; XI, 160; *Conn. Rec.*, I, 384; M.H.S. *Proc.* (1869-1870), 344.

[42] Winthrop Mss., XI, 160; XVIII, 30; M.H.S. *Coll.*, 5th ser., VIII, 75-76; *Hutchinson Papers*, II, 104-105; Wilbur C. Abbott, *Colonel John Scott of Long Island* (New Haven, 1918), pp. 7-23.

this, and in November 1662 voted to defer all negotiations over possible union with Connecticut until Governor Winthrop's return. On December 12, Secretary Allyn of Connecticut wrote John the unpleasant news that on Long Island "there is some kinde of disturbance. . . .By Reason of Captain Scotts Informing of them that they are not Included in Our Charter . . . .as allsoe that he Informes that New haven Jurisdiction is by our soveraign the king excluded our charter. . . ." Allyn went to Long Island to find whether it was true that the New Haven and Long Island colonists had commissioned Scott as their London agent to procure charters for them. John was warned to be on guard. "I suppose you will soon see the Captain after his arrivall," Allyn said. "It would be good to take the first oppertunety to treat with him, that soe you might understand his designe."[43]

In talking with the Narragansett proprietors, Scott varied his tune, telling them that Winthrop was weakening to Clarke's pressure and might surrender the Narragansett Country to Rhode Island. Lord Chancellor Clarendon, said Scott, had asked Clarke in public audience "iff he were not ashamed so Impudently to Vilify and acuse Mr. Winthrop (and Mr. Winthrop being present). . .he wondered how Mr. Winthrop Could have the patience to bare itt." The Narragansett proprietors wrote to John more insistently than ever "to yield no way to Road Island, for they are not rational." John was told (December 25, 1662) "of the love we have had from our noble freind Captain Scott, who is really desirus that we may not be injured by Roade Iland men." The proprietors were so affected by his love that they admitted Scott into their partnership and sent him back to England as their personal agent with instructions to assist Winthrop in the battle against Clarke.[44]

John was not very kindly disposed to Scott when the Captain reappeared in London, February 1663. Through the fall and winter of 1662-1663, he had been continuing the haggle

---

[43] Winthrop Mss., x, 17-18; Calder, *The New Haven Colony*, pp. 232-36. Lilian T. Mowrer, in *The Indomitable John Scott* (New York, 1960), presents a much more favorable interpretation of his role.

[44] N.Y.H.S. *Coll.*, II, 47; M.H.S. *Coll.*, 5th ser., IX, 37-45; Winthrop Mss., XIV, 60-61.

with Clarke. In October the Rhode Island agent tried to obtain a hearing before a committee of the Privy Council, and after that failed there were further attempts at private arbitration. Always Winthrop insisted that his Narragansett partners be guaranteed the undisturbed enjoyment of their property.[45] John was heartily sick of the controversy and wanted nothing so much as the liberty to sail home. He knew that if Clarendon should now receive Scott's complaints from New Haven and Long Island against Connecticut, the charter itself might be in jeopardy. He must come to separate terms with both Scott and Clarke.

John had no intention of abandoning union between New Haven and Connecticut. In a memorandum of 1662 he had written: "New Haven within Connecticut patent. and alsoe desired to be comprehended within that patent." But he was annoyed at the Hartford government's roughshod tactics in his absence, their admitting freemen and appointing officers in several New Haven towns. On March 3, 1663, he met with Scott and two other spokesmen for New Haven at the house of William Hooke, Davenport's former colleague now in hiding because he had been Cromwell's chaplain. John put his signature to a letter which Scott and his companions had drafted and which was posted to the Connecticut General Court, requiring that all attempts to coerce New Haven be stopped immediately. In this dictated letter John said, "I gave assurance before authority heere that it was not intended to meddle with any towne or plantation that was settled under any other government; had it been otherwise intended or declared, it had beene injurious, in taking out the patent, not to have inserted a proportionable number of [New Haven] names in it." In a covering letter to Hartford, John explained why he had pledged New Haven's status quo. Let them join us of their own volition, he argued, even if it takes a little longer. He implored the Connecticut government to stop stirring up trouble with New Haven, Long Island, and the Dutch. "I beseech you," he said, "consider what may be most for your present

[45] *Ibid.*, XI, 151-62; XII, 24; M.H.S. *Coll.*, 5th ser., VIII, 79-80.

peace and peaceable settlement." John secured a promise in writing from Scott that he would not prosecute for a New Haven charter.[46] Convinced that New Haven could not long resist, he rightly felt that he had the best of the bargain.

In settling with Clarke, however, John had to make a real concession. On April 7, 1663, the two agents finally agreed to a boundary settlement worked out by a panel of five arbitrators which included John's friends, Dr. Benjamin Worsley and Sir William Brereton. Despite the valiant efforts of the panel, however, this final settlement was too janus-faced to be workable. The Pawcatuck River was made the boundary between the two colonies (as it is between the two states today), preserving Rhode Island's limits as patented by Roger Williams in 1644. On the other hand, all property holders were to be left undisturbed, and the Narragansett proprietors were to be permitted to join Connecticut's jurisdiction if they chose, in which case the choicest part of the Narragansett Country would be taken from Rhode Island. Finally, John's personal property along the border at Quinebaug and Fisher's Island was specifically allocated to Connecticut. John himself considered this private settlement to be less binding than a Privy Council order, especially since his legal advisers told him that the Connecticut charter could not be altered without destroying its validity. He foresaw accurately that the Connecticut people could only be persuaded to accept narrower boundaries "if they shall se his majesties pleasure of so farr shorting them declared in a new grant to them."[47] He had no intention of suing for a second Connecticut charter.

John's final act in England was to solicit the crown on Clarke's behalf for the long awaited Rhode Island charter. The two men were now reconciled, and the home government issued this charter (July 8, 1663) largely on the strength of "the good opinion and confidence wee had in the said Mr Winthropp." Yet the crown officials were even more skeptical than

[46] Winthrop Mss., XII, 25; XIX, 54; *Cal.S.P.Col., 1661-1668*, pp. 125-27; *Cal. S.P.Dom., 1663-1664*, pp. 63-65, 98, 117; M.H.S. *Coll.*, 4th ser., VII, 594; VIII, 174; 5th ser., VIII, 77-81.

[47] *Ibid.*, 76, 82-83; Winthrop Mss., V, 35; XII, 25.

John that the boundary dispute was finally settled. The long quarrel with Clarke had helped to persuade Clarendon that it was necessary to send a royal commission over to New England and straighten out the mess there. John was made to promise before he left that when these royal commissioners came out, the colonists would submit to "any alteration at that tyme, and upon such a visitation, as if no Charter were then passed to them."[48]

Free at last, John departed for home in April, as soon as he had settled with Clarke. It was his seventh and final transatlantic voyage. At the behest of the Royal Society he conducted experiments en route in sounding the depth of the ocean. Like most of his scientific efforts, the experiments "proved successless." In his English sojourn John had already won enough success, in fact too much. He had enlarged Connecticut's territory and entrenched her right of self-government. He had extracted essentially the same privileges from Charles II in 1662 that the Massachusetts Bay Company got from Charles I in 1629. The sum of his experience at court was that New Englanders need not feel distressed by the Restoration. The home government's chaotic colonial attitude had indeed tempted John to be too clever for his own good, to ask for too much from the King, but it was not the mercantilists or courtiers of Whitehall who checked Connecticut's ambitions; it was the protests of New Englanders in London. All in all, the Merry Monarch had proved to be a dangerously casual master.

[48] Winthrop Collection, I, 47; *N.Y.Col.Doc.*, III, 55.

7. The Royal Commission of 1664

UPON the completion of his mission to obtain a royal charter for his colony, John Winthrop, Jr., reckoned that he had fulfilled his public responsibility and was entitled to retire to private life. Since his estate was mortgaged to English creditors and he had two grown sons and four daughters to provide for, John had good reason for wanting to concentrate on his long neglected business affairs. "Let me begg," he wrote the Connecticut magistrates in March 1663, a month before sailing home, "that you will please at your next election to leave me out." Yet when he landed at Boston in early June, to be escorted in triumph to Hartford, he found that the colony freemen had re-elected him governor *in absentia* on May 14. Once again he asked for his release. "Being newly arrived," he wrote the Council on June 30, "and very much businesse depending which must of necessity be attended I must begg your favour that I may have dismission from attending the public affaires," or at least a leave of absence.[1] John may have been allowed a few weeks to straighten out his personal affairs, but he was not permitted to retire. Getting the Connecticut charter was only the first half of his job. Now the colony required his special talents to enforce the charter.

❧ IN 1663-1664, under John's reluctant management, Connecticut tried simultaneously to annex New Haven and to wrench the Narragansett Country from Rhode Island and Long Island from the Dutch. John was made uneasy by the greed, bitterness, and brutality which his benevolent deed, the Connecticut charter, was generating. Having fostered Connecticut's expansionist ambitions, he was now unable to restrain his fellow colonists' roughshod treatment of their neighbors. John

[1] M.H.S. *Coll.*, 5th ser., VIII, 80; Winthrop Mss., V, 37.

consistently advocated a limited and tactful Connecticut policy on union with New Haven, on disposition of the Narragansett Country, on annexation of Dutch territory. In each case he was overruled. His position was more than a little awkward. Though the Connecticut people insisted on his remaining as governor and were exploiting his large prestige in the neighboring colonies, they continually undermined his efforts at peacemaking.

The most critical issue was the union with New Haven Colony. Since 1661 it had been John's aim to amalgamate the two governments. His charter of 1662 incorporated New Haven, and his bargain with Scott in 1663 blocked New Haven's quest for a separate charter. Though he had effectively eliminated the New Havenites' freedom of choice, John wanted them to join with Connecticut voluntarily, not by force. He knew that most of them were amenable to union, despite Davenport's insistence that Connecticut's loose discipline would vitiate their church. Unfortunately, John's extra year in England fencing with Clarke ruined all hope of a quiet settlement. In his absence, the Connecticut government adopted strong-arm tactics, receiving four defecting New Haven towns into her jurisdiction, and the remaining New Havenites naturally rejected her brusque terms of surrender. By the time John reached Hartford in June 1663, Governor Leete and Master Davenport were both far too angry to admit that New Haven's situation was hopeless. They each appealed to John personally for redress. Leete said he had always been confident of John's "acting in the Pattent businesse . . . without any intendment to infringe our liberty or priviledges in the least thereby," while Davenport knew "it was not the Kings purpose, nor yours, to destroy the distinction of Colonies, nor our Colonie-state."[2]

John attempted to introduce his intended policy of amicable union with New Haven. He made it clear to both Leete and Davenport that he wanted to consolidate the two colonies, but stressed the necessity of friendly mutual consent. "The more I looke upon the weakened condition of the plantations, in this wildernesse," he wrote Davenport on August 11, 1663, "the more need does appear to be of . . . union amongst these . . . plan-

[2] M.H.S. *Coll.*, 4th ser., VII, 521-24, 550-51.

tations." Leete, he knew, would be easier to deal with. The New Haven governor found John's letter "very acceptable," and said John's idea of union was kindred to his own proposal back in 1661 "to make your Pattent a covert, but no controule to our Jurisdiction, untill we accorded with mutual satisfacon to become one. . . ." John persuaded the Connecticut council to send a committee on "a loving visit" to New Haven in late August. Unhappily John himself was off in Boston. Still, the Connecticut committee offered to retract Hartford's authority over the four defecting New Haven towns until union was reached.[3]

All of John's efforts were spoiled when the quarrel was aired at the annual September meeting of the New England Confederation commissioners in Boston. As Connecticut's spokesman, John argued that union was now almost achieved, but the New Haven commissioners were encouraged by Massachusetts and Plymouth to stiffen and to demand that Connecticut stop trespassing on her jurisdiction. In October 1663 the Connecticut General Assembly called for New Haven's categorical submission. John sent the Assembly a vain message of protest: "for the plantations that are chelonged by New-Haven, or the Dutch, untill his majesties pleasure concerning them be further knowne, I must dissent from any actions towards them otherwise then by amicable treaties that may tend to a peaceable issue of things by mutuall consent."[4] But bitterness on both sides now reached its climax. The New Haven court voted to raise £300 for its own charter and ordered those persons who had defected to Connecticut to pay their share within six days. An armed gang of Connecticut men (among them young Wait Winthrop) rode down to protect the defectors at Guilford and almost precipitated a battle with the loyalist New Haven militia. In February 1664 John again suggested a "loving and friendly conference" with Leete.[5] By this time New Haven Colony had only a penniless shadow govern-

---

[3] Winthrop Mss., v, 36; M.H.S. *Coll.*, 4th ser., VII, 552; *New Haven Colony Records, 1653-1665*, pp. 493-96.

[4] Winthrop Mss., v, 39.

[5] *Ibid.*, v, 37, 40; *Conn. Rec.*, I, 415, 588-89; *New Haven Colony Records, 1653-1665*, pp. 502, 511-15, 527-28.

ment, but new negotiations only led to new friction, so in June 1664, one year after John's return, the amalgamation of the two colonies seemed no closer than ever.

Meanwhile Connecticut was jousting with Rhode Island over the Narragansett Country. Here John's aim was to guarantee the property rights of the present Narragansett landholders, himself included. Accordingly he tried to carry out his treaty of April 7, 1663, with John Clarke in England, whereby the Narragansett Country was assigned to Rhode Island but his fellow Narragansett proprietors were given the option of attaching the choicest land in the area to Connecticut jurisdiction. As soon as he landed at Boston, John told his partners of their option. On July 3, 1663, they voted to join Connecticut. However, the Winthrop-Clarke compromise, which had cost John so much time and labor, was already being ignored by his government. The Hartford magistrates, in accepting jurisdiction over the Narragansett proprietors, announced that it is "abundantly apparent by our Ample and firme Charter" that the whole Narragansett Country belongs to Connecticut. They appointed officers for the Boston Neck plantation and named it Wickford, after Mrs. Winthrop's English home, Wickford, Essex.[6]

Any lingering hope of a quiet Narragansett settlement was blasted by the work of Captain John Scott and Dr. John Clarke in England after John's departure. Scott, acting as agent for the Narragansett proprietors, wrote them that he could not "deem those terms Mr. Winthrop made with Clarke any way to answer your desires, were there a certainty in what Clarke hath granted." Hardly had Winthrop's ship weighed anchor when Scott, through backstairs maneuvering and £60 in bribes, began negotiations for a royal letter (dated June 21, 1663) to the New England Confederation "filled with authorizing expressions" to protect the proprietors against Rhode Island. It was typical of England's colonial policy that Scott's letter conflicted directly with another royal document, the Rhode Island charter, which finally passed the seals two weeks later on July

[6] M.H.S. *Coll.*, 5th ser., IX, 31-32; Winthrop Mss., XII, 25; *Conn. Rec.*, I, 407; "The Fones Records," *Rhode Island Colonial Gleanings*, I, 23-25.

8, 1663. In drafting this charter, Clarke had delineated Rhode Island's territorial limits very carefully, and had inserted a clause explaining that the Connecticut agent had agreed to fix the boundary between the two colonies at the Pawcatuck River, any statements in the Connecticut charter to the contrary notwithstanding. Fisher's Island was specifically exempted from Rhode Island limits, but Clarke inserted nothing whatsoever about the Narragansetts proprietors' option.[7]

When Rhode Island received her charter she ignored Connecticut's pretensions and Scott's royal letter and tried to force the Narragansett proprietors to submit to her jurisdiction. Physical violence broke out at the Pawcatuck River, where Rhode Island planters on the east side (the present town of Westerly) were feuding with Connecticut planters on the west. The people of Wickford soon complained that Winthrop was not giving them adequate protection against the marauding Rhode Islanders. John himself complained to Dr. Benjamin Worsley in England that Rhode Island had flagrantly violated the purpose of his agreement with Clarke, to protect the present owners' undisturbed enjoyment of property in the Narragansett Country. John's own government viewed his treaty with Clarke as invalid anyway, on the grounds that his agency for Connecticut expired with the passage of the charter. Even Roger Williams was none too hopeful of composing the Narragansett quarrel between the two colonies. "Sir," he wrote John on May 28, 1664, "when we that have been the eldest, and are rotting, (to-morrow or next day) a generation will act, I fear, far unlike the first Winthrops and their Models of Love: I fear that the common Trinity of the world, (Profit, Preferment, Pleasure) will here be the *Tria omnia*, as in all the world beside: . . .that God Land will be (as now it is) as great a God with us English as God Gold was with the Spaniards. . . ."[8]

In Connecticut's third quarrel, with New Netherland, Governor Winthrop again took a more moderate stance than his fellow colonists. John intended the charter of 1662 to embrace

[7] M.H.S. *Coll.*, 5th ser., IX, 53-55; *R.I. Rec.*, II, 18-20.

[8] *Ibid.*, I, 515-17; II, 65-70; M.H.S. *Coll.*, 5th ser., IX, 59-62; Winthrop Mss., V, 40; XVII, 113; Winthrop Collection, I, 48; *Publications* of the Narragansett Club, VI, 319.

the English villages on the east end of Long Island, and so he inserted several Long Island planters in the roster of charter magistrates. His Hartford colleagues were more ambitious. They saw the chance to annex the west end of Long Island also, and the mainland coast as far as the Hudson River. One of the Connecticut magistrates, Samuel Willys, wrote John in September 1662, as soon as the precious charter had arrived, to say how "those of Longe Island that I have spoke with all Like well that our pattent should include them as the words seeme fully to doe." Actually the document does not mention Long Island by name. The following month a Long Island planter named John Younge sent a circular letter to the five villages on west Long Island settled by Englishmen within Dutch territory, notifying them that they were now under Connecticut jurisdiction. When Winthrop in England heard of this, he begged his colleagues to stop, but by the time he got home, the Connecticut General Assembly had also claimed authority over the village of Westchester, north of Manhattan Island.[9]

John's efforts to paper over this explosive situation were singularly unsuccessful. In the manner of Leete and Davenport, Governor Stuyvesant appealed to him in June and July 1663, requiring to know whether the boundary agreement of 1650 between New Netherland and the New England Confederation was still in force. John suggested that the Dutch governor bring the matter up at the September meeting of the Confederation in Boston. Stuyvesant did so. He must have been very angry when John and the other Connecticut commissioner said they were not prepared to discuss the New Netherland boundary and had it postponed for a year.[10] In desperation, Stuyvesant sent a delegation of three Dutchmen to the October session of the Connecticut General Assembly. These delegates could win no guarantees for the west end of Long Island even

[9] Winthrop Mss., XX, 50; Winthrop Collection, I, 1-2, 4; M.H.S. *Coll.*, 5th ser., VIII, 79; *Conn. Rec.*, I, 387-88, 403; Calder, *The New Haven Colony*, pp. 217-18, 240-41.

[10] *Conn. Rec.*, I, 406-07; M.H.S. *Coll.*, 4th ser., VI, 526, 534-35; 5th ser., I, 395-97; IX, 55-58; Hazard, *Historical Collections*, II, 479-83; *N.Y.Col.Doc.*, II, 385.

when they agreed to surrender Westchester. John told the Assembly that he dissented from taking Dutch (or New Haven) territory by force, and one evening at supper with the Dutchmen "he expressly declared: that the intent of the [Connecticut] Patent was by no means to claim any right to New Netherland, but that it only comprehended a tract of land in New England &c." When, however, his guests asked to have this statement in writing, "he declined, saying it was sufficiently plain from the Patent itself." Winthrop's view was dismissed by his colleagues. The Assembly told the Dutchmen that "the Governor is but one man." Unless New Netherland relinquished her authority over the English towns on Long Island, Connecticut would occupy the whole island. A troop of 100 Englishmen moved through these towns ousting the Dutch officials, and Stuyvesant was forced on November 15, 1663, to acknowledge this *fait accompli* in the hope that he could save his Dutch settlements.[11]

Though Connecticut seemed on the verge of possessing all Long Island, she now received a foretaste of trouble to come from England with the reappearance on the scene of John's nemesis, Captain John Scott. Having left England more recently than Winthrop, he had found out that the home government was plotting to conquer New Netherland and turn it into a proprietary colony for the King's brother, the Duke of York, the future James II. Scott hoped that if he posed as the Duke's agent and chased the Dutch officials out of their remaining Long Island villages before the arrival of the Duke's invasion fleet, he might be given title to the whole island as a reward for his service. John knew that the home government was thinking of sending over a royal commission to investigate New England, but he was ignorant of the impending attack on New Netherland. Scott slyly offered to help the Connecticut government secure full possession of Long Island. He accepted a commission as a Connecticut magistrate, gathered 150 men, and paraded through the five English and five Dutch towns at the west end of the island in early January 1664. "I will stick my rapier," he shouted in Dutch, "in the guts of any man

[11] *Ibid.*, II, 389-92; XIV, 537-39; Winthrop Mss., V, 39; *Conn. Rec.*, I, 411-14.

who proclaims the States [the Dutch States-General] here, or says this is not the King's land." Scott also came to the Connecticut towns at the east end of the island, to tell the inhabitants that he was the King's sworn servant, and that the Hartford government was acting rebelliously. His purpose was not to drive the Dutch completely off Long Island, but to gain personal control over the English villages now under Connecticut jurisdiction. Stuyvesant reached an agreement with Scott, recognizing him as President of the English on Long Island on condition that he cease molesting the five remaining Dutch towns. President Scott appointed local officers in his English towns, and proclaimed Long Island's allegiance to the Duke of York.[12]

When Fitz Winthrop, John's elder son, reported that Scott was establishing his own private state on Long Island, the Connecticut leaders were furious. Scott explained airily to John that a laudable excess of loyalty to England had moved him to rival Connecticut's concern for the Long Islanders' liberties, but in March 1664, a squad of Connecticut men captured Scott and carried him to Hartford for trial, where he was found guilty of usurping the King's authority. This stirred violent protests from New Haven, since Scott had been New Haven's agent in England, and made union between Connecticut and New Haven that much more difficult. Connecticut felt free to deal roughly with Scott because there was yet no word of the Duke of York's intentions. The General Assembly declared, May 1664, that Long Island was within her charter limits. The following month John himself visited the disputed English villages on the west end of the island and replaced Scott's officers with new ones. Stuyvesant met him there and protested vainly against his intervention. It was now clear to the Dutch that Governor Winthrop, for all his conciliatory tone, would not or could not check Connecticut's imperialism.[13]

John had been made uneasy by Scott's performance. He

[12] *N.Y.Col.Doc.*, II, 394; XIV, 544-45; Winthrop Collection, I, 6; C.H.S. *Coll.*, XXIV, 10-11; Mowrer, *The Indomitable John Scott*, pp. 103-23.
[13] *Conn. Rec.*, I, 420-30; Winthrop Mss., XVII, 85; XVIII, 29; C.H.S. *Coll.*, XXI, 152-58; Calder, *The New Haven Colony*, pp. 242-46; *N.Y.Col.Doc.*, XIV, 552.

asked Thomas Breedon, a Boston merchant just returned from England, whether Scott actually had been delegated any authority by the Duke of York. Breedon replied on June 6 that Scott might well be employed by the Duke, who had a patent for Long Island and other territory. He also told John that the royal commissioners were on their way to America, that "the Honnorable Governor Nickalls with other Commissioners are comeing over with there friggatts and intended first for Longe Iland. I know hee [Scott] will bee very joyfull to see them there."[14] As matters stood in June 1664, New Haven was still balking at union with Connecticut, Rhode Island was still determined not to surrender the Narragansett Country, and the Dutch were still contesting Long Island. It was a singularly embarrassing time for the home government to send over commissioners to possess all Dutch territory (including Long Island) for the Duke of York, and to arbitrate New England boundary disputes. Clearly Connecticut must belatedly rely on her governor's personal influence and diplomatic skill, if all was not to be lost.

⫻ THE Royal Commission of 1664 was the net result of various conflicting colonial attitudes in circulation at Whitehall during the early years of the reign of Charles II. To capture New Netherland from the Dutch suited the London merchants; to award this stolen territory to the King's brother as a proprietary colony suited the courtiers; to inquire into and report on the state of affairs in New England suited the bureaucrats and statisticians; to crack the recalcitrant Puritan colonists' autonomy suited the Anglicans and archroyalists; and to expend the smallest possible amount of men and money suited the King's exchequer. The voice was Jacob's voice, but the hands were the hands of Esau. The Commission's first and chief task was the conversion of New Netherland into New York. As Sir George Downing and other imperialists had argued, the Hudson Valley was the economic and strategic key to North America, and its retention by the Dutch prevented the effective application of the Navigation Laws in English America. Fur-

---

[14] Winthrop Mss., XI, 42.

thermore, New Netherland was ripe for the plucking. Although England was at peace with the United Provinces, Charles II in the spring of 1664 ordered a force of four frigates and 400 soldiers to take New Netherland. The commander, Colonel Richard Nicolls, was to govern the captured territory as the Duke of York's deputy and also to head the four-member commission of inquiry into the state of New England. Nicolls was forty years old, a lifetime servant of the royal family who had fought in the Civil War, followed the Duke into exile, and come back to England as a member of his household. He was able, tactful, and loyal, an excellent man for the job, but he had been given too much to do.

The King granted the territory of New Netherland to his brother in a proprietary charter very hastily passed through the seals in early March 1664. This instrument was nearly as obnoxious to the New Englanders as to the Dutch. It deliberately encircled and encroached on the New England plantations. The Duke was given, in addition to Dutch territory, a large section of Maine, Martha's Vineyard, Nantucket, Long Island, and all of the mainland west of the Connecticut River! The charter declared that the Duke's grant superseded any previous English grant which might conflict with it.[15] Not only was Long Island thus taken from Connecticut, but the western half of the colony, containing every significant town except New London. Considering that Winthrop had spent much time and money in wheedling the Connecticut charter from the King less than two years before, the issuing of the Duke of York's patent was a horrid example of government by caprice. All through the rest of his life John would have to exercise his diplomatic skill in order to get back and keep as much Connecticut territory from the Duke as possible.

When Nicolls' squadron sailed for America in May 1664, it carried letters to John from Lord Chancellor Clarendon, Robert Boyle, and Sir Robert Moray, President of the Royal Society, all urging him to receive the commissioners cordially.

[15] Francis Newton Thorpe, *The Federal and State Constitutions, Colonial Charters, and Other Organic Laws of . . . the United States of America* (7 vols.; Washington, 1909), III, 1637-1640.

"I know," Clarendon wrote, "you will give that reception & welcome to the commissioners, as is due to the quality they come to you in, and. . .as may give a good example to the rest" of the New England governments. After Nicolls' squadron arrived, John replied to his eminent English patrons that he had been delighted to welcome the commissioners as honored guests. "Your Lordships Commands," he told Clarendon, "shalbe attended with all imaginable indeavours," and he talked warmly to Moray of "the happy arrival of our noble friend Colonell Nicolls."[16] This was no pose. Nicolls shared John's intellectual tastes, travelled in the London circle which John had unwillingly abandoned, and was in fact a real friend. John had long been on good personal terms with one of the other three commissioners, the anti-Puritan New Englander Samuel Maverick.

While John adopted his customary conciliatory policy, most of the other New England leaders showed signs of panic. The coming of the Royal Commission unwittingly proved a great boon to Connecticut in settling her amalgamation with New Haven. The New Haven General Court grudgingly agreed in August 1664 to submit at least temporarily if Connecticut would protect her in the forthcoming royal inspection. At the New England Confederation meeting in September, Massachusetts and Plymouth urged a more complete submission, and finally in December the five remaining New Haven towns voted to yield to Connecticut's terms.[17] Some New Havenites never surrendered. Abraham Pierson led a band of the faithful off to New Jersey in 1666, and two years later the spiritual leader of the defunct colony, John Davenport, moved to Boston, a defeated and bitter old man. On the other hand, New Haven's political leader, William Leete, succeeded John as governor of Connecticut, and for most colonists the rancor of 1661-1664 quickly died away.

Meanwhile the royal commissioners arrived. Nicolls sailed

[16] M.H.S. *Proc.*, 1st ser., VII, 377; XVI, 223; 2nd ser., XIII, 455; M.H.S. *Coll.*, 5th ser., VIII, 90-92.

[17] *Mass. Rec.*, IV, pt. 2, 101-102, 157; *New Haven Colony Records, 1653-1665*, pp. 544-53; Hazard, *Historical Collections*, II, 496-97; *Conn. Rec.*, I, 437.

into Boston harbor on July 23, presented his credentials to the Bay magistrates, announced that his first task was to take New Netherland, asked for additional troops, and proceeded at once with his fleet to the west end of Long Island. John joined him there about the middle of August. He gave Nicolls valuable assistance in securing the painless surrender of New Amsterdam. The English expeditionary force, with headquarters near Coney Island, was far more than a match for Stuyvesant's crumbling defenses. But when Nicolls demanded Dutch surrender, guaranteeing full civil and property rights to the inhabitants, Stuyvesant stalled for time and acted as though he would put up a fight. John served as mediator. He wrote a letter to Stuyvesant and his council on August 22 urging them to accept Nicolls' generous terms. Otherwise, he said, "you may be assured, that both the Massachusetts Colony and Connecticut, and all the rest are obliged & ready to attend his Majesties service: and if you should by wilful protraction occasion a generall rising of the English Colonies, I should be sorry to see the ill consequences which you will bring upon your people thereby . . . a needlesse warre, with all the evills & miseries that may accompany the same, when nothing but peace and liberties & protection is tendered."[18]

Three days later, John rowed over to Manhattan under a white flag. He tried to argue the Dutch leaders into surrendering, and gave Stuyvesant his letter. John's words carried weight in New Amsterdam, even though he had done as much as any man to undermine the colony. Stuyvesant tore up the letter, but the outcry from the burghers was so great that he feared they would mutiny. He was compelled to piece the torn letter together and let everyone see it. On August 27, with the English forces drawn menacingly close to Fort Amsterdam, Stuyvesant gave up without a shot being fired. John was one of the six Englishmen to sign the articles of capitulation. New Amsterdam had become New York.[19]

With Manhattan in the hands of the Duke of York's repre-

[18] *Mass. Rec.*, IV, pt. 2, 117, 120-26, 157; M.H.S. *Coll.*, 4th ser., VI, 528; 5th ser., VIII, 90-91.

[19] *N.Y.Col.Doc.*, II, 250-53, 411, 444-45; III, 103.

sentatives, John's next task was to secure Connecticut's western boundary on as favorable terms as possible. If worst came to worst, Connecticut could surrender Long Island. But she absolutely could not admit the Duke's claim to the Connecticut River. John returned to Hartford in September 1664 and tactfully sent his congratulations to each of the royal commissioners on hearing that they had captured the remaining Dutch outposts on the upper Hudson and the Delaware. To Nicolls, he remarked that by bringing the whole northern continent of America under the King's obedience, "your honor hath happily laid a foundation for much enlargments of his Majesties Dominions, and the generall future good of all the English. . . ." The Connecticut Assembly met on October 13, ordered that 500 bushels of grain be sent to the commissioners as a present from Connecticut, and delegated Governor Winthrop, Captain Fitz Winthrop, and five others to pay a state visit to New York, congratulate the commissioners on their victory, and "if an oppertunety offer itselfe," resolve the boundary dispute between the Connecticut patent and the Duke's patent.[20]

The Connecticut envoys came to terms with the commissioners in New York, November 1664. John and his colleagues argued their right not only to the western half of the Connecticut mainland but to the eastern two-thirds of Long Island, where they had been exercising authority for twenty years. John sweetened his argument by presenting each of the commissioners with a horse from his Fisher's Island stud farm. Maverick, however, said he could not accept the horse as a bribe from Connecticut Colony, but only as a personal gift from John. "I know the Duke of Yorke his right," Maverick said, "and the trew intent of your pattent to well to consent to what I perceive will be demanded"—i.e., Long Island. On November 30, the two parties signed a New York-Connecticut boundary agreement. Long Island was to be part of New York, "as is expressed by plain words" in the Duke's patent, though Nicolls announced that the civil administration and property ownership on the island, as previously settled by Connecticut, should con-

---

[20] *Ibid.*, II, 414; XIV, 557; Winthrop Mss., V, 44, 199; XV, 163; M.H.S. *Coll.*, 4th ser., VII, 309-10; *Conn. Rec.*, I, 433-35.

tinue unchanged. All offshore islands, even Fisher's Island only two miles from the Connecticut coast, were assigned to the Duke's jurisdiction, though again Nicolls confirmed John's title to Fisher's Island in return for a nominal quitrent of one lamb per annum. It was some consolation to Winthrop that John Scott's pretensions to the presidency of Long Island were also dismissed. Nicolls rapidly decided that the Captain was a knave, and Scott skipped off to the West Indies. In the mainland settlement Connecticut won her essential point. The commissioners dropped the Duke's claim to the Connecticut River, and in fact were misled by the Hartford delegation into drawing the New York-Connecticut boundary at Mamaroneck River, further west than the Dutch-English boundary of 1650.[21]

Richard Nicolls was a loyal servant to the Duke of York, but he was also a reasonable man, and he had no desire to ruin Connecticut or perpetrate "a manifest breach of their late patent." He explained to his master "that to the East of New Yorke and Hudsons River nothing considerable remaines to Your Royal Highness except Long Island and about twenty miles from any part of Hudsons River; I looke therefore upon all the rest as onely empty names and places possesst forty yeares by former graunts and of no consequence to Your Royal Highness except all New England could be brought to submit to Your Royal Highness his patent."[22]

Within four months after the conquest, Nicolls promulgated a special law code known as the Duke's Laws, modeled largely on New England codes, for use in the English towns on Long Island. Nicolls' behavior was as generous as Winthrop could reasonably expect, and he thanked the Colonel for his "entertainment and many favours to my selfe and company" at New York.[23] The treaty of November 30, 1664, was the basis of the present New York-Connecticut boundary. Unfortunately, it did not fully satisfy either party, and within ten years Connecticut would make an effort to regain eastern Long Island,

---

[21] Winthrop Mss., v, 46; M.H.S. *Coll.*, 4th ser., VII, 311; Trumbull, *History of Connecticut*, I, 525-26; *N.Y.Col.Doc.*, III, 86, 105, 136; XIV, 561; N.Y.H.S. *Coll.*, II, 76.

[22] *N.Y.Col.Doc.*, III, 106.

[23] *Ibid.*, 91; XIV, 564-66, Winthrop Mss., v, 47.

while the Duke would reopen his claim to the western half of Connecticut.

❧ THE Royal Commission's second task, inspecting and regulating New England, turned out to be considerably more difficult than the establishment of New York. The head commissioner, Nicolls, was busy reorganizing the ducal proprietary, so most of the New England work devolved on his three colleagues, Sir Robert Carr, Colonel George Cartwright, and Samuel Maverick. This trio was uniformly intemperate and grossly partisan. Lord Clarendon realized too late the unwisdom of appointing Maverick, with his background of strong personal enmity toward the Bay government, and warned him "if you should reveng any old discourtesies, at the King's charge. . . the King would take it very ill, and do himselfe justice accordingly." The appointment of Sir Robert Carr introduced New Englanders to the new breed of crown colonial officers who aimed at making their fortunes in America by fleecing the yokel planters. Carr went to the Delaware allegedly to establish the Duke of York's authority over the Dutch outposts there, but ("tumbling in plunder," as Maverick told Winthrop) settled down to the business of staking out his own Delaware estate. Nicolls had to go down himself and drag Carr back. On a later occasion in Boston, Sir Robert engaged in fisticuffs with a local constable trying to chase him out of a tavern at closing time.[24]

The commissioners' chief target was to be Massachusetts. Clarendon's public instructions, to be displayed to the New England governments, explained that the King had no doubt of his colonists' loyalty, and was demonstrating his paternal solicitude by sending over commissioners to hear complaints, settle disputes, and generally remove all jealousies between old and New England. Clarendon's secret instructions, on the other hand, directed the commissioners to exert private pressure for the election of magistrates and deputies "of the best quality" who would agree "to renew their Charters and to make such

[24] *N.Y.Col.Doc.*, III, 87; M.H.S. *Coll.*, 4th ser., VII, 309-10; Winthrop Mss., XVII, 87.

alterations as will appeare necessary for their own benefit," such as giving the King a casting voice in the selection of governors, and lengthening the governor's term to three or five years. The King would like Massachusetts to elect Nicolls as her governor and Cartwright as the commander of her militia. The commissioners were told to insist upon religious toleration in New England, especially for Anglicans, at the very time when the Clarendon Code was enforcing intolerance in England.[25]

The only special instructions concerning Connecticut were: (1) to find out how her civil and religious structure differed from Massachusetts', and (2) to settle her boundary dispute with Rhode Island. The commissioners were to remind Mr. Winthrop, "if he be still Governor there, of whome wee have had a good opinion," that he promised before leaving England that Connecticut would submit to any boundary settlement made by the commissioners "as if no Charter were then passed to them; which wee cannot but expect at their hands." The commissioners were advised to reject the claims of both Connecticut and Rhode Island to the Narragansett Country, and award the disputed territory directly to the crown. They were instructed not to disturb any property holders in the area.[26]

Winthrop, who may have guessed the nature of these Narragansett instructions, conducted Connecticut's policy toward the commissioners with finesse. Everything conspired against him, however. He tried in October 1664 to reopen direct negotiations with Rhode Island over the boundary dispute, to forestall outside arbitration. The two colonies' aims were still mutually exclusive, and the new peace conference broke down. Next, John urged Nicolls to visit Connecticut before Rhode Island and advised him to hold a hearing on the Narragansett Country in Boston, which happened to be the home of most of the Narragansett proprietors. Since Nicolls could not get away from Manhattan, Carr, Cartwright, and Maverick began their inspection of New England without him. They went first

[25] *N.Y.Col.Doc.*, III, 57-63; Trumbull, *History of Connecticut*, I, 523-24; M.H.S. *Proc.*, 1st ser., VII, 377.
[26] *N.Y.Col.Doc.*, III, 55-56.

to Boston, where their reception was exceedingly frosty. Cartwright was accused of being a papist, and Carr of keeping a naughty woman. The commissioners moved down to Rhode Island in early March 1665. Here they were welcomed wholeheartedly, since the Rhode Islanders looked to them for protection from the tyranny of the New England Confederation. The commissioners announced that they would judge the Narragansett Country dispute, and asked Connecticut to send a delegation to present her side of the case. The settlers at Wickford implored John to come in person. John did set out as fast as he could, and though choking ice made the Connecticut River temporarily impassable and a late fall of snow blocked the path, he managed to send a message by Indian runner, beseeching the commissioners that his tardiness "may be no prejudice to this colony nor the people there whom it concernes."[27]

He might as well have stayed in Hartford. On March 20, 1665, the commissioners, following Clarendon's instructions, decreed that the Narragansett Country belonged to neither Connecticut nor Rhode Island but directly to Charles II, and named it King's Province. Since they had dispossessed Rhode Island of half her territory, they authorized the Rhode Island magistrates to govern King's Province until further notice. This decision was at least as workable at the Winthrop-Clarke agreement of 1663, and might possibly have been accepted had the commissioners followed Clarendon's injuction not to disturb property holders. Instead, they listened to Rhode Island's charges that Atherton and his partners had defrauded the Indians when they bought the land in 1659, charges which John himself did nothing to deny. They voided these purchases and ordered the Narragansett proprietors (John, of course, being one of them) to leave King's Province by the following September. Sir Robert Carr promptly asked his superiors in England for title to a large tract of the choicest Narragansett graz-

[27] *Conn. Rec.*, I, 435; *R.I. Rec.*, II, 71-76; Winthrop Mss., V, 46-47, 49; XIV, 61; *N.Y.Col.Doc.*, III, 94; M.H.S. *Coll.*, 5th ser., IX, 62-66; *Cal.S.P.Col.*, *1661-1668*, pp. 274-75.

ing land.[28] The creation of King's Province had the long range effect of buttressing Rhode Island's authority over the Narragansett Country, but it by no means settled the matter. John protested vigorously to Nicolls, "I beseech your honor to settle some way for [the Narragansett planters'] peaceable possession of what they have . . . their eyes are towards your honor for reliefe." Nicolls got the other commissioners to reverse their position and order Rhode Island not to disturb property possession in King's Province.[29] With his partners protected, John felt reasonably satisfied. The Connecticut government, however, had no intention of surrendering her claim to the Narragansett Country so easily, and refused to acknowledge the verdict of Carr, Cartwright, and Maverick on the grounds that Nicolls, the chief commissioner, was absent when the case was heard.

The commissioners gave Connecticut a more cursory inspection than the other New England colonies. They were escorted by John to New London in late March 1665. They did not bother to summon the Connecticut General Assembly, but they presented to John several requirements: that all Connecticut householders take the oath of allegiance, that "all men of competent estates and civil conversation" have liberty to vote and hold office, that "all persons of civil lives" have complete religious liberty, and that all laws derogatory to the King be altered or repealed. Nothing was said about the Navigation Laws. The Connecticut General Assembly composed an address to the King, thanking him for his "special grace in sending your commissioners, and assuring your poore planters heere that their priveledges Civill and Ecclesiasticall shall not be violated in the least degree." The Assembly explained that Connecticut was already practicing the civil liberty required by the commissioners, which was true, as well as religious liberty, which was untrue. The Connecticut people were not rigid Pres-

[28] *Mass. Rec.*, IV, pt. 2, 175-76; *R.I. Rec.*, II, 93-94; *N.Y.Col.Doc.*, III, 55-56, 97, 109; N.Y.H.S. *Coll.*, II, 90-91, 107-108.

[29] Winthrop Mss., V, 52; M.H.S. *Coll.*, 4th ser., VII, 573; *N.Y.Col.Doc.*, III, 158; *R.I. Rec.*, II, 94-95.

byterians, as Sir Robert Carr ignorantly reported home, but they were certainly rigid.[30]

The commissioners' visit to New London raised the troublesome question of the crown's authority to review colonial court decisions, which New England had so far successfully resisted. In 1662, while John was away in England, a determined royalist named William Morton had tried to prosecute some New London persons for treason because they had spoken ill of the King. Morton was foiled first by the local magistrate, John Tinker, who was also John's steward. He was foiled next by the Hartford Council, where Secretary Allyn allegedly threatened him with hanging. He then went to England to appeal for justice, and the Privy Council ordered the royal commissioners to review Morton's case.

Fortunately for Connecticut, when Carr, Cartwright, and Maverick visited New London, Morton had not yet returned from England. John assured the commissioners he would reexamine the case.[31] In October 1665, a special committee of the Connecticut General Assembly granted Morton a new hearing which apparently satisfied him. John pointedly thanked Clarendon for suspending judgment against his remote servants and for directing "the further disquisition of the case heere, where the due testimonies may be produced *face to face*, and both parties may be heard together." He was telling the Lord Chancellor, as openly as he dared, how much Connecticut disliked royal interference in local court decisions.[32]

After their visit to New London, the royal commissioners returned to the main business and confronted the Massachusetts General Court in May 1665. Unlike the smaller New England colonies, the Bay government was girded for battle. Governor Bellingham acted in the vein of the elder Winthrop in 1635. The Massachusetts court asked the King to recall his

[30] M.H.S. *Coll.*, 5th ser., IX, 73; *Conn. Rec.*, I, 439-40; II, 27; C.H.S. *Coll.*, XXIV, 11-12; Winthrop Mss., V, 203; *Cal.S.P.Col., 1661-1668*, p. 341.

[31] Caulkins, *History of New London*, pp. 149-50; Winthrop Mss., V, 199; XI, 7; M.H.S. *Proc.*, 1st ser., VII, 346; *N.Y.Col.Doc.*, III, 97.

[32] M.H.S. *Proc.*, 2nd ser., XIII, 455-56; *Conn. Rec.*, II, 27; Winthrop Mss., V, 206.

Royal Commission because it was infringing the colonists' liberties. Learning that Robert Boyle had written Winthrop the previous year of Clarendon's friendly intentions toward New England, the court also boldly appealed to Boyle for his help. Boyle, a prerogative man, was insulted. "I did not imagine," he replied stiffly, "that what I occasionally writt to Mr Winthrop. . .upon the score of haveing been my particular acquaintence, should have been taken notice of by so considerable an assembly as yours. . . ." The Massachusetts government's latest petition to the King, he said, was "more unexpected than welcome."[33]

Nevertheless, the Massachusetts General Court fought the royal commissioners to a standstill. It refused to adopt an oath of allegiance to the King, to permit religious liberty for the Church of England or appeals to the crown. It blocked the commissioners' attempt to sit as an appellate court. In the fall of 1665 the commissioners dispersed, helpless to do more. In their formal report to the home government they praised the cooperative attitude of the three southern colonies, recommended direct royal government for New Hampshire and Maine, and the revocation of the Massachusetts charter. On April 10, 1666, Charles II ordered Massachusetts to send agents to England to answer the commissioners' charges. The Bay government coolly refused. The General Court's only concession was to ship the King two large masts in September 1666 as a present for the royal navy. Nothing further was done to force Massachusetts' obedience. Governor Bellingham and his cohorts had dared to challenge the Royal Commission and they had won.

Governor Winthrop seemingly had gained much less than Massachusetts by staking his policy on friendship with the commissioners. He obviously had more to lose by trying to fight them. And John had solidified his colony's good reputation at Whitehall. Nicolls reported home that there was "not the least appearance of a refractory disposition" in Connecticut. Robert Boyle told John he had spoken to Clarendon of "your Respectfulnes to his Majesty's Commissioners, which his Lordship was

---

[33] *Hutchinson Papers*, II, 113-14; M.H.S. *Coll.*, 5th ser., I, 400-401.

pleas'd to let mee know, that he was inform'd of it otherways, & that it was very wellcome to him." Clarendon himself wrote John that the commissioners said they had been "very civilly treated by you, with which his Majestie is well pleased." Charles II's official letter of April 10, 1666, to Connecticut reiterated his pleasure at the colony's reception of the commissioners, "set off with the more lustre by the contrary deportment of the colony of the Massachusetts."[34] All this good will might have seemed of little consequence in 1666, but it helped Connecticut to escape the brunt of the attack when the home government systematically broke down New England's autonomy in the 1680's and 1690's. In the long run it helped Connecticut retain a larger measure of self-government than Massachusetts.

In the case of Connecticut, the Royal Commission of 1664 counterbalanced the Royal Charter of 1662. Charles II's careless generosity had inflamed the colony's expansionist ambitions, but his commissioners' settlement of New England boundary disputes effectively dampened her inordinate hopes. As for John Winthrop, Jr., he rejected his father's precept, in 1664 as in 1662. He worked on the principle that New England's liberty and prosperity was better promoted by cooperation with the home government than by defiance. Events proved that he was correct.

[34] N.Y.H.S. *Coll.*, II, 114; M.H.S. *Proc.*, 1st ser., XVI, 224-26; 2nd ser., XIII, 455; Winthrop Mss., XI, 36; Trumbull, *History of Connecticut*, I, 537; M.H.S. *Coll.*, 4th ser., VII, 313.

8. *Under the Stuart Shadow*

ON the eve of the annual Connecticut election in May 1665, Governor Nicolls of New York extended an invitation to his friend John Winthrop, Jr. "If your resolutions are not to accept of the Government of Conecticott the Yeare Ensuing," Nicolls wrote, "I would begg the favour of you, to resolve of setting at New Yorke with your family. . . . I doe promise you, that in fourteene daies Notice I will provide for your selfe and family one of the best houses in New Yorke, which shall cost you nothing but the acceptance. . . ."[1] John wanted to escape the burdensome honor of re-election, but being nearly sixty years old, with more property in Connecticut and Massachusetts than he could handle, he quelled his strong migratory impulse and stayed in Hartford. Nicolls' effort to lure him was, however, indicative of New York's strong pull upon Connecticut. It was no light matter to live next door to the Duke of York. The Duke's management of New York, and his relationship with New England, prefigured his colonial policy in the 1680's when he became King. John Winthrop, Jr., for his part, tried hard to keep good relations with Stuart New York. During the final dozen years of his life, 1664-1676, John's dealings with three successive ducal governors—Nicolls, Lovelace, and Andros—occupied the central place in his affairs.

⟨⟨ THE English seizure of New Netherland in 1664 provoked a general war, the second Anglo-Dutch war of 1665-1667. Charles II's government tried to enroll the colonials actively in her war plans but with scant success. The New Englanders' performance in this war expressed very well their position midway between the first generation planters, who had escaped entanglement in international conflict, and the third

[1] Winthrop Mss., xv, 165.

generation, who would have to serve on the front line in the great Anglo-French war of 1689-1713. The King's spokesman in America was Governor Nicolls, who called for united New York-New England action against the Dutch and French. The New Englanders, especially Massachusetts, preferred neutrality. John Winthrop, Jr., assumed the difficult task of liaison between Nicolls and the New England governments.

Upon the outbreak of the war, Nicolls tried to follow the home government's orders for intercolonial defense against a Dutch counterattack on New York. In June 1665 he asked John to alert the Connecticut militia in the towns bordering New York to come to the aid of Manhattan when warned of the enemy's approach. "I have made some former proposalls to you," Nicolls complained, "of Mutuall Assistance upon such occasions, but I could (hitherto) never obtaine a Satisfactory Answer." He could not obtain one this time, either. John assured him that the Connecticut magistrates were "very zelous for his Majestie interest," but in fact their zeal only extended to the defense of Connecticut. Nicolls wrote home that, thanks to Connecticut, he must rely on the handful of soldiers he had brought from England, dispersed in four widely separated garrisons, and so he had no hope of securing New York against the Dutch.[2] Fortunately for all concerned, the Dutch attack never came.

When France also entered the war against England, the home government in February 1666 instructed the New England colonies to organize an expedition for the conquest of Canada if possible. Nicolls was in favor of this. Again, John assured Nicolls (June 2, 1666) that Connecticut "wilbe as forward as any to joyne with the rest of his majesties colonies" against the French, but the General Assembly, meeting the next month, decided that the need for manpower at harvest time and the danger of Indian raids into Connecticut made it impracticable for the colony to join in an invasion of Canada.[3]

[2] *Ibid.*, 166; *Cal.S.P.Col.*, *1661-1668*, p. 272; *Conn. Rec.*, II, 19-21; M.H.S. *Coll.*, 5th ser., VIII, 96-98; *N.Y.Col.Doc.*, III, 114-15.

[3] *Cal.S.P.Col.*, *1661-1668*, pp. 349, 357-58; Winthrop Mss., v, 55, 57-59; *Conn. Rec.*, II, 43-46; M.H.S. *Coll.*, 5th ser., VIII, 99-101.

John personally did do valuable work for the English cause. In August he went up the Connecticut River to Springfield, Massachusetts, and managed to dissuade a large party of local Indians from joining the French in upper New York. He also sent out a few horsemen to reconnoiter the overland passage to Canada, although they turned back only 120 miles from Hartford. John went on to Boston, consulted with the Bay leaders, and drafted letters to the King and the two secretaries of state (October 25, 1666), explaining that the New England colonists had not invaded Canada because instructions from home had arrived too late in the summer for adequate preparations. Besides, the overland route to Canada was almost impassable and warships were needed for an attack by sea.[4] Thus the first English project to drive the French out of North America came to nothing.

The war crisis continued until mid-1667. John's colony followed Nicolls' example by reorganizing the militia into squads of mounted dragoons specially designed to meet sudden enemy raids. In the spring of 1667, Connecticut and Massachusetts received new instructions from the King to ship down victuals, arms, and men for the relief of the West Indies islands under Dutch and French attack. The home government could scarcely have expected this order to be obeyed, but it shows which of her colonial possessions she valued most. Once more John went to Boston, consulted the Bay leaders, and sent letters of excuse to England. The New Englanders, he said, were very anxious to help their dear countrymen in the Caribee Islands, but could not possibly do so. They had no spare manpower, were short of food and ammunition themselves, and had no shipping available.[5] When the war closed with the Treaty of Breda (July 21, 1667), the English government surrendered Acadia to France in exchange for three West Indies sugar islands.

Since the New Englanders had done almost nothing to help their side win, Nicolls had good reason to complain about their war effort. He found fault also with other aspects of New Eng-

---

[4] Winthrop Mss., V, 58, 60, 62-64; M.H.S. *Coll.*, 5th ser., VIII, 101-103.

[5] Winthrop Mss., V, 65a-68a; *N.Y.Col.Doc.*, III, 167; M.H.S. *Coll.*, 5th ser., VIII, 105-14, 117-19; *Cal.S.P.Col.*, *1661-1668*, pp. 357-58.

land behavior. John was endlessly having to placate him. Nicolls wanted to break up the New England Confederation, which he saw as an instrument of Puritan autonomy. John justified the Confederation to Nicolls as having "hitherto beene usefull for the keeping peace with the Indians" and urged the New York governor to collaborate with the Confederation commissioners in Indian negotiations. When the commissioners met every September to oversee the business affairs of the Society for the Propagation of the Gospel in New England, John assured him that these were not full meetings of the Confederation.[6]

Nicolls was also deeply suspicious of the Connecticut clergy. Was it true, he asked John in 1667, that Master Davenport "hath furiously rayled at the Government in England both Church and State" in a recent sermon? "No Charter doth priviledge any Man to speake Treason," Nicolls said. "I beseech you Sir that your Court may bee mooved to testify against such seditious discourses." Hearing that a convention of ministers at Hartford were debating the sacrament of baptism, Nicolls wanted assurance that they would not "bee suffer'd to make any decree against the Generall Use of that Sacrament, for which his Majestie hath so amply declared himselfe." John sought to calm his fears on both points. He talked to Davenport about the treason charge and felt sure that it was pure slander. Perhaps, John suggested to Nicolls, the New Haven minister might have preached "against the popish Antichristian Roman Hierarchy (though mr Davenport remembers not any late occation that way.)" As for the baptism debate, John laughed it off. An assembly of ministers had indeed been called by the Connecticut General Assembly, but "these ancient men who were heere could not well beare the hot weather heere, and began to be ill. . .and nothing was done in publiq."[7]

In spite of all, Winthrop and Nicolls continued to like and trust each other. When the colonel was relieved of his governorship in 1668 and sailed back to England, John sent him a farewell letter full of sadness at his departure and "humble

---

[6] Winthrop Mss., V, 52-53.
[7] *Ibid.*, 68a, 175; XV, 163; M.H.S. *Coll.*, 5th ser., VIII, 126.

thankes for your good affection alwaies exprest to this colony."
Would Nicolls do one further favor for Connecticut, namely,
help her get control of the Narragansett Country? John hoped
"your Honor will represent the case so cleerly to his Majestie
that he may be pleased to give his Royall order for the confirmation of it" to Connecticut. Two years passed, another peace
conference between the two colonies failed, and Richard Smith,
the leading Wickford planter, went to England. Again John
wrote Nicolls, asking him to help Smith at court.[8] John himself by this time was unwilling to press his colony's claim to
the Narragansett Country too hard. He told the Connecticut
Assembly in 1670 that he dissented from its efforts to exercise
jurisdictional power east of the Pawcatuck River "untill his
majesties pleasure be further knowne, or the matters issued by
a treaty betweene some impowred from this colony and Road
Iland." The two old adversaries, Winthrop and Clarke, wrote
to each other, both anxious "to forget these tedious and troublesome contests which faithfulness to our trust (as charity bids
us believe) put us upon beyond the seas. . . ."[9] But the contest
was only well started. Not until Connecticut finally reconciled
herself to the Pawcatuck River boundary in 1728, more than
fifty years after John's death, was a permanent solution found
for this problem which he had done so much to create.

John talked of making another trip himself to England, to
clear his heavy private debts with Henry Ashurst and John
Harwood in London. The war of 1665-1667 had been a disaster, costing him personally several thousand pounds. Two
ships in which he had large cargo or interest were taken as
prizes by the Dutch. He told Nicolls that his private affairs
"have for a good while suffered so exeedingly that I cannot
longer omitt to take more particular. . .care about them without a totall ruine." Accordingly, when the Connecticut freemen
re-elected him in 1667, he told the Assembly it would be "an
absolute impossibility" for him to continue in the governorship.
Nevertheless, when the Assembly freed his estate from taxation
and raised his salary to £112 per annum, he consented to stay.

[8] Winthrop Mss., V, 81, 92; M.H.S. *Coll.*, 5th ser., VIII, 126.
[9] Winthrop Mss., V, 90; XI, 158.

In 1668 he again wanted freedom from office so that he could visit England. He took the governor's oath with the stipulation that he might have leave of absence at any time.[10] By 1670 John had paid off all but £100 of his £484 debt to Ashurst, but the £1500 debt to Harwood was still outstanding, and he owed money also in Boston. He went to Massachusetts, trying to settle with his local creditors, and sent a letter of resignation to the Connecticut General Assembly. There was a necessity, he wrote, "eyther of a voyage into England, or much longer stay in the Massachusetts, then I intended." The resignation was turned down as usual, and the court again raised his salary to £150 per annum.[11] John continued in harness, dropped the projected voyage to England, and delegated the management of his tangled business affairs to his two sons.

Like his father before him, John Winthrop, Jr., ended his days a triple prisoner, bound by his private debts, his public responsibilities, and his people's love. There are worse fates.

❧ THROUGHOUT his declining years, John's chief delight was in keeping his active association with the Royal Society. Tied permanently to Hartford, he felt increasingly the isolation of the new world, where the physical horizon was so vast and the intellectual horizon so narrow. There was a current of loneliness, almost of pathos, in his anxiety to stay in touch with European science and technology. Looking back on his English trip of 1661-1663, John told the secretary of the Royal Society, Henry Oldenburg, of his great happiness "when for that short time I sojourned in London they were pleased to permitt me to wait upon them at Gresham Colledge (unworthy I acknowledge of that honour), nor can I possibly (though thus farre distant) forgett my duty to that Society."[12]

Too old and disillusioned to try any further industrial experiments in New England, John endeavored to fulfill his duty to the Royal Society by sending reports on his scientific observations and especially by shipping a wide sampling of curiosi-

[10] *Ibid.*, v, 67, 81; M.H.S. *Coll.*, 5th ser., VIII, 120, 134; *Conn. Rec.*, II, 64.
[11] Winthrop Mss., v, 93; X, 88-90, 122; XIV, 13-14; M.H.S. *Coll.*, 5th ser., VIII, 137; *Conn. Rec.*, II, 145, 153.
[12] M.H.S. *Coll.*, 5th ser., VIII, 131.

ties from the American wilderness. One of his proudest possessions was a three-and-a-half foot telescope, a present from
Dr. Benjamin Worsley. "Be assured (Deare Sir)," he wrote
Worsley, "I seldom looke upon the constellations of the
heavens, or the planetts, especially Jupiter with my telescope,
or the glorious constellation of Orion, but the most gratefull
memory of yourself is fresh to my thoughts, and soule, besides
a thousand other tymes." Through this instrument he had seen
five satellites around Jupiter "very distinctly," though it was
more than two hundred years before any other astronomer was
able to observe Jupiter's fifth satellite. He was himself suspicious of "such a novelty of my singular observation," and asked
for confirmation from stargazers in England with bigger tele-
scopes. In 1672 he gave his telescope (along with other astro-
nomical instruments) to Harvard College, and immediately
wanted to know what the scholars at Cambridge could see
through it.[13]

During the Dutch War of 1665-1667 John's letters and contributions to the Royal Society were mostly captured or lost
at sea, a heavy blow, accentuating his remoteness "from that
fountaine whence so many rivelets of excellent things doe
streame forth, for the good of the world." The vast ocean bar-
rier had given John a sense of isolation almost directly contrary to the splendid isolation of his father's city upon a hill.
When the war was over, he prepared and shipped to the Society several collections of New England flora and fauna. In
1669 four boxes of assorted "rarities or Novelties" were sent
in the care of his nephew Adam Winthrop, such things as dwarf
oak trees (whose acorns he feared would shake off during the
voyage), samples of spring and winter wheat, and porcupine
quills. Secretary Oldenburg told John how extremely successful his "American Curiosities" had been: "His Majesty himselfe, hearing of some of the rarer things, would see them, and
accordingly the Extraordinary Fish, the dwarf-oaks, the
gummy fragrant Barke, with knobbs, the silken podds, the
baggs with litle shells in them, etc., were carried to Whitehall,

[13] Winthrop Mss., V, 70, 94; M.H.S. *Coll.*, 5th ser., VIII, 93-94; M.H.S. *Proc.*,
2nd ser., IV, 265.

where the King saw them with no common satisfaction, expressing his desire in particular to have your Stellar fish engraven and printed. . . . his Majesty would be well pleased, if you sent over such a quantity of your silkpods, as would make him a pillow. It may occasion his Majesty to think on you as often [as] he lays his head on a pillow." These silk pods were evidently milkweed pods. As soon as the milkweed along the New England roadsides ripened in the fall of 1670 and the pods burst, John collected a barrel full of down and shipped it to England. The home government was most anxious to promote the production of silk, or a viable substitute, in the colonies. The King and Sir Robert Moray hoped that the down from John's pods would be spun into thread or used for making hats. Short experimentation convinced Moray that New England "silk" was insufficiently tough or resilient for any useful purpose. Apparently the royal pillow was never made.[14]

John shipped other New England curios to the Royal Society in 1670: two rattlesnake skins, and "the nest of a small bird (an humming bird so called from the humming noise it makes whiles it flies)," John wrote to Oldenburg; "it is an exeeding little bird and only seene in summer and mostly in gardens flying from flower to flower and sucking hony. . . ." Oldenburg reported back that the "Humbird-nest was also shew'd to his Majesty, who was as much pleased with it as the Society." The most pleasing specimen of all was the carcass of a horseshoe crab, or (as John named it) a horsefoot crab. The gentlemen of the Society questioned whether what John called the creature's long tail was not actually its head or nose, to which John answered that its "progressive motion is alwaies the other part the round part forward, when they goe, they draw that sharp spike after them, as I have my selfe seene often and thousands of others." In succeeding years he sent over poison ivy plants, and a pig born without ears. In exchange he received the annual *Transactions* of the Royal Society (in which several of his contributions were printed) and other scientific publications. When Oldenburg pressed him to write a

[14] Winthrop Mss., V, 88-89, 92, 163; M.H.S. *Proc.*, 1st ser., XVI, 230, 244-45, 249; Birch, *History of the Royal Society*, II, 418-21.

natural history of New England, he said he was collecting the materials for it, but the interior of the country was not yet well enough explored to warrant such a work.[15]

John also corresponded with Robert Boyle on the New Englanders' progress in civilizing and converting the heathen, work which Boyle's Society for the Propagation of the Gospel in New England was subsidizing. The Society sponsored the publication of John Eliot's Indian Bible, originally dedicated to Parliament in 1659 and tactfully readdressed to Charles II after the Restoration. Boyle presented the King with a copy of the Eliot Bible: "he looked a pretty while upon it, & shewd some things in it to those that had the honour to be about him in his bedchamber." John sent Boyle two Latin compositions written by Indian students at Harvard. The Indians, he reported, gave him prompt answers "in Latin to many questions that I propounded to them in that language, and [I] heard them both express severall sentences in Greke also."[16] It must have been a wonderful scene.

Governor Winthrop's continued comradeship with Boyle, Moray, and Worsley was a bridge between two increasingly divergent societies. Unlike John, most New England preachers and public officers still carried the intellectual baggage, shabby and patched, which their fathers had brought over before the Civil War. In Restoration England, there was a new climate of opinion, combined with an overwhelming concentration of social and political power in the property-owning upper half of society, the aristocrats, gentry, and merchants. New England was far more egalitarian. To be sure, an increasingly self-conscious colonial elite, consisting of the Winthrop family and a few score of others, sat on the colony councils, owned the Boston warehouses, or held title to the hugest tracts of empty land. Yet with free land everywhere available, and with far more widespread participation in church and state management

[15] Winthrop Mss., V, 76, 89, 92, 100, 106, 159; M.H.S. *Proc.*, 1st ser., XVI, 245, 249-51; Birch, *History of the Royal Society*, II, 448, 499; John Lowthorp, ed., *The Philosophical Transactions and Collections* [of the Royal Society] (Abridged, 3 vols.; London, 1716), II, 630-34, 832-33, 854; III, 564-65.

[16] M.H.S. *Proc.*, 1st ser., V, 376; M.H.S. *Coll.*, 5th ser., VIII, 84-85; Winthrop Mss., V, 76, 92.

than at home, there was no possibility of the English extremes in wealth and social status. "No house in New England," it was reported to the colonial office in the 1670's, "hath above 20 Rooms: Not 20 in Boston, which have above 10 Rooms each . . . .The worst cottages in New England are lofted. No beggars. Not 3 put to death for theft."[17] Here was the real difference between the old world and the new.

Considering this widening intellectual and social breach, Massachusetts' insolent treatment of the royal commissioners, and New England's refusal to participate actively in the war of 1665-1667, Charles II's government might be expected to take strong measures against the Puritan colonies. Instead, the King abandoned his interventionist policy of 1664-1665. One reason is that Clarendon fell from power in 1667, and his successor as the royal minister principally interested in plantation affairs was Lord Ashley, himself an active colonial entrepreneur in Carolina. Ashley wanted personal freedom to test his political, social, and economic ideas in Carolina; he shared the New Englanders' jealousy of centralized royal control. While Lord Ashley dominated the King's plantation councils, 1667-1673, the home government left the New England colonies to their own devices. Richard Smith of Wickford brought the Narragansett Country dispute to Ashley's attention. "Severall Gentellmen in England of nobell Qualaty did inquyer for you," Smith reported to John Winthrop, Jr. "I had much discourse with my Lord Anthony Ashly Copers Hounor concerning. . . the discent betwene Coneticott and Rode Island. He wished your selufe there." Ashley's Plantation Council favored commissioning representatives from the two colonies to settle the argument, implicitly abandoning the royal commissioners' decision of 1665 and explicitly leaving the problem to the colonists. Likewise, in 1671 the Council advised the King to send over new royal agents to Massachusetts who should be temperate men, "not too much contrary to the present humour of the people"—in other words, more conciliatory than the royal com-

[17] David Ogg, *England in the Reigns of James II and William III* (Oxford, 1955), pp. 33-35; Robert N. Toppan and Thomas S. Goodrick, eds., *Edward Randolph* (7 vols.; Boston, 1898-1909), II, 200 (hereafter referred to as *Randolph*).

missioners of 1664. The Council, fearing that the Bay colonists were already "almost upon the very brink of renouncing any dependence on the Crown," wanted to discover whether the New Englanders "were of such power as to be able to resist his Majesty and declare for themselves as independent of the Crown." No agents were actually sent.[18]

This weak and vacillating treatment of New England reflected the general aimlessness of Charles II's conduct at home during the first fifteen years of his reign. Only in the mid-1670's did the King find enough money and political security to assert his absolutist instincts openly, at home and in the colonies. Then at last Charles II's government launched a consistent attack on the chartered autonomy of the New England colonies. But before the attack had well begun, John Winthrop, Jr., was dead.

◆ THE final episode in John's relations with the mother country was the New York crisis of 1673-1675. Richard Nicolls' successor as governor of New York in 1668 had been another career servant of the royal family, Colonel Francis Lovelace. This gentleman administered the Duke's province in the same style as his elder brother, Richard Lovelace, wrote Cavalier poetry, with elegance and flippancy. Lovelace kept in amicable correspondence with John, but he was not a real friend as Nicolls had been.[19] Probably he suspected that Winthrop was encouraging rebellion among the English towns on Long Island, particularly East Hampton, Southampton, and Southold on the east end, not reconciled to being taxed by the Duke without a representative assembly. When Lovelace burned their "seditious" protests, the people of East Hampton, Southampton, and Southold appealed to the King, "praying that they might be continued under the Government and Patent of Mr Winthrop," or else be given their independence. In July

[18] C. M. Andrews, *British Committees, Commissions, and Councils of Trade and Plantations, 1622-1675*, pp. 104, 136-39; Daniel B. Updike, *Richard Smith* (Boston, 1937), p. 87; Ralph P. Bieber, "The British Plantation Councils of 1670-4," *E.H.R.*, XL, 105; *Cal.S.P.Col., 1669-1674*, p. 244; Louise F. Brown, *The First Earl of Shaftesbury* (New York, 1933), ch. IX.
[19] Winthrop Mss., V, 89, 92, 96; M.H.S. *Coll.*, 3rd ser., X, 79-82.

1672 the Privy Council referred this petition to the Plantation Council.[20]

Before the Council could reach a decision, the situation in America had drastically altered. A new Anglo-Dutch war broke out in 1672. Governor Winthrop called a special session of the Connecticut Assembly and readied the colony defenses against a Dutch attack. Since Lovelace did not try to organize a joint plan of action among the English colonies as Nicolls had, and since the New England Confederation was now moribund, there was even less effective preparation than for the last war. Lovelace did institute a monthly post between New York and Boston, and on hearing of a large enemy fleet bound for the West Indies, he wrote to John that the time had come "for us to begin to buckle on our armor, and to put ourselves into such a posture of defense as is most suitable to our several conditions."[21] Unfortunately he did not follow his own advice. In midsummer 1673, a Dutch squadron several times more powerful than Nicolls' fleet of 1664 was plundering Virginia and heading north; Lovelace chose this moment to visit John at Hartford. He stayed at John's house for four days, had a pleasant time, and was ceremoniously escorted part-way from Hartford to New Haven. When Lovelace got to New Haven he learned that the Dutch fleet had sailed into New York harbor and was besieging Fort James (July 30). He talked gallantly of raising the Long Island militia, but it was already too late. The outmanned English garrison had surrendered New York after putting up token resistance. The Dutch had regained their province as easily as they had lost it. Rumors flew that they had landed three thousand men, and would soon move on to New England. As John's son Fitz wrote him from New London on August 3, "what the intentions of soe great a fleete may be, I believe you have considered; and how lyable (these parts perticulary) wee are to the Injury of an Enimy is easily seene."[22]

[20] John Brodhead, *History of the State of New York* (2 vols.; New York, 1853-1871), II, 172-73; *N.Y.Col.Doc.*, III, 198; *Cal.S.P.Col., 1669-1674*, p. 381.

[21] *Conn. Rec.*, II, 180-83, 559-61; M.H.S. *Coll.*, 5th ser., IX, 83-86.

[22] *Ibid.*, 5th ser., VIII, 148-50; IX, 87-92; 6th ser., III, 435-44; Winthrop Mss., V, 109; VI, 12, 21; XII, 108; XIII, 101; XIX, 73.

Immediately after the capture of New York on July 31, 1673, the Dutch occupied Fort Albany, took ex-Governor Lovelace into custody and reestablished their old government throughout the Duke of York's domain. Only among the Duke's most dissatisfied subjects on eastern Long Island, ironically enough, was there any resistance. On August 7 the people of East Hampton and Southampton appealed to Hartford for protection. In an emergency session, the Connecticut Assembly mobilized the militia, set up a council of war, and dispatched two emissaries to the Dutch commander to protest against Dutch pretensions to eastern Long Island, which had never been in Dutch hands before, and also to sound out the enemy's further intentions. Representatives of the New England Confederation met at Hartford on August 27 and announced that Massachusetts, Plymouth, and Connecticut would stand together if any one of them was invaded. By this time, however, it was fairly clear that the enemy was not planning to invade New England. Despite Dutch threats "to doe all manner of dammage" to the enemies of the United Provinces, the issue had narrowed down to who was going to control the English villages on the east end of Long Island. The Dutch asserted that they would force East Hampton, Southampton, and Southold to submit, and "shall not be afraid to goe against those that shall seeke to maintaine the said villages in their injustis."[23]

Governor Winthrop wanted his colony to stand up to the enemy. In his first flush of anger at the fall of Manhattan, he told John Pynchon of Springfield that the English should spend £20,000 in equipping an army to drive out the Dutch and as much per annum in garrisoning New York to keep them out. On second thought he reflected whether "it be not duty, as well as good manners, and safe also to acquaint our superiours [in England] first and obteine leave and particular commission."[24] The Dutch fleet sailed away in September 1673, greatly reducing the enemy's potency. In October the people

[23] Winthrop Collection, I, 14-20; *Conn. Rec.*, II, 203-208, 561-63; Brodhead, *History of the State of New York*, II, 210-16; *N.Y.Col.Doc.*, II, 584-86.
[24] Winthrop Mss., V, 204.

of East Hampton, Southampton, and Southold refused point blank to take an oath of allegiance to the Dutch governor, Anthony Colve, and again asked Hartford to help them stand for the King "and for our owne honest previlidges." John gave the Connecticut magistrates his personal pledge that, if soldiers were sent to Long Island, the cost would be reimbursed. He said he had "pregnant reasons" for helping the Long Islanders.[25] One of the most pregnant was that Connecticut would be strengthening her English claim against the Duke of York for jurisdiction over these towns.

The Connecticut Assembly followed her governor's advice and undertook to protect the three towns. Governor Colve was warned (October 21, 1673) to keep away from eastern Long Island; Colve replied that he took "little notice of your strange and threatening expressions." Actually Colve was afraid of inciting the New England Confederation to attack New Netherland, while on the English side, Massachusetts turned down Connecticut's request for military support. The Long Islanders asked that John's elder son, Fitz, who was managing the family estate at New London, be made their commander. The Connecticut council of war commissioned Fitz Winthrop, and Samuel Willys, a magistrate, to take fifty or sixty militiamen over to Long Island and arrange a treaty with the Dutch commanders if possible, immunizing the disputed area. John instructed his son to be careful to act in the name of the King.[26]

From October 1673 to April 1674, Long Island was a battlefield. Repeatedly Colve sent sorties against the English towns, and at each emergency Fitz Winthrop and Samuel Willys would race across the Sound with Connecticut volunteers. On November 6, for instance, a Dutch ketch sailed through Plum Gut into Gardiner's Bay, sighted a sail, gave chase and intercepted a sloop carrying Winthrop and Willys over from New London. Both ships landed at Southold. The Dutchmen found nearly one hundred mounted cavalry and foot soldiers in arms

[25] *Ibid.*, 192; Winthrop Collection, I, 22; M.H.S. *Coll.*, 3rd ser., X, 87, 89; 5th ser., VIII, 152-58; 6th ser., III, 445; *N.Y.Col.Doc.*, II, 601-602, 620, 638-42; *Conn. Rec.*, II, 212.

[26] M.H.S. *Coll.*, 5th ser., VIII, 158-61; IX, 93-96; 6th ser., III, 444-45; *Conn. Rec.*, II, 214-20, 563-66; Winthrop Mss., V, 165; X, 21.

at the service of Winthrop and Willys, and not one person willing to swear allegiance to the States-General. The Dutch
thought of visiting other villages, to see whether they were as
firmly united as Southold, but when a Southampton man in
the crowd shouted, "take care that you come not with that Flag
within range of shot of our village," they decided instead to
sail straight back to Manhattan.[27]

Colve became more belligerent. Dutch raiders captured English shipping in the Sound and threatened to plunder the Connecticut coastal towns. The eastern Long Islanders retaliated
by raiding the west end of the island, forcing the angry Dutch
farmers to retire with their grain and livestock behind the walls
of the fort on Manhattan.[28]

In late February 1674 there was a pitched battle of sorts
between the Dutch and English. Stirred by the seizure of a
Dutch vessel off Shelter Island, Colve dispatched the strongest
force which he could muster: one ketch and two sloops. When
the alarm came, Fitz Winthrop received authorization from
Hartford to take over another party of New London militia,
and soon reached Southold. With droll humor, Fitz described
what happened next. The Dutch squadron drew up before the
town, and the commander proclaimed that if the English should
refuse to surrender, "he would destroy them with fire and
sword: As soon as I received this message I informed the officers and soldiers thereof, who unanimously resolved to oppose
them to the utmost hazard of their lives. . . . [the Dutch]
filled their sloops with men, and made all preparations to land;
which we readily perceived, and were ready to entertain them
with 50 men, which I placed a forlorn hope. . . . he fired one
of his great guns upon us; but the shot grazing by the disadvantage of the ground did no hurt to our men. Having received this kindness I gave order to return him thanks by firing
a piece of ordnance upon him; but the shot falling at his fore
foot did him no hurt—whereupon he fired 2 more great guns,

[27] Winthrop Collection, I, 24; *N.Y.Çol.Doc.*, II, 648-58; J. T. Adams, *History of the Town of Southampton* (Bridgehampton, L.I., 1918), 90-92.
[28] Winthrop Mss., V, 118; XIII, 103; *N.Y.Col.Doc.*, II, 662-64, 669-70; M.H.S.
Coll., 5th ser., VIII, 272-73.

and his small shot, which fell thick but did us no hurt—We then presently answered. . . . Many of our small shot hitting the ship as we could perceive, but know not of any hurt done him—Whereupon he presently weighed and set sail. . . ."[29]

Although the Dutch had again been driven off, many people in the mainland towns along the Sound anticipated further attacks. Fitz and his men were anxious to get back to New London, but at the request of the Hartford council they remained on Long Island until mid April. In May all hostilities between Dutch and English ceased, as word was received that the two home governments had signed the Treaty of Westminster, February 9, 1674.[30]

When the Connecticut General Court assembled in May, Governor Winthrop had just learned that the terms of this treaty required the Dutch to hand back New York to the English, and that a new ducal governor of New York was said to be ready to sail for America. Nevertheless, he hoped to detach eastern Long Island from the Duke's province and reunite it with Connecticut. East Hampton, Southampton, and Southold applied for membership in Connecticut's government, and their application was accepted "as farr as shalbe in our lawfull power from his Majesties gracious grant in his Charter. . . ." The three towns voted in June 1674 to petition the King that they might be continued within Connecticut's jurisdiction, and raised £150 to cover the cost of petitioning.[31]

John knew that Connecticut's best chance of keeping eastern Long Island lay in a direct appeal to the Privy Council. He spoke to Fitz "of the necessity & utility of an handsome, true & full narrative to be drawne of matters that have fallen out since the suddaine surprise of New Yorke by the Dutch, especially in reference to those famous townes of the East end of Long Iland by whose loyalty, prudence & valour the honour of the English hath beene maintained in these parts of the world

---

[29] *Ibid.*, 3rd ser., X, 93-94; Winthrop Mss., V, 104; XIV, 83.

[30] *Ibid.*, V, 105; VI, 15; XVI, 60; Winthrop Collection, I, 26; II, 156; M.H.S. *Coll.*, 3rd ser., X, 95-106; 5th ser., VIII, 274-77.

[31] *Conn. Rec.*, II, 222, 226; M.H.S. *Coll.*, 3rd ser., X, 105-106; *Records of the Town of East-Hampton, Long Island* (5 vols., Sag Harbor, L.I., 1887-1905), I, 370-71.

. . . ." John himself started to compose a narrative; among his papers are some random notes on the Dutch invasion and an unfinished draft of the narrative itself in his handwriting.[32] He intended to emphasize in about equal proportions the strength of the enemy fleet, the heroism of the east Long Islanders, and the patriotism of Connecticut in coming to their aid. He told how the Long Islanders in 1673 were determined to stay loyal to the King and therefore turned for help to Connecticut, "especially understanding they had a . . .charter from his majesty which according to the woords of their charter did comprehend the Ilands of the maine land." John wanted to present this narrative to the Privy Council, coupled with the eastern Long Island towns' petition for union with Connecticut.

In October 1674, John's son-in-law, Edward Palmes, went to England, and John entrusted him with Connecticut's appeal to the Privy Council. He gave him a letter of introduction to Robert Boyle. Palmes proved an ineffective agent. Six months after reaching England he wrote Winthrop that he had not yet seen Boyle, and there is no evidence that he was ever admitted before the Council to tell his story.[33]

John's plans for annexing eastern Long Island were checkmated by the Duke of York. As soon as the home government heard in 1673 that the Duke's province had been captured, an expedition was proposed to regain it, and when a few months later New York was peaceably restored by the Treaty of Westminster, the Duke was granted a new charter reiterating all his old province boundaries. Major Edmund Andros was sent out as the new governor, an able and efficient administrator with a heavy sense of the responsibility of government, but a complete autocrat who refused to share or delegate power. John would find such a neighbor less understanding than Nicolls and less easy-going than Lovelace.

[32] Winthrop Mss., V, 162, 197. John's title is: "A narrative of the proceedings of the Generall Assembly and Councell of Connecticut colony in reference to the English plantations upon the west [sic] end of Long Iland. . . ."

[33] M.H.S. *Coll.*, 3rd ser., X, 110-11; 5th ser., VIII, 161-62; Winthrop Mss., V, 128; XVI, 65.

The new governor arrived at New York, November 1, 1674, and received the province from Colve. John had heard that Andros was "a very civill person & well disposed," and that "the Plantations at the Easterne End of Long Iland are well countenanced by the great ones in England." This encouraged him to hope that if the eastern Long Islanders petitioned Andros for permission to join Connecticut, Andros would acquiesce. In December he sent his son Fitz and Samuel Willys to visit New York as a courtesy to the new governor, and then hurry to the east end of Long Island and advise the people there how to deal with him. It was too late. Andros had already learned that East Hampton, Southampton, and Southold had been received into Connecticut jurisdiction. He wrote bluntly to John that if "there be any pretended Engagement betweene you (which cannot now be valid) I doe hereby desire . . . that you will send to disabuse any such persons at the East End of Long Island." The day before the two Connecticut delegates arrived to welcome him, Andros set out himself for eastern Long Island. With firmness and skill he persuaded the three towns to accept his authority and won over the chief property owners in the area. Returning to Manhattan, he found Fitz Winthrop and Willys waiting for him, and also an angry letter from John. The brave Long Islanders "deserve the greatest favour," John wrote. "What is meant by disabusing of them I doe not well apprehend, not knowing that they have been misled by any of this colony. . . ." Andros, however, was now in a contented mood. He thanked the two delegates for honoring him with their visit, and complimented Connecticut, Governor Winthrop, and Fitz Winthrop on having done the King such good service. He could afford to be generous.[34]

Having reasserted the Duke's authority over Long Island, Andros proceeded to revive the Duke's claim to the western half of mainland Connecticut. In this, he was anticipating his master's wishes. The Duke of York in April 1675 wrote to compliment Andros on "reduceing to obedience those 3 factious

[34] *Ibid.*, V, 121, 124, 136-37, 162; X, 67-69; XI, 73; M.H.S. *Coll.*, 3rd ser., X, 114-17; 5th ser., VIII, 165, 277-78; M.H.S. *Proc.*, 2nd ser., IV, 284-85; Brodhead, *History of the State of New York*, II, 274-75.

townes at the East end of Long Island" and spoke also of the boundary settlement of 1664 with Connecticut, which he had never confirmed. The Duke said, "my opinion is 'tis best only to make accomodations of this kind temporary, soe if possible to preserve the utmost limitts for me that my Patent gives me a title to." Even before receiving this letter Andros had discarded Nicolls' settlement of 1664. On May 1, 1675, he wrote to the Hartford Assembly, saying he had discovered that a great part of the Duke's territory was at present being ruled by Connecticut, since New York's eastward boundary was the Connecticut River. "I doe therefore," said Andros, "desire (and will not doubt, from so worthy an assembly,) that . . . you will give present and effectual orders for my receiving, in his Royal Highnesse behalfe, that part of his Territories as yet under your Jurisdiction."[35]

John and his colleagues must have been staggered by this crisp command to hand over half their territory and almost all their towns. They replied politely (May 17) that doubtless Andros was not aware of Connecticut's royal charter, and that the present boundaries had been agreed upon by His Majesty's Royal Commission. Andros would not be so lightly put off. On June 2 he reiterated his demand that western Connecticut be surrendered, arguing that the Connecticut charter obviously does not counter the Duke's title to this area. "I . . . cannot find one word in't comprehending any part of his Royall Highnesse territories." Furthermore, Andros said, the royal commissioners in 1664 had no authority to alter the Duke's boundaries, and their settlement was never confirmed. John and his fellow magistrates met on June 16 and composed another firm but temperate reply, refusing to surrender any territory, but suggesting a "neighborly conference" if Andros remained dissatisfied.[36]

By now the whole colony was tensely waiting for Andros' next move. Having once taken a bold stand, he could neither retreat gracefully nor submit to a conference where nothing would be settled. Edmund Andros was a man of action. Diplo-

[35] *N.Y.Col.Doc.*, III, 231; *Conn. Rec.*, II, 569.
[36] *Ibid.*, II, 570-74; Winthrop Mss., V, 145; X, 71; XX, 53.

matic negotiations having proved worthless, he chose to stake out the Duke's claim to the Connecticut River, and at a singularly nasty time for doing it.

In late June 1675 the most terrible of New England Indian wars, King Philip's War, broke out in Plymouth Colony. Hartford immediately passed the alert to New York. On July 7 the Connecticut Council received a reply from Andros, stating that "upon this extraordinary occasion" he was hastening his troops "to Connecticutt River his Royall Highnesse bounds there." Whether Andros' soldiers were to be used against the Indians or against the Connecticut government was unclear, but the Council members could guess. They sent a company of militia commanded by Captain Thomas Bull to Saybrook, with instructions to protect the seacoast from "the approach of an enemie"—either redskinned or redcoated. The next morning, before Bull's men could reach Saybrook, Andros sailed into the broad, flat mouth of the Connecticut River with two sloops full of soldiers. The Saybrook trainband, however, had been hastily roused, and stood in arms, joined by militia from neighboring towns, watching while a boat was lowered from the governor's sloop.

Messengers, who carried ashore another bullying letter to Hartford, said their master had come on a visit, and to lend aid against the Indians. Andros himself was vexed at seeing the whole river mouth in arms against him. Why, he asked, were the militia not off fighting Indians? Evidence from his own memoranda indicates Andros' intention, had he found Saybrook undefended, to take possession of the local fort. Apparently he supposed that the colonials would run away at his show of force. Instead, the Connecticut militia was unlimbering the cannon in the fort. The governor kept to his ship.[37]

In Hartford, the Connecticut General Assembly was gathering for an emergency session to consider the twin crises posed by the Indians and Andros. Captain Bull was given fresh instructions. If Andros really wanted to fight Indians, he should be directed to the seat of war in Plymouth Colony. If, on the other hand, he tried to land his soldiers at Saybrook, Bull was

[37] *Conn. Rec.*, II, 333, 579-82; Winthrop Mss., XI, 47, 135.

to forbid their landing. "And in generall, whatsoever shall be done or attempted in opposition to the Government here established by his Majestie, you are to declare against, oppose and undoe the same. . . . But you are in his Majesties name required to avoyd strikeing the first blow; but if they begin, then you are to defend yourselves and doe your best to secure his Majesties interest and the peace of the whole Colony of Connecticott in our possession."[38]

Captain Bull followed these orders. On July 12 he handed Andros a letter from the Assembly, promising that the colony would defend herself against his intrusions. It was now clear, even to Andros, that if he wanted to take Saybrook Fort he would have a bloody fight on his hands. Outbluffed at last, but anxious to retrieve his exit with a final flourish, Andros and his officers came ashore the next day and ceremoniously published the Duke of York's charter and his commission to the silent, hostile crowd. Before the Connecticut troops escorted their stiff-necked guest back to his sloop, however, they made him listen to the Connecticut court's proclamation against him. Since Major Andros has chosen, the proclamation read, to molest us "in this juncture, when the heathen rage against the English . . . and still are carrying their heads about the country as trophies of their good success," Connecticut publicly protests against his illegal actions, warns him to desist, and orders all subjects of the colony government "utterly to refuse to attend, countenance or obey the sayd Major Edmond Andross or any under him. . . . God save the King."[39]

He had been slandered, Andros said, and sailed away. It was the closest that the New England planters had yet come to fighting a pitched battle for their chartered liberties. Governor Winthrop found at the close of his life that the only way to win an argument with Edmund Andros was to use brute force. His

[38] *Conn. Rec.*, II, 334.

[39] The Hartford council reproved Captain Bull, afterwards, for listening silently to the Duke's charter and commission. The militia should have drummed or shouted Andros down! (*Ibid.*, II, 262, 342-43, 582-85; M.H.S. *Coll.*, 4th ser., VII, 137.) Trumbull's account of this Saybrook episode (*History of Connecticut*, I, 328-30) is somewhat inaccurate and highly colored.

experience with Andros in 1675 was a somber foreshadowing
of the Dominion of New England ten years later.

⟪⟫ BY THE time of the New York crisis, John Winthrop,
Jr., was an old man, broken in health. On December 1, 1672,
his wife Elizabeth had died, his companion of nearly forty
years. All through the same winter he himself was desperately
ill. "I have been downe in the lower roomes several tymes this
last weeke," he wrote forlornly to his son Wait in February
1673, "but have not beene yet one stepp abroad, nor can abate
any thing yet of my usuall clothes day or night, exept by the
fire side for a very small tyme."[40] He never did fully recover.

John was still saddled with debt. In these last years his correspondence was full of schemes to borrow money and sell land.
The Connecticut Assembly helped him in 1674 by voting to
meet out of tax money "some debt that the Governor contracted
when he was procuring our Charter." John was most grateful.
The Assembly "was very free and most of them unanimous in
this thing," he told Wait. "I looke at it as their greater and
more signall manifestetion of good will and loving respect."
Yet in May and June 1675, just before the Saybrook incident,
he attempted once more to resign the colony governorship, so
that he could make a trip to England for health and business
reasons. As before, the Assembly would not release him.[41]

In the hectic days of July 1675, John presided over only a
few of the Hartford Assembly and Council meetings. He complained to his sons of how he longed for a rest. He felt faint
and weak from the unusually hot weather. Since he continued
to talk of going to England, the Assembly commissioned him
to protest against Andros to the home government. A narrative
was prepared, similar to the narrative of Connecticut's patriotic defense of eastern Long Island that John had drafted the
year before, which complained of Andros' "high handed dealings" at Saybrook, "much unlike the neighborhood we enjoyed

[40] Winthrop Mss., V, 77.
[41] *Ibid.*, V, 89-90, 96a, 105-106, 119-20, 156, 193; M.H.S. *Coll.*, 5th ser.,
VIII, 166, 168-70, 383-95; *Conn. Rec.*, II, 231.

from the Honorable Collonell Niccols and Collonel Lovelace." It requested, in so many words, that the King order Andros to leave Connecticut alone. Not knowing when John would be able to sail, the Connecticut Council forwarded to friends in London the documents prepared against Andros. The whole crisis faded away when the Duke of York ordered his governor to drop the fight over western Connecticut. In January 1676 the Duke told Andros he was glad the issue had been raised in order to preserve his charter rights entire, but until "more convenient means of adjusting the Boundaryes in those parts" were found, he was willing to keep Nicolls' settlement of 1664.[42] The net result of two years' agitation over the New York-Connecticut boundary was to leave everything as it had been, the Duke keeping Long Island and Connecticut keeping her mainland territory.

John never did take his trip to England. As King Philip's War grew steadily more serious, he went to Boston in September 1675 and joined the other New England Confederation commissioners in organizing men and supplies. In October he wrote an English friend that he had a new fit of illness and was hardly capable of an Atlantic voyage before winter. He explained how Connecticut had been disquieted during the summer by the governor of New York, who "sent to demand the cheife part of that colony, although the distinct bounds were orderly settled betwene these colonies by the former governor Colonell Nicols, and all the rest of his Majesties commissioners unanimously under their hands and seales. I am bold humbly to request your labour in behalfe of that colony."[43] These are John's last recorded remarks about Andros. Deliberately understated, they convey the sadness of a tired old man who had spent many years trying to keep a balance between colonial freedom and responsibility to the home government. John stayed in Boston through the winter. He caught cold in late March, and died on April 5, 1676.

Coming in the midst of King Philip's War, the death of

[42] *Ibid.*, II, 263-64, 338-44; Winthrop Mss., V, 148; M.H.S. *Coll.*, 5th ser., I, 431; *N.Y.Col.Doc.*, III, 235-36.
[43] Winthrop Mss., V, 150-52, 157.

John Winthrop, Jr., seemed like part of God's judgment against New England. William Hubbard, writing a narrative of the Indian war in 1677, paused to elegize the well-loved son of a much revered father: "the loss of Mr. *John Winthrope* the late worthy Governour of the Colony of *Connecticut,* is as it ought, much lamented by all. . . . The memory of the Father, though he dyed so long ago yet lives still in the minds of the surviving Generation, and is like to continue much longer, by the remembrance of the eminent virtues found in this the eldest of his off-spring, . . . being so well furnished with many excellent endowments, as well moral as political and philosophical, which rendred him most fit to be an healer of that people."[44]

Though he left his people when his healing power was most sorely needed, when it seemed that the society which he had helped to build was falling apart, perhaps John found comfort in the adjuration he received shortly before his death from another old man in Rhode Island. "Dear Sir," Roger Williams wrote, "if we cannot save our patients, nor relations, nor Indians, nor English, oh let us make sure to save the bird in our bozome, & to enter in that straight dore & narrow way, which the Lord Jesus himselfe tells us, few there be that find it."[45] Roger Williams had originally come to America, like the elder Winthrop, to prepare himself for entry into that strait door and narrow way. In this religious context the colonists had insisted upon freedom from home interference. Now, forty years later, the fire had greatly faded. New England society was already metamorphosing from Puritan to Yankee. Yet is not the continuity in the tradition of freedom as important as the changing basis for it? The elder Winthrop's Massachusetts government had mobilized the militia against a governor general in 1635; the younger Winthrop's Connecticut government stood equally firmly against Andros in 1675. In this sense, Puritan New England had *not* fought a losing struggle.

[44] William Hubbard, *A Narrative of the Troubles with The Indians in New-England* (Boston, 1677), pp. 114-15.
[45] M.H.S. *Coll.,* 4th ser., VI, 306.

BOOK THREE

FITZ WINTHROP

1638 - 1707

&

WAIT WINTHROP

1642 - 1717

9. *Two Cavaliers in Israel*

THE leitmotiv of Cotton Mather's massive *Magnalia Christi Americana* is his effort to shame his third-generation New England audience for the "visible shrink in all Orders of Men among us, from that *Greatness*, and that *Goodness*, which was in the *first* Grain, that our God brought from *Three sifted Kingdoms*, into this Land. . . . What should be done for the stop, the turn of this Degeneracy?" The reverend author answers his own question. "I'll shew them, the *Graves* of their *dead* Fathers." John Winthrop, Jr.'s two sons, Fitz and Wait, were excellent examples of Mather's "degeneracy."[1] They were men of ordinary talent, lacking their grandfather's driving moral purpose and their father's breadth and creative intelligence. Both brothers were humorous, easy-going and self-indulgent, half-aware of their many absurd quirks of character. Fitz's and Wait's conduct betrayed a fundamental moral confusion. Both men made enemies for trivial reasons and nourished longstanding grudges; they were susceptible to flattery and manipulation by cleverer and stronger persons. The accumulation of real estate was their main object, and the conduct of lawsuits over disputed land claims was among their main occupations. The brothers also displayed an acute awareness of their status as gentlemen and the necessity of living in style. They were always exceedingly anxious to hear about the latest London fashions in waistcoats and wigs. The Winthrop dynasty was definitely on the wane.

Yet Fitz and Wait Winthrop, in their selfish, petty, and confused behavior, accurately mirrored the social temper of late seventeenth-century New England. It was a time of rapid expansion in population, wealth, ease, and comfort, in which the

---

[1] Cotton Mather, *Magnalia Christi Americana* (London, 1702), Bk. III, p. 11. A word of apology is necessary for my designation of Fitz-John Winthrop as "Fitz." He signed himself "John Winthrop" and was always addressed as such, never as "Fitz-John." To avoid hopelessly confusing him with his father and grandfather, I have adopted his boyhood nickname of "Fitz."

colonists were nevertheless sorely buffeted by strange new external pressures, dubious about their inherited values, ashamed of their parochialism, and utterly bereft of first-class leadership. By the turn of the century, the problem of reconciling New England's heroic Puritan mission with her dependent status in the English imperial system had produced an acute crisis, yet (as Cotton Mather complained), the colonists could find no leaders of the stature of John Winthrop or John Winthrop, Jr., to help them. Due to their family pedigree, Fitz and Wait were called upon to perform greater public services than their talents warranted. They were elected to high office and entrusted with political responsibilities as important as anything their father or grandfather had undertaken. Actually, the brothers accomplished a great deal in their long and eventful public careers. Despite their preoccupation with private interest, they proved to be better guardians of New England's chartered liberties than of their own family fortune. But Fitz and Wait are chiefly significant as representative third-generation New Englanders, expressing the tensions and fumblings of a society in flux and epitomizing the final secularization of the New England conscience, the completed evolution from Puritan to Yankee.

⚫ᴿ As YOUNG MEN, Fitz and Wait Winthrop found it very hard to accept their New England environment. Like many colonials of their generation, they looked enviously to English standards of taste, to English aristocracy, wealth, and power. They resented the psychological distance between London and New London. Far from living in a godly community for all the world to look at, the brothers rusticated in an outlying province of a great empire. They grew up a couple of Cavaliers in Israel. It was going to take all of Cotton Mather's help in solemnizing the graves of their dead fathers to bring them back to the family tradition of championing New England's political and religious privileges.

The brothers were much alike, physically, and emotionally. Both were homely men, indeed almost comic looking. Both were full-faced, with weak mouths, big eyes, and (chief family trait) the wonderfully long, wide-flanged Winthrop nose. Wait's earliest surviving letter was to his brother Fitz in England. "I hope," seventeen-year-old Wait wrote, "that that vast sea which is betweene us shall never make me forgetfull of you. I can scars yet digest it, that thare being but two of us in the world that we should live soe many thousand milles asunder . . . ."[2] Actually, Wait was not so alone; he had five sisters. But his bond with Fitz was exceptionally strong. The brothers were to quarrel with many people, not least with members of their own family, but all through their lives they maintained a close relationship with each other.

Fitz-John was born in Massachusetts in 1638, at the time when his father was restlessly shuttling between Ipswich, Salem, and Boston, experimenting with salt making and looking for new horizons. The infant was christened John, but to avoid confusion was called Fitz by the family. In 1642 came Waitstill, born seven months after John Winthrop, Jr., had sailed for England in search of money and equipment for a New England ironworks. The meaning of this second son's Christian name is in dispute. One theory is that he was named in honor of friends, the Wait family from Essex and the Still family, connected by marriage with the Winthrops. More probably his name was a characteristically Puritan invocation to wait still for the Lord, with the poignant added plea (in an era of terrible infant mortality) to wait still for the mortal father to come home from across the ocean and see his child.[3] The boy soon became known simply as Wait Winthrop and kept this shortened form all through his life.

Little is known of the two boy's early years. When John Winthrop, Jr., moved to Pequot in 1646, he took eight-year-old Fitz down with him and left Wait and the girls with relatives in Boston. The whole family soon gathered in the straggling new town. Here the boys grew up amidst their father's sprawling domain, with thousands of acres of wild, rocky, un-

[2] M.H.S. *Coll.*, 5th ser., VIII, 382.

[3] On September 27, 1642, seven months after the baby's birth, John Winthrop, Jr.'s sister-in-law wrote to him in England, saying how lonely his wife was, and "therefore I pray hastin to us and let not watestill wat any longer. you know I soppose your sones name is so." *Winthrop Papers*, IV, 354-55.

developed farmland to explore, with the thickets and pastures of Fisher's Island just offshore, and bands of Indians squatting and hunting on the periphery. This was always to be Fitz's home, and he and Wait both loved the place.

It soon appeared that Fitz was best suited to an active, outdoors life, while Wait was somewhat more of a scholar. John Winthrop, Jr., naturally wanted his boys well educated, but there was no school at Pequot. Samuel Fitch kept a school at Hartford, and in September 1652 he offered John to "entertain your sonns into my house and educate them to my utmost." The two boys lived with Fitch for a year and a half, during which time Fitz made friends with John Haynes, the son of the Connecticut governor. "Sir," the schoolmaster reported to John Winthrop, Jr., in August 1653, "your sonn Wait is at present ill, has been drooping 4 days passd, listless & sleeping, unwilling to stirr about. I fear'd wormes, wherefor I gave him wormseed, he complain'd of trouble in his belly . . . and he has voided by vomitt one worme." It was the season for pilfering from fruit trees.

The following year John transferred the boys to Cambridge, where they boarded together with a local family and spent some of their spare time at Ten Hills, the family farm on the Mystic River which their grandfather had first planted. Twelve-year-old Wait was enrolled in Elijah Corlett's grammar school, and it was hoped that sixteen-year-old Fitz could be admitted to Harvard College. President Dunster said that Fitz was by no means ready for Harvard, so the young man's cousin Thomas Dudley undertook to tutor him. It was no easy task. "His mind," Dudley wrote guardedly to John, "seems not altogether adverse to what may seem for the present to be out of his reach, but willing to do its utmost."[4] When Fitz fell ill (perhaps he was mostly homesick), his father wrote in a somewhat different spirit from the parental adjurations which he himself had received as a youth, to caution Fitz against morbid fear of death, a delusion of Satan. Fitz came home after a year of tutoring at Cambridge, his formal education ended. His

---

[4] Winthrop Mss., XIII, 65-67; M.H.S. *Coll.*, 4th ser., VII, 460, 466; 6th ser., III, 424-25.

younger brother made better progress. Wait performed cred-
itably at the Cambridge grammar school for four years, and
entered Harvard with the class of 1662 in the fall of 1658.
His father paid an extra fee in order to give him the advanced
social rank of fellow commoner at the college. He was inclined
to follow the parental example and study medicine.[5]

While Wait continued his schooling in the late 1650's, Fitz
was having as much trouble settling down to a permanent career as his father had had thirty years before. At this time in
New England a young gentleman had the narrow practical
choice of entering the ministry, setting up as a merchant, or
becoming a farmer. Fitz was not enough of a scholar to pursue
the first alternative and apparently was not drawn to the second,
for he passed by an opportunity in 1656 to go to Barbados as
a junior partner in Richard Leader's salt manufacturing enterprise.[6] The most obvious choice was the third one, helping his
father raise cattle on Fisher's Island and operate the unwieldy
family estate. But Fitz wanted to do something more adventurous, and in the fall of 1657, when he was nearing his twen-
tieth birthday, he set sail for England. John warned him that
once he crossed the Atlantic he would have to pay his own bills.
There were, however, plenty of friends and relatives in England to help him find adventure and employment. By January
1658 he reached London safely and presented himself to his
uncle Colonel Stephen Winthrop and Hugh Peter.

Young Fitz wanted to join the army, not because he felt any
special allegiance to Lord Protector Cromwell, but because
army life was glamorous. "I see your son," Hugh Peter wrote
to John on March 1, 1658. "Hee is well growne, and is much
affected to horse, & therefore your brother meanes to put him
into his Regiment, though your brother is but weake himselfe
& (I feare) not long lived." Colonel Winthrop attached his
nephew to his regiment at Gloucester, though there is no record

[5] *Ibid.*, 5th ser., VIII, 43, 62; M.H.S. *Proc.*, 2nd ser., I, 119-20; Winthrop
Mss., V, 14, 16, 19; J. L. Sibley, *Biographical Sketches of Graduates of Harvard
University* (9 vols.; Cambridge, 1873-1956), I, 579; C.S.M. *Publ.*, XXXI, 264-65;
Samuel Eliot Morison, *Harvard College in the Seventeenth Century* (2 vols.;
Cambridge, 1936), I, 59.
[6] M.H.S. *Proc.*, 2nd ser., III, 193.

of his procuring Fitz a commission. In a few months Colonel Winthrop died, and Fitz then went up to see his other military uncle, Colonel Thomas Reade, who was governor of Stirling on the River Forth in central Scotland. The Protector's standing army in Scotland was being gradually cut in size to save expenses, and Reade at first had no vacancy for his nephew. Then in September 1658 Fitz was commissioned a lieutenant of foot, less glamorous service than the cavalry, but a good post as adjutant to his lieutenant colonel.[7]

Oliver Cromwell had just died, and for the next fifteen months the English political situation was wildly unstable, but the Scots were kept quiet, though untamed, by the garrison rule of General Monck. Colonel Reade was a loyal follower of Monck. Most of his regiment was quartered at Stirling, but several companies were stationed at small neighboring posts such as Cardross on the River Clyde, where Lieutenant Fitz Winthrop held his first command over fifty men during the winter of 1658-1659. His parents were comforted to hear that he was serving under his uncle's command, for they were afraid that he might have been tempted into fast company and evil habits in England. Both mother and father exhorted him to seek the Lord. "I have often forewarned you, and persuaded you against wine and strong drinke," John wrote on one occasion, explaining that liquor "never agreeth with the constitution and lungs of any of our family."[8]

Certainly Fitz was a quick tempered and arrogant young man, overly conscious of his social rank. When it was arranged in 1658 that his older sister Elizabeth should marry the minister at Wenham, Massachusetts, a man named Antipas Newman, Fitz distressed his parents (to say nothing of the bride) by writing disdainfully that he would refuse to acknowledge such an inferior person as his brother-in-law. He had to be

---

[7] M.H.S. *Coll.*, 4th ser., VII, 115, 203; 5th ser., I, 44-47; VIII, 45-46, 49-50; 6th ser., III, 426-27; Winthrop Mss., V, 16; XVII, 35; Firth and Davies, *Regimental History of Cromwell's Army*, II, 566.

[8] M.H.S. *Coll.*, 4th ser., VII, 116-17; 5th ser., VIII, 45-46; 6th ser., III, 430; Winthrop Mss., XII, 6-8; C. H. Firth, ed., *Scotland and the Protectorate, 1654-1659* (Scottish Historical Society Publications, XXXI [1899]), pp. 368, 370.

persuaded to swallow his pride and accept the match. Family friends in England complained to John that his son did not bother to visit them. John himself complained to Fitz that he should write home more often and let his family know how he was being affected by the political upheaval in England.[9] Fitz hardly demonstrated the maturity which his father had shown as a similarly young man in 1630.

In the winter of 1659-1660 Fitz did help in a small way to terminate the arid struggle for power in England. Fitz's general, George Monck, broke the deadlock between Army and Parliament. In January 1660 he marched unopposed with ten loyal regiments from Scotland to London and, having thus established himself as the strongest man in the realm, began dictating a reconstitution of Parliament that quickly resulted in the restoration of Charles II. Colonel Reade's regiment marched south with Monck. In reorganizing his army just before leaving Scotland, the general promoted Fitz to the rank of captain-lieutenant, and after reaching London, he raised him again to a full captaincy. This rapid promotion had nothing to do with Fitz's military prowess; it was a political maneuver, for Monck was dismissing all officers who might possibly challenge his authority, and young Fitz could be depended on to obey his uncle.

Fitz was quartered in several different taverns on the Strand and at Covent Garden. His correspondence shows no political awareness. On May 8, 1660, the day that Parliament proclaimed the King, he sent off an affectionate letter to his brother with absolutely no news in it beyond a postscript hint that he would be coming home next year and wanted a good horse reserved for him. During June and July, the critical months in which Charles II was settling into power, Fitz was happily romancing. The gallant young cavalier rode up to Cambridge to visit his boyhood friend, John Haynes, at the university, and afterwards Haynes told him of "the sweet parcell of Ladys"

[9] M.H.S. *Coll.*, 5th ser., I, 47-51; VIII, 45-49, 68-69; Winthrop Mss., V, 16, 18, 19.

who were yearning to "obtaine that patterne of perfection Captain Winthrop."[10]

Fitz's commission as captain was renewed in the name of the King in June 1660, but it was obvious that he would soon lose his job, since the new government was disbanding almost the entire standing army. Fitz was no more settled in a career than he had been three years before. He asked his father whether he should return home, and suggested, alternatively, that he might continue a military life by fighting free lance in some foreign army. John Winthrop, Jr., was unenthusiastic about the latter proposal, "exept your call be very cleere," and he rather urged Fitz in September 1660 to stay in England until the following year when he himself would be coming over. Fitz did stay on. The London atmosphere was now supercharged with royalism. In October a soldier in his company named Arthur Allen was seized by a constable and thrown into Westminster gatehouse for saying during a drinking bout that Charles II "was not King till hee was Crownd." Poor Allen wrote Captain Fitz from prison, begging him to attend his trial at Old Bailey and lend him six shillings for expenses.[11] After Colonel Reade's regiment was mustered out in the same month, Fitz kept his London lodgings, ran up debts, and continued in the social whirl without finding any new employment. Perhaps he was something of a libertine; some love letters from a lady named Von Limburg were destroyed by the family in the nineteenth century as "too confidential." He had at least one chance for a new job. His cousin Sir George Downing, the King's ambassador to The Hague, paid two calls on Fitz in London with the intention of inviting him to Holland as his companion, but either Sir George did not find the young New Englander at home or was rebuffed by him. Fitz was

[10] M.H.S. *Coll.*, 5th ser., VIII, 266-67; 6th ser., III, 428-29; M.H.S. *Proc.*, 2nd ser., I, pp. 122-23; Firth and Davies, *Regimental History of Cromwell's Army*, II, 566-68.

[11] M.H.S. *Coll.*, 5th ser., VIII, 69-72; Winthrop Mss., X, 16. On November 19, 1660, Allen was given his terminal pay and discharged from the army, having apparently escaped further punishment.

still foot-loose in England when his father arrived in September on his quest for a Connecticut charter.[12]

John brought along Fitz's brother, nineteen-year-old Wait, on this trip. After entering Harvard College in 1658, Wait had dropped out two years later without a degree. "Mr Waite is this winter at home at Hartford," a family friend reported to Fitz in December 1660, adding, "he groweth to be a very serious gentleman." When Wait arrived in London, however, John Clarke of Rhode Island found him a bold and confident young fellow, an accomplice of Captain Scott, working to defeat any compromise settlement of the Connecticut-Rhode Island boundary dispute. When the colony agents were willing to come to terms, Clarke complained that "those two young ones bestirred themselves" and prolonged the quarrel.[13]

As for Fitz, he complained to his father (now that his military pay was gone) about his poverty and uncertain future. One of John's chief objects during this English visit was to establish Fitz securely by arranging a good marriage for him. He can hardly have been pleased when Fitz said he wanted to sow a few more wild oats, and "spend som few yeares more in travell." Though he would obey any commands, Fitz said, he was most unwilling to be tied down to a wife, a remedy worse than the disease of poverty. He admitted to spending a great deal of money, but justified it in terms of Aristotle's golden mean: "Sir, I am soe well acquainted with your scarsity of mony (as to myself), that I could be well satisfied without it, did not pressing necessityes many tymes require a supply . . . . I allwaies kept a just decorum betwene those extremes, and, as I did never prodigally spend, soe I did never basely spaire, which is most hatefull to my naturall inclination." Unless he could live in high style, Fitz also found it hateful to return to New England. "I had far rather," he said, "content myself with a meare competensye in a strange countrye than in a citty or place where I am knowne, and where every judge-

[12] M.H.S. *Coll.*, 4th ser., VII, 117; 5th ser., I, 52; VIII, 267-68; 6th ser., III, 429-30; Mayo, *The Winthrop Family in America*, p. 83.
[13] Winthrop Mss., XI, 160; XVII, 109.

ment will pass theire virdict upon me." When he asked permission to go to France with John Haynes, his father replied that a journey to France would be much more expensive than Fitz imagined. But he may have let Fitz visit the continent in 1662.[14]

Fitz escaped being married, but he did not escape returning to New England. In April 1663 both brothers sailed home with their father. So far life had been adventurous enough, especially for Fitz. Even if neither of the young colonials felt much personal involvement in the collapse of the Commonwealth and the restoration of the monarchy, both of them were lastingly impressed by the drama, glitter, and style of life in London. They had to adjust now to a much more humdrum world.

On RETURNING to New England, Fitz and Wait took up the task of earning a livelihood on the colonial frontier. For twenty years or more after 1663, they were chiefly occupied with the management of the family estate. Here they echoed their father's early career, for John Winthrop, Jr., had been more attracted to business than to public service when he first came to New England. Fitz and Wait went even further; they deliberately avoided participating in the local colony governments. Since they were born into the ruling class, the brothers might easily have worked their way onto the Connecticut board of magistrates. Twice, in 1671 and 1678, Fitz was a deputy from New London, but because he took no interest in the Hartford court sessions he was not re-elected. As for Wait, he divided his time between New London, Hartford, and Boston until 1670, after which he lived mostly in Boston. Wait did not take the covenant; he did not join a Boston church; he was a second-class citizen. Occasionally he was called on to act as Connecticut's representative in intercolonial dealings with the Massachusetts government. In military matters, naturally, Fitz was called on as a specialist. In 1672 he was designated com-

[14] M.H.S. *Coll.*, 5th ser., VIII, 268-71; Winthrop Mss., V, 31.

mander of the New London county militia, and when the Dutch
retook New Netherland in the following year, he was commissioned sergeant major of the English forces on eastern Long
Island and led the people of East Hampton, Southampton,
and Southold in their resistance to Dutch rule.[15] As long as
their father was alive, Fitz and Wait Winthrop performed useful but secondary services for the New England governments.
They showed no desire to play a more commanding role. They
chose to spend the prime years of their lives in relative obscu-
rity, immersed in family business affairs.

It was high time for someone to take the family business affairs in hand, especially after John Winthrop, Jr., lost several
thousand pounds in cargo to enemy privateers in the Dutch
war of 1665-1667. Though he held title to many thousand
acres of land in Connecticut and Massachusetts, most of it was
either undeveloped or leased at low rents to tenant farmers.
John had difficulty converting his wealth into cash, because the
land could only be sold at a ruinous loss. Year after year his
grain crop failed, and most of his revenue (apart from his salary as governor) came from stock farming on Fisher's Island.
Having borrowed £1,500 from the London merchant John
Harwood in 1663 by mortgaging Fisher's Island and his Tantiusques black lead mine, John was unable to raise enough cash
to redeem this property within the six-year time limit, even
though Harwood was willing to settle for £1,200. When John
defaulted, Harwood empowered his brother-in-law, Hezekiah
Usher, of Boston to receive Fisher's Island and 900 head of
livestock. Winthrop hung on to his estate by promising to meet
the debt. He would have sold Ten Hills farm to Usher, except
that Usher's price of £2,200 was too low. He mortgaged Ten
Hills to Samuel Shrimpton of Boston for £500. Harwood grew
increasingly anxious and sent an agent to New England in
1672. Since Winthrop was now being harassed by Shrimpton

and other creditors to whom he owed at least £1,000, Harwood's agent returned to England empty handed.[16]

In 1663 Fitz took over the management of his father's principal property in and around New London. No crops were raised on Fisher's Island, but large herds of sheep, cattle, and horses ranged there. It was a large operation: Wait spoke once of wintering "som hundreds" of cattle and slaughtering the rest. Generally, Fitz shipped them live by water to Boston where his brother would sell them or graze them at nearby Ten Hills until the Boston market was right. Wait also handled the rent and occasional sale of his father's property in the Bay area and dickered with his father's creditors. Meanwhile, he built up his own mercantile interest, buying shares in overseas trading ventures.[17]

The debt-ridden Winthrop estate had to supply inheritances for seven persons, Fitz and Wait and their five sisters. This was a source of great trouble. Three of the girls, Elizabeth, Lucy, and Margaret, married young. Lucy's husband was a strong-minded New London merchant named Edward Palmes, and when Governor Winthrop settled part of his New London property on the newlyweds, Palmes thought he had stinted while Fitz and Wait complained that he was overly generous. Was Fisher's Island also to be given away? The old Governor assured Fitz that the island was his and gently pleaded with him to remember his sister's welfare: "where God denies extent of wealth there is no helpe for it, and everything must be proportioned according to those dimentions that are within our compasse."[18] The brothers would not be so philosophical.

When their father died in 1676 Fitz and Wait were unhappy with the terms of his will, which divided the estate equally among all his children "after all debts are paide." As Wait explained to his brother, "only yourselfe and I to have as much more as any of the rest, which we neede not boast of." In the process of settling the estate Fitz and Wait forfeited some of

[16] Winthrop Mss., Deeds, p. 48; v, 105-106, 120; XIV, 13-18; M.H.S. *Coll.*, 5th ser., VIII, 144-45, 393-95; *Mass. Rec.*, IV, pt. 2, 466; Frank E. Bradish and William B. Trask, eds., *Suffolk Deeds*, III (Boston, 1892), 137.

[17] Winthrop Mss., XIX, 125; M.H.S. *Coll.*, 5th ser., VIII, 254, 466.

[18] Winthrop Mss., V, 132, 134, 202.

their father's property, but they managed to retain a surprisingly large portion of it. The creditors were naturally more insistent than ever, especially Harwood in London, whose son came to Boston in 1677. "Here is little Mr Harwood com with greate demands," Wait told his brother, "but I hope I shall make a good issue with his merchantship." The brothers sold Ten Hills farm for £3,300, and two warehouses and a wharf in Boston for £345. This gave them enough cash to redeem the £1,500 Harwood mortgage with a bargain settlement of £1,150, to redeem Shrimpton's £500 mortgage and other old debts, and to make cash settlements with their sisters. The two unmarried girls (Martha and Anne) got £1,000 apiece, while Elizabeth and Margaret got smaller amounts to supplement their marriage portions. Lucy and Edward Palmes were considered to have received more than their fair share already, and so got nothing.[19]

Edward Palmes was not the man to accept this verdict. When Lucy died a few months after her father, the Winthrop brothers and "Sir Hude" (as they nicknamed Palmes) began an outrageous quarrel over her inheritance which continued intermittently for forty years. In 1679, for instance, Fitz discovered that Palmes' servant was fencing in a tract of Winthrop land in New London and sharply told his brother-in-law to take his claims to the courts.[20] Fitz kept truce with Palmes in the 1680's, but this was only temporary. In their declining years, the two men feasted on litigation against each other.

In 1677, Wait married Mary Browne, the daughter of a prominent Salem merchant. The newlyweds settled in Boston. Their first son died in 1680, but a second (John) was born the next year. Meanwhile Wait's sister Martha was married to Richard Wharton, one of the biggest entrepreneurs in New England, with whom Wait had long had commercial dealings.[21] Obviously Wait was trying to reconstitute the tattered family fortune by allying with the merchant circle. Men such as

[19] *Ibid.*, Deeds, 54, 66; M.H.S. *Coll.*, 5th ser., VIII, 404-408; 6th ser., III, 453-56; *Suffolk Deeds*, III, 141; X, 102-104, 163, 167, 192.

[20] Winthrop Mss., VI, 27, 29, 32.

[21] *Ibid.*, X, 33; XIX, 125; M.H.S. *Coll.*, 5th ser., VIII, 419.

Browne and Wharton, large-scale overseas traders and internal land speculators, had discovered in the Restoration era a far more viable road to prosperity than John Winthrop, Jr.'s primitive experiments at colonial self-sufficiency. Their commercial system hinged on close ties with London factors and London patronage, and accordingly they had little sympathy with Massachusetts' policy toward the home government. The Winthrop marriage alliance into this increasingly ambitious merchant group strongly bound Wait's future conduct.

As for Fitz, it is amusing to find that the man who castigated his sister's marriage to a clergyman should himself perpetrate a serious blot on the family escutcheon. Sometime in the 1670's Elizabeth Tongue, an obscure New London girl, bore him a daughter named Mary. Fitz and Elizabeth lived together in New London, evidently in common-law marriage. Elizabeth signed a release of dower, specifying that she would make no claim on Fitz's estate. In his will, Fitz carefully refers to her as "my daughter's mother, Mrs. Elizabeth Winthrop." Years later, an enemy accused Fitz of having "lived in open adultries in despight of [Connecticut] lawes."[22] There is no surviving evidence of adultery, but certainly Fitz's domestic arrangements did shock his neighbors, relatives, and friends, and contributed to his long estrangement from colony affairs. Years passed before even Fitz's closest correspondents deigned to ask after "Mrs. Elizabeth" or "Mrs. Betty" in their letters. Wait never did accept the lady as his sister-in-law. When necessary, he referred to her stiffly as "Madam Winthrop," in what we may take to be a double-entendre.[23]

The dominant topics in Fitz's and Wait's correspondence in the 1660's and 1670's were the price of horseflesh and the buying and selling of real estate. Still, the brothers found the colonial routine of farming and marketing monotonous, and the formalism and complacent sobriety of middle-aged New England Puritanism distinctly irritating. To Fitz, in particular,

[22] E. B. O'Callaghan, ed., *Documentary History of the State of New York* (3 vols.; Albany, 1849-1850), II, 301-302. The enemy was Jacob Leisler. See p. 293.
[23] Winthrop Mss., VI, 15; X, 23, 39, 41, 45; XIX, 36; Lawrence H. Leder, *Robert Livingston, 1654-1728, and the Politics of Colonial New York* (Chapel Hill, 1961), p. 159.

any echo of his past Army and London life was welcome. He was delighted with the arrival of Colonel Nicolls' squadron in 1664, attended Nicolls during the capture of New Netherland, and did his best to ingratiate himself with the colonel. Nicolls invited him to sail from New York to Boston in April 1665. With "the good Company of your son," Nicolls wrote Governor Winthrop from the Bay, "I have had no unpleasant voyage." Fitz went with Nicolls to Fort Albany for a conference with the Indians, and was subsequently entrusted with several errands by the ducal governor. He became a familiar guest at New York. His letters to Nicolls were overwhelming in their sophomoric self-depreciation and fawning adulation. "I hope," Fitz wrote characteristically, "your honor will believe that I esteme the losse of my Life the least expression of my affection (please to pardon that too familiar word) which since I cannot live to serve you as I should, I would gladly dye to avoyde the torment of my farther Ingratitude." Fitz did not talk that way to his fellow colonials. Again he writes: "I must ever owne them blest that had the honor to attend you whilst I sneake aweaye my dayes in a melancholy retirement with a pining apprehention of my want of quallity to recommend me to that honor of that duty."[24]

Fitz was similarly drawn to Colonel Lovelace, Nicolls' successor, who was likewise a more stylish figure than his homespun neighbors. In July 1673, on the eve of the Dutch reconquest of New York, Fitz was invited to come speedily "once more to New York, where you may rest confident to receive as hearty a welcome as ever, both from the Governor and others."[25] Instead, it was the Dutch who seized the invitation, and Fitz had to help the eastern Long Islanders defend themselves. When the Dutch vacated the colony the following year, however, Governor Winthrop sent Fitz with Samuel Willys to welcome the new ducal governor, Edmund Andros. Fitz was in an irritable mood. His service against the Dutch had been tedious, and he was casting about for an excuse to travel abroad. He protested against the indignity of waiting upon the new

---

[24] *Ibid.*, V, 52; VI, 8-9; XII, 103; XV, 165; M.H.S. *Coll.*, 5th ser., VIII, 272.
[25] *Ibid.*, 5th ser., IX, 87; 6th ser., III, 433-34.

governor; it was a "sleeveless errand." Yet the two majors got along very well when they met. Andros was about Fitz's age; he had a military background; he was a courtier; he knew how to be charming. Once he had firmly quashed the east Long Islanders' notion of seceding from New York, he complimented his visitor on leading their defense against the Dutch.[26] Fitz returned to New London satisfied that the new ducal governor was as attractive as his predecessors.

IN THE last week of June 1675, Fitz lay sick in bed at his New London farm, slowly recovering from a dangerous fever and his brother's medicines. It was a poor time to be ill. Messengers came pounding down the Pequot path spreading the alarm that Philip, chief of the Wampanoags, was on the warpath in Plymouth Colony. They were announcing the start of the most desperate and bloody episode in seventeenth-century New England, King Philip's War.

King Philip started on the warpath because his tribe was being squeezed. Land hungry entrepreneurs (such as the Winthrop's Narragansett Company) carving out tracts along Narragansett Bay had hemmed in the central Indian hunting grounds of southeastern New England. Once Philip's tribe had opened the attack, therefore, the prime question was how to keep the war localized. New London, eyeing her Pequot, Mohegan, and Narragansett neighbors with suspicion, called to Hartford for help. Since Fitz was ill, the Connecticut council appointed Wait on July 1 to take his place as commander of the county militia. Immediately Wait plunged into his new responsibilities. Having toured the Pequots, Mohegans, and Niantics, he marched east with sixty militiamen and a similar number of Pequot and Mohegan scouts, to confront the Narragansetts, the toughest tribe in southern New England, and make them pledge neutrality. Fitz from his sickbed sent Wait his well worn carbine, much battered, whose stock was split "but is glued, & if kept from the rayne may hold: as you ride," Fitz recommended, "it will be best to rest it upon your horse

[26] Winthrop Mss., v, 202; x, 69; M.H.S. *Coll.*, 3rd ser., x, 114-17; 5th ser., VIII, 277-78.

neck. The bullets goe in very hard but may be forst downe."
Since the bullets were lost in transit, the carbine was useless.
But Wait did not need it. He met Captain Hutchinson's troop
from Massachusets, and together they concluded a treaty with
the Narragansett sachems on July 15. The Narragansetts
promised not to aid Philip, and to deliver any of his wounded
warriors to the English.[27] Had the Narragansetts honored this
treaty, King Philip's War would soon have ended. Unhappily,
Wait's efforts were wasted, the Narragansetts joined Philip,
and the war spread. By September, towns all along the Massachusetts frontier were raided and sacked, and savages were
murdering up and down the Connecticut Valley.

Meanwhile, Governor Andros of New York had sailed into
Saybrook harbor with two sloops full of soldiers, demanding
that Connecticut cede him the western half of her territory.
Amid the general alarm and the abuse showered on Andros, at
least one Connecticut man remained unperturbed—Fitz Winthrop. "I believe," he wrote Wait on July 8, "those soldiers
which are with him are more for handsomnes and guard to his
person then any other purpose." Andros solicitously sent one
of his sloops from Saybrook to New London to inquire, as he
said, "of Major Winthrops health and indian intelligence that
way."[28] Fitz was identified as the New York governor's friend
at a time when Andros was doing everything possible to show
his hostility toward the New England colonies. While the New
Englanders pooled their resources and grimly mounted a coun-
teroffensive against Philip, Andros kept New York on the side
lines. The only shots he fired during King Philip's War were
verbal ones against the Connecticut government.[29]

In a series of bloody battles through the winter and spring
of 1675-1676, the New England militia methodically destroyed
the Indians' bases, killed their women and children, and reduced the warriors to starvation and eventual surrender in the
summer of 1676. It was a dirty and dangerous job requiring

[27] *Conn. Rec.*, II, 331-32, 337-38; M.H.S. *Coll.*, 5th ser., VIII, 170-74, 279-80,
401-404; Winthrop Mss. V, 149; D. E. Leach, *Flintlock and Tomahawk: New
England in King Philip's War* (New York, 1958), pp. 56-62.
[28] M.H.S. *Coll.*, 5th ser., VIII, 279; Winthrop Mss., VI, 20; X, 72.
[29] *Conn. Rec.*, II, 397-98, 404.

the participation of every able-bodied man, and the best available military leadership. But Fitz Winthrop, one of the top four officers in the Connecticut militia and among the few experienced soldiers in New England, took no active part in any of the fighting. Connecticut supplied one-third of the troops for the confederated English army, Major Treat and Major Talcott conducted the chief campaigns, Major Palmes (the Winthrops' brother-in-law) managed the commissariat, and the New London militia went out on a series of bloody forays in which they claimed to have killed 239 Narragansetts. It is true that Fitz was still in poor health, but he was well enough to take eighty Pequots and Mohegans up to Hartford on one occasion, and to perform various other rearguard services, such as keeping guard over Indian prisoners and distributing cloth coats as payment to the loyal Indians who brought the captives in.[30] Wait Winthrop took more active part. In September 1675 he attended his father to Boston, where the New England Confederation held an emergency session to declare war against Philip. He sat as Connecticut's second commissioner, helping to supervise the winter campaigns. Father and son were still in Boston, with the war far from over, when Governor Winthrop fell mortally ill and died on April 5, 1676.[31]

Friends of the old Governor hated to see the Winthrop sons slipping out of the family tradition of public service. "Sir," the Hartford magistrate John Allyn wrote to Wait in June 1676, "your father tould me it was his desire that his sons might serve God & his people in this country. . . . the good people of this towne doe earnestly desire you would com & take up your aboad amongst us. . . . Pray, Sir, please to come up & make a tryall amongs us." In 1680 there was talk of electing Wait a Connecticut magistrate ("being a very sober discreet gentleman, much advantaged by his parentage, as well as his abillitys and fullnesse of estate"), in order to induce him to

---

[30] *Ibid.*, 345, 379, 408, 435, 479; Winthrop Mss., x, 22-26; M.H.S. *Coll.*, 6th ser., III, 448-51; Hubbard, *A Narrative of the Troubles with the Indians in New-England*, postscript, p. 9.

[31] *Conn. Rec.*, II, 271-72; M.H.S. *Coll.*, 4th ser., VII, 581; *Records of Plymouth Colony* [Acts of the Commissioners of the United Colonies of New England] (2 vols.; David Pulsifer, ed., Boston, 1859), II, 456-61.

move to Connecticut. But Wait stayed in Boston. Fitz, once his father was dead, began quarreling more openly with the Connecticut government. There was some unpleasantness over Fitz's receipt of Indian prisoners captured during the war. The Connecticut council permitted him to keep several captives for his own use on Fisher's Island, and Fitz bought ten others from the colony, which he shipped to Barbados to be sold as slaves. When rumors circulated that he was appropriating further captives, Fitz's highly inflammable pride was ignited. There have been too many insinuations, he wrote John Allyn in March 1677, that "I medled with Matters out of my Capassity. . . ; but I know I have been faythfull in all occasions wherein I have been engaged for the interest of the country. . . ."[32]

Noticeably more pleasant were Fitz's dealings with Andros in the late 1670's. The New York Governor kindly offered to visit Fitz while he was mourning for his father, and though Fitz tactfully declined this offer, he added gratefully that "noething could have been more reviving to my dead heart than the honr of yor letter & kinde expressions therein." Fitz was one of the few colonials whose company Andros cordially liked, and he was several times the Governor's guest at New York.[33] In 1680 Fitz deliberately allied himself with Sir Edmund (recently knighted) against his own Connecticut government in a territorial dispute over Fisher's Island.

The Winthrops had title to Fisher's Island from Connecticut, but the royal commissioners in 1664 had awarded it to the Duke of York. Four years later, Governor Nicolls offered John Winthrop, Jr., a New York patent by the terms of which he would enjoy the island as a free gift. Fisher's Island was to enjoy the privileges and immunities of any New York town and was exempted from all military obligations and taxes except for a nominal acknowledgment of one lamb per annum upon demand. Winthrop was uncertain what to do, since his island was obviously in Connecticut rather than New York waters, but the Connecticut council was not greatly concerned

[32] M.H.S. *Coll.*, 5th ser., VIII, 282; 6th ser., V, xiv, 5; Winthrop Mss., VI, 24; X, 32.

[33] M.H.S. *Coll.*, 5th ser., VIII, 283; 6th ser., III, 452; M.H.S. *Proc.*, 2nd ser., IV, 287-88; *N.Y.Col.Doc.*, III, 257, 260.

over the matter, and so he accepted Nicolls' patent. The Connecticut government had never actually recognized New York's authority over the island, and when a ship, the *Providence*, was wrecked along its shore in the winter of 1680, Governor Leete issued a warrant for the salvage of the wreck. Fitz refused to accept the warrant. He wrote a diplomatic letter to Leete (March 10, 1680), saying how happy he would be "to have my vine kindly secured under yor authorety," but pointing out that New York had a claim on the island. He left immediately for Manhattan to consult Andros on the matter. If Andros "gives not up his clame easely," Fitz told Wait, "I may have better opportunety to make conditions with this [Connecticut] government."[34]

Fitz should have known what a hornet's nest he was stirring up. He found Sir Edmund determined, of course, to assert his authority over the island. Andros wrote Governor Leete, sharply ordering him to withdraw his warrant. He dispatched a sloop to Fisher's Island in April to salvage the wreck and to receive a lamb from Fitz as acknowledgment of his tenure. Leete retorted to Andros that the Nicolls patent was merely "a paper of Civility," and the Connecticut General Court rose to the occasion on May 20 with a proclamation couched in language reminiscent of their manifesto against Andros' proceedings at Saybrook. All persons on Fisher's Island were forbidden to yield "obedience to any authority whatsoever save the authority of his Majestie vested in the colony of Connecticut."[35] Fitz professed his neutrality, but when Sir Edmund's sloop arrived, a constable for the island was sworn in under oath to the Duke of York. Governor Leete reproachfully asked Fitz to exhibit something "of yor fathers virtues & cordiality of love to this colony." Unfortunately for Leete, Fitz preferred New York. He told Manhattan friends that he was looking for an escape from the hands of the Philistines and jested with them over the Connecticut court's "wonderful pro-

[34] Winthrop Mss., XV, 142; M.H.S. *Coll.*, 5th ser., VIII, 285-86, 294-95, 420.
[35] *Ibid.*, 5th ser., VIII, 286; 6th ser., III, 460-61; Winthrop Mss., XIV, 131; XV, 126; *Conn. Rec.*, III, 64, 283.

test" against Andros.[36] He was anxious enough to know what further steps the Connecticut government might take, but nothing further happened. Since Andros' claim in 1680 was much better justified than in 1675, and since Fitz was cooperating with him, Connecticut had to swallow her anger and silently concede Fisher's Island.

When Fitz learned that his patron, Sir Edmund, was being recalled to England in 1680, he told Andros how he longed for his speedy return, "since noething can be thought successfull to any that is not under yor honrs present influence, and blest with your generous & successfull hand. . . ." Fitz very well knew the man he was flattering. He knew that Andros claimed to be governor not merely of Fisher's Island, but of mainland Connecticut. Andros himself had written Fitz in June 1680: "I shall nott be wanting on occasion efectually to serve you, perticularly for sufficiently fitt authority (when you give me the opportunity) nott only for yor island, but other parts of the government; which I thinck none cann blame you for, . . . & pray I may heare from you of itt."[37] When Sir Edmund was next given the opportunity to serve Fitz with sufficiently fit authority, he was sitting in Boston as royal governor of the Dominion of New England.

[36] M.H.S. *Coll.*, 5th ser., VIII, 287-92; 6th ser., III, 461-65; Winthrop Mss., VI, 37-38; X, 35; XIV, 131.
[37] M.H.S. *Coll.*, 5th ser., VIII, 293; 6th ser., III, 464.

10. *Edward Randolph and the "Moderates"*

ONE June morning in 1676, barely two months after John Winthrop, Jr., had been buried in the family plot at his father's side, a London ship inaptly named the *Welcome* made her way into Boston harbor. On deck a special envoy of Charles II caught sight of Castle Island, portal of Massachusetts Bay Colony, looming up-channel with thirty-eight cannon poking out from the bastioned stone fort. Somewhat to his surprise, a royal ensign fluttered out over the fort, and the ship's captain obediently struck his flag. As they passed, the traveler observed that there were only two men along the ramparts of the fort. Docking at last among the jutting wharves and warehouses of the wooden town, he noted the cluster of ships in Boston harbor. Foreign ships were trading freely, and New England ships were bringing in cargoes of wine, oil, and silk from Spain and France in exchange for local fish and timber, all in violation of the English navigation laws. The envoy had been sent to investigate Massachusetts' misdeeds. His name was Edward Randolph.[1]

Randolph's arrival signalized the home government's new policy of thoroughgoing imperial centralization. The next ten years saw an unparalleled assertion of royal power in English America and a corresponding invasion of colonial liberties. The highlight of Charles II's new imperial policy was Randolph's attack on the self-governing chartered corporations of New England. The years 1676-1686 put the first Winthrop's policy of splendid isolation to the acid test. Randolph did not work alone; he recruited allies among the colonials, so-called "moderates" who were willing to support his campaign against the New England charters. Fitz and Wait Winthrop were two of these. The great founder's grandsons were caught in open apostasy.

---

[1] *Randolph*, II, 195, 203, 237, 249-50.

Edward Randolph and the "Moderates"

꿔 AFTER 1675, Charles II became increasingly intent on crushing all opposition to the authority of the crown at home and in the colonies. With the close of the Third Dutch War in 1674, the King stopped trying to be all things to all men, and aligned himself with the Earl of Danby and his Anglican, divine right supporters. One aspect of Charles' and Danby's centralization of power was the establishment in 1675 of a new Privy Council committee, the Lords of Trade and Plantations, with broader authority and more effective organization than any previous colonial council. The Lords of Trade aimed to improve upon their predecessors' ineffective regulation of the plantations. Their greatest obstacle was the fact that two-thirds of the plantations were in the hands of private companies or proprietors. Hence the Lords' ultimate objective was the destruction of all colonial charters.[2]

As their title suggests, the Lords of Trade were much more interested in regulating colonial commerce than in other areas of colonial life. Overseas trade was the most vigorously expanding aspect of the English economy. The King's strength depended on his ability to tap this wealth. New England's violation of the navigation acts and encroachment on the home merchants' West India trade was reckoned by Randolph to cost the King "in his Customs above £100,000 yearely and this Kingdome much more." In addition, King Philip's War in New England and Bacon's Rebellion in Virginia, both raging in 1676, seemed proof of gross mismanagement by the colony governments. The Earl of Anglesey, a member of the Lords of Trade, rebuked Governor Leverett of Massachusetts: "you are divided among yourselves. . . . you are poor and yet proud."[3] The Virginia rebellion caused greater alarm, for Charles II drew £100,000 per annum in revenue from this one colony, equal to his secret subsidy from Louis XIV. The "ill news from Virginia and New England," according to an English letter of 1676, "doth not only alarm us but extremely abate the customs so that notwithstanding all the shifts Treasurer

[2] Michael G. Hall, *Edward Randolph and the American Colonies, 1676-1703* (Chapel Hill, 1960), pp. 18-20; Philip S. Haffenden, "The Crown and the Colonial Charters, 1675-1688: Part I," *W.M.Q.*, 3rd ser., XV, 297-311.

[3] *Randolph*, II, 266; Hutchinson, *History of Massachusetts-Bay*, I, 262.

can make this Parliament or another must sitt. . . ." Royal commissioners were sent with eleven ships and 1,130 soldiers to Virginia. New England did not warrant such generous attention, but in March 1676 the Lords concluded "that this is the Conjuncture to do something Effectual for the better Regulation of that Government, or else all hopes of it may be hereafter lost."[4]

A peremptory royal letter was drafted, ordering the Massachusetts government to send agents to England to answer charges against the colony. The Lords of Trade appointed a special representative to carry over the letter and to bring back information about such topics as: "What Laws and Ordinances are now in force there, derogatory or contradictory to those of England. . . . what notice is taken of the Act of Navigation. . . . How they generally stand affected to the Government of England?"[5] Edward Randolph, chosen as the King's messenger to Massachusetts, was the first of the new style colonial officials to come to New England. He was not a colonist coming back to avenge mistreatment at the hands of fellow New Englanders like Samuel Maverick, nor a disreputable adventurer like Sir Robert Carr. He was a professional civil servant, presenting himself with pride as entirely the King's man, and devoting his career consistently to the increase of crown revenue and the extension of royal authority. To Randolph, the colonies existed only for the profit of the mother country. If the colonists held opinions different from those in Whitehall, such opinions were *ipso facto* wrong. Randolph was a fanatic, a fitting antagonist for the fanatics he would find presiding over the Massachusetts government.

Randolph's first day in Boston, June 10, 1676, set the tone for his entire stay in New England. He presented himself to Governor John Leverett, an unreconstructed Puritan who regarded the King as a sort of Santa Claus: one received presents from him, but one was not bound by a sense of duty. Nothing in Leverett's experience of Charles II had taught him to love

---

[4] Wilcomb E. Washburn, *The Governor and the Rebel* (Chapel Hill, 1957), pp. 93, 214; *Randolph*, II, 196.

[5] *Ibid.*, 197-99.

the King, to feel the need of his help or the fear of his anger. "At the beginning of the reading of your Majesties letter," Randolph reported to the King, "the whole councill being covered, I put off my hat; whereupon three of the magistrates tooke off their hats and sate uncovered; but the governor with the rest continued to keep their hats on. Your Majesties letter . . . being read in my hearing, the governor told the councill that the matters therein contained were very inconsiderable things and easily answered." When Randolph informed the council that "they were to give me a full answer to his Majesties letter with all convenient speed, they asked me by what Order I made that demand. . . . I replied that what I had there demanded I would answer at Whitehall." A few days later, on Randolph's complaint that Massachusetts seemed to be violating the navigation laws, Leverett "freely declared to me that the Laws made by Our King & Parliament obligeth them in nothing but what consists with the Interest of New England . . . ." The Bay governor was so utterly oblivious to criticism that he supposed a troubler of Israel, like Randolph, must recognize the probity of Massachusetts' conduct. At Randolph's departure, after a six weeks' visit, Leverett "intreated me to give a favourable report of the country and the magistrates thereof, adding, that those that blessed them God would blesse, and those that cursed them God would curse."[6] If so, Edward Randolph was certainly a damned man.

One week after landing in Boston, Randolph had written to the Secretary of State, urging that Massachusetts be reduced to obedience by force. Since the colonists were distracted by the Indian war, he argued, "3 ffrigats of 40 Guns with 3 Ketches well manned Lying a League or two below Boston with his Majesties express Orders to seize all Shipping & perform other Acts of hostility aganst these Revolters would . . . do more in One Weeks time then all the Orders of King & Councill to them in Seven years."[7] The argument was undoubtedly correct, but his method was much too drastic for the Lords of Trade. In order to make Massachusetts look especially black, Randolph reported that the other New England governments were

[6] *Ibid.,* 203, 205, 217, 224.   [7] *Ibid.,* 208.

eager to show their obedience to England and panting for a royal governor general.[8] Yet the nub of his charge was indisputably true. Politically, religiously, and, most important of all, economically, Massachusetts flouted Charles II's wishes and instructions and pursued her own independent course. The two agents sent by the Massachusetts General Court to counter Randolph in London were unable to dodge or deny this fact.

From late 1676 until mid-1679, the Massachusetts agents tried strenuously to shake Randolph's credit with the Lords of Trade and to forestall further action against their colony. They could not arrest the Lords' evolving attack upon all corporate and proprietary charters. The Lords were meeting frequently and planning actively, and Randolph had a better entree than his enemies to the colonial offices in Scotland Yard. By the spring of 1678, the Lords had about decided that Massachusetts was incorrigible. They requested an expert opinion on the validity of the Massachusetts charter. The Attorney General and Solicitor General advised that they had sufficient grounds to sue for repeal of the charter by the *quo warranto* procedure attempted in 1635, if they could prove that the Bay government was guilty of the misdemeanors charged against her.[9] There the matter rested for another four years.

Meanwhile, the Lords of Trade did insist on the immediate commercial regulation of New England. "Wee have had more light and information from Mr. Randolph," the Lords said, "then from any person else . . . in this matter." They recommended in 1678 that he be the man to enforce the navigation acts as Collector of His Majesty's Customs at Boston, sweeping aside the Massachusetts agents' bitter protest. The policy of the Lords of Trade toward Massachusetts was temporarily neglected when Titus Oates produced his Popish Plot in September 1678. But Randolph soon headed back to Boston in October 1679 as the first salaried civil servant to be stationed by the King in New England. A situation beyond compromise

[8] *Ibid.*, 222-23, 258; Hall, *Edward Randolph*, pp. 26-29.

[9] *Randolph*, II, 297-98; III, 3-5. For details on the organization and effectiveness of the Lords of Trade in the late 1670's, see Hall, *Edward Randolph*, ch. 2, and Ralph P. Bieber, *The Lords of Trade and Plantations, 1675-1696* (Allentown, Pa., 1919).

was shaping up. The home government had entirely rejected New England's existing structure and, though declining Randolph's precipitate methods, had plainly endorsed his goal of a royal government responsible to the King rather than to the colonists. Either the colonists or the King would have to make a total surrender.

As Edward Randolph saw the situation there was no real problem, because New England would welcome royal government. He argued that only a rather small Puritan "faction" defied the Lords of Trade. New England was divided into two parties, this "faction" and the "honest and good" remainder, who were the actual majority, very loyal to the King, groaning under the Puritan yoke, and "in dayle hopes and expectations of a change, by his Majesties reassuming the authority and settling a general government over the whole country. . . ." The spokesmen for this suppressed majority Randolph discovered among the discontented non-Puritan merchants and land speculators. Such men, chiefly distinguished for their property and English connections and not for parochial loyalty to the local church-state system, seemed to him the rightful leaders of colonial society. Several times, when drawing up plans for New England's surrender to the King, Randolph sent home lists of persons suitable for offices in the new royal regime. He named both Fitz and Wait Winthrop to this select circle.[10]

These colonial friends of Randolph have been the subject of scholarly discussion which has produced more heat than light. Thomas Hutchinson was apparently the first historian to identify them as the "moderate" party, and all subsequent writers agree that they had a decisive influence on the course of events in the 1680's. The moderates allied with Randolph in order to get into power in 1686, but reversed themselves in 1689, joining the rebellion against the royal Dominion of New England. Critical estimate of the moderates is sharply divided. To John Palfrey, the nineteenth-century Puritan apologist, these men were corrupted by wealth, "timid, timeserving, and sordid." Viola Barnes and James Truslow Adams, reacting against such

[10] *Randolph*, II, 253; III, 40; VI, 93.

Puritan hagiography in the 1920's, preferred to extoll the moderates' loyalty to England and their liberal stand against Puritan intolerance. Perry Miller has identified them as "men disgusted with the arrogance and presumption of democracy. They were . . . authoritarians, ready to give up the charter because, in their experience, it supported elected officers and rampaging parsons who could not keep the populace in order." The most recent interpretation, by Bernard Bailyn and Michael Hall, stresses the economic platform of the New England merchants, their common aim to make the best of their position on the edge of a mercantilist empire by dominating the local government and cultivating English officials.[11] The only common ground among all these commentators is their starting point: Randolph's division of New England society into two distinct parties.

Yet this notion of anything so clear-cut as a party rivalry in the 1680's is misleading. Certainly a sizable number of colonists cooperated, or appeared to cooperate, with Randolph. The role of these men in establishing and destroying the Dominion of New England was indeed decisive. But they were too multifarious to form a party. Massachusetts had only one party with clear-cut beliefs and organization, and that was the venerable ruling alliance of magistrates and ministers. Many merchants (though by no means all), some magistrates, and some church members were disenchanted, in varying degrees and for various reasons, with this ruling alliance. Some wanted closer ties with England, some wanted religious toleration, some wanted aristocratic government, some (like Joseph Dudley, Randolph's leading colonial adherent) simply wanted political power. Almost any explanation of the "moderates" will contain an element of truth, for they were even more widely assorted than the Remonstrants of forty years before. It is noteworthy that while Randolph referred endlessly in his letters and papers to "the faction" as shorthand for the whole system which he

[11] Hutchinson, *History of Massachusetts-Bay*, I, 279; Palfrey, *History of New England*, III, 359; Barnes, *The Dominion of New England*, pp. 8-10; Adams, *The Founding of New England*, pp. 394, 408; Miller, *The New England Mind: from Colony to Province*, p. 141; Bailyn, *The New England Merchants in the Seventeenth Century*, pp. 189-92; Hall, *Edward Randolph*, pp. 58-60.

was trying to destroy, he had no blanket symbol for the alleged majority who groaned for a change in government. Only rarely did he discuss the men he approved of, and always he identified them as individuals. Randolph hoped to create a moderate party, but he did not find one ready at hand. The essence of the situation was the fluidity among the moderates.

The Winthrop brothers' connection with Randolph between 1676 and 1686 illustrates very well the nature of the moderates' role in New England's mounting crisis.

Before Randolph arrived, Fitz Winthrop in particular had already demonstrated considerable hostility toward the established New England system and an awe of English officialdom. He and his brother were snobs, protesting against the egalitarian and provincial tendencies in their society. Fitz's grandfather had disdained democracy but had willingly tied himself to public service in New England because he believed that his city on a hill was worthy of his fullest efforts. John Winthrop, Jr., with his cosmopolitan tastes, had been naturally more reluctant to confine himself to New England and to public service. Fitz and Wait rebelled even more sharply against the accepted New England scale of values and exhibited a stronger pride in wealth and status. The brothers would not solicit for the public office which was their due, nor would they forgive New England for passing them by. The longer the Winthrop family lived in America, the stronger its feeling grew—in inverse proportion to the talents of each succeeding generation—that New England was too small a stage and that the family pedigree was insufficiently honored by their fellow colonists. Edward Randolph seemed to have a better sense of the Winthrop family's value.

Actually, in the Winthrop brothers' correspondence during the late 1670's there is scarcely a hint that Fitz and Wait knew Randolph existed, let alone that they knew of the decision of Charles II's government to terminate New England's commercial and political independence. "Deare Brother," Wait scribbled characteristically one June day in 1679, while the carrier waited for his letter, "I received from England two wiggs and a wast belt of the better sort, but I know not whether you will like it. . . . if it be, as it seemes, the generall mode, it may be, when you se it, you will not so much dislike it."[12] Indian corn is selling for twelve-pence a bushel, black peas sell for nothing, the barrel of pickled beef has arrived safely from Fisher's Island, the tallow shortage in Boston continues, and the candles from the island are "so intimately mixt with straw and joined together, that they weare good for little." This was the sort of thing about which Fitz and Wait wrote to each other.

The best index to Fitz's and Wait's relationship with Randolph is to trace the three men's involvement in the continuing struggle for control of the Narragansett Country between 1678 and 1683. King Philip's War, with the bloody conquest of the Narragansett Indians, opened the long disputed grazing land to real settlement for the first time. One of the Narragansett Company proprietors warned in 1679 that "Rhod island setells dayly in Naragansett; if no stop be made, it will be hard to remove them." The Narragansett Company expanded its membership to include more than twenty partners, most of them Boston merchants. Fitz and Wait held three shares, and their brother-in-law Richard Wharton (a newcomer to the enterprise) quickly established his leadership. The proprietors decided to promote a new plantation on their land and to ignore Rhode Island's suzerainty on the grounds that she had abandoned defense of the area in King Philip's War.[13]

On behalf of his fellow proprietors, Wait Winthrop petitioned Connecticut in 1678 to put the company plantation under Hartford jurisdiction. But he soon found that Connecticut could neither protect the proprietors from Rhode Island, nor persuade the Lords of Trade to reverse the royal commissioners' 1665 decision.[14] Matters were complicated when Connecticut's agent to England, William Harris, was captured by Barbary pirates. In February 1680 poor Harris was sold

[12] M.H.S. *Coll.*, 5th ser., VIII, 417.

[13] *Conn. Rec.*, III, 269; *Rhode Island Colonial Gleanings*, I, 30-31; Winthrop Mss., V, 35; M.H.S. *Coll.*, 5th ser., IX, 98, 111; *Cal.S.P.Col., 1677-1680*, pp. 271, 403.

[14] *Conn. Rec.*, III, 15-16, 32, 257-58, 267-69; *R.I. Rec.*, III, 18-19, 40-63; *Cal.S.P.Col., 1677-1680*, pp. 270-71, 282-83, 398, 422.

into slavery on the Algiers market. His Algerine owner demanded a ransom of £300 within one year. "If you faile mee of the said sum and said time," Harris wrote the Connecticut magistrates, "it is most like to be the loss of my life, he is soe Cruell and Covetous." During his captivity Harris lived on bread and water (partly out of Yankee thrift and partly to avoid catching the plague) and indefatigably called for additional documents which he needed to prosecute the Narragansett case. The Connecticut government and Narragansett proprietors finally secured Harris' release in June 1681 by borrowing the necessary redemption money in London. All in vain, for Harris died three days after reaching England.[15]

The Narragansett proprietors decided to try the new style in dealing with Whitehall and established connections with crown servants who had entree to the Colonial Office. Edward Randolph was one of the men they approached for help. There is an unaddressed letter of his, dated July 18, 1678, which was evidently written to Richard Smith, who was in London at the time, petitioning for the proprietors. Randolph's message was as follows: "I feare . . . that I shall not gett a positive direction from the King as you intended, but feare not but I will gett you into some place of profitt & advantage, & am therefore petitioning the King, for the better observation of the laws of trade, to have all the forts & castles by his commission put into the hands of such as I may answere for. . . . What money I lay out in your business shall account at our next meeting."[16]

Randolph did try to get Smith a place of profit and advantage. When he proposed to the Lords of Trade in 1679 that they appoint sixteen officers to command the New England militia until the arrival of a governor general, his candidates

[15] *Conn. Rec.*, III, 37-38, 51, 72, 169, 272-80, 303-307; *Rhode Island Colonial Gleanings*, I, 31; R.I.H.S. *Coll.*, X, 322-26, 333-34, 350-51; *Cal.S.P.Col.*, *1677-1680*, p. 454; M.H.S. *Coll.*, 6th ser., V, 8. The cost of Harris' redemption, including bills of exchange and interest, was £459, which was eventually repaid to Connecticut out of his estate.

[16] *Ibid.*, 6th ser., III, 457. Several historians have quoted this letter as from Randolph to William Stoughton, Massachusetts' agent in London. But internal evidence makes it far more probable that Smith was the addressee. See Hall, *Edward Randolph*, p. 47.

included Richard Smith, Fitz Winthrop, and two other Narragansett proprietors. In 1680 Randolph specifically endorsed the proprietors' plans for an independent Narragansett charter, telling the Lords "that it would be farr more conducing to the Planting that [Narragansett] Country if it were a distinct government by itself, It belonging to many gentlemen of good Estates & quality."[17]

The proprietors clinched the interest of the Lords of Trade by getting two royal governors to solicit on their behalf. In 1680 Fitz Winthrop asked Sir Edmund Andros to support the proprietors' petition for a new royal commission to settle the Narragansett Country. "Shalbe ready," Andros replied, "in what you desire relating to your interest in Narragansett & to serve you in what I may." Andros added his regret that Fitz was "nott in another place & from your retirement as I have long desired."[18] Fitz's brother Wharton had meanwhile been applying to Lord Culpeper, the governor of Virginia, who stopped at Boston in 1680 on his way to England. "His Lordship," he told Fitz, "promises to be our sollicitor for settlement of Narragansett, and to send an effectuall answere to our peticion sent this summer." Lord Culpeper was made a partner in the Narragansett Company. On his return to England, he recommended to the Lords of Trade eight "substantial, able and (as I was informed in the place) uninterested persons, fit to be Commissioners in the Narragansett affair." His list included such uninterested persons as Fitz Winthrop, Fitz's brother-in-law Palmes, and Edward Randolph.[19]

The Lords of Trade accepted Culpeper's recommendation to reopen the 1665 Narragansett settlement. Wharton sent via Randolph a letter to William Blathwayt, secretary to the Lords, discreetly intimating that the proprietors would pay Blathwayt "due acknowledgments" for promptly dispatching the commission. On April 7, 1683, the Lords appointed nine men, headed by the royal governor of New Hampshire, Edward

[17] *Randolph*, III, 40, 59; *Cal.S.P.Col., 1677-1680*, pp. 612-13.

[18] M.H.S. *Coll.*, 5th ser., VIII, 292-93; 6th ser., III, 469.

[19] *Ibid.*, 5th ser., IX, 111; 6th ser., III, 466; *Cal.S.P.Col., 1677-1680*, pp. 609-11; *1681-1685*, pp. 29, 34; *Randolph*, III, 110.

Cranfield, but otherwise following Culpeper's list, to investigate the rival claims to the Narragansett Country. It was a stacked group. Yet the only common bond between the English and colonial members of the Commission was their willingness to fleece Rhode Island. Otherwise, they worked at cross-purposes. Governor Cranfield wrote William Blathwayt that huge sums of money could be milked from the gullible colonials by negotiating their local disputes in the name of the crown. "The Narragansett Countrey lyes betwixt severall claimours," he told Blathwayt; "both parties have mony and 3 or 4000: li will not be felt in the disposeing those Land's . . . ."[20] When the Narragansett commission was delivered to him in July 1683, Cranfield entered into his task with some enthusiasm.

The proceedings of the commission were farcical. Richard Wharton urged Fitz Winthrop to be sure to join the commission when it visited the Narragansett Country in August. Fitz stayed in New London, but his presence was not needed. When Cranfield and his colleagues gathered at the house of one of the proprietors, attended by Wait Winthrop and five other Narragansett partners, the exasperated Rhode Island government challenged their proceedings and ordered them to get out of her jurisdiction. Filled with righteous indignation, Cranfield's party moved back to Boston and tore up the settlement of 1665. They found that the Narragansett proprietors had title to the disputed soil and were under the jurisdiction of Connecticut rather than Rhode Island. Cranfield reported the decision to Blathwayt, explaining that the proprietors "doe all intend to complement you with a parcel of land within their claime."[21] What sort of complement the proprietors made to the head commissioner, Cranfield did not say.

Edward Randolph was unable to join the Narragansett commission, for he was in England on weightier business, the repeal of the Massachusetts charter. On October 26, 1683, a few days after the commissioners had written their report, he was

---

[20] *Cal.S.P.Col.*, *1681-1685*, pp. 270, 417, 449; *Randolph*, VI, 138-39, 142.

[21] M.H.S. *Coll.*, 5th ser., IX, 112-44; *R.I. Rec.*, III, 127-47; *Conn. Rec.*, III, 324-25; *Randolph*, VI, 148-50.

back in Boston with a writ of *quo warranto*, which he served against the Bay government. Randolph also demonstrated the superficiality of his alliance with the Narragansett proprietors. He told Cranfield that he was the Duke of Hamilton's agent, and laid claim (on the basis of the Duke's 1635 patent) to the whole area between the Connecticut River and Narragansett Bay. Cranfield washed his hands of the matter, telling the Narragansett proprietors and the Connecticut government to draw up formal answers to Randolph's claim and to transfer the case to England.[22] Randolph's espousal of the Hamilton claim was, of course, quite incompatible with his strenuous efforts to consolidate New England into a single royal colony. He was playing both ends against the middle. The Hamilton claim might be a useful speculative venture in case the Lords of Trade gave up their attack on the Massachusetts charter. Meanwhile, it served to keep the colonists on the defensive.

The experience of the Narragansett proprietors demonstrates that these colonial "moderates" really had less in common with Randolph, Culpeper, Cranfield, and Blathwayt than with their neighbors, the dispossessed Puritan "faction." The proprietors had arrived at a very tenuous alliance with Randolph, and then only after they had tried several other avenues. Each party was trying to exploit the other. The proprietors cultivated Randolph as a means of advancing their local business interests, whereas he cultivated them as a means of imposing imperial controls (at a personal profit) upon such local interests. Any such partnership was necessarily flimsy and ephemeral. Furthermore, in the case of the Narragansett proprietors, the very term "moderate" seems a misnomer. There was nothing moderate about the proprietors' appetite for land, though to be sure in this respect they were badly outdistanced by royal officialdom.

❧ ON OCTOBER 23, 1684, one year after the Narragansett commissioners had completed their task, the Massachusetts charter was at last declared vacated by Court of Chancery. In

[22] *R.I. Rec.*, III, 145; M.H.S. *Coll.*, 5th ser., VIII, 439-40; IX, 114-16; *Conn. Rec.*, III, 136, 333-36. Randolph never strongly advocated the Hamilton claim, and dropped it as soon as his campaign against charter government succeeded in 1684.

January 1685, Wait relayed rumors of momentous change to Fitz in New London: "that this charter was condemned the last terme; that one Collonell Kirke that was Governor of Tangere is coming Governor here, som report with six or 7 frigotts and 5000 men, Mr. Randolph to be secretary and register, and several gentlemen here to be of the Councill."[23] Wait's picture of immediate military dictatorship was wide of the mark. Though the Lords of Trade were in fact projecting an absolutist government for New England, they were very slow in sending over the new governor general, and eventually equipped him with only 120 soldiers.

The Lords had not yet decided at the time of the Massachusetts charter's annulment just what the constitution of the new royal government of New England should be. In 1683 Randolph worked out with Joseph Dudley, his chief colonial confederate, a set of proposals which indicates what some of the "moderates" wanted: a single governor for New England, an elected council without legislative assembly, a notably high property qualification for freemanship (£400 in land or personal estate), and an annual quitrent on all land.[24] Fitz and Wait might boggle over the last feature of this plan, considering their large holdings of undeveloped land. Otherwise, such a government would have seemed to them a great improvement over the existing charter governments.

The Lords of Trade, as their plan took shape in 1684, tightened the Randolph-Dudley proposal. They agreed to concentrate power in a governor and council without representative assembly (at the special motion of the King), but they also provided an appointed rather than elected council. Governor and council would legislate, tax, regulate trade, enforce a system of quitrents, and foster the Church of England. Details

---

[23] M.H.S. *Coll.*, 5th ser., VIII, 451. Fitz considered Wait's report sufficiently important so that he passed it on to at least three Connecticut and New York correspondents (*Ibid.*, 5th ser., VIII, 300; Winthrop Mss., VI, 50-51).

[24] Michael G. Hall, ed., "Randolph, Dudley, and the Massachusetts Moderates in 1683," *N.E.Q.*, XXIX (1956), 513-16. I cannot agree with Mr. Hall that these proposals were "radically different from the eventual and disastrous constitution of the Dominion government," since they embodied the Dominion's most controversial features—abolition of the popular assembly, and imposition of quitrents on settled properties.

were worked out casually. Indeed the master plan was revised and extended until the eve of the Glorious Revolution. Since the Connecticut and Rhode Island charters were still intact, the Lords started by joining together Massachusetts, New Hampshire, and Maine and, as an afterthought, added the Narragansett Country. After listening to the Narragansett commissioners' report in favor of the Narragansett proprietors, the Lords stipulated that the governor should confirm all titles of land quietly possessed, on payment of a quitrent, and that disputes about title were to be settled by governor in council.[25] In keeping with these drastic changes, Charles II picked Colonel Percy Kirke to be his governor, a tough and seasoned officer who had just concluded a rugged tour of duty as commander of the English military outpost at Tangier. At this point, however, the King's death in February 1685 postponed all further action for six months.

The new King was, to say the least, a firm advocate of colonial centralization, but James II and his advisors had enough discernment to see that Kirke would make an unsuitable governor for New England. Having helped to crush Monmouth's Rebellion in July 1685, Kirke treated his prisoners with flagrant brutality. "I could not at any tyme believe he would make a fitt Governor for those people," said Edward Randolph, "but now since the great carnage he has made in the West, he will be much more arbitrary and oppressing." Randolph spurred the Lords of Trade into ending the paralyzing legal vacuum in New England with the appointment of a provisional royal government staffed by loyal colonists. Following his recommendations, the Lords commissioned (September 27, 1685) a president and council to manage Massachusetts, New Hampshire, Maine, and the Narragansett Country until a governor general could be sent over. Joseph Dudley was the president, Randolph was the secretary, and the Winthrop brothers were among the sixteen councilors. Wait was to sit for Massachusetts, and Fitz for the Narragansett Country.[26] Due to the usual transoceanic delays it was May 1686 before Randolph could deliver his commission to Dudley. The provisional gov-

[25] *Cal.S.P.Col.*, *1681-1685*, pp. 706, 718, 726, 731, 752.
[26] *Randolph*, IV, 29, 44, 51-58; *Cal.S.P.Col.*, *1685-1688*, pp. 77, 80.

ernment lasted only a few months, but its members continued in office as councilors in the permanent royal government established in December 1686 with the arrival of the governor general, James II's old and trusted servant, Sir Edmund Andros.

During this period of flux Fitz Winthrop prepared for his new career in royal government by fawning on the New York governor and snarling at the Hartford magistrates. When Governor Thomas Dongan notified Fitz that he was redistributing patents to all New York lands not improved within four years, a policy which imperiled the Winthrop claim to lands on Long Island and even to Fisher's Island, Fitz did not protest. Instead, he hastily visited Dongan in 1685 "to receive your honors comandes," as he explained, "and perticulerly for the best Methode of proceding in such a way of Improovement as may be most acceptable to your honors inclinations, and most safe to secure my intrest."[27] On the other hand, he was furious when his title to a small tract on the Mystic River was disputed in 1681, which necessitated his bringing suit in Connecticut court. Fitz spoke darkly of those "in authorety" who were crossing him. "I doe resent their base abuse soe highly that I cannot forget it." Certainly he was not very badly abused, for he won the case. Three years later, Secretary Allyn forlornly urged him to visit his Hartford friends who still respected him; "had you been at the election you would have seen it by their voteing."[28] The time had not yet come when Fitz would participate in Connecticut elections.

The Winthrops were overshadowed by their extremely ambitious and energetic brother-in-law, Richard Wharton, and it is striking how Wharton's attitude toward Randolph changed with the creation of the Narragansett commission in 1683 and especially with the annulment of the Bay charter. Earlier, stung by Randolph's efforts to enforce the navigation laws, Wharton had written private jokes to Fitz, toasting him with "a glass of such wine as Mr Randolph will allow," or speculating as to whether "all [Randolph's] Eggs are addeld." When

[27] Winthrop Mss., VI, 51-54; X, 41; M.H.S. *Proc.*, 2nd ser., IV, 290; M.H.S. *Coll.*, 5th ser., VIII, 297-99; 446-47.

[28] Winthrop Mss., VI, 42; X, 41; M.H.S. *Coll.*, 5th ser., VIII, 295-97; *Conn. Rec.*, III, 88.

he saw that royal regulation of New England was certain, with the prospect of political power for the non-Puritan merchants, he cultivated Randolph in earnest, drafting proposals for the reorganization of New England. He explained how the loyal colonists (as distinguished from the factious Bay government) submitted to the King's will, praying for pardon, religious liberty, and, last but not least, confirmation of property. The Narragansett proprietors, he said, humbly accepted the payment of quitrents. On learning of the accession of James II, Fitz Winthrop and nine other proprietors lost no time in announcing to the new King that he had been solemnly proclaimed in the Narragansett Country.[29]

To judge by their letters, Fitz and Wait were relatively indifferent about the coming of royal government. From 1680 to 1686, they continued to talk mostly about the marketing of their Fisher's Island horses and cattle in Boston, or the current fashions in gentlemen's suits and belts. Wait forwarded to his brother whatever gazettes he could get from England. Only occasionally did he mention in passing the latest arrival of Edward Randolph or the latest stratagem of the Bay government to parry him. There is no evidence of close friendship with Randolph. This may be deceptive. Possibly the brothers were secretly cultivating Randolph. Yet surviving evidence indicates that Fitz and Wait felt less deeply engaged in the New England crisis of the mid-1680's than many of their neighbors.

In the new royal government which Randolph had so ardently propounded for New England, everything hinged on cooperation between an authoritarian English governor and a council of colonial "moderates" such as Fitz and Wait. There was little reason to suppose that such an arrangement would work. The Winthrop brothers had indeed detached themselves from the indigenous New England political system in favor of crown officials and London-centered merchants. Their break with family tradition was real, but it can easily be exaggerated. As events would soon prove, Fitz and Wait were feeble pillars upon which to build the Dominion of New England.

[29] Winthrop Mss., XIX, 133, 138; *Cal.S.P.Col., 1681-1685*, pp. 746-47, 757; *1685-1688*, p. 65.

11. *The Dominion of New England*

THERE is an extraordinary parallel between the course of events in England and New England between 1685 and 1689. On opposite shores of the Atlantic, James II and his deputy Sir Edmund Andros governed in such a highhanded and authoritarian fashion as to alienate their subjects, particularly those persons in the upper level of society who were used to sharing political power. The Dominion of New England had all the unpopular features of James' home government. Just as the King broke with Parliament in England, so he abolished representative institutions in New England. While James II whipped up religious hysteria in England by appointing Catholics to high offices, Sir Edmund was fostering the Anglican service in Boston, which in Puritan eyes was little better than the Whore of Rome. Andros was buttressed by a troop of redcoats in Boston, equivalent to James' standing army at Hounslow Heath. In England, seven Anglican bishops were prosecuted for challenging the government's religious policy; in New England, Master John Wise and others were prosecuted for challenging the government's tax policy. Even Harvard College felt her independence threatened, as did Oxford and Cambridge.

Nor does the parallel end here. On both sides of the Atlantic this unpopular government was overthrown by revolution: November 1688 in the mother country, and April 1689 in America. Neither revolt was spontaneous. Both were precipitated by external circumstances; the landing of William of Orange galvanized the English rebels, and the news of William's landing spurred on the colonists. James II and Sir Edmund Andros were both unseated easily and without bloodshed. There was no popular or social upheaval. The revolution was carefully managed by those with the greatest stake in society, the great aristocratic landholders in England, merchants and clergymen in New England, who were not so much fighting for a noble cause as for their personal entrenchment. Finally, on both sides of the Atlantic a number of the principal actors engaged in double-dealing. Lord Churchill, for instance, the future Duke of Marlborough, pledged himself to both James and William and slipped over to William's side only at the last minute when he was sure that James would lose. Similarly, in the far smaller world of Boston, Wait Winthrop remained a member of Andros' Dominion Council until the day the revolt broke out, when he abruptly became a member of the Council of Safety, which directed the rebellion, arrested Andros, and took over the government.

The Winthrop brothers' participation in and last-minute revulsion against the Dominion of New England marked the great turning point of both their careers. The momentous events of the 1680's taught them a hard lesson: the danger of dependence on the home government. Despite all the parallels between the situation in England and New England, the revolutionary crisis forced Fitz and Wait Winthrop to identify themselves as either Britons or colonials, to decide whether their prime loyalty was to the imperial service or to their local society. The Winthrop brothers decided that they were New Englanders.

⌘ THE atmosphere was peculiar in Boston when the new royal government supplanted the old charter government in May 1686. The defeated orthodox party was bitterly unhappy. Magistrate Samuel Sewall tells in his *Diary* how the last session of the Bay court was closed "by the Weeping Marshal-Generall. Many Tears Shed in Prayer and at parting." But the jubilation of Randolph's circle was oddly muted. Month after month had passed without the arrival of either royal frigates or royal governor. Everyone was straining for news. In March, Wait wrote to Fitz: "Here is little new since my last to you, only . . . a coppye of the commission for the Government of this Collony, the Province of Maine, New Hampsheir, and Kings Province or Narrogansett country. . . . The commission is to Mr Dudly, as President till the chiefe Governor come, and to the rest named as of Counsell, whereof you are one, who are . . . to do all things with respect to the Government of the forenamed places as the commission largly directs."[1] Wait did not bother to mention that he also was named to Dudley's council. Another month passed, and Wharton wrote Fitz that Boston was in an uproar: "some pray for Kirke, & some for Dudley, and as many curse both." At last on May 14 Edward Randolph debarked from the frigate *Rose* and took a coach for Joseph Dudley's house in Roxbury to present him with the Commission for the President and Council of New England. Three days later, as secretary of the council, Randolph curtly informed Fitz of his appointment and pressed him to come to Boston as quickly as possible.[2]

Dudley's provisional government held office from May to December 1686. There was a distinctly new atmosphere in Boston, but by no means a wholesale transformation of Massachusetts society or institutions. By firmly refusing to dicker with members of the defunct charter government, Joseph Dudley was able to supplant them with a minimum of friction. His council was installed on May 25. When the new officers took their oaths before a public assembly in the Boston Town House, Dudley established the tone for the administration in his inaugural address. It was every colonist's duty to support the King's aim, which he defined as "the happy increase and advance of these Provinces, by their more immediate dependence upon the Crown of England." Obviously ruffled by his personal unpopularity, Dudley endeavored to meet his critics half-way, by promising that the transition from old government to new would be "as plain and easie as is possible."[3]

The transition was suspiciously easy. With ten days of hard work, the council fulfilled its instructions to reorganize local government, the judicial system, and the militia. Many of the old officeholders were reappointed. Only a handful of men were haled before the council for contempt; one man was im-

[1] M.H.S. *Coll.*, 5th ser., V, 140; VIII, 459-60.
[2] Winthrop Mss., XIX, 141; M.H.S. *Coll.*, 5th ser., V, 137; *Randolph*, IV, 74-75.
[3] M.H.S. *Proc.*, 2nd ser., XIII, 226-27.

prisoned and fined for speaking sedition.[4] Samuel Sewall, whose sensitivity to innovations was exceptionally delicate, did complain about the new regime in his *Diary* but only on religious grounds. Sewall was upset by Anglican services in the Town House, by several Prayer Book marriages and burials, and by the insidious reappearance of the popish St. George's cross in the colony flags. Chiefly he was scandalized by the uninhibited behavior of Samuel Shrimpton and other nonpuritan Boston gentlemen, who seized the opportunity to "drink Healths, curse, swear, talk profanely and baudily to the great disturbance of the Town and grief of good people. Such high-handed wickedness has hardly been heard of before in Boston."[5] Sewall had not seen anything yet.

Ironically, by the time Dudley's council had held office for a few weeks, Edward Randolph was more critical of the new regime than was Samuel Sewall. Randolph speedily discovered that his colleagues were more interested in the perquisites of office than in fundamental reform programs. After only four council meetings, he was finding that his supposed ally, Richard Wharton, "has carried himselfe very odly," thwarting the appointment of Randolph's nominee as Captain of Castle Island in Boston harbor. Instead, Wharton secured this strategic post for his brother-in-law. "The Castle of Boston," explained the council to the Lords of Trade on June 1, "a place of great importance to this Country, is now put under the care and Command of Captaine Wait Winthrop, a person of known Loyalty."[6] When Randolph saw that the council was unwilling to foster the Church of England actively, and that most of the councilors, being merchants, would only pay lip service to the Navigation Acts, he felt horribly cheated. New Moderate was but Old Faction writ large.

---

[4] *Ibid.*, 229-46, 262-64; M.H.S. *Coll.*, 5th ser., v, 138-41.

[5] *Ibid.*, 142-43, 147, 151.

[6] Wait seems also to have been given immediate supervision of the Boston militia. It was his job, for instance, to arrange a military escort for President Dudley's installation. His command of the Castle did not require him to live on the island; his lieutenant was expected to stay with the garrison. Wait's appointment was delayed, since the former commander did not surrender the Castle to him until September. (*Randolph*, vi, 172; M.H.S. *Proc.*, 2nd ser., xiii, 240, 269; M.H.S. *Coll.*, 5th ser., v, 140-41, 152, 154; Winthrop Mss., Deeds, 63.)

Week by week, Randolph's frustration mounted. Initially merely complaining that Dudley had outmaneuvered him in the division of spoils, he was soon wildly slandering the President as "a man of base, servile and antimonarchial principle." Wharton he found not merely an engrosser of great land tracts and a smuggler, but a seditionary, for Wharton "did openly declare that his Majesty, in appointing me his Secretary and Register, intended to inthrall this people in vassalage." Writing home in August, Randolph summed up his predicament: "I am attack'd from every part: the Ministers quarrell for my bringing in the Common prayer, the old magistrates and freemen for vacating their Charter: the mobile are troubled that the Lawes of England are in force; & the Merchants for putting the acts of trade in full execution: by which they have lost severall ships & large quantityes of Goods. . . . such is their implacable malice, that Oliver the late Tyrant was not more ingrateful to the Royalists then I am to the most of the people. . . ." Randolph called for a sweeping counterattack. An English governor general must be immediately dispatched who could displace uncooperative council members and "hold the raines of Government in his hands & restrain the liberty of Conscience which they now grosly abuse."[7]

Too drastic for Sewall, not drastic enough for Randolph, Dudley's council offered no real policy because it had no real power. Not daring to levy direct taxes without an assembly, it had almost no funds. The councilors, who were unsalaried, resented having to neglect their personal affairs in order to meet at Boston. After the initial burst of activity, meetings were held only about once a week and often lacked the prescribed quorum of eight members. According to Randolph, the councilors were jealous of Dudley's powers and fought passionately among themselves. "Wee have very seldome Councills and then little done besides quarrelling: and agree in nothing but Sharing the Country amongst themselves and laying out Larg tracts of lands . . . . I am forcd to say little," he added, "in regard wee have

[7] *Randolph*, IV, 89, 92, 108-109, 114-15, 131-32; VI, 199. Michael Hall argues that Randolph's break with Dudley's regime was not so extreme (*Edward Randolph*, pp. 100-107).

but a very thin Councill . . . and I feare they will throw all up."[8] As usual, Randolph was exaggerating. Yet Dudley's care-taker government was manifestly incapable of handling any emergency. Left indefinitely to its own devices, the council might have disintegrated completely.

Of the two Winthrop brothers, Wait was much more active in Dudley's council. Like a number of his colleagues, Fitz lived so far from Boston that his membership was perfunctory. He came up from New London for the organizational meetings of the council, May 25 to June 3, 1686, and then went home again. Wait, being a Boston resident, was one of the half-dozen most faithful councilors and missed only six of the forty-four meetings. In addition to his appointment as Captain of the Castle, Wait served on a number of committees. He was not aggressive enough, however, to benefit from the council's pleas-ant habit of voting land, commercial privileges, and cash rewards to its members. Wait missed the opportunity to confirm the title to his father's lead mines because he did not have the deeds and Fitz did not send him attested copies.[9] Among the core of councilors Wait was clearly a less forceful personage than either President Dudley, Deputy-President Stoughton, or Richard Wharton. Randolph never bothered to insult him in his letters home.

The Winthrop brothers were particularly concerned in the council's handling of the perennial Narragansett Country prob-lem. Inevitably, with the Winthrops and several of their fellow councilors being Narragansett proprietors, the council deter-mined to enforce Cranfield's 1683 judgment in their favor. On June 23, Dudley, Fitz Winthrop, Randolph, and Wharton held court at Kingston and reorganized the whole Narragansett Country government. They announced that anyone settling without permission on the Narragansett proprietors' lands must make prompt composition by purchase or rent. Fitz presided over a second Narragansett court session in October. The Rhode

[8] *Randolph*, IV, 99-100; VI, 187-88, 192; Barnes, *The Dominion of New England*, pp. 57-59.
[9] M.H.S. *Proc.*, 2nd ser., XIII, 256, 269, 274-75, 279, 281; M.H.S. *Coll.*, 5th ser., VIII, 463, 474.

Island government did not dare to contest this action because Randolph had a writ of *quo warranto* against their charter. By cooperating with the council, they hoped to avoid complete surrender. The proprietors, losing no time in turning their land to advantage, contracted to sell to a group of French Protestant refugees a tract near Kingston at £20 per 100 acres, for the plantation of a new town. In fact, the proprietors were pushing too far too fast. When dispute arose over the eastern limits of the Narragansett Country, their inveterate enemy John Greene of Warwick took ship for England and petitioned the King that the proprietors were usurping royal land. The question of the Narragansett land title was fatally left open for Sir Edmund Andros to decide.[10]

In 1686 the Winthrop brothers also figured in the council's efforts to annex Connecticut to the Dominion of New England. There were strong arguments for ending Connecticut's political autonomy. With the collapse of John Winthrop, Jr.'s 1662 plan to make the Long Island Sound area an economic unit, the colony was an agrarian backwater. Some Connecticut planters were actively criticizing the existing charter government, in the manner of Randolph's circle of Boston moderates. Two men close to Fitz and Wait, their brother-in-law Edward Palmes of New London, and Fitz's hunting and fishing partner Samuel Willys, of Hartford, especially resented being excluded from the Connecticut council. Palmes, who had been unsuccessfully nominated for the magistracy a number of times, petitioned in 1685 against the arbitrary irregularity of the colony's judicial system. Willys, dropped from the magistracy in 1685, complained to Fitz that Connecticut was ruled contrary to English law. Undoubtedly Sir Edmund Andros "hath a sense of my sufferings," said Willys.[11]

[10] *Ibid.*, 5th ser., VIII, 467; IX, 152-57, 171-73; M.H.S. *Proc.*, 2nd ser., XIII, 235, 280; *R.I. Rec.*, III, 193, 197-202, 221; *Rhode Island Colonial Gleanings*, I, 179; *Randolph*, VI, 178-79.

[11] Winthrop Mss., XX, 54; *Conn. Rec.*, III, 193. The three most vigorous critics of Connecticut's resumption of charter government after 1689 were all well treated by the Connecticut court in 1686. Palmes and William Rosewell both had petitions granted, and Gershom Bulkeley was licensed as a physician. (*Ibid.*, III, 200, 216, 218.)

Edward Randolph and Wait Winthrop tried in different ways to make the Connecticut government surrender, and with equal lack of success. Randolph's technique was bullying, if not dishonest. He had two writs of *quo warranto* against the Connecticut charter, and one against Rhode Island, but by the time he reached Boston in May 1686 all these writs were invalid, because their time of return had lapsed. Randolph wrote Governor Treat that if Connecticut were so foolish as to resist the *quo warranto* proceedings, she would be punished by being partitioned between New England and New York. But Treat played off New York against Boston. He hinted to Governor Dongan that if he could offer better terms than Randolph, Connecticut might ask to be joined to New York. The Connecticut General Court met on July 6, and petitioned the King to recall his attack upon their charter. Now Randolph was forced to come to Hartford, on July 20, and deliver his worthless writs. Treat told his visitor how he honored all representatives from the imperial crown, and raised Randolph's hopes for a humble surrender. Actually, Randolph's visit stirred the Connecticut government into looking for an English agent to defend the charter at law.[12]

Randolph claimed that Dudley's council was secretly advising the Connecticut leaders to stall, in order to delay or prevent the coming of a permanent governor general. He was probably correct. For Dudley's council was trying to arrange an alliance with the Connecticut government, which was certainly somewhat contrary to Randolph's purpose. On July 21, while Randolph was safely off in Connecticut, the council decided to send three of its members, Wait and Fitz Winthrop and John Pynchon, on a separate mission to Hartford. These three missionaries bore instructions to dwell on Connecticut's New England heritage of religion and liberty, as well as her economic ties with Massachusetts. They were to urge that Connecticut petition the King, requesting that in case the charter was annulled, she would like to join Massachusetts rather than New York.

[12] *Ibid.*, III, 207-13, 352-62; *Cal.S.P.Col., 1685-1688*, pp. 205-206; *Randolph*, IV, 100-101, 113; VI, 191.

The trump card was to propose sending a joint Massachusetts-Connecticut agent or agents to England, probably Richard Wharton and Fitz Winthrop, for both men were talking of sailing to England in the fall.[13] Surely the main aim of such an agency would be to persuade the home government to continue the Dudley government indefinitely, with a few salutary modifications such as the reestablishment of a legislature and the removal of Edward Randolph.

The trouble with the councilors' plan was that they had nothing attractive to offer Connecticut. Wait Winthrop and Pynchon went to Hartford without Fitz, who became violently ill while setting out from New London. Fitz wrote Wait that he would welcome "any expedient, that might conduce to the continuance of the hapiness, and prosperity, of this good Collony; whose welfare wee are obliged to intend, haveing our intrest wrapped up with them in all Respects." However, he suggested no expedients. On August 3 Wait and Pynchon were politely received at Hartford, but came away with neither an alliance nor an agreement on a joint agent. "We must tell you we love our own things, if we may injoy them," the Connecticut magistrates wrote pointedly to Dudley, "but if we be deprived of them, . . . the will of the Lord be done." Treat and his colleagues were almost as suspicious of Dudley as of Randolph, and they knew that the tenure of his government was extremely uncertain. Not that they intended to ally with New York. Instead they commissioned a London merchant, William Whiting (who had been John Winthrop, Jr.'s landlord in 1661-1663), as their agent, and petitioned the King once more to recall his attack. In the instructions to Whiting, however, they did take one agonized glance into the future; if Whiting could not defend their charter, they wanted Connecticut joined to the royal government of New England, rather than to New York.[14]

On August 25, 1686, just as the Connecticut government was drafting its instructions to Whiting, Randolph jubilantly wrote to Fitz, "I send you for a cordiall the good newes that Sir Ed-

[13] *Ibid.*, IV, 97; VI, 191, 194, 196; M.H.S. *Proc.*, 2nd ser., XIII, 259, 262; *Conn. Rec.*, III, 358-59, 363-64; Winthrop Mss., XII, 143.
[14] *Ibid.*, VI, 56; *Conn. Rec.*, III, 364-75; *N.Y.Col.Doc.*, III, 429.

mund Andros is appointed our gouvernor." He expected Andros to reach Boston in a fifty-gun frigate sometime in November. Wait, less enthusiastic than Randolph, told his brother that Andros' commission "differs not much from that which is here already, the same councill, Pemaquid and Plimouth added. . . . The procedure against Conecticutt and Rode Island to be this next terme. Quo waranntose out against Pensillvania, East and West Jarsey, Carolina, &c. . . . It will be best to be prepared to be here at the first notice after Sir Edmond comes." Wait's letters in late 1686 plainly reveal his awe of Sir Edmund. He could see that however similar Andros' commission was to Dudley's in form, it was quite different in spirit. The new appointment signalized the home government's decision to rely on trusted royal servants to carry through a new policy of tight, unified control over all the colonies. The Dudley council's talk of sending an agency to England had abruptly become irrelevant. After waiting nearly four months for their new master, Wait and some of his colleagues went out to Nantasket on December 19 to greet Sir Edmund's incoming ship. "He inquired for you as soon as I came on bord," Wait told Fitz, "and sayes you must come, being of the Councill. I told him I expected you this week; therefore hope if this finds you not on the roade you will make all the hast you can after you receive this."[15] The salad days were over.

◀ ANDROS' administration lasted just over two years, from December 1686 to April 1689. Despite this brief period of power, Sir Edmund's regime has fascinated historians, and properly so. It represents a forceful effort to reconstruct, radically and quickly, an established social order. Sir Edmund's break with New England's past was more radical than James II's parallel innovations at home, but because New England was a smaller society, her local traditions less virile, and Andros an abler man, he was able to accomplish more positive and lasting results.

[15] M.H.S. *Coll.*, 5th ser., VIII, 464, 468, 471; 6th ser., III, 476-77; *Randolph*, VI, 205.

Unlike Dudley, whose policy had been to make the transition from old to new government as easy and slight as possible, Andros made a grand entrance, marching in a laced scarlet coat through an honor guard of militia to the Boston Town House, escorted by the local dignitaries and merchants, while the rest of the populace huzzaed. Every action was masterful. He immediately asserted his superiority over his councilors by standing with his hat on when they took their oaths. He threw the congregational clergy, his chief potential source of opposition, on the defensive by coolly demanding that the Anglicans be given one of their three Boston meetinghouses.[16] Perhaps Andros thought back to his first reception by New Englanders, at Saybrook in July 1675. He had not changed much since then. Always Andros' greatest strength and greatest weakness was his extreme self-confidence. With his knighthood, court connections, and two companies of English soldiers, he cut a far more imposing figure than had Dudley. He had no need for Randolph's supercharged self-pity. Andros' letters to the Lords of Trade breathed crisp efficiency. He told briskly of how he was carrying out the Lords' plans, and he minimized his difficulties. Andros was not trying to deceive the Lords of Trade; he was deceiving himself.

Andros' greatest success came in the opening year of his administration, when his energy and decision made the Dominion of New England for the first time a reality. Plymouth and Rhode Island were quietly annexed. Andros shrewdly capitalized on the divisions within his unwieldy council, Puritans against Quakers, landowners against merchants, to ram through a program favorable to the prerogative, tackling issues upon which Dudley's Council had temporized. The New England court system was made conformable to English practice, the Anglican Church was protected and encouraged, the Navigation Acts were enforced, the printing presses were censored, and most crucial of all, revenue was provided by a direct land tax and increased import duties. This produced an estimated rise in revenue from £2,466 to £3,846 per annum. To be sure, most

[16] *Ibid.*, 207; M.H.S. *Coll.*, 5th ser., v, 159-62; A.A.S. *Proc.*, N.S., XIII, 240-41.

of the towns in Essex County tried to resist this taxation without representation, but Andros quickly silenced opposition in his most famous display of arbitrary power; he imprisoned the ringleaders, secured their conviction, and fined them heavily. As he explained to Fitz, the Essex people soon paid their taxes, with "all persons well disposed & satisfied." Sir Edmund, being a soldier first and foremost, was less upset by the colonists' refractoriness than by their feeble defenses against French attack. In the fall of 1687 the militia was mobilized to construct a palisade fort at the south end of Boston, on Fort Hill, commanding both the sea and land approaches to the town. Stronger batteries at Castle Island were also built.[17] As it turned out, Andros' energies were here misapplied, for the French in America did not have the resources to mount direct attacks on English seaports and instead harried the inland frontier, where Andros' defensive forts offered little protection.

The diarist Sewall tells how he called at Wait Winthrop's house on January 7, 1687, and found Governor Andros there. "Capt. Winthrop had me up to him, so I thankfully acknowledged the protection and peace we enjoyed under his Excellencie's Government." Sewall felt less thankful when Andros decided to hold Anglican services in Sewall's South Meetinghouse until an Anglican church could be built. South Meetinghouse became a busy place every Sunday. The Anglicans and Congregationalists both held morning and afternoon meetings, and each group regularly accused the other of violating the agreed time limits.[18]

Edward Randolph had more cause than Sewall to acknowledge gratitude, and indeed Randolph did admit that Andros "is ready att all tymes to favour me and is very solicitous on my behalfe." But he was still unhappy. With its trade decaying as a result of the enforcement of the Navigation Laws, New England seemed unable to support Andros' ambitious military program. The golden spoils of office were likewise illusory. Randolph raised the schedule of fees for work done by his

[17] *Ibid.*, 249, 256-64, 477-82; M.H.S. *Coll.*, 5th ser., V, 190, 194-95; 6th ser., III, 482; *Randolph*, IV, 183; VI, 211-12; *Cal.S.P.Col.*, *1685-1688*, pp. 350, 422, 472-74.
[18] M.H.S. *Coll.*, 5th ser., V, 164, 171-72, 176-77, 180, 216-19.

secretary's office but still failed to make money and soon leased out the secretary's post. Meanwhile he saw almost all the councilors continuing clandestinely to undermine the Dominion. Randolph could only sadly conclude that "His Excellency has to do with a perverse people."[19]

Fitz Winthrop, a long-standing disciple of Andros, played a larger role in his council than he had in Dudley's. As before, Fitz lived too far from Boston to attend council meetings regularly. He was at most of the important organizational meetings, between December 31, 1686, and March 12, 1687, and joined in the work of collecting and revising the laws of the former New England governments and in reorganizing the militia. Sir Edmund was genuinely fond of Fitz, probably more so than of any other New Englander. In recognition of his military experience, he named Fitz in January 1687 as colonel of the Rhode Island and Narragansett Country militia, the most responsible office Fitz had yet held. In April Fitz exercised his troops, and was warmly thanked by the Governor "for your going by Roode Island & setling things as you did."[20]

Fitz did useful work for Andros in trying to bring Connecticut into the Dominion. The Hartford leaders had no loving memory of Sir Edmund, and continued to procrastinate. After receiving a third (and valid) writ of *quo warranto*, they wrote to Secretary of State Sunderland in January 1687 that, if necessary, they would submit to Andros' government. As a result of this letter, the home authorities did not bother to pursue the legal forfeiture of their charter. Yet when Andros wrote four separate invitations to submit and finally sent Randolph to Hartford in June 1687, Connecticut's answer was invariably that she would continue in her present station until she received new directions from the King. Resistance was cracking, however. Secretary John Allyn asked Fitz to provide him with ammunition to convert the General Court. In reply, January 13, 1687, Fitz indicated his disappointment at Connecticut's intransigence. The colony was going to have to surrender, "'it

[19] *Randolph*, IV, 147-48, 160-63; VI, 215-19, 225-26, 235, 251.
[20] A.A.S. *Proc.*, N.S., XIII, 245-46, 466; M.H.S. *Coll.*, 5th ser., VIII, 477-79; 6th ser., III, 477, 481.

being his Majesties pleasure to make some alteration in all his governments in America; and it will be pitty that many of yourselves should not be continued in place of trust." Connecticut's behavior might provoke Andros into refusing to give the present colony leaders positions on the Dominion council, so that "many persons possibly may be imposed upon you that your selves may not think suitable." Fitz praised the generous constitution of the Dominion: "All things that will really conduce to the growth and prosperety of the people . . . will readely be granted by his Excellency." On March 30, Allyn and two other magistrates publicly declared their desire for immediate submission, but the majority in the General Court remained blind to Fitz's arguments. Allyn could only ask Fitz to be patient, and to explain Connecticut's conduct to Andros as favorably as possible.[21]

Diplomacy having failed, Andros went to Hartford in October 1687 and seized the Connecticut government. The situation had indeed become unseemly; Governor Dongan was insisting to the Lords of Trade that New York needed the province more badly than did Massachusetts. He, too, had been writing the Connecticut Governor and General Court and had even sent three councilors to drum up sentiment for surrendering to him rather than to Andros.[22] On October 18 Andros received instructions from home to annex Connecticut, and the next day, before discussing the matter with his council or notifying Governor Treat, he wrote Fitz at New London to be ready to join him in Hartford. Precisely what happened on Andros' arrival, the evening of October 31 at Hartford meetinghouse, is shrouded in legend. He failed to confiscate the Connecticut charter; it was placed before him (so the story goes), but the candles were suddenly blown out and the precious document spirited away by Joseph Wadsworth to a hollow oak tree in Samuel Willys' yard. This story ignores the lack of contemporary substantiation, or the fact that Willys was

[21] *Conn. Rec.*, III, 222-38, 375-83; M.H.S. *Coll.*, 5th ser., VIII, 300-302; 6th ser., III, 478-80; Bates, *The Charter of Connecticut*, pp. 34-35; Winthrop Mss., X, 44.

[22] *Conn. Rec.*, III, 386-87, 464; *Cal.S.P.Col.*, *1685-1688*, pp. 364-65, 370-71, 375.

one of Andros' warmest admirers. Otherwise, the Hartford status quo was much less disturbed than in Boston in 1686. Fitz attended the two council meetings in Hartford at which Treat and Allyn were sworn in as his colleagues, and all the other former magistrates made justices of the peace. Andros did, however, appoint as justices several other men who had been at odds with the old government, most notably Fitz's brother-in-law Edward Palmes, and the former minister of his New London church, Gershom Bulkeley.[23]

With Andros' annexation of Connecticut, Fitz Winthrop gained new power and prestige. The Governor and his suite toured the principal Connecticut towns, establishing local courts, militia, and customs officers for the Dominion government. In New London on November 10 Andros gave Fitz command of the militia in Connecticut in addition to Rhode Island and the Narragansett Country, and promoted him to Major General. Fitz was (after the Governor himself) the highest military officer in New England, in charge of 3,800 men. John Allyn thanked Fitz for securing him Andros' patronage, and William Jones, a magistrate of long standing in the old Connecticut government, asked the Winthrops' favor in obtaining the probation and registry of wills for one or several counties. As a New York friend noted in congratulating Fitz on "the new honour which your meritts have acquired you in his Majesties service, . . . The times are well alter'd in the reception of Sir Edmund Andros in those parts now, to what they were formerly."[24]

In contrast to Fitz, Wait Winthrop found that the change in administration took away much of the responsibility he had had under Dudley and placed him in an increasingly awkward position. One of Andros' first acts was to order Wait to deliver Castle Island to Captain Nicholson, commander of his bodyguard. The new Governor pointedly observed that the Castle

---

[23] *Ibid.*, *1685-1688*, pp. 472-73; M.H.S. *Coll.*, 5th ser., V, 193; 6th ser., III, 482-83; *Conn. Rec.*, III, 248-49, 387-88; C.H.S. *Coll.*, III, 137-41; A.A.S. *Proc.*, N.S., XLVIII, 279.

[24] M.H.S. *Coll.*, 6th ser., III, 483-85; *Cal.S.P.Col.*, *1689-1692*, p. 261; Winthrop Mss., XIV, 86.

was in wretched repair.[25] Wait continued to be one of the most diligent councilors, attending sixty-three of the seventy-nine recorded meetings in 1687. But he was no longer given special committee assignments, and he was unhappily conscious of becoming a cipher.

In 1690, safely after Andros' overthrow, Wait joined four other Dominion councilors, William Stoughton, Thomas Hinckley, Bartholomew Gedney, and Samuel Shrimpton, in *A Narrative of the Proceedings of Sir Edmond Androsse and his Complices*. The authors complained that Andros had habitually overruled or side-stepped council debate, that important bills were privately drafted and unexpectedly presented for discussion, that the Governor listened only to a small clique of outsiders and ignored the majority of his council. In Wait's case, there is more justification than with last-minute converts like Stoughton or Shrimpton for reading back into 1687 the complaints voiced in 1690. The *Narrative* condemns Andros' restriction of local self-government, permitting only one town meeting per year, and it is interesting to find that Wait attended the annual Boston town meetings in 1687 and 1688, the only councilor to do so. Again, the *Narrative* objects to the way Andros rammed through his tax legislation, as well as his technique of bypassing local courts in order to bring critics of his regime to trial before the council at Boston, so it is interesting to find that Wait did not attend the council meetings or the special Boston court of oyer and terminer which punished the leading Essex County rebels. Perhaps it was not accidental that he chose this time to visit New London. If Wait felt troubled by Andros' policy, he also found himself uncomfortably identified as Andros' creature by the man in the street. He complained to Fitz in 1687 of never getting news from Connecticut, since "no body has the manners to come nere me unless I mete with them accidentally."[26]

Unquestionably, Wait's greatest grievance against Andros

[25] A.A.S. *Proc.*, N.S., XIII, 241; Winthrop Mss., Deeds, 63; *Cal.S.P.Col.*, *1685-1688*, p. 350.

[26] W. H. Whitmore, *The Andros Tracts* (3 vols.; Boston, 1868-1874), I, 133-47; A.A.S. *Proc.*, N.S., XIII, 481-86; Barnes, *Dominion of New England*, p. 89; M.H.S. *Coll.*, 5th ser., V, 170, 213; VIII, 476, 479; 6th ser., III, 482.

was the royal Governor's land policy. At first, the issue was simply that Sir Edmund halted the Dudley councilors' practice of feathering their own nests. A case in point was his crushing rejection of the Narragansett proprietors' title to their land. Andros sifted the rival claims to the area, including Wharton's plea for the proprietors, and then recommended to the Lords of Trade that all unimproved land titles should be dismissed. In thus reversing the Cranfield judgment of 1683, Andros argued (no doubt correctly) that the settlement of the Narragansett Country had been hindered by the proprietors' speculative claims. Wharton got a patent for only 1,700 acres of Narragansett land, which was under cultivation, on payment of an annual quitrent of ten shillings. The Winthrops got nothing.[27]

Andros' rebuff of the Narragansett proprietary, together with his hostility toward Wharton's similar scheme for developing a vast tract at Pejepscot in Maine, drove Wharton to England in June 1687 in the hope of persuading the home government to reverse Sir Edmund's land policy. Wharton began playing a double game, superficially a cordial colleague of Andros and Randolph, yet trying to ambush them at Whitehall. The man who had been more conspicuously enthusiastic about the Dominion than any other New Englander in 1686 was the first colonist to take positive measures to circumvent it. When Wharton reached England, he sent Wait a copy of Andros' report on the Narragansett claims, which he believed "may prove more to our advantage then was intended. My Lord Culpepper promises to make the best on t." Culpeper joined Wharton in petitioning the King that Andros be instructed to grant the proprietors patents for 60,000 acres of Narragansett land. The Lords of Trade actually drafted a letter to this effect on April 10, 1688. But by this time Wharton told Wait, "I dispair of bringing [the Narragansett business] to any good head," and for some unexplained reason his scheme was stalled.[28]

Wharton, however, had become engrossed in a grander ven-

---

[27] *Cal.S.P.Col.*, *1685-1688*, pp. 423-24; A.A.S. *Proc.*, N.S., XIII, 470; M.H.S. *Coll.*, 5th ser., IX, 167-70; Winthrop Mss., XIX, 142.

[28] M.H.S. *Coll.*, 5th ser., VIII, 475; 6th ser., V, 9-10, 14; *Randolph*, VI, 222; *Cal.S.P.Col.*, *1685-1688*, pp. 486-87, 527.

ture, which also concerned the Winthrops. This was the creation of a joint-stock company, to be chartered by the King and generously capitalized by subscribers on both sides of the Atlantic, to develop New England's mines and naval stores. Wharton exhibited specimen ores and resins in London, and Wait supplied him with an optimistic report on ore found at Woburn. Money was no problem, for Wharton had the promise of £25,000 from English investors, a far larger opening stock than John Winthrop, Jr., had been able to raise for his ironworks. Wharton told Wait, in March 1688, "I have subscribed £200 for you in the new company, and shall give you my vote for president. You will have roome to subscribe £1,600 more when the patten comes out, if you please. Pray faile not to satisfy yourselfe as privately as you can what the Wooborne oare will yield. . . . indeed, if you . . . have had a cheat put upon you, as I am something fearfull, I shall suffer much in my reputacion heer, and great discouragement will fall upon the undertakeing."[29] Wharton petitioned for incorporation in February 1688, and the Lords of Trade ordered a patent to be drafted, August 10, 1688. At the point of success, Wharton's scheme again stalled, this time probably because of the impending revolutionary crisis in England.[30]

Meanwhile, back in New England Governor Andros was encountering increasing difficulties during 1688. His wife died in the middle of her first Boston winter. His most powerful Puritan adversary, Increase Mather, the pastor of Boston North Church, escaped surveillance and fled to England. Edward Randolph was getting thoroughly jealous of Andros' New York favorites, John West, John Palmer, and James Graham, and he complained to England that "now the Governor is safe in his New Yorke confidents, all others being strangers to his councill."[31] A more fundamental problem was that Andros was being given too much work for any one man. Hardly had he

[29] M.H.S. *Coll.*, 6th ser., V, 11-15.
[30] *Cal.S.P.Col., 1685-1688*, pp. 496, 564, 577, 581; *Randolph*, IV, 221; Bailyn, *New England Merchants*, pp. 173-74.
[31] *Randolph*, IV, 197, 199, 226-27; VI, 250-51.

finished inspecting his most northerly territories in New Hampshire and Maine, in the spring of 1688, than his jurisdiction was greatly extended southward by the addition of New York and the Jerseys to his Dominion. These territories he proceeded to annex and reorganize in August and September, with much the same pomp and circumstance as in Connecticut the year before, though with less tranquillity, since there was no love lost between Dongan, the supplanted New York governor, and Andros. On the top of everything else, Sir Edmund had to guard his sprawling Dominion against the mounting threat of attack from the French in Canada and their Indian allies. In 1688 trouble was brewing at all points along the English frontier where the raiders from the North could most easily strike— in Maine, the Connecticut Valley, and the Hudson Valley.

Fitz continued to be active in Andros' service. The two men corresponded on how to train the militia and how to manage the Indians. In all his extant letters to Andros during 1688, Fitz harped on a single theme: his gratitude over Andros' paternal care for New England, "& those designes your Excellency layes to settle a lasting hapines to the posterety of this country." Andros called for Fitz at New London on his way to New York in August 1688, and for the next two months Fitz travelled in the Governor's party. He joined in parleys with the chiefs of the Five Nations at Albany and in less ceremonious parleys with Dongan, who wanted the Dominion government to reimburse him for the £6,482 which he claimed to have spent in New York's defense. The high point of Fitz's stay in New York came with the news of the birth of the Prince of Wales, the event which triggered revolutionary preparations in England. Sir Edmund stood in Fort James amid his councilors and local dignitaries, and when he proposed the new Prince's health, the guns in the fort were fired, the soldiers volleyed, and all the ships in the harbor echoed their guns in salute. Then followed general feasting, bonfires, "and nothing but God blesse the prince and drinking his health and loud acclamations were heard that night." The scene was a little different in Boston, where none of the Congregational churches chose to observe the absent Governor's proclamation for a day of public thanksgiving.[32]

The touchstone to New England's temper on the eve of the Glorious Revolution was her reaction to Andros' land policy, the most authoritarian aspect of his general program. The Dominion had been designed to be financed largely from quitrents, thus calling for a profound change in New England land tenure. At first Andros applied this system only when he was asked (as by the Narragansett proprietors) to grant titles for vacant or disputed lands. By 1688 he was calling into question all property titles issued under the old charter governments, many of which he asserted to be defective. If landholders wanted secure titles, they must petition for new patents at a uniform quitrent of 2s. 6d. per hundred acres. Only about two hundred persons in the whole Dominion actually did petition for such patents during Andros' administration. These included Edward Randolph, whose petitions for commons land belonging to the towns of Lynn, Watertown, and Cambridge were naturally not very popular, and Joseph Dudley, whose petition that his estate be repatented "for his owne benifitt, and for a good Example to others, But he would not have his lands Surveied," was concisely judged by his enemies: "Oh the poyson of a Serpent is deadly."[33]

Another petitioner was Fitz Winthrop. In an undated letter he asked Andros to confirm the whole Winthrop estate, since "'tis his Majestyes grace to give renewed title to all our possessions." This letter marks the peak of Fitz's subservience to Andros and to the home authorities, and it suggests other things as well: Fitz's thinly veiled greed for land, his frustration at falling behind pushing entrepreneurs such as his brother Wharton in the race for power and wealth, and, in general, the long distance travelled between the first and third generations of his family. As Fitz states the case to Andros, the present Winthrop property is at best a poor reward "for the waste of that plentifull estate which my predecessors joyfully layde downe

[32] M.H.S. *Coll.*, 5th ser., VIII, 485; 6th ser., III, 486-90; Winthrop Mss., VI, 162; XI, 101; *Cal.S.P.Col.*, *1685-1688*, p. 601; *Randolph*, VI, 263-65.

[33] Barnes, *Dominion of New England*, ch. 8; *Andros*, I, 160.

to begin the growth & prosperity of this country. . . . I am not myselfe sollicitous for the sweete of this world; but, being now ready to leave it, and haveing two nephewes, the hopes of our family, I would gladly leave a settled and sure title of such accommodations at I have. . . . It will be great in your Excellency to build up the ruines of our family, whose decay was one of the greatest supplyes that gave life to the beginning and growth of these plantations, since tis soe much in your power, whose generous hand is allwayes ready to doe good. . . . [May it] please the King to continue you a shield to the people under your Government. I beg your Excellency will not please to let me fall. . . ."[34]

In his desire to have Andros build up the ruins of the Winthrop family, Fitz was even out of step with his own brother. Wait Winthrop saw that if the reconfirmation of land titles enabled Sir Edmund to build up, it also enabled him to tear down. The Winthrop property was peculiarly vulnerable to demolition. Many of the family's extensive claims were to unimproved, unsurveyed lands which had been vaguely deeded to John Winthrop, Jr., many years before by Indians. Wait was more aware than his brother seems to have been that rival speculators in eastern Connecticut lands, such as James Fitch of Norwich or their own brother Palmes, were being given a golden opportunity by Andros to secure confirmation of properties which the Winthrops also claimed. In July 1688, Wait explained to Fitz why he was delaying coming down from Boston to New London: "J. F. [James Fitch] is here, but I beleive is scared with the charge of taking patents. He is not going home yet, and I am willing to se him gon before I goe. I am very desireous to se some ships from England also before I come. My last letters from thence give me grate hope of a

---

[34] M.H.S. *Coll.*, 6th ser., III, 492-93. Andros' reply to Fitz has not survived. The only evidence which I have found of Sir Edmund's confirmation of the Winthrop property is his order, March 5, 1688, that seven square miles in the Nipmuck Country, granted to John Winthrop by the Indians, be surveyed and patented to Fitz's sisters. [Winthrop Mss., Deeds, 102.] But the volume of "Sir Edmund Andros Land Warrants, 1687-1688" in the Massachusetts Archives, which includes this Nipmuck warrant (p. 79), is evidently incomplete, stopping at July 28, 1688.

generall confirmation from his Majesty of all lands according to former useage."[35]

During 1688 New England landholders of every political shade began banding together in opposition to Andros' repatenting program, and Wait Winthrop was among them. In July Andros tried to force a general application for new titles by instituting test cases of eviction against properties held by Samuel Sewall and Samuel Shrimpton, prototypes respectively of the old psalm-singing orthodoxy and the new swash-buckling, episcopalian, mercantile aristocracy. The result was decisive. Sewall petitioned for a new title, but he immediately wrote to Wharton in London for help, offering to subscribe £50 or £100, and in November he was sailing himself for England. Shrimpton refused to petition for a new title, and announced that he would carry his appeal to the King if necessary. Sewall and Shrimpton even dined together, and in company with Cotton Mather "Had Sturgeon, Wine, Punch, Musick." The property issue likewise produced a coalition among diverse New Englanders in London. Wharton dropped his Narragansett and mining projects to join Increase Mather in attendance on James II, and together they beseeched the King to deliver New England from oppression. Optimistic as always, Wharton wrote Wait on October 18, 1688, the day before William of Orange's fleet set sail for England, by which time James II was making desperate concessions and "hath often assured us our propertyes shall be continued and confirmed." Wharton felt sure that Andros' arbitrary rule would be investigated by Court or Parliament, but he and Mather would need at least £2,000 in subscriptions from New Englanders to support their agency. "If other men of estate," he told Wait, "would give the same assurance you have done to contribute, wee would find creditt heer. . . ." Wait Winthrop was now actively enrolled in the attack upon the Dominion.[36]

Men as dissimilar as Wait Winthrop and Increase Mather were drawn together on the property issue not merely because

[35] M.H.S. *Coll.*, 5th ser., VIII, 484.
[36] *Randolph*, VI, 281-82; M.H.S. *Coll.*, 5th ser., V, 219-21, 228-32, 236; 6th ser., V, 17-18.

they disliked a new tax nor because they feared that their dubious land titles would be exposed, important as both these considerations undoubtedly were. Wait and his fellow councilors, in their *Narrative*, later summed up their objections to Andros' policy: "The purchasing of the Natives Right, was made nothing of, and next to a Ridicule. The Enjoyment and Improvement of Lands not inclosed, and especially if lying in common amongst many was denied to be possession;. . . . Many were Solicited, and Encouraged to Petition for other mens Lands, and had a shameful Example set them by some of the chief Contrivers of all this Mischief. When some men have Petitioned for a confirmation of their own Lands, a part of these only was offered to be granted to them, and another part denied. Nor could any mans own Land be confirmed to him, without a particular Survey of every part and parcel of them first made, the great charges whereof, and of other Fees to be taken would have been to most men Insupportable."[37] In short, Andros' land policy created a state of war between the government and each individual property holder. Wait Winthrop can hardly be blamed for concluding that such a situation was intolerable.

⤷ IN APRIL 1689 Wait Winthrop actively participated in overthrowing the Dominion of New England. Fitz Winthrop passively accepted the turn of events. As in any revolutionary episode, there are a number of mysteries about this Boston coup d'état, but the Winthrop brothers' role in the affair is reasonably clear. It is certain that Wait's and Fitz's desertion of Andros marked the watershed in both brothers' lives.

In a sense, it was Fitz who inaugurated the revolution. In October 1688 came the Dominion's first and only serious military test, when Indian outrages began multiplying alarmingly along the frontier settlements in the Connecticut Valley and in Maine. Andros called an emergency session of his council in Boston, at which it was agreed to send 300 militia immediately to the eastern frontier. Andros offered the command of this expedition "upon very good terms" to Fitz. According to Randolph, Fitz "at first assented but afterwards declined it wholly";

[37] *Andros*, I, 143.

no other councilor being willing, the Governor accepted their advice to take command himself. Why did Fitz back out? The official reason is that he fell sick. Fitz frequently fell sick on such occasions. Certainly he was not very sick this time. He was able to travel back to New London in mid-November, just as Andros was heading up to Maine, and in his correspondence with Wait in the next few weeks the most urgent topic was his selection of a new winter coat and waistcoat. Fitz's refusal forced Andros to depart into the Maine woods on a four-month winter campaign, at the critical time when rumors of William of Orange's successful invasion of England were stirring up the discontented colonists. Fitz's behavior also demonstrated that there was now almost no New Englander whom Andros could depend upon. As Randolph said, "his Excellence discharges all offices: from Generall to Sutler."[38]

Wait Winthrop was later accused of plotting with the Congregational ministry to strike against Andros as early as January. The anonymous author of *New England's Faction Discovered* notes meaningfully that the warrant for public observance of the martyrdom of Charles I on January 30 "was called in and suppressed by Captain *Waite Winthrop*, one of the Council, who in the Commotion appeared the chief Man and Head of the Faction against the Government, which he twice swore to maintain. . . ."[39] Wait's extant letters from the winter of 1688-1689, however, indicate that he was not engaged in long-range plots with Cotton Mather and the old charter party, though they do confirm his estrangement from Andros. He wrote tartly to Fitz on the inconclusiveness of Andros' Indian campaign. "If you had gon," he said, "it would have bin counted ill conduct if all the enemys had not bin destroyed before this between us and the north star." He gave no hint of believing, as the more credulous Puritans did, that Andros was betraying the militia to the popish French. Wait quoted approvingly from Wharton's letter of the previous October, reporting progress in the New England agents' campaign

[38] *Randolph*, IV, 276-77; VI, 281-82; *Andros*, II, 181; M.H.S. *Coll.*, 5th ser., V, 236; 6th ser., III, 492; Winthrop Mss., VI, 60.

[39] *Andros*, II, 212.

against Andros, and by mid-December he was getting the first stories of William of Orange's invasion. Yet he told Fitz, "tis generally feared the Duch are landed in England before this," as though the invasion was bad news. On January 28 he reported that Andros was embargoing all ships for England, "which I understand the meaneing of no more than of many other things. . . . He has communicated nothing which came by the last ships to any of the councill here that I know of."[40] Wait's prevailing tone of helpless mystification is inappropriate to a conspirator.

Like most rebellions, the Boston outbreak was precipitated by the increasingly nervous behavior of an administration which knew it was losing effective power. Andros' efforts to embargo news from England and to punish William of Orange's partisans for sedition completed the fatal division between colonials and outsiders and turned his government into a naked army of occupation amid a potential mob. New England was saturated with rumors. "We have no certainty of any thing," John Allyn wrote Wait on April 15, "but great talkes there is that things will be as sometimes they have bin by reason of a proclamation made by his Majestie October last that restores charters; but when it will be I know not, & what new changes ther may be I canot tell, & wither that proclamation reacheth us I know not. . . ." Allyn had not heard about the latest sensation, that a copy of the Prince of Orange's Declaration, even more exhilarating than James II's restoration of charters since it instructed unjustly expelled magistrates to resume their offices, had been smuggled into Boston on April 4. Andros, who had returned to Boston from the frontier in late March, sensed that trouble was brewing. "There's a general buzzing among the people, great with expectation of their old charter, or they know not what," he wrote just two days before the revolt. In a desperate effort to restore authority, he decided to try Cotton Mather at a special council meeting, April 18, on the charge of preaching sedition.[41]

---

[40] M.H.S. *Coll.*, 5th ser., VIII, 486-90.

[41] *Ibid.*, 6th ser., V, 19; C. M. Andrews, ed., *Narratives of the Insurrections, 1675-1690* (New York, 1915), p. 167; Hutchinson, *History of Massachusetts-Bay*, I, 316; *Andros*, II, 211-12; III, 23, 145.

The revolt that cut short Andros' plan was effected by a combination of spontaneity and planning. There was no dominant rebel leader. Wait Winthrop and the other dissident Dominion councilors drew up plans with a few of the old charter leaders for the management of a coup d'état. Cotton Mather tells us in his *Magnalia* that "some of the Principal Gentlemen in *Boston* consulting what was to be done in this Extraordinary Juncture," they agreed that if it proved necessary "to prevent the shedding of *Blood* by an ungoverned *Mobile*, some of the Gentlemen present should appear at the Head of the *Action* with a *Declaration* accordingly prepared." Undoubtedly the "Principal Gentlemen" played a more active hand than Mather cared to admit. Their problem was how to make Andros' two garrisons at Fort Hill and Castle Island and the frigate *Rose* capitulate without bloodshed. To prevent the *Rose's* escape, the first step in the coup was the seizure of her commander, Captain George, as he came ashore about eight o'clock on the morning of April 18. Over a thousand Bostonians rushed to arms by beat of drum and formed themselves into companies. Militia from the neighboring towns streamed in with suspicious alacrity. According to a hostile reporter, Wait Winthrop was designated as the commander of this army, and "had bin with the conspirators of the North end [of town] very early that Morning. . . ." When he saw the armed mob come "to his house requesting Him to bee their Commander and lead them, with abundance of Modesty and no less hypochrisy refused the offer. But at length pretending he was wearied with their importunity's, and to doe the Governour a signall kindness, he condescended to accept of the office, and walk'd before them." Boston was thus easily occupied, though Randolph, West, Graham, and Palmer had managed to reach Fort Hill, where they found Andros with a garrison of fourteen soldiers.[42]

The mob and its leaders gathered at the Town House and listened to Cotton Mather's windy Declaration, which announced that the colonists, in imitation of the Prince of Orange and the English people, were resolved to seize "the Persons

[42] Mather, *Magnalia Christi Americana*, Bk. II, 45; Andrews, *Narratives of the Insurrections*, pp. 200-201.

of those few *Ill Men* which have been (next to our Sins) the
grand Authors of our Miseries; resolving to secure them, for
what Justice, Orders from his Highness, with the *English Parliament* shall direct. . . ." Thus had New England's revolutionary credo been transmuted since the 1630's. In the council
chamber, Wait joined a carefully balanced panel of fifteen men
(five Dominion councilors, five charter magistrates, and five
merchants who had never held office), the fruition of the anti-
Andros coalition which had been uniting almost all New Englanders during the past year. These men drew up a letter summoning Andros to surrender, arguing disingenuously that the
mob action had totally surprised them, that the mob was prepared to storm Fort Hill, but that they could promise security
to Andros' party if he delivered up his government and fortifications. Sir Edmund tried to escape to the *Rose*, but when
the colonials chased his handful of redcoats inside the palisade
and trained the shore batteries on it, he led his loyal councilors
to the Town House, where they were made prisoners and ha-
rangued by their former colleagues. None of the contemporary
narratives tell whether Wait supervised the investment of Fort
Hill, nor whether he joined in insulting the captive governor.
The next day, Castle Island and the *Rose* also surrendered, and
the bloodless revolution had been achieved.[43]

The establishment of a new government over the excited
Massachusetts populace promised to be a harder job than the
overthrow of Andros. On April 20 Wait and the other gentlemen who had managed the coup styled themselves a provisional
Council for the Safety of the People and Conservation of the
Peace. They invited "such other of the old Magistrates Or
such other Gentlemen as they shall Judge meet" to join the
council, enlarging their membership to thirty-seven and retaining the balance between old and new enemies of Andros.
Former Governor Simon Bradstreet, eighty-seven years old,
was chosen president, and Wait Winthrop was appointed commander of the militia. The composition of this Council of
Safety was extremely significant. It heralded Massachusetts'
new ruling class, the combination of former charter magistrates,

[43] *Andros*, I, 3-8, 18-20; II, 196-97.

former Dominion councilors and heretofore private citizens who would hold power under the new charter of 1691. Nine of the fifteen men who summoned Andros to surrender, for instance, would sit on the Bay council in 1692, and ten of them in 1696. The only prominent Massachusetts man to be conspicuously excluded from the Council of Safety was Joseph Dudley. He had been out of town when the revolt occurred, but was caught and carried to the Boston common jail, where he was kept for over nine months until he was shipped to England with Andros and the other prisoners. He was the one "moderate" who had irretrievably committed himself to English over colonial interests. Dudley never forgot his bitter humiliation, and the remainder of his career may be seen as a calculated revenge on the Massachusetts rebels. But for the moment the Council of Safety had the triumph. On May 20 an address to William and Mary was prepared. It explained how the Bostonians had risen "as one Man" in emulation of their Highnesses' "late glorious Enterprise," though happily the people were "so Overruled by the Interposition, and prudence of some Gentlemen upon the place; that the thing was Effected without the least Bloodshed or Plunder." The council asked for the restoration of Massachusetts' charter and English liberties. Meanwhile, Edward Randolph joined Dudley in Boston jail. He gave his address to correspondents as "the Common Gaol in New Algiers."[44]

The Council of Safety itself lasted only five weeks. Lacking instruction from England, the council sought to imitate the Prince of Orange's Convention of January 1689 by calling a similar assembly of representatives from forty-four towns at Boston on May 9. Here the English parallel ends, for the great majority of the towns wanted immediate resumption of the old charter government. This naturally displeased most of the councilors such as Wait, who were nonfreemen or at least had not held office under the charter. A vocal minority of the towns wanted to continue the Council of Safety. The anti-Andros coalition seemed to dissolve completely when Bradstreet and the charter magistrates of 1686 agreed on May 24 to resume administration under the old form. However, Wait Winthrop,

[44] M.A., Court Records, VI, 2-3, 23-24; *Randolph*, IV, 305; VI, 289.

Samuel Shrimpton, and nine other excluded councilors signed a Declaration to the charter party, May 25, pledging to support their administration "in this dangerous conjuncture," and promising to try "to pacifie the dissatisfied in our regards, and promote the publick tranquility as far as in us lies." For a week Wait retired from the council. Then a new Convention of deputies from the towns made a modest concession by choosing Winthrop, Shrimpton, and three others to join the 1686 panel of charter magistrates. Wait was not yet a freeman, and he did not become one until 1690. Still, on June 7, 1689, he took his oath as an Assistant in the charter government and as Major General of the Massachusetts militia.[45]

Indeed, it was only in the aftermath of the Boston revolt that Wait became a first-class citizen of his colony. The Reverend John Higginson renewed his former plea that Wait follow Christ's command, as well as the example of his grandfather and father, and "joyn your self in full communion with Mr Willard's church (where you do constantly attend)." Three weeks later, on August 25, 1689, he was admitted to South Church. As he read the humble thanks of another clerical correspondent, Samuel Stow, that "the Lord . . . raised up your noble heart to do worthyly for his poor people in the spring,"[46] Wait might be pardoned for thinking that in Massachusetts life begins at forty-five. At last he was securely launched as a popular public man, the role he would play for the rest of his life. Wait's performance in 1689 illustrates how the overthrow of the Dominion, while much in character with the Glorious Revolution at home, had insensibly widened again the transatlantic gap. The old orthodoxy and the new moderates of Boston, by learning to submerge their differences in common cause against Andros, were solidifying the instinct for local self-determination within their provincial society.

[45] M.A., Court Records, VI, 11-12, 17-18, 27-28, 34-36, 130; Barnes, *Dominion of New England*, pp. 244-47; Hutchinson, *History of Massachusetts-Bay*, I, 324-28.
[46] M.H.S. *Coll.*, 6th ser., V, 21-23.

12. *A Small Practitioner in Physick*

THE Glorious Revolution started Wait Winthrop off in an entirely new direction. Not only was he henceforth an active public figure, regularly elected to the Massachusetts council from 1689 till his death in 1717, but he became increasingly a champion of Massachusetts' "antient liberty," the religious orthodoxy and chartered privileges established by his grandfather. Having at last joined the church, Wait became the protégé of Cotton Mather, a zealous judge in witchcraft trials, a pious critic of his colleagues' self-seeking greed in office, and a stern defender of the old-time New England virtues. By 1701 he proclaimed that the only way of reviving his people's precious heritage of liberty and morality was to offer himself as governor of Massachusetts and try to restore the Massachusetts Bay Company's charter of 1629.

However, postrevolutionary Massachusetts was a far cry from the first Winthrop's city on a hill. The Bay colonists were now subordinate members of a complex imperial system, closely bound to the home government by the new royal charter of 1691. Splendid isolation was out of the question; a Massachusetts politician was as strong as his connections with the colonial office in England. Furthermore, Wait Winthrop was by no means a man of his grandfather's stature. In politics, he proved to be a pawn of Cotton Mather. Undercutting his talk of preserving Massachusetts' "pure order of the Gospell," his chief motivating impulse was really hurt family pride. In a crisis, he disdained to fight hard for his new-found cause. Faced with greater obstacles than the Founder had ever encountered, Wait dissolved (in Edward Randolph's contemptuous phrase) into "a small practitioner in physick."[1]

[1] *Randolph*, v, 267-68.

A Small Practitioner in Physick

THE key to Wait Winthrop's initial success and eventual failure in postrevolutionary Massachusetts politics was his central position in the coalition which seized power from Andros in 1689 and ruled the province till 1702. This coalition consisted of "moderates" drawn from the Dominion of New England, old-style Puritans drawn from the pre-1686 charter government, and Boston merchants without previous public office. In the dozen years following the Revolution, Massachusetts had three constitutions and four governors, but Winthrop and his fellow coalition members were always in power. Wait obtained a council seat under the old charter in 1689, and served in this capacity for three years, until Sir William Phips arrived with the new charter. Since he was named to Phips' council in the new charter, he continued in office, to be re-elected annually by a big vote. Throughout the crisis years of the 1690's, Wait was a pivotal figure in Massachusetts' ruling caste.

No one would guess from Wait's extant correspondence of the 1690's that he held any public office. He was a rather negligent councilor, attending only about 60 percent of the Massachusetts council meetings. Some of his short absences from Boston are explained by his duties as a judge, riding on circuit. The longer gaps were caused by his trips down to New London to visit Fitz and check the family estate. Personally this was a tragic season for Wait. His wife Mary died of smallpox in 1690, leaving him with four small children, two of whom also soon died.

Wait's business life in these years is hard to reconstruct. The pattern of his Fisher's Island partnership with Fitz was not altered by the Revolution. Sometimes the brothers had several thousand sheep on the island, as well as cattle and horses. Fitz sold the wool locally, and Wait exported the livestock from Boston to the West Indies. The brothers were always complaining about the tenant farmers who decimated their herds. Wait bought shares in ships and cargo, as in 1695 when he hoped to realize £400 on the voyage of the *Mehitabel* from Barbados to London. He also invested in land. By 1692 he owned the whole fifteen-mile chain of Elizabeth Islands north-west of Martha's Vineyard. Edward Randolph insinuated that he used these lonely islands as a base for smuggling Virginia tobacco into Scottish ships. But Wait's chief income was not from trade, illicit or otherwise, but rather from agriculture. In 1698 he complained, no doubt with exaggeration, that he had sacrificed £6,000 by living in Boston rather than improving his country estate.[2]

By the 1690's Wait was best known as an amateur physician. He was frequently called Doctor Winthrop. He carried on his father's benevolent practice of medicating large numbers of friends and neighbors. Cotton Mather in 1689 speaks of "the many hundred Sick people, whom your charitable and skilful Hands have most freely dispens'd your no less generous than secret Medicines to." Wait's top secret medicine was *rubila*, a red powder of niter and antimony which John Winthrop, Jr., had taught him to make. Another favorite concoction was horehound shredded into warm milk from a red cow, which cured Wait's consumptive cough in 1694 "almost to a miracle (God be praised)." Undoubtedly his medical practice was cruder than that of his learned and inventive father. Wait asked Fitz in London to send him the English translation of the chemist Glauber's works; John Winthrop, Jr.'s library had Glauber only in Latin. Wait also asked his brother for a camlet cloak, a summer suit, a hat and—most important—two wigs, since he had recently cut off his hair.[3]

In the aftermath of the Boston revolution, Wait was an uneasy celebrity. It was reported in New York that "Capt. Winthrop, Coll. Shrimpton, Coll. Page, John Nelson, &c., ware the chief actors in this affaire." Wait wrote to Andros' New York councilors, explaining that the Council of Safety could neither restore nor release Sir Edmund.[4] The Massachusetts coalition

[2] Wait was not a prominent investor in Boston shipping. The Massachusetts shipping register, 1697-1714, records sixty-nine men who invested in ten or more vessels, but Wait Winthrop was not among them. See Bernard and Lotte Bailyn, *Massachusetts Shipping, 1697-1714* (Cambridge, 1959), pp. 128-33. Also, M.H.S. *Coll.*, 5th ser., V, 323; VIII, 493-98, 510-12, 535; Winthrop Mss., X, 5; Deeds, 76, 80; *Randolph*, V, 216-17.

[3] G. L. Burr, ed., *Narratives of the Witchcraft Cases, 1648-1706* (New York, 1914), p. 94; M.H.S. *Coll.*, 5th ser., VIII, 502-503, 511-12.

[4] Hutchinson, *History of Massachusetts-Bay*, I, 321, 327-28; N.Y.H.S. *Coll.*, I, 244, 251, 266; M.H.S. *Coll.*, 5th ser., I, 437; Winthrop Mss., XI, 89; XII, 135-36.

was bound together in 1689 by fear of counterrevolution. When Cotton Mather published his *Memorable Providences* two months after the revolt, he ostentatiously dedicated it to Wait Winthrop, "whom I reckon among the Best of my Friends, and the Ablest of my Readers"—and Mather might have added, the newest convert to orthodoxy. In December 1689 Wait helped gather and prepare evidence against his former colleagues, Andros, Randolph, and Dudley. The next month, at the request of the General Court, he joined four other turncoat Dominion councilors—William Stoughton, Samuel Shrimpton, Thomas Hinckley, and Bartholomew Gedney—in writing an exposé of Andros' regime. Long before the Boston revolt, it seems, these patriotic councilors had become "much dissatisfied and discouraged" with Andros' arbitrary conduct, "and had little reason to wonder that soe great a number of the People were soe too." Plaintively, they described how Sir Edmund had ignored and overruled them in council meetings, and how they had vainly disapproved of his tax and land policies. "The Places that we held were rendred exceeding uneasie to us," the authors concluded. Their statement evidently pleased the Massachusetts government, for it was published in Boston in 1691.[5]

For seven months after Andros' overthrow, the Massachusetts rebels waited tensely for endorsement from William III's rebel government at home. It was December 1, 1689, before orders were received from the King to continue the existing colony administration until further notice, and to send Andros, Randolph, Dudley, and the other Dominion prisoners back to England for trial. Once they were put on shipboard in February 1690, the worst danger seemed over, and the Massachusetts coalition was dominated for the next two years by exponents of the old orthodoxy. The aged Bradstreet continued to be reelected a figurehead governor, two-thirds of the Assistants were holdovers from 1685, and the deputies in General Court kept agitating for royal confirmation of the charter.[6] Wait Winthrop

[5] Burr, *Witchcraft Cases, 1648-1706*, p. 94; M.A., Court Records, VI, 35-36, 93-94, 98; *Andros*, I, 133-47. There is a copy of the Dominion councilors' statement, dated January 27, 1690, in Winthrop Mss., X, 80.

[6] Hutchinson, *History of Massachusetts-Bay*, I, 331; *Cal.S.P.Col., 1689-1692*, pp. 196-97, 205-206, 214-16, 272; M.A., Court Records, VI, 104-105, 197-98.

was the only ex-Dominion councilor to be returned to the bench of Assistants in every election, 1689-1692. He was named Major General every year also, and served on various military committees. But when Massachusetts joined Connecticut and New York in an ambitious three-pronged invasion of Canada in 1690, Wait took no part in the campaign. The Massachusetts hero in 1690 was Sir William Phips, a lucky, plucky sailor who captured Port Royal, though he was totally unable to take Quebec. The attack on Canada ended in failure, but to the confused and rudderless people of Massachusetts, Phips (with no experience in pre-1689 politics) looked like the rising man. Wait Winthrop's popularity, however, was slipping. In the 1691 nominations for the magistracy, Wait polled 942 votes, more than any other candidate except Bradstreet, but election returns for 1692 show that he was twelfth among the eighteen Assistants, and Phips was first.[7] In the Massachusetts crisis atmosphere, Wait was being shouldered aside by more energetic men.

The colonists' hopes and fears were jangled by the home government's imposition of a new, restricted royal charter. This charter of 1691 was a product of England's ambiguous postrevolutionary colonial policy. At first, spokesmen for the colony had hoped that the Convention Parliament would pass a corporation act declaring that corporate charters could not be forfeited, thus restoring the old Massachusetts charter along with the many other charters annulled by Charles II and James II. The new King objected to this infringement of his prerogative. The charter issue had been blunted in England by James II's last minute restoration of all the forfeited English municipal charters, and William III killed the corporation bill by dissolving Parliament in February 1690. Thereupon, advocates of imperial centralization hoped that the King would restore the Dominion of New England. When Andros, Randolph, and Dudley arrived to tell their tale in April 1690, the Lords of Trade quickly dismissed charges against them. Andros' sup-

[7] M.H.S. *Coll.*, 5th ser., v, 360; 6th ser., v, 26-27; M.A., Court Records, vi, 35, 73, 117, 133, 140, 183, 214-15; Winthrop Mss., x, 7-8; *Cal.S.P.Col., 1689-1692*, p. 410.

porters in Massachusetts heard in 1691 that Sir Edmund was returning to Boston with a regiment and reported that "young Mather, Dr. Winthrop and several others are on the wing for England, fearful that when the Governor arrives they may be brought to the test."[8] But King William settled on a compromise that satisfied neither Puritans nor Tories. He granted Massachusetts a new royal charter with more generous boundaries than the old, since it incorporated Plymouth, Maine, and Nova Scotia, but less generous political privileges. The new royal province of Massachusetts was a more manageable unit than the Dominion of New England, and it offered its inhabitants far more self-government.

The most important feature of the 1691 charter was that the Governor and Lieutenant-Governor were royally appointed instead of popularly elected. The Governor's independence was greatly increased, and also his exposure. He named all military and judicial officers, called and dissolved the General Court, and vetoed legislation. More nakedly than before, he was the servant of two masters—of the King, who appointed him, sent him orders, and reviewed his decisions; and of the House of Representatives (equivalent to the old Deputies), which paid his salary. The new charter curtailed the independence and weight of the Council (equivalent to the old Assistants), though this was not to be apparent during the administrations of Phips, Stoughton, and Bellomont, 1692-1702. The new Council had twenty-eight members rather than eighteen; it was elected by the General Court (subject to the Governor's veto) instead of by the freemen; its judicial business was taken over by the newly created Massachusetts Superior Court; its executive powers were very largely absorbed by the Governor. The new charter also broadened the franchise by requiring only a modest forty shilling property freehold, providing almost universal male suffrage. However, the first beneficiaries from this change were not the small farmers but the Boston merchants. Paradox-

---

[8] *Ibid.*, pp. 563-64. Wait Winthrop's brother-in-law Richard Wharton, who in 1688 had helped Increase Mather to lobby against Andros in London, died in May 1689, when negotiations with William III were only just beginning.

ically, while the 1691 charter distributed power to the Governor and Representatives, weakening the basis for a Massachusetts ruling caste, its immediate effect was to consolidate the colony's postrevolutionary oligarchy.

Sir William Phips was nominated by Increase Mather as the first royal governor. To complement Phips, Mather's choice as lieutenant-governor was William Stoughton, who had managed to participate in every Massachusetts government throughout the revolutionary crisis. Mather likewise named the twenty-eight charter councilors, to serve until 1693. He selected Winthrop as well as several merchant "moderates" from the Council of Safety who had been left out of office since 1689, and he excluded six Assistants in the Bradstreet regime who had most tenaciously fought for the continuation of the old charter.[9] In every way, the new charter and Mather's nominations swung Massachusetts away from her traditional social pattern. Everything seemed designed to the perfect taste of Wait Winthrop.

◆? WHEN Sir William Phips and Increase Mather arrived in Boston late one Saturday in May 1692, the Governor ordered the ceremonial cannon salutes to be postponed till Monday, so as not to violate the Sabbath. Clearly Massachusetts was not yet entirely reconstructed. Phips assured his fellow colonists that he was God's instrument for the preservation of their ancient privileges. He was also the King's lieutenant, the most dominating executive Massachusetts had yet seen except for Andros. Wait Winthrop took a principal part in the administrative reorganization. He helped to revise the colony laws, and in July 1692 Phips reappointed him commander of the colony militia. Wait was now regarded as the senior councilor.[10] Apparently he was entering into a secure and solid regime. Actu-

[9] Hutchinson, *History of Massachusetts-Bay*, II, 4-9; *Cal.S.P.Col., 1689-1692*, p. 545; K. B. Murdock, *Increase Mather* (Cambridge, 1925), pp. 251-52. For an analysis of Massachusetts' potential political democracy under the 1691 charter, see Robert E. Brown, *Middle-Class Democracy and the Revolution in Massachusetts, 1691-1780* (Ithaca, 1955), chs. 2-6.

[10] *Cal.S.P.Col., 1689-1692*, p. 653; M.A., Court Records, VI, 222-37; Winthrop Mss., Deeds, p. 72.

ally, Phips' governorship was a disaster and lasted only two years.

Sir William had the misfortune to enter office in the midst of colonial New England's ugliest panic, the witchcraft epidemic at Salem Village. Accusations had started in February 1692, and by the time Phips arrived, Salem jail was full and the mania was spreading to other towns. An outsider like Andros or Bellomont, however much he believed in witchcraft or feared being himself labelled a witch, could have seen that his duty as governor was to give the accused common-law justice and to restore peace and order. Sir William Phips was an insider, or rather, he wanted to become an insider. Unsure of his administrative responsibilities, deferential to the clergy on spiritual matters, he was peculiarly ill equipped, psychologically and intellectually, to handle this crisis. The morbid fantasies of the Salem people were symptomatic of Massachusetts' general social malaise, torn between the dead Puritan formulas of the past and an unknown, seemingly purposeless future. The new Governor's sponsors, Increase and Cotton Mather, not only shared the almost universal belief in witchcraft but had long been preaching that, unless New Englanders confessed their sins and repented, God in His wrath would let loose the Devil in the shape of Indian massacres and witch torments. The Mathers' only recipe for handling the scores of alleged Salem witches was the traditional covenant formula of prayer, confession, and repentance. In the frenzy of 1692, this meant that innocent persons accused of witchcraft must either imperil their souls by making lying confessions of guilt, or imperil their lives by standing trial for the capital offense of witchcraft.

About fifty of the accused did confess to being witches, and turned into witnesses against the other witches. But some of the accused obdurately protested their innocence. Immediately upon Phips' landing, and before the General Court convened, the council persuaded the Governor to issue a special commission of oyer and terminer to seven councilors who would try the unrepentant witch suspects. Phips wrote Blathwayt that the seven judges were "persons of the best prudence and figure that could then be pitched upon"; they were also a perfect microcosm of the Massachusetts ruling coalition. Stoughton was chief judge; Wait Winthrop and Bartholomew Gedney were old "moderates"; Samuel Sewall, John Richards, and Nathaniel Saltonstall were old "orthodox"; Peter Sergeant was a merchant newcomer to the council. Phips left the whole matter to his judges' discretion and took up the more congenial business of fighting Indians in Maine. The court opened at Salem on June 2, 1692.[11]

The commission of oyer and terminer was by far the most important judicial action Wait Winthrop ever participated in. The court sat at Salem, the center of the hysteria. It operated under the rules of the defunct charter government, with jurors drawn only from church membership rolls and the defendants permitted no counsel. The Boston clergy urged "exquisite caution": spectral evidence is insufficient for the conviction of witches, since the Devil may torment his victims by taking the shape of innocent men. But the judges thought they knew better, that the Devil cannot impersonate the innocent, and so they wantonly depended on spectral evidence. The prisoners were often chained to stop them from tormenting their alleged victims, and the jailors found that when they were fettered neck and heels they were more likely to confess their witchery.

Wait Winthrop and his fellow judges were caught in the hideously rising tempo of panic. The court began by sentencing Bridget Bishop to death in early June. One month later, it condemned five women, inducing the jury in the case of Rebecca Nurse to reverse its original verdict of not guilty. In August, six men and women (including the Reverend George Burroughs) were sentenced at the court's third session. In September there were two sessions, and the court condemned fifteen persons. By September 22, 1692, the judges had tried twenty-seven suspects, all of whom denied being witches and all of whom were sentenced to death. Nineteen had actually been hanged, and Giles Corey had been pressed to death for refusing to stand jury trial. None of the fifty confessed witches had been tried or executed, but there were another one hundred accused in prison waiting trial, and two hundred more accused

[11] Burr, *Witchcraft Cases*, pp. 93-95, 112-13, 196, 355.

who had not yet been imprisoned. Among the new suspects were Lady Phips and the Reverend Samuel Willard of Wait Winthrop's Boston South Church. The judges, as though bewitched themselves, could only drive on and on. By October, Increase Mather was throwing his influence against the court's continuation, and Thomas Brattle, in a famous public letter, was censuring it openly. The Governor finally stepped in and called a halt. The commission of oyer and terminer never reconvened in Salem after September 22.

Obviously Wait Winthrop's tragic work at Salem was closer in spirit to his grandfather's prosecution of Antinomians than to his father's protection of Quakers. Still, according to the contemporary accounts of the Salem proceedings, Wait played a relatively inconspicuous part. He did not resign from the court in disgust, like Nathaniel Saltonstall, nor did he exhibit the conspicuously vengeful zeal of magistrates John Hathorne and Jonathan Corwin, who arraigned most of the suspects, and Chief Judge Stoughton, who presided over their execution. Nor did he have the courage or conviction to admit publicly that he had done wrong at Salem, like Judge Sewall, who stood up in South Meetinghouse in 1697 and asked to take the shame and blame.[12]

For three months after Phips stopped the commission of oyer and terminer, the witch trials hung in abeyance. In November and December the General Court rearranged Massachusetts' judicial system in keeping with the 1691 charter, and Phips' council voted for five justices to staff the new Superior Court. Four of the five appointees, including Wait Winthrop, were Salem judges, but their procedure was altered. Under Phips' orders to ignore spectral evidence, the Superior Court took up the witch trials at Salem in January 1693. It considered the cases of more than fifty witch suspects, dismissed half of them for lack of evidence, tried twenty-six, and sentenced three women to death. Phips reprieved even these, to Chief Justice Stoughton's great rage. The witch hangings were over, and the panic passed. It left indelible, hidden scars. In political terms, the Salem tragedy shook Phips' coalition administration and

[12] Burr, *Witchcraft Cases*, pp. 184-85, 200, 206, 212-13, 251, 351-52, 358-59, 363, 373, 385-88; M.H.S. *Coll.*, 5th ser., V, 309-10.

especially damaged the credit of Increase and Cotton Mather. Champions of the old charter and Boston merchants inclined toward the new Toryism were alike critical of the witch trials, and by 1693 were actively campaigning against Governor Phips.[13]

The King was likewise quickly disenchanted with Sir William's administration of Massachusetts. Phips' stop to the witch trials was about the only thing he did that the home government approved. Complaints reached London that the choleric Governor had dragged Jahleel Brenton, the customs collector, around a Boston wharf, thrashing him with his cane and fists. There was a similar street scuffle with Captain Short, commander of the royal frigate *Nonesuch*, in which Phips knocked Short down, hit him over the head with his cane, and threw him into jail "among witches, villains, negroes and murderers" for nine months. Phips was said to be personally engaged in illicit trade and to have sponsored a colony law exempting Massachusetts from the requirements of the navigation acts.[14] When the speaker of the House of Representatives, Nathaniel Byfield, agitated for closer political dependence on England, with Joseph Dudley as royal governor, Phips expelled him from the House. But in February 1694, the King recalled Phips to England to answer charges of misconduct.[15]

Sir William acknowledged the King's summons in July 1694 but delayed sailing in order to rally the General Court into giving him a vote of confidence. Phips still had the Mathers' blessing and enough general popularity to provide him with a slim majority in the lower house. But the upper house wanted to get rid of him. Stoughton was bitter over the witch reprieves, and most of the councilors were disgusted with the Governor's bumpkin statecraft. Finally the General Court agreed on an address (October 31, 1694) to the King and Queen, which asked

[13] Burr, *Witchcraft Cases*, pp. 184, 200-201, 382-83; M.H.S. *Coll.*, 5th ser., V, 366-67, 370-71; M.A., Court Records, VI, 280; Hutchinson, *History of Massachusetts-Bay*, II, 52-53.

[14] *Cal.S.P.Col.*, *1693-1696*, pp. 5-6, 63-64, 67-68, 209-10, 246, 250.

[15] *Ibid.*, *1689-1692*, pp. 408-409; *1693-1696*, pp. 224, 294-95; Bailyn, *New England Merchants*, p. 192; Hutchinson, *History of Massachusetts-Bay*, II, 59-60; Robert E. Brown, *Middle-Class Democracy and the Revolution in Massachusetts*, pp. 63-64.

that Sir William be kept on as governor. Phips sailed on November 17, reached London in January 1695, and died almost immediately, on February 18, before the Lords of Trade had time to hear his case.

Wait Winthrop had been a silent participant in the uproar about Phips' regime. He was not even present during the General Court session in the fall of 1694; he considered it more important to visit New London and check on his brother's affairs, since Fitz was away in England. Fitz expressly hoped that the King would not dismiss Phips. He accompanied Phips to Whitehall, nursed him in his illness, and wrote feelingly to Wait upon his death.[16] Wait must have shared Fitz's sorrow. For Phips' downfall imperilled the Massachusetts coalition and and undermined Wait's middling political philosophy. Now he must decide whether to peg his political future on the new Toryism, or revert to the old orthodoxy.

During the half-dozen years following Phips' recall, Wait Winthrop was gradually drawn into the climactic episode of his public career—a duel with Joseph Dudley for the governorship of Massachusetts. The rivalry had been growing since 1689, when Winthrop staked his future on serving the local electorate and Dudley staked his on serving the crown. While Wait was entrenching himself in the Massachusetts council, Dudley schemed against Phips in England and tried to get appointed as Sir William's successor. The home government procrastinated, and Lieutenant-Governor Stoughton took charge of the Bay colony from November 1694 to May 1699. Stoughton's council reverted to the formula of Dudley's council in 1686: a body of New England gentlemen managing the colony quietly and expediently in the name of the King but to the benefit of themselves. Wait Winthrop had not joined effectively in the spoils system of 1686, and again in the late 1690's he stood aside, half-jealous and half-contemptuous of his more purposeful colleagues. It greatly upset Wait to see Stoughton cultivate Byfield and keep in touch with Dudley.

<hr />

[16] M.A., Court Records, VI, 363, 370-71, 374-75; *Cal.S.P.Col.*, *1693-1696*, pp. 309, 390; M.H.S. *Coll.*, 5th ser., VIII, 326, 501-502.

"I believe it is not my opinion alone," he wrote in 1699, "that the ruine of the antient liberty of this country is instrumentally owing to the pride, ambition, avarice, of som such. . . ."[17] More and more, Wait Winthrop became a defender of the old New England verities.

Everything about Stoughton's government seemed less happy than Phips' regime to Wait. He kept his appointment as justice of the Massachusetts Superior Court, but his name disappeared from council and General Court committee lists in 1695. "We are under ill circumstances here," he grumbled to Fitz, "and poore management with respect to the Indian warr." As a member of Stoughton's council, he found himself isolated from the lower house and the general populace. More plainly than ever before in the history of the Massachusetts General Court, the Lieutenant-Governor and council formed an inner coterie, espoused the prerogative, and pitted themselves against the representatives, who stood for local self-determination. In 1696 the representatives voted that an agent be sent to England to work "for restoration of the Ancient Priviledges of the Colonies of the Massachusets, and New Plimouth, with further Additions of Power, and Government." The council vetoed the plan. Wait was absent on this occasion, but he doubtless sympathized with the representatives. Connecticut's charter privileges, he told Secretary Allyn in 1696, ought to be preserved "for the sake of an honest and good people, who would serve God according to his own institutions, for which our fathers left all that was desirable to com hither, and which will in liklyhood in a grate measure be lost if these constitutions should chang, which I pray God yet to continue if it be his will."[18]

In 1698 Wait established an alliance with Massachusetts' London agent, Sir Henry Ashurst, against "the Jacobites," as he called Dudley, Stoughton, and Byfield. Ever since the Revolution, Sir Henry had made himself the Whitehall missionary for Massachusetts Puritanism. He helped Increase Mather negotiate the 1691 charter. But how could he save New Eng-

---

[17] M.H.S. *Coll.*, 6th ser., v, 50.
[18] Winthrop Mss., Deeds, p. 82; M.H.S. *Coll.*, 5th ser., VIII, 514, 522-23, 525-26; M.A., Court Records, VI, 492-93.

land when Stoughton's administration threatened to drop him as the Massachusetts agent? Ashurst had to find backing within the colony, and to do so he opened correspondence with Wait Winthrop. "I have heard of your great fidelity to your country in the worst of times," Ashurst wrote Wait, "and of your zeale and piety, which makes me value you much and desire your frendshipp." Wait assured Sir Henry that "all the good people" of Massachusetts applauded his work in England. Then he poured out his own pent-up complaints against the Massachusetts ruling clique. Wait told Ashurst of Byfield's rising power: speaker of the House in 1698, councilor in 1699, with his daughter married to Stoughton's nephew. "Thay are fast to their own interest, but I know not to whose else." More broadly, Wait denounced the "factors and strangers" in Massachusetts, "who have in a little time got more by the government then all that have bin before. . . . [who] eat up the poor as bread and squeese them to death by virtue of an office. . . . but if I have bin any wayes instrumentall to save the best interest here and keep this people from that slavery which they were growing under and have almost forgot alredy, I am satisfyed."[19] Wait's woolly lamentations show that his politics hinged on family pride. The old charter government, for all its faults, had at least perpetuated his grandfather's moral cause. The new charter government jettisoned the Winthrop legacy and imported the modern English political vocabulary of *place*, *interest*, and *connection*.

Yet Wait himself in 1699 secured a place as judge of the Admiralty Court, thanks to his connection with Ashurst. When the Navigation Act of 1696 authorized the establishment of American vice-admiralty courts, which were special prerogative courts without juries, to try cases of illicit trade, Edward Randolph nominated Byfield as judge of the Massachusetts and New Hampshire Admiralty Court. Byfield presented his commission to the Massachusetts council in March 1698. Stoughton wanted to swear him in, but the council majority wanted to postpone the new court as long as possible. Wait complained to Ashurst, who expressed amazement at Byfield's

---

[19] M.H.S. *Coll.*, 5th ser., VIII, 533-35; 6th ser., V, 37, 39-41.

appointment. "I have bin laboring to the utmost of my power," Sir Henry told Wait in May 1699, "to get Byfield's place for you, and I have now atained itt to my great satisfaction, and your comition is a drawing; and I am glad I had an oppertunity to serve so good a man." Wait's commission (May 2, 1699) was broader than Byfield's. The King gave him jurisdiction over New York as well as Massachusetts and New Hampshire, with liberty of deputation. "I know not what profit it will be," Wait wrote Fitz as he took his judge's oath in October 1699, "but it breakes the measurs of the Jacobites." He thanked Ashurst and, while admitting his ignorance of admiralty procedure, promised the Board of Trade to serve the King faithfully "in that Station, as I have don in others, and not knowingly made any wrong step." Randolph was naturally not very pleased. The smugglers on the Bay council, he snorted, have "turn'd out Mr. Byfield a man zealous for haveing the Acts of Trade duly executed. . . . And made Mr. Waite Winthrop (a small Practitioner in Physick) to be Judge of That Court Tho' in no Sort qualifyed for the Office. . . ."[20]

The Winthrop-Ashurst alliance benefited Winthrop more than Ashurst. Wait undoubtedly was instrumental in getting the Massachusetts General Court to vote Ashurst £500 for his past services, but he could not prevent the court from dropping Ashurst in 1699 as the colony agent. "The truth is," he told Sir Henry, "we have a smale party . . . who have this many years don all thay could against your interest and ours too, hopeing to get their comrade Mr. D. to be Governor here and so drive on their private interest with the ruine of this people's libertyes. . . ." Massachusetts had no agent in London, 1699-1701. Ashurst kept pressing Wait for his reinstatement on a regular salary; Wait tried to move the General Court in 1700 and again in 1701, without success. Fortunately, just as Ashurst was being dismissed by Massachusetts, Fitz Winthrop asked him to become Connecticut's agent, and Sir Henry's hurt

[20] *Cal.S.P.Col.*, *1696–1697*, pp. 382-83; *1697–1698*, p. 141; *1699*, pp. 281, 457; M.H.S. *Coll.*, 5th ser., VIII, 533-34, 560-61; 6th ser., V, 40-45, 49, 56; Winthrop Mss., VII, 74a; VIIb, 50; *Randolph*, V, 267-68.

pride was a good deal eased on receipt of £200 in bills of exchange from Hartford.[21]

Ashurst took personal credit for the Board of Trade's appointment of the Earl of Bellomont, instead of Dudley, as governor of Massachusetts in 1697. He commended Bellomont to Wait as an honest man of sound principles, a real friend to New England. No doubt Wait relished the prospect of Bellomont rescuing Massachusetts from Stoughton, Byfield, and the other local placemen, yet the Board of Trade's appointment also illustrated Massachusetts' subordinate status. Bellomont was an outsider imposed on the colonists by the King, and (as in the Dominion of New England) he was given control of a vast territory: New York, Massachusetts, and New Hampshire. In 1698, Wait journeyed down to New York with two other delegates from the General Court to greet Bellomont, and he later told Ashurst that he found "his Lordship every way to answare the noble carracter your selfe with others have given him." A year passed before Bellomont came north to Boston, but at last in May 1699 he staged a grand entry. Much of the history of late seventeenth-century Massachusetts is compressed into the successive tableaux of new governors landing at Boston—Andros and his martial invasion of enemy territory in 1686; Phips and his homespun deference to the Sabbath in 1692; Bellomont and his Whiggish *noblesse oblige* in 1699. There was new ceremonial and new hierarchy in the General Court. Bellomont administered the oath of office to Lieutenant-Governor Stoughton; Stoughton administered the oath of office to the councilors; and four of the councilors administered the oath of office to the representatives. In his opening speech, Bellomont graciously thanked the Bay people for their welcome and daringly evoked the memory of 1688 by attacking Charles II and James II as "Aliens . . . [who] have not fought our Battles." He took William III as his model of the perfect governor: a noble patron of religion, liberty, property—and strong central authority.[22]

[21] M.A., Court Records, VII, 46; *Cal.S.P.Col.*, *1699*, pp. 352, 425, 432; M.H.S. *Coll.*, 6th ser., V, 42-43, 46-47, 60, 71, 80-83.

[22] *Ibid.*, 5th ser., VIII, 533; 6th ser., V, 42-43, 60; M.A., Court Records, VI, 566-70; VII, 1-9.

Bellomont evidently liked Wait Winthrop. He used his services much more than had Stoughton. In 1699 and 1700, Wait attended Bellomont on his travels to New Hampshire, Rhode Island, and New York. He was judge of both the Massachusetts Superior Court and the Admiralty Court, and since the Governor delegated a great deal of council work to committees, Wait sat on many committees also. Wait participated in the examination and arrest of the notorious Captain Kidd in 1699, and was disappointed when Bellomont sent Kidd to England for trial. "If the pirates and their goods had bin tryed here," he remarked to Ashurst, "as som people thought thay ought, there might have bin more advantage [i.e., profit for Admiralty Judge Winthrop] then ever is like to be again."

Wait was exceedingly deferential, not to say obsequious, toward the Earl of Bellomont. There are hints, however, of inner resentment, as toward Sir Edmund Andros ten years before. Bellomont was a far more benevolent viceroy than Andros; he sought popularity from the colonists as well as obedience to the King, and since he was often ill or absent, left most of the business of running Massachusetts to the council. But even by May 1700 he was greeting his second General Court less warmly, irked (despite his handsome £1,500 salary) by the opposition to his program. In July 1700 he departed for New York, never to return. He died in March 1701. After Bellomont's death, Wait wrote circumspectly to Ashurst: "The Truth is I was a little surprised to see som alterations in our Governors apprehensions (as they seemed to me at least) before he left this place . . . , but he has since left us all."[23]

Bellomont's death returned Massachusetts to the political pattern of 1695-1699, with Lieutenant-Governor Stoughton as regent. From Wait Winthrop's point of view, the situation in March 1701 was exasperating in the extreme. Ten years of the new charter had convinced him that the old charter was preferable, but by now most of the colonists had become reconciled to the new one! Obviously the Board of Trade would soon pick Bel-

[23] Winthrop Mss., Deeds, p. 84; M.A., Court Records, VII, 17, 52, 73-75, 121, 134-35; M.H.S. *Coll.*, 5th ser., VI, 20; VIII, 555, 561-66; 6th ser., V, 72-74, 81, 83.

lomont's successor, and Joseph Dudley (now living in England, with good connections at Whitehall and a seat in Parliament) was the leading candidate. Wait's opinion of Dudley was emphatic; he called him "a venimous serpent" in 1701. Stoughton was Dudley's friend, and the colony had no accredited agent in London. But Stoughton was nearly seventy years old and sickly. Wait calculated that there was enough personal dislike and fear of Dudley among the councilors and representatives so that, if he took the lead, a majority would rally behind him against Dudley. For years, Wait had deplored Massachusetts' clumsy dealings with the home government. Now, in the most daring stratagem of his career, Wait volunteered to go to England himself as Massachusetts' agent.

The news of Bellomont's death reached Boston on March 15, 1701, just as a General Court session was breaking up. Anticipating Wait's plan, Stoughton proposed to dissolve the court, thereby postponing discussion of the succession question until a new General Court was elected in May. After heated argument, the council got the Lieutenant-Governor to summon a special April session of the court. In this session, Wait overrode Stoughton's active opposition and called a conference between the two houses to formulate the colony's policy on a new Governor. The conference was a total failure. Bucking against the council's efforts to dictate policy, the representatives perversely voted an address to the King, asking that Stoughton be promoted to governor. The council rejected this idea. At the representatives' request, Stoughton dissolved the General Court.[24]

Two months passed, with Stoughton sinking into his last illness, and the succession crisis getting more acute. When the issue was revived in the next General Court, Wait had better success. Once more he was chairman of a joint committee, and this time his committee recommended (June 25, 1701) "that it is now a propper time to petition his Majestie for a restoration of some of our former priviledges, viz. the choosing of our Governor Lt Governor and Secretary, and such others as this Court shall think fitt." The council approved this recom-

[24] *Ibid.*, 5th ser., VI, 33; 6th ser., V, 83, 91, 93; M.A., Court Records, VII, 179-84.

mendation; the representatives rejected it. The deadlock of 1696 was reversed, with the upper house now championing local self-determination and the lower house upholding the prerogative; but the paralyzing effect was the same. However, on June 30 both houses agreed to send Wait Winthrop to England as the General Court's agent. Wait told Fitz that the decision was almost unanimous. "I have bin a little surprised about it, being altogether without my expectation. . . ." He asked Fitz's advice, obviously wanting to be urged to go. Lieutenant-Governor Stoughton adjourned the General Court without consenting to Winthrop's agency. But Stoughton could delay proceedings no further. On July 7 he died.[25]

By the process of elimination Wait Winthrop had become the leading man in Massachusetts. The council notified the Board of Trade (July 10, 1701) that the colony was without an executive and decided to carry on a stopgap administration by meeting every Wednesday and acting by majority rule. Since Wait was the senior ranking councilor, he performed when necessary as the chief executive. The council elected him to Stoughton's post as chief justice of the Superior Court. When the General Court reconvened on July 30, Wait gave the opening speech, reminding the representatives that his agency was not yet settled. Both houses voted to commission him as Massachusetts' agent and drafted his instructions. Wait asked for sweeping powers, proposing on August 6 that the court give him the authority and the money to obtain "a lasting settlement" from the King, based on "the enjoyment of the pure order of the Gospell which [our fathers] here set up, and has been ever since practised in the generallity of these churches." In plain language, Wait wanted to restore the 1629 charter.

As in June, the representatives would not consent to such conditions, so Wait withdrew his proposition on August 8. Sewall reports that Wait was forced to yield in order to get a majority, even in the council, to sign his commission. As it was, only fourteen of the twenty-two attending councilors did sign; Elisha Cooke was Wait's chief supporter; conspicuous among the eight abstainers was Nathaniel Byfield. The cost of the

[25] M.H.S. *Coll.*, 5th ser., VI, 38; 6th ser., V, 87; M.A., Court Records, VII, 202, 215-26; XX [Foreign Relations], 51-54; Winthrop Mss., VII, 113; X, 9.

agency was another vexed question. The court offered Wait £500, with an additional £500 in reserve, but Wait wanted to protect himself against a new governor, such as Dudley, cutting off his source of supply, and so he asked the court for £1,000, and an additional £1,000 "to be sequestred in sombody's hands." He was still hoping to amend or annul the 1691 charter. The representatives wanted time to consider Wait's terms, and the General Court was prorogued till September. "I suppose," Wait told his brother, "thay will comply therabouts; otherwise I think I shall not goe." Wait's twenty-year-old son, John, was very hopeful. As he told Uncle Fitz, "It will be a very advantageous oppertunity for me to see the world."[26]

Wait had procrastinated fatally. By the time the General Court reconvened in September 1701, the news of Dudley's appointment as governor had reached Boston. Wait tried to tell the court that the need for an agent was as strong as ever, but the representatives had lost all interest. The General Court did decide in October to hire an English agent, in order to defend Massachusetts against the 1701 parliamentary bill attacking charter colonies. But Wait could not even persuade the representatives to appoint Ashurst, and £100 was sent to Constantine Phips, Jacobite cousin of the late Massachusetts Governor. Wait was exceedingly mortified. He had taken the field against Dudley and the 1691 charter, only to find that he had no troops. The Massachusetts people, he complained to Fitz, have squandered "the opertunity which God had by a very extraordinary Providence given them, to adress for what they wanted there being nobody left to hinder them and thay will never have the like again. . . ." As months passed by with no sign of Dudley's arrival, Wait felt more and more frustrated. He wrote Fitz (October 27, 1701): "your Government are as senceless as ours and I think it is time for us to looke to ourselves since nothing but private interest is regarded."[27]

Sir Henry Ashurst did all he could to help Wait in England.

[26] M.A., Council Records, III, 218-19, 224; Court Records, VII, 225-37; XX [Foreign Relations], 56, 59-60, 64; M.H.S. *Coll.*, 5th ser., VI, 40; VIII, 572; 6th ser., V, 93-98, 513-14.

[27] M.A., Court Records, VII, 238-48; XX [Foreign Relations], 76-78; M.H.S. *Coll.*, 6th ser., III, 77-78; V, 98-100; Winthrop Mss., VII, 117-19.

As soon as he heard of Bellomont's death, Ashurst started working frantically to block Dudley. His hope was to keep the Massachusetts governorship vacant, as after Phips' death, and to put Winthrop in Stoughton's place as lieutenant-governor. In June 1701 the King decided to appoint Dudley governor, but Ashurst managed to suspend Dudley's commission for five months by petitioning the Lords Justices against him. Had Wait arrived in London as late as November 1701, he would have found Dudley's appointment still reversible. Sir Henry claimed that with a minimum of help from Massachusetts he could have defeated Dudley altogether. "If either your Counsel or Representives," he told Wait in 1702, "had addressed against him & sent itt to mee, he could not have gon." But Dudley pointed out to the Lords Justices that Ashurst was not Massachusetts' accredited agent. Dudley had powerful friends in the ministry, he had the Board of Trade's approval, as well as letters from Massachusetts supporters (including the Mathers—insulted by the General Court's selection of Wait Winthrop instead of Increase Mather as colony agent), and on December 11, 1701, his commission as governor and commander in chief of Massachusetts and New Hampshire was finally issued. There was further haggling over Dudley's Lieutenant-Governor. Ashurst pushed as hard as he could for Winthrop; Dudley pushed as hard as he could for Byfield. In April 1702, the post was given to an English army officer, Captain Thomas Povey. "If Mr. D. doe not pleas you," said Ashurst, "you may thank yorselves."[28]

One contributing factor in Dudley's victory of 1701 was that his two chief opponents, Winthrop and Ashurst, worked at cross purposes. Sir Henry, convinced that he was the only man with enough influence to stop Dudley, thought it was foolish for his provincial friend to take over the colony agency. "I am sorry you thinke of coming this dangerous season," he wrote Wait tartly on November 2, 1701. "I wish these were your friends that were for sending you out of the way to be agent. I am

[28] *Cal.S.P.Col.*, *1701*, pp. 304-305, 325, 610, 670; *1702*, p. 216; M.H.S. *Coll.*, 6th ser., v, 84-85, 88-92, 109; Hutchinson, *History of Massachusetts-Bay*, II, 92, 96; Everett Kimball, *The Public Life of Joseph Dudley* (New York, 1911), p. 75.

sure they were Mr. D.'s friends." Ashurst was horrified by Wait's apparent aim of restoring the 1629 charter. "Whoever advised the addressing for the old [charter], had a mind, in my humble opinion, to ruine your countrey; nothing could further D.'s going more effectually than that." Ashurst told Wait that Dudley had been able to veto his appointment as lieutenant-governor by producing "leters that said you moved in the Counsel that now thare Governer & Lef Governer was dead they might take upon them thar old charter." Wait hotly denied that he had made or heard any such motion, but his program in 1701 *did* hark back to Massachusetts' good old days, "as in their beginning when men were not seekers of themselves but spent (som of them) great estates to serve the publick interest."[29]

Wait's effort to resurrect Massachusetts' traditional orthodoxy and her traditional freedom from outside control was supported neither by the House of Representatives, bastion of self-government, nor by Sir Henry Ashurst, pillar of Puritanism. His duel with Joseph Dudley for the leadership of Massachusetts in 1701 was simply no contest. After the collapse of his agency plan, Wait never again presumed to speak for New England.

꙰ THE rebuff of 1701 marked the first time that the New England colonists had ventured to reject the leadership of the Winthrop dynasty in a time of crisis. Wait took his children down to New London for a long visit, thus avoiding the unpleasantness of Dudley's grand entry into Boston (June 11, 1702). He considered the possibility of staying in Connecticut permanently.[30]. Though he returned to Massachusetts and took his seat on Dudley's council, he found that the political power he had enjoyed for the last dozen years was gone. Under Dudley, he compromised his credo of "antient liberty" by becoming the Governor's placeman. He devoted his old age to petty quarrels over the disposition of the family estate, despite his

[29] M.H.S. *Coll.*, 6th ser., III, 86; V, 100-101, 109-11; Winthrop Mss., VII, 138.
[30] M.H.S. *Coll.*, 5th ser., VI, 57-60; 6th ser., V, 109-13.

scorn for "private interest." The final years of Wait's life were a continuous, painful retreat from his platform of 1701.

Governor Dudley's arrival was the most important political event in Massachusetts since the Glorious Revolution. Dudley broke up the loose coalition which had ruled Massachusetts since 1689 and consolidated the political and social division between court (the Governor and Council) and country (the House of Representatives). He insisted on loyalty and subservience from his councilors, prohibiting secret balloting in council meetings. Dudley tried to cow the lower house in similar fashion, by sending endless messages of instruction, challenging its privileges, and scornfully criticizing its performance. The representatives, with their separate corporate identity and their power of the purse, fought back in what would become the standard eighteenth-century pattern, by starving Dudley on an annual salary of £300 or less. The charter of 1691 was at last in full operation.

In the new political pattern, Wait Winthrop was shunted aside. The Governor let Wait keep his council seat, no doubt preferring to have him under his thumb without making him a popular martyr. But Dudley did drop Wait from the Massachusetts Superior Court, and the Board of Trade commissioned William Atwood in Wait's place as judge of admiralty for New England and New York. Wait professed to be happy to surrender the Admiralty Court, "having never bin reimbursed halfe the charge I have bin unavoydably put upon," but he complained soon enough to Fitz that Atwood was tyrannically abusing his jurisdiction.[31]

During the first five years of Dudley's governorship, Wait attended about half the council meetings and headed a good many committees. He seldom spoke out in debate and took no important part in directing Massachusetts' defense against the French and Indian attacks in Queen Anne's War. His letters to Fitz and to Ashurst were discreetly silent about Dudley's administration. "The times are so hazardous," he wrote Ashurst, "that I can not give you account of many things as I

[31] M.A., Council Records, III, 341, 349, 362, 365-67; M.H.S. *Coll.*, 6th ser., V, 84, 97, 101-102; Winthrop Mss., VII, 120; X, 124; *Cal.S.P.Col., 1702-1703*, p. 557.

would, therefore must be excused." The colonists' docile submission to Dudley baffled and angered Sir Henry. "Thar is little couradge amounge you," he replied to Wait; "if you boldly oppos, D. could doe you no harme." And again, "I doe hope you will see a new Governour, but you deserve none for being so poor spirited."[32]

In 1707, Wait had a chance to turn tables on Joseph Dudley. The Massachusetts Governor was in serious trouble: the French war had gone very badly, the General Court had punished four of Dudley's merchant friends for trading with the enemy, Cotton Mather had published a scandalous diatribe in London against him, Nathaniel Higginson and others had petitioned the Queen for his removal, and Dudley's supporters on the Board of Trade had been dismissed. In September 1707, Ashurst gave Wait "the joyfull newes that I have, after all my paines, expence, & labor for so many yeares removed for-ever from being your oppressive Governor Mr. D. I doe hope to send you a new comition to bee Left. Governer of New England [i.e., Massachusetts] & New Hampshire."

But Wait Winthrop had chosen another road to Damascus. At the very time Ashurst was writing his premature news, Wait was coming to terms with "Mountseer" as he nicknamed Dudley. His son John revealed in August 1707 that he and Anne Dudley were in love; the two fathers agreed to the match in September, and the wedding took place on December 16. The political consequences of this Winthrop-Dudley marriage were almost indecently rapid. On February 11, 1708, Governor Dudley asked Wait to write on his behalf to Ashurst—"Sir Hary would beleive your representation of mee as an honest man." Two weeks later, Wait Winthrop was restored to his old office of chief justice of the Massachusetts Superior Court.[33]

After 1707 Wait Winthrop played a double game, encouraging Ashurst to continue working against Dudley in England, while keeping on good terms with Dudley in Massachusetts.

---

[32] M.H.S. *Coll.*, 6th ser., V, 128-32, 138. My estimate of Wait's role in Massachusetts, 1702-1707, is based on a survey of the court and council records for the period, on Wait's correspondence (M.H.S. *Coll.*, 6th ser., V, 115-51), and on Sewall's *Diary* (*Ibid.*, 5th ser., VI, 60-195).

[33] *Ibid.*, 5th ser., VI, 196-218; 6th ser., V, 151-53, 163-64; Winthrop Mss., Deeds, p. 90.

When he saw that Sir Henry had not succeeded in removing Dudley, Wait wrote in March 1708 that he would accept only the governorship of Massachusetts, not the lieutenant-governorship: "if I am fit for that, I am as fit for the other, if the charge of procuring it be not over great." The Lieutenant-Governor, Wait explained, has no power nor salary unless the Governor is absent or dead, "and thay that wait for such shoose may go barefoot." Wait insisted that, though his son had married Dudley's daughter, he was no apostate. "I confesse," Ashurst replied, "your son's marrying D.'s daughter did coole & startle me; but your letter hath fully satisfied me." Ashurst was likewise cooled and startled upon discovering that the Massachusetts council in 1707 unanimously dismissed the Nathaniel Higginson petition, which charged Dudley with personal involvement in enemy trade, as scandalous and wicked. Wait privately excused himself to Ashurst. The Privy Council dismissed all charges against Dudley, but Ashurst continued to agitate singlehandedly for his removal and to address Wait mawkishly as the only true man left in New England. It was an absurdly illusory yet potent friendship between two men who never met, and Wait genuinely mourned for Sir Henry when he died in 1711.[34]

Dudley urged Wait to move to New London in 1707 after Fitz Winthrop's death, and take up his brother's office as governor of Connecticut. Wait did spend much of his last years in New London, but he continued as Massachusetts councilor and chief justice. In the years 1709-1710 he joined more actively than before in Dudley's administration, and helped plan the capture of Port Royal in 1710.[35] Much had changed in Massachusetts since 1702: Winthrop was now the Governor's henchman, while Byfield had become Dudley's bitter enemy. On the whole, the political tension had notably eased. The Governor and representatives, having long tested each other's strength, learned to work together against French Canada.

[34] M.A., Court Records, VIII, 318; M.H.S. *Coll.*, 5th ser., VI, 202; 6th ser., V, 165-66, 173-75, 180-81, 199, 214, 226-27, 255, 281-83; Winthrop Mss., VIII, pt. 2, p. 59.

[35] M.H.S. *Coll.*, 6th ser., V, 161, 164, 185-90; M.A., Court Records, VIII, 420, 447, 492, 500, 506; IX, 64.

Between 1711 and 1713 Wait stayed mostly in New London. Having been absent for over a year, he was dropped from the Massachusetts council in the May 1713 election. Sewall deplored this. "He was the great Stay and Ornament of the Council," Sewall wrote in his *Diary*, "a very pious, prudent, Couragious New-England Man. Some spread it among the Deputies, that he was out of the province, and not like to Return." When Wait did return to Boston, Dudley called an unprecedented special session (August 6, 1713), to replace a councilor who had died, and Wait was given back his council seat. From 1714 to 1717, he lived in Boston and attended council meetings regularly, despite painful illness (strangury) and gathering old age. He had the satisfaction of outlasting Governor Dudley, who was retired from office in 1715 at the accession of George I. Winthrop and Dudley remained on good, if not intimate terms. When the council, headed by Wait, briefly assumed control of the province in 1715 because the Governor's commission had expired, Wait was evidently no longer eager to dispossess Dudley. "I am sorry no orders are com about the Government," he wrote his son, "the councill all would have been glad the Governor might have . . . kept the place but it was thought inconsistent with the charter." Dudley's successor, Governor Samuel Shute, reissued Wait's commission as chief justice of the Massachusetts Superior Court. For much of his tenure, 1707-1717, Wait must have been an absentee chief justice. After his death, Sewall told Shute that "by reason of the inability of the late honorable Chief Justice Winthrop to ride the remoter Circuits, I have frequently presided."[36]

Wait's overriding concern in his last years was the preservation of his family estate. His marriage in 1707 to Katherine Brattle, a rich widow, entailed neither profit nor loss, since Wait and Katherine each renounced all claim to the other's estate. Fitz's death, on the other hand, placed the bulk of the Winthrop property in Wait's hands, but also saddled him with large debts and a violent family feud. According to Fitz's will

[36] M.H.S. *Coll.*, 5th ser., VI, 385, 392; 6th ser., II, 90; V, 230, 243, 267, 303-305; M.A., Court Records, IX, 312-15; Winthrop Mss., VIII, pt. 2, p. 79; Deeds, pp. 94, 96.

(March 14, 1702), his New London house and considerable adjoining property went to his daughter Mary Livingston, but Wait contended that he had held the Winthrop estate in joint tenancy with his brother, which invalidated Fitz's bequest to Mary Livingston. Governor Dudley officiously supported Wait. Having "had near fifty years a perticular intimacy & freindship" with Fitz Winthrop, Dudley testified that Fitz always intended to make John Winthrop his sole heir. "Sir," he wrote to Governor Saltonstall of Connecticut in 1708, "you will give me leave to tell you that [it] is the first family in this Province, and more then the first in your Collony. . . . We are some of us English gentlemen, . . . & we should labor to support such famalyes because truly we want them."[37] Wait's battle over Fitz's will was long and litigious. He continually suspected Governor Saltonstall of trying to injure him. The reverse was more true, since Wait did not pay Saltonstall his £500 bequest until 1715. Wait succeeded in retaining possession of the Connecticut property, but at the great cost of irritating Saltonstall, the New London people, and the Hartford Assembly.[38]

Never an efficient man of business, Wait Winthrop procrastinated hopelessly in his old age. Dudley urged repeatedly that he sell enough wilderness land to pay off his debts, that he settle with his tenants and with the Livingstons, and above all that he make his will. When Wait sold a farm in 1714 for £1,100, Dudley directed John Winthrop to "thank him heartily, & pray him that he will please with that money to put himself out of debt, & that he will execute a will and keep it always by him. . . ." But in 1715 Wait was borrowing more money, his brother's debts were still largely unpaid, and though he did draft a will (September 28, 1713), he left it unsigned and unwitnessed, and died intestate.

On October 28, 1717, Wait wrote his weekly letter to John in New London, cheerful and disconnected as usual, and concluding as he often did: "I long to see the poor children." Four

[37] M.H.S. *Coll.*, 6th ser., III, 413-20; V, 154-60, 164, 167-70; Winthrop Mss., VIII, pt. 2, pp. 26, 85; XVI, 70.
[38] M.H.S. *Coll.*, 6th ser., V, 257-60, 271, 278, 284-94; Winthrop Mss., VIII, pt. 2, pp. 48, 67-68, 72, 83, 85, 106.

days later he took to his bed, and on November 7 he died. Wait was seventy-five years old. His funeral was ceremonial and expensive. Governor Shute and ex-Governor Dudley led the procession through the crowded Boston streets, and Cotton Mather preached the sermon. His old friend Sewall succinctly eulogized Wait Winthrop: "for parentage, piety, prudence, philosophy, love to New England ways and people, very eminent."[39] It was true, as Sewall said, that Wait had grown into a New England Yankee. But his public life since 1689 had been a revealing story of failure. Trying to resurrect his grandfather's conception of liberty and authority within the framework of Massachusetts' 1691 charter, Wait Winthrop lost ignominiously, and ended his days as Governor Dudley's creature in the brave new world of place, interest and connection.

[39] M.H.S. *Coll.*, 4th ser., VIII, 27; 6th ser., V, 267, 283, 352-70; Winthrop Mss., VIII, pt. 2, p. 85; XII, 170. Sewall's unsuccessful courtship of Wait's widow, Madam Winthrop, in 1720 is the most celebrated passage in the Judge's *Diary*.

13. Salvaging the Connecticut Charter

FITZ WINTHROP'S postrevolutionary career was notably more successful than his younger brother's. Like Wait, he found that the Glorious Revolution opened a new world to him. He became the governor of Connecticut colony and the champion of her traditional liberties. He spent the last fifteen years of his life fighting off a wide variety of attacks upon the royal charter which John Winthrop, Jr., had obtained in 1662. The two brothers adopted the same formula after 1689; the great difference was that Fitz's colony was less affected by the English imperial reorganization than Massachusetts, and better able to stay free from home control.

It took much pressure to convince Fitz that he must champion Connecticut's chartered privileges in the 1690's. He had been more hostile than his brother to New England's pre-1686 charter government and less distressed than Wait by Andros' Dominion of New England. He tried in 1689 to be neutral and stay out of politics. Yet increasingly he felt forced, like his brother, to stand for a middling political program between two enemy camps. On the one hand, Gershom Bulkeley and Edward Palmes were appealing to England for continuation of royal government in Connecticut, or at least the curtailment of the colony's autonomy. On the other, James Fitch was appealing to the common people in the colony for democratic reforms of the charter government, thus winning great popularity and large land tracts from the General Assembly. Fitz's hostility to both of these programs explains his increasingly prominent role in Connecticut affairs during the 1690's. It is the thread connecting his three most conspicuous deeds in the decade after the Revolution: his military expedition against French Canada in 1690; his agency in England to preserve his father's charter,

1693-1697; and his assumption of the Connecticut governorship in 1698.

◄ℛ Fitz took no part in the Revolution of 1689 in Connecticut. Having turned down Andros' request that he command a campaign against the Indians in Maine, Fitz spent the winter of 1688-1689 in New London. There is a dark passage in Gershom Bulkeley's *Will and Doom*, describing "J.W. his going to Boston . . . so near about the time of Sir E.A. his apprehension, for he came to Boston the very day that Sir Edmund was apprehended; his siding with the transaction, taking advice there, and busy promoting of the revolution here after he came back. . . ." Since Andros had summoned out-of-town councilors to meet in Boston, April 18, 1689, we might deduce that Bulkeley was talking about John Winthrop. But he was not. At the time of the Boston coup, Fitz was once more conveniently sick in New London. "I hope in God the worst is over" his brother Palmes wrote Wait on April 23, "and that hee will bee soone able to walke abroad."[1]

The political effects of Andros' surrender were very much the same in Connecticut as in Massachusetts. The immediate question was how should the colony be governed, and to this there were three contrary answers. Those led by James Fitch, who regarded Andros' annexation of Connecticut in 1687 as usurpation, wanted direct resumption of charter government and called for the annual election of new colony officers at Hartford on May 9, 1689. They hoped to exclude men like Secretary Allyn and Samuel Willys, to say nothing of Fitz Winthrop, for collaborating with Andros. At the opposite extreme, Gershom Bulkeley of Wethersfield wanted to continue the Dominion administration and persuaded his townsmen to boycott the Hartford election. Bulkeley wrote a tract entitled *The People's Right to Election Argued*, contending that the Connecticut corporation was dissolved in 1687 while the Dominion was still in force, since its power derived from the King whether or not Andros surrendered his governorship.[2] A mid-

---

[1] C.H.S. *Coll.*, III, 151; Winthrop Mss., XVI, 67.
[2] C.H.S. *Coll.*, I, 62-69; III, 154-55.

dle party, whose leaders included Allyn, Willys, and the Reverend Timothy Woodbridge of Hartford, wanted the charter restored but also wanted to share in the new government and feared the consequences of Fitch's sudden election held in an atmosphere of mob hysteria. These men, whose position resembled the Council of Safety in Boston, turned to Fitz for help.

About May 1, 1689, Allyn and Woodbridge each asked Fitz to come to Hartford for the election, in the hope of "chooseing your selfe Governor." Their invitation found Fitz in a discouragingly nebulous mood. He had refused to join Andros' four councilors in New York in planning how to continue royal government in the southern half of the Dominion, but his replies to Allyn and Woodbridge were not very helpful either. He seemed to say that Andros' overthrow was a good thing, but it would be best to retain the Dominion administration until instructed from England, yet "there is noe striveinge against the streame of popular resolution" if the people insist on a hasty election, and, while his illness must excuse him from coming to Hartford, he hoped Allyn and Willys would accept office. This did not satisfy Allyn. "If you fayle of coming," he wrote Fitz on May 6, more sharply than ever before or after, "I beleive you will repent of it, for . . . I know you can doe as much towards the preventing of inconveniences & defeating the designes of Colonel Fitch & those with him here & elswhere, as any man amongst us. Sir, you must not desert your friends, or not let them want your assistance at such a time as this." Fitz did start out for Hartford, but fell sick again at Middletown and got no further.[3]

The Connecticut election on May 9, 1689, was a compromise. The freemen protested vociferously against restoring to power the men who had betrayed their charter to Andros, yet they were prevailed upon to re-establish Governor Treat and his 1687 panel of magistrates, so that Allyn and Fitch were both on the council. Fitz and Willys were made magistrates, to fill two vacancies. According to Bulkeley's *Will and Doom*, the free-

[3] Winthrop Mss., X, 46, 47; *N.Y.Col.Doc.*, III, 591; M.H.S. *Coll.*, 6th ser., III, 33, 497-501.

men were only given the option of approving or rejecting the whole panel, without being allowed to vote down individual magistrates. It is probable that Fitz and Willys were not the people's choice. The election of 1689 broadened the old charter government (as in Massachusetts), to include a Dominion councilor like Fitz Winthrop, who had never been a Connecticut magistrate before. However, Fitz did not yet choose to join the charter government; he ignored his election to the magistracy. And Gershom Bulkeley, one of the few Dominion officeholders to be excluded from the 1689 compromise, was entirely dissatisfied. Bulkeley prepared (October 1689) a statement of dissent from the new government, which he wanted endorsed by all Connecticut gentlemen who objected to "the methods that are used since the late Revolution of Government, more & more to abuse & indeed to invassall this poore people." He specially asked Fitz to champion his protest movement, "your Honor being one of the Kings Councill, your power & influence is of a larger extent" than that of most other right-minded men. He also invited Fitz's brother Palmes.[4]

Called upon from all sides for his help, Fitz finally entered public service in 1690 by joining the grand scheme of the New England and New York governments to conquer French Canada. The seventy-year Anglo-French war for North America had begun in earnest as in Europe William III brought England into his alliance system against Louis XIV, and in America Count Frontenac seized the opportunity afforded by the Dominion's collapse to strike against the English colonists. Andros' defense system had been prostrated by the Revolution. The provisional Massachusetts government withdrew Andros' troops from Maine, while in New York, where the radical Jacob Leisler had expelled the Dominion administration, all the colonists

---

[4] *Conn. Rec.*, III, 250-53; C.H.S. *Coll.*, III, 155-59, 190; Winthrop Mss., X, 47; XI, 90. Bulkeley also wrote to Wait Winthrop, October 11, 1689, on hearing that Wait had seen a manuscript copy of *The People's Right to Election*, and "allso that you have somewhat reflected upon my sending or suffering of it so to goe abroad. . . .And now I heare that some do intend to print it. I assure you sir, that it is no desire of mine, & if your Honor can do anything to hinder that, I shall take it as your kindness: for in my opinion, the season of doing any good by that paper is now past. (*Ibid.*, XI, 89.) Bulkeley's tract *was* printed in 1689, but in Philadelphia rather than Boston.

were too engrossed in the bitter civil war between Leisler's Committee of Safety and the Andros stronghold of Albany to guard the Hudson Valley. On February 9, 1690, some 250 French and Indians made a daring and brutal attack on Schenectady, massacring sixty persons, taking twenty-seven captives, and burning the town. Fitz, who had visited Schenectady with Andros in 1688, was disgusted "that a place so well fitted for defence, soe well enclosed with stockadoes . . . should be soe poorly defended, or rather not at all disputed." The Canadians were said to be expecting twelve frigates and 2,000 soldiers from France.[5] Delegates from Massachusetts, Plymouth, Connecticut, and New York agreed (May 1, 1690) to strike back fast with a three-pronged invasion of Canada. One column would attack Montreal by the Champlain route, another would make a diversionary feint in Maine, while the largest force would assault Quebec by sea. The conquest of Canada, a stroke beyond the dreams of Andros' Dominion, would prove to William III the loyalty and worth of the revolutionary colonial governments. It was the boldest, most imaginative, and unfortunately also the most intricate campaign yet attempted in North America.

Fitz took command of the overland attack upon Montreal, but there were ominous difficulties over his appointment. New York was to contribute 400, Connecticut 200 and the Five Nations nearly 2,000 men. Connecticut did not want to place her troops under Leisler, especially when Leisler's chief enemy, Robert Livingston, a rich Albany merchant, fled to Hartford and implored the government to insist that a New Englander lead the campaign. On May 15 the General Assembly nominated Fitz the Connecticut commander, which honor Fitz accepted with unwonted dash. "It is now noe tyme to make excuses," he replied, and he announced himself ready to hazard his life for the people's safety, though his phrasing to Wait was more restrained: "if all things be well managed, I know not, but I may assist them." The Hartford magistrates were pressing Leisler to accept Fitz as commander in chief of the

[5] Francis Parkman, *Count Frontenac and New France under Louis XIV* (Boston, 1898), pp. 221-27; Winthrop Mss., X, 50; M.H.S. *Coll.*, 6th ser., III, 507-508.

whole Montreal expedition. Leisler viewed all former Dominion councilors as traitors, but he consented, on condition that Fitz obey the orders of New York's Committee of Safety, and that during the campaign he follow the advice of his Council of War, consisting of all commissioned officers. Fitz, for his part, entertained Robert Livingston at New London and cordially reciprocated Leisler's ill will, especially after a New York sloop stole thirty sheep and ten calves from Fisher's Island. "Tis better to be robed by the French," he told Wait on May 29, "then those that pretend to be our freindes." At the last minute, in July, he was trying to back out of his command, but the Hartford magistrats "lay hold of my promise . . . soe that I can finde noe way to put it of." Hardly a promising start.[6]

It is abundantly clear from Fitz's letters that he was not joining the attack on Canada in order to justify the New England Revolution to William III. He referred slightingly to "all those who pretend government in the severall parts of the country," and he hoped that the next ships from England would bring "something for our better settlement."[7] He threw his prestige and military experience into the campaign of 1690 in the hope of averting the disaster into which he felt the weak revolutionary governments were drifting. Fitz wanted to enlist every fifth militiaman in the colonies for a massive effort. This helps explain his sickening disappointment over the wretched preparations for the Montreal expedition. On reaching Albany, July 21, he wrote the Connecticut council, "I found all in confusion, and not now to be recovered." No rendezvous had been arranged with the Five Nations. No canoes had been built to transport the army up Lake Champlain and the River Richelieu. New York had not met her troop quota. Connecticut soldiers were dying of smallpox. The worst trouble was the mutual hostility between Fitz, Livingston, and the Albany burghers on the one hand, and Leisler's soldiers on the other. To Fitz, who established his Albany headquarters in Livingston's

[6] *Ibid.*, 5th ser., VIII, 303-307; 6th ser., III, 508-510; *N.Y.Col.Doc.*, III, 727-31; C.H.S. *Coll.*, XXIV, 31-32; Winthrop Mss., VI, 65, 68; X, 50; XII, 29; Deeds, 70; Leder, *Robert Livingston*, pp. 70-73.

[7] M.H.S. *Coll.*, 5th ser., VIII, 304; Winthrop Mss., VI, 65.

house, Leisler had now revealed himself to be the "worst of vipers."[8]

On a firm foundation of unyielding despair, Fitz set out with 500 men on August 1, north along the Hudson and overland through pine swamps, camping on August 7 along Wood Creek, which empties into Lake Champlain. He had come about 100 miles, only one-third of the distance to Montreal but the hardest stage of the trip since the rest of the way would be by water. At Wood Creek an advanced party had built ten canoes, less than half enough to carry the army. It was too late in the season to make more, for the bark would not peel from the trees. Only seventy Indians had come from the Five Nations, and when they were reproached for not keeping their promise, "the Indian Captains Answered we can not help it. it is not our fault, nor your fault, but God almightys pleasure." The Indians went down the creek, pretending to make canoes, but did nothing. After a week's fruitless encampment, Fitz's supply of biscuit and fishy pork was running low, and his men were steadily sickening. Poor Fitz was in a miserable predicament. Couriers brought letters from the Massachusetts and Connecticut governments, beseeching him to continue the expedition lest he fatally endanger Sir William Phips' naval attack on Quebec. They also brought word that he was needed back in New London, where four French ships had entered the town harbor on July 17, raided Fisher's Island, burned his house, killed some of his livestock and terrorized all his tenants into running away. At last, on August 15, Fitz's Council of War agreed it was impossible to pursue the campaign. To achieve some small part of his original purpose, Fitz authorized John Schuyler to enlist 40 whites and 100 Indians, as many men as there were canoes for, to raid the Montreal area. He himself retreated south with the rest of his forces, and camped outside Albany on August 20.[9]

After his long years of easy prestige as Cromwell's captain and the victor over the Dutch on Long Island, Fitz's biggest chance to prove his military prowess had turned into a galling

[8] M.H.S. *Coll.*, 5th ser., VIII, 308-309; *N.Y.Col.Doc.*, III, 752.
[9] M.H.S. *Coll.*, 5th ser., VIII, 310-19, 493-94; 6th ser., III, 3-12; Winthrop Mss., VI, 69; X, 7, 52; XII, 30.

fiasco. Undoubtedly in 1690 Fitz lacked energy, the very fault which he had charged against revolutionary New England's over-all military program, but he was also a victim of circumstances. If he had managed to get his army to Montreal, it would have been dangerously outnumbered. As soon as French scouts reported his advance, Frontenac was able to raise 1,200 men to defend the place. Fitz might have put more colonial troops into his raiding party and led it himself, for Schuyler's raid inflicted much less damage than had the French at Schenectady. When Phips reached Quebec in October, his assault was so inadequate that he was lucky to get most of his ships and men back to Boston. The English, by bungling their 1690 invasion, lost a matchless opportunity to end the struggle for Empire in North America with a single stroke.

The worst of Fitz's troubles came with his return to Albany. Leisler rushed up to confront him. He had found Fitz an "excellent person" two months earlier, but now he made him a prisoner. "From the 27 of August," Fitz recorded on the last page of his campaign journal, "early in the Morning that Captain Lesler arrived herr from New York to the 2d of September the whole Citty has been in a flame, . . . the principle and worthyest of the Burghers . . . dragd to Confinement, and unmercifully treated; I am myself detayned by force under a strict gaurd; and soe disabled from taking care of their majesties forces." Leisler's intention was to court-martial Fitz for concocting with his Albany friends a Jacobite plot to scuttle the invasion. He accused Fitz of refusing to swear allegiance to William III and of bribing the Five Nations to stay away from their rendezvous. He raked up old scandal by calling him an adulterer, and the subverter of civil government and Christianity. In short, Fitz was a public enemy.[10]

Fitz was freed from confinement after several days, not by his 200 Connecticut troops, but by a large delegation of Indians who happened to be in Albany at the time. Leisler tried to make Fitz pledge his return to New York for trial. "Never," Fitz told Wait, "did I see such a pittifull beastly fellow; as-

---

[10] *Ibid.*, VI, 170; *N.Y.Col.Doc.*, III, 752-53; O'Callaghan, *Documentary History of New York*, II, 265, 301-302.

sure yourself noething can Appeare Against me. . . . Man could not doe more then I did." When he got back to Hartford with his men in mid-September, he tried to soothe his pride by sending elaborate defenses of his conduct to the Connecticut and Massachusetts governments, in which he laid special stress on the impudent insult of his confinement. He was pathetically eager for the Connecticut General Court's official testimonial (October 1690), upholding his fidelity, valor, and prudence, and branding his arrest as injurious and dishonorable to himself and to New England. The court even gave him £40.[11] When a royal governor took charge of New York the following spring and immediately tried, sentenced, and executed Leisler for treason, Fitz was assuredly not among the mourners.

◄℞ THE Montreal fiasco was Fitz's single entry into public affairs in the four years following the Revolution. Since he did not bother to attend any of the Connecticut council meetings after being elected magistrate in 1689, he was not re-elected. His only office was Colonel of the New London County militia.

In these years, James Fitch, chief architect of the Revolution in Connecticut, was the dominant man of the colony. "Captain fitch will be the great Minister of state a little while," Allyn had predicted to Fitz after the 1689 election, "but I thinke his time is allmost out." Allyn was wrong. Governor Treat continued in nominal command, but it was Fitch who controlled the council, since by 1692 only half the magistrates were holdovers from before the Revolution, and the new councilors were Fitch's men. The colony franchise was enlarged by requiring only a 40s. freehold for admission to freemanship, and a strikingly democratic election system was devised: each freeman at his town meeting wrote out a list of twenty nominees for the magistracy, and, after the individual nominations were pooled at Hartford into a collective list of the twenty highest candidates, the freemen in a second series of town meetings balloted

[11] Trumbull, *History of Connecticut*, I, 384, 540-41; M.H.S. *Coll.*, 5th ser., VIII, 320-24; Winthrop Mss., VI, 71, 177; X, 53-54, 62; *Conn. Rec.*, IV, 38-39. For a contrasting view of Fitz's relations with Leisler, see Jerome K. Reich, *Leisler's Rebellion* (Chicago, 1953), pp. 93-105.

from this list for governor, deputy-governor, and twelve magistrates. Fitch had warmly applauded Leisler's seizure of power in New York. He unfolded a philosophy of government similar to Leisler's in a bellicose tract, "A Plaine Short Discourse," unfortunately now lost, in which he is quoted as saying that the duty of those in authority is "to screw up the inkhorns, still the tongues, empty the purses, and confine the persons" of colonists who dare oppose the restoration of the charter. In order to force disaffected colonists into obedience, the General Assembly in 1689 and 1692 ordered that persons refusing to render to the tax lists a true account of their property would be rated "will and doome," by having their cattle, swine, and horses confiscated.[12]

To Fitz Winthrop, this program, though aimed against Gershom Bulkeley's party, savored unpleasantly of Leisler's demagogy. Besides, the Winthrop brothers and James Fitch were rival claimants to land along the Quinebaug River, forty miles northeast of New London. The Winthrops' Indian purchase of ten square miles had been confirmed by the Connecticut court in 1659, but Fitch was settling tenants on the best meadowland along the river. Fitch offered to pay them £100 for seven square miles of their claim, but they preferred to enter the real estate business themselves and began selling lots to prospective tenants from Stonington. By 1693 each party was separately trying to promote a new town in Quinebaug.[13]

Fitz was also feuding with Edward Palmes. In 1689 a New London merchant, John Liveen, made a deathbed revision of his will, giving only one-third of his estate to his disgruntled widow and the rest to the local ministry. The estate, when debts were cleared, was about £1,500. The Liveen case became more important the longer it remained in dispute. Liveen's three executors were Fitz, Palmes, and the widow, a curious trio. Fitz was happy with the bequest to his young friend the Reverend Gurdon Saltonstall, while Mrs. Liveen and Palmes declared that Liveen was *non compos mentis* when he made the

[12] *Conn. Rec.*, IV, 6, 11-12, 22, 41-42, 51, 65, 80-81; C.H.S. *Coll.*, III, 84, 159-60, 249-53; *N.Y.Col.Doc.*, III, 589, 595, 598.

[13] M.H.S. *Coll.*, 5th ser., VIII, 499; Winthrop Mss., VI, 76; XIII, 47-48, 62; Deeds, 72; Winthrop Collection, I, 114.

will. For a year and a half the will was not probated. Palmes refused to recognize the validity of the Connecticut courts under the restored charter government. Much to Fitz's and Saltonstall's vexation, Mrs. Liveen and her two sons by a previous marriage, John and Nicholas Hallam, were holding the property. In March 1691, Saltonstall won suit in New London County court against the executors, and just as Nicholas Hallam was about to sail his stepfather's ship to Barbados, the constable seized it. There were cries of robbing a poor widow, but the General Assembly upheld the local action. For Palmes, the fight had just begun. He joined Gershom Bulkeley in an active campaign to end Connecticut's despotic government by restoring royal administration to the colony.[14]

This internal resistance to the charter came at a critical time, for Connecticut's status with William III's government was growing increasingly dubious. The colony sent three addresses to the new King between 1689 and 1692 without receiving any reply. Her efforts to establish recognition at Whitehall, or even to find out whether the charter was still valid, were hamstrung by lack of money and poor tactics. The former Connecticut agent, William Whiting, grumpily resigned, though he wrote Governor Treat that he supposed the charter was still good. His successor, James Porter, was of no use, being "an inferior officer in the custom house" without court connections. Increase Mather resented Connecticut's aloofness from his efforts to restore the Massachusetts charter, but he nevertheless brought some comfort to Hartford by obtaining (August 2, 1690) a unanimous opinion from three eminent lawyers, including the King's Attorney General and the King's Solicitor General, "that you may go on with your charter government as formerly, & [they] say, that you are very weake men if you do not so."[15] Connecticut occupied much the same anomalous position within the Empire as during James II's reign. William III's government wanted to keep the Dominion's centralized defense system against the French, and Massachusetts and New York

[14] *Ibid.*, III, 291-92, 297; C.A., Miscellaneous, I, 96-98, 101-102; Winthrop Mss., VI, 72; *Conn. Rec.*, IV, 39, 48-49.

[15] *Ibid.*, III, 463-66, 469-70; C.H.S. *Coll.*, XXIV, 24-31, 37-39; Winthrop Mss., X, 49; C.A., Foreign Correspondence, II, 25d.

continued their agitation of the 1680's for annexation of Connecticut. Sir William Phips arrived in Boston, May 1692, as the first royal governor under Massachusetts' new charter, bearing a commission as commander-in-chief of all forces in New England, specifically including Connecticut. He notified Hartford to account to him for her military establishment. As Bulkeley put it, "the militia is a principal flower of the crown, and if they let that go they had almost as good let all go." With only one dissenting vote the General Assembly agreed that it could not submit to Phips. He complained to England of Rhode Island's disobedience, but said nothing about Connecticut's parallel conduct.[16]

Gershom Bulkeley was almost as disgusted with Phips as with the Hartford government, and he saw that if Massachusetts were to annex Connecticut, Fitch's rule might well be actually strengthened. He turned to New York, where the newly arrived Governor Benjamin Fletcher was more than willing to patronize him. Bulkeley, Edward Palmes, and William Rosewell of Branford petitioned William and Mary (September 16, 1692) to restore royal administration to Connecticut. "It is impossible," they explained, "for us to serve two masters, your royall Majesties & this soveraigne corporation," and in an accompanying brief they reviewed the Connecticut corporation's misconduct since 1689. Fletcher sent these documents to the Lords of Trade. By December 1692, Bulkeley had expanded his argument into a full book, written (as an enemy admitted) "with great cunning and art," and entitled *Will and Doom, Or the Miseries of Connecticut by and under an Usurped and Arbitrary Power.* In this fascinating polemic he courageously set out to shatter all the idols of his local tradition, harking back to the golden days of Andros and ridiculing Connecticut's canting religion and her levelling democracy.[17] *Will and Doom* had no immediate effect for it remained in manuscript and was not even presented to the home government until 1704. Bulkeley claimed to speak for a sizable party, and he did collect thirty-

[16] *Cal.S.P.Col., 1689-1692,* p. 572; *1693-1696,* pp. 28-29; *Conn. Rec.,* IV, 77, 85; C.H.S. *Coll.,* III, 240-48; XXIV, 52-56.

[17] *Cal.S.P.Col., 1689-1692,* pp. 704-707; C.H.S. *Coll.,* III, 77, 93-95, 101, 195, 199, 236-37, 244; XXIV, 49-52; *N.Y.Col.Doc.,* III, 849-54.

five signatures on a petition to Governor Fletcher.[18] At least two-thirds of these petitioners were Wethersfield men, which suggests that Bulkeley's influence was largely confined to his own town. Nevertheless, his alliance with Fletcher precipitated a crisis for Connecticut in 1693.

Prompted by Fletcher's complaints that Connecticut refused to help defend Albany and by Bulkeley's appeals against the charter government, the Lords of Trade decided to make Connecticut into a satellite of New York. On March 3, 1693, the Connecticut government was ordered to aid the Governor of New York against the French whenever required, and to establish with Massachusetts, Pennsylvania, Maryland, and Virginia a quota system of troops for the defense of Albany. This royal order was not addressed to the Governor and Company, but to "such as for the time being take care for preserving the peace and administring the laws" in Connecticut. A second royal command was more explicit. On May 1, 1693, Phips' command over Connecticut's militia and fortifications was revoked, and Fletcher was commissioned commander-in-chief in his place. Fletcher was not altogether satisfied. "If I have not the absolute government of Connecticutt," he wrote Blathwayt, "t'will be hard to bring them to any thing." The effect of the news in Connecticut was that the General Assembly in emergency session voted to send an agent to England.[19]

The choice of Fitz Winthrop as agent was arranged very suddenly. In May 1693 he had been elected to the Connecticut council but did not bother to take his oath of office. As late as August 4, Allyn wrote him of the universal desire "that you would please to take the oath & serve God & your Generation." Two weeks later the Secretary wrote again to tell of Fletcher's commission, and that the governor and council were polling the people in each town to find out how many were willing to pay for an agent to defend the charter against Fletcher. Fitz suddenly assumed a new role as champion of the charter. "I am sincerely concerned," he told Allyn on August 25, "for the

[18] Winthrop Collection, II, 212.

[19] *Cal.S.P.Col.*, *1693-1696*, pp. 16, 19-20, 26, 173-74; C.H.S. *Coll.*, XXIV, 56-57; *N.Y.Col.Doc.*, IV, 29-31, 36-37.

preservation of that conciderable part of the Government soe conduceing to the safety of the whole Charter," and he pledged "that I will readely joyne with them to support every part of the Government and will readely contribute all the intrest I have for the advantage of their service." When the General Assembly gathered in special session on September 1, 1693, it was discovered that 2,182 of the approximately 3,100 adult males in the colony had endorsed the agency. Few of the 900 who had not voted were actually opposed to the scheme. The assembly felt directed to go ahead with a new petition to the crown and chose Fitz Winthrop as their agent to present it to William and Mary. He was commissioned (September 2) to obtain royal approbation of Connecticut's charter government and particularly to secure the continuation of the colony's control over her militia. The assembly levied a special tax of a penny on every pound of ratable estate in order to raise £500 for Fitz's expenses.[20]

Fitz did not undertake the agency out of sheer altruism. Sad experience had taught him that a man with property interests as large as the Winthrops', living in a community as small as Connecticut, must either assume the responsibilities of leadership or suffer damage from those who do so. Forced to choose between Bulkeley and Fitch, he used common sense in aligning himself with the overwhelmingly preponderant party. Fletcher approached him, on September 9, 1693, with the offer of a commission as his deputy-commander of the Connecticut militia.[21] But Fletcher's suzerainty over Connecticut was by no means as full or certain as Andros' had been in 1687. To accept his commission would mean declaring war against Hartford, and, even worse, it would mean an alliance with Edward Palmes. By rescuing the charter party in its hour of need, Fitz could hope to end James Fitch's dominance in the colony. There was, of course, the risk that his diplomacy at Whitehall might backfire as miserably as his generalship at Wood Creek. Yet certainly no one else in Connecticut could match his credentials as English ambassador.

Preparations for Fitz's journey were rushed through so that

[20] *Conn. Rec.*, IV, 91, 93, 101-104; Winthrop Mss., VI, 76; X, 57; Deeds, 78.
[21] M.H.S. *Coll.*, 5th ser., I, 444-45.

he could sail before winter. In the Connecticut Archives there is a list of the twenty-five documents which the council sent with him: a copy of the charter, a file of all the correspondence between the colony and the crown since 1662, narratives of Connecticut's past military achievements, a book of the colony laws showing the constitution of the militia, various letters to persons in England, and three copies of Connecticut's new petition to William and Mary. Fitz was empowered to revise this petition, but he did not get the plenary commission which he wanted from Hartford to make further petitions in the name of the colony. He thought that Connecticut was not giving him enough money, as well he might, remembering how his father had gone to England with £580 in 1661 and yet ended his agency £1,500 in debt. At Fitz's request, the General Assembly asked Gurdon Saltonstall to accompany him to England. But since the colony refused to pay his passage, Saltonstall stayed home.[22]

The most interesting feature of Fitz's preparations for departure was his private effort to reach a modus vivendi with Bulkeley's party and to win their acceptance of his agency. Five men had been jailed in March 1693 for defying the charter government, and Samuel Willys, the magistrate most sympathetic toward Bulkeley and critical of Fitch, had been dropped from the council in May. Willys was furious. Charter government in Connecticut, he told Fitz, was languishing "to almost the lowest ebb of Democracy if it doth not border upon Anarki." It would be worse than useless to get the charter merely confirmed. What was needed to restore orderly government was an exposition of the charter by the King, binding Connecticut to: (1) provide a stated honorable maintenance for the clergy, to prevent their salaries being dependent on "the arbetrary humors of the vulgar sort of people"; (2) observe fully all English common or statute laws, to prevent their infringement or abolition by Connecticut laws; (3) settle "persons of good parintage, education, abilitye, and integrity" in the chief colony offices, to prevent the election of "persons of mean & low degree." The affinity between Willys' proposal and Bulkeley's

[22] C.H.S. *Coll.*, XXIV, 57-77; Winthrop Mss., X, 57-58; *Conn. Rec.*, IV, 105, 107.

Will and Doom is obvious. Fitz gave Willys the impression that his agency would aim at Willys' goal. On October 8, shortly before Fitz left the colony, Willys wrote him: "In obedience to your commands, I have discourst mr Buckely and mr Woodbridge . . . and shall move Mr Elliott and Mr Roswell and other leadinge men who are sensable of . . . the privelage of the English lawes and Libertys to acquiesce in your Motion and to perswade those . . . on whom they have an Influence to doe the like in full Confidence that you will be Instrumentall to Ease the Spirits of A very considerable part of the most prudent and knowinge persons of the Colony. . . ."[23] Fitz may have compromised his commission and instructions from the Connecticut government, but he was trying to make his agency a rallying point for all colonists, and thus to ease the threat of civil strife.

On the eve of Fitz's sailing, an insurrection almost did occur when Governor Fletcher attempted to enforce his command of the Connecticut militia. On October 13, 1693, Fletcher set out to publish his commission in Hartford, collect as many Connecticut troops as possible, and take them to winter quarters in Albany. Fletcher had good reason to be exasperated by Connecticut's meager support of Albany, and especially by the rumor that the eastern towns on Long Island were once again trying, through Fitz's agency, to rejoin Connecticut.[24] Fletcher's exasperation was one thing; his insufferable arrogance was another. Cut from very much the same cloth as Sir Edmund Andros, Benjamin Fletcher demonstrated plainer contempt for the colonials than any royal official yet to appear in New England.

Fletcher's sloop reached New Haven on October 15, and he found that the General Assembly was meeting in Hartford. He notified the assembly to stay in session, kept it waiting for him a week, and then asked that it adjourn to New Haven since his horses were delayed. Upon eventually reaching Hartford on October 23, however, Fletcher was all bustle. He insisted that

---

[23] *Ibid.*, IV, 88, 91; *Cal.S.P.Col.*, *1693-1696*, p. 73; M.H.S. *Coll.*, 6th ser., III, 16-17; Winthrop Mss., XX, 56.
[24] *N.Y.Col.Doc.*, IV, 55-56.

the assembly immediately comply with his orders lest he be hindered from hastening in the King's service to the defense of Albany. His commission was read to the assembly. The Connecticut government told him that they would continue to control their own militia until further orders from England. Fletcher assured the Hartford magistrates that he would reappoint all present militia officers, and that he had no power or inclination to invade Connecticut's civil rights. But he was writing the Lords of Trade that Bulkeley, Palmes, and Rosewell would be the fittest candidates for his council if Connecticut were annexed to New York. On October 26, Fletcher reiterated his demand for obedience, "and expect a speedy replye in two words, Yes or No." The assembly offered £600, or fifty men, for Albany. Forty people came to the New York Governor's lodgings at the Hartford inn to register their obedience to his commission. One fellow dared to taunt his alleged authority and Fletcher threw him down the stairs. On the night of October 27 men in arms began menacing the inn, and by October 30 Bulkeley was certain there would be bloodshed if his Wethersfield friends tried to guard Fletcher. The next day, having sent to Allyn his proclamation forbidding all persons to execute or obey Connecticut's chartered militia commission, he left—for Manhattan, not Albany. "I never sawe the like people," said Governor Fletcher.[25]

With his colony in turmoil, Fitz journeyed up to New Hampshire, where the mast fleet was gathered in the Piscataqua River, and boarded the frigate *Samuel and Henry*. In a tender valedictory, Governor Treat told Fitz how he was carrying with him the "hope of all the good people of the Colonie, which is ground of encouragement to you, being not onely so freely & generally called to this great work, but also many prayers will goe along with you for your good protection & prosperity therein." The fleet set sail on November 10.[26]

◄ℛ Fitz's four-year visit to England, December 1693 to November 1697, coincided with a formidable reorganization of

[25] *Ibid.*, IV, 69-72; *Cal.S.P.Col.*, *1693-1696*, pp. 193-99; *Conn. Rec.*, IV, 111-17.

[26] *Winthrop Mss.*, VI, 77; *M.H.S. Coll.*, 6th ser., III, 18.

colonial administration by King and Parliament which completed the century-long evolution of the English imperial system. In spite of this, Fitz managed to achieve his aim of salvaging the Connecticut charter of 1662. Partly his success was due to his skillful presentation of Connecticut's case. More important was the fact that the home government's attitude toward the plantations had subtly shifted since the Revolution. Whereas the Stuart colonial policy, 1675-1688, had been basically authoritarian, aiming to tighten the King's political and economic control over the plantations, after 1689 the impetus was power politics, to achieve effective world-wide competition with France for trade and empire. More than ever the plantations were seen as commercial and strategic investments. Their trade must be regulated so as to return profits to the mother country, and their local governments must be made to cooperate in fighting the French war. The new Navigation Act and the new Board of Trade, both of 1696, were wartime measures to strengthen England against Louis XIV. William III's government halted Charles II's and James II's attack on colony charters and rescinded their tamperings with the colonists' religion, representative institutions, and property. In the case of Connecticut, which was less engaged in commerce than probably any other English plantation and less in contact with the French enemy than most, the imperial reorganization of 1696 imposed fairly slight limitations on her autonomy.

In the Connecticut government's letter to former agent Whiting, Fitz was candidly introduced as a man "long absent from England & possibly not soe well acquainted with the methods & customes now in use at court." It was over thirty years since Fitz's last visit, and he must have felt a total stranger. He was, however, acquainted personally or by reputation with many of the men employed by the colonial office, for the Revolution had not brought a turnover in its personnel. William Blathwayt was still secretary to the Lords of Trade. Most of the crown officers stationed in New England in the 1680's had now been promoted to higher posts in more southerly latitudes. Sir Edmund Andros was governor of Virginia, Francis Nicholson (deputy-governor of the Dominion of New England) had just been made governor of Maryland, Edward Randolph was surveyor-general of the customs in America, with headquarters on Chesapeake Bay, and even Edward Cranfield (governor of New Hampshire) had fulfilled his wish for a balmier climate by getting an assignment to Barbados. On hearing of Fitz's Connecticut agency, Randolph wrote uncharitably to the plantation office: "he is a great coward & Hopes to be made therefore Governor of that Colony." In Randolph's judgment, Fitz Winthrop and Sir William Phips both deserved the whipping post, but on second thought, he recommended that two such clowns be given wooden swords.[27]

At the time of Fitz's arrival, English colonial administration was aimless and inefficient. The King was too busy with the war and too little interested in the plantations to impose a clearcut policy of his own. The Lords of Trade drifted along a rudderless course. In the case of New England, it was as yet unclear in 1693 whether the Dominion idea had been completely or only partially rejected. By the time of Fitz's departure, all this had changed. Spurred by the House of Commons' resolve (January 1696) to create a parliamentary council which would more actively advance and protect English trade, William III issued his own new commission of trade and plantations, May 15, 1696, establishing the body known as the Board of Trade. With the creation of this agency, the King both prevented Parliament's encroachment on his supervision of trade and reformed English colonial administration. The Board of Trade encompassed the promotion and regulation of plantation affairs, though the King's instructions heavily emphasized trade.[28] The board consisted of eight lay experts, including William Blathwayt and John Locke, who were each paid a good salary of £1,000 and expected to work full time. The board members were not Privy Councilors and their function was purely advisory. Fitz found the Lords of Trade in the first years of his agency much more amenable to his arguments than the Board of Trade would be in 1696-1697.

In 1693 William III's colonial administration was heavily

[27] C.H.S. *Coll.*, XXIV, 72; *Randolph*, VII, 451.
[28] Stock, *Proceedings of the British Parliaments*, II, 156-58, 213-16.

strained, like almost everything else in England, by the French war, the biggest war England had yet fought. The war was going poorly on land and especially at sea. The navy was unable to control the English Channel, let alone the world sea lanes, so the loss of shipping to French privateers was terrible. Merchantmen were forced to sail in convoys, such as the mast fleet Fitz travelled with. The large percentage of mail lost between Fitz and his New England correspondents testifies to the inadequacy of even this convoy system. English merchants, whose political voice had been strengthened by the Revolution, were demanding parliamentary action to improve the protection of trade. The one requirement which the Lords of Trade definitely insisted upon from the northern colonies was an effective, unified defense against Canada. It was obviously inexpedient for Fitz, in protesting against Fletcher's command over Connecticut's militia, to stand upon his colony's chartered right to maintain her own military establishment completely independent of the neighboring colonies. He adjusted his tactics accordingly.

Fitz went to work quickly against Fletcher. A six weeks' passage brought him to London just before Christmas, and in January 1694, having delivered his credentials to the Lord President of the Council and to the Secretary of State who supervised the plantations, he presented Connecticut's petition to the King. Fitz adroitly revised the line of argument which the colony government had agreed upon in September 1693. He said that his government readily accepted the current wartime plan for cooperation against France, with a single commander drawing quotas of troops from each colony. He admitted Fletcher's command over a limited body of Connecticut men, but insisted that the New York Governor's commission made him merely a minister under the Hartford government. If Fletcher should be permitted unrestricted power over the Connecticut militia, he being "a souldier of fortune, not their Governour, & upon that account not responsible for any inward consumption of the Colony . . . though he should prove of an abstinence unusuall in this age," yet he would inevitably call too freely on Connecticut's troops for his colony's use and neglect the defense of Connecticut's own frontier. Fletcher threatened to "become perfect master of the lives, libertyes & estates" of the Connecticut people. Fitz's argument exposed very effectively the dangers of Fletcher's broad commission. He asked that the King restrict Fletcher's command to a specified number of Connecticut men, to be drawn in proportion to the quotas from other colonies.[29]

On January 29, 1694 the Privy Council referred Fitz's petition to the Lords of Trade, who in turn relayed it to the Attorney General and Solicitor General. It was the third time in four years that these officers had been asked to interpret the legal powers of the Connecticut charter. Fitz paid "a tedious & continued attendance" on the Attorney and Solicitor Generals, and was rewarded when their report of April 2 supported the argument in his petition. The King, they said, may authorize a wartime commander to draw specified quotas from Connecticut and Rhode Island, but in peacetime the militia ought to be left to the disposition of each government. Fitz got the Lord President to call a meeting of the Lords of Trade on April 13, where the report was accepted, and Fletcher's command was limited to a wartime quota of 120 Connecticut troops, a number suggested by William Blathwayt.[30]

Though Fletcher warned that Connecticut had given no military assistance to New York, and that the confirmation of her commonwealth charter would greatly damage their Majesties' interest in America, the King in Council approved Connecticut's 120-man quota on April 19, 1694, just before William III left for Flanders. Similar quotas were fixed for all the other colonies from Virginia to Massachusetts, providing a total of 1,898 men for the defense of Albany. On June 21, parallel letters were issued from Queen Mary to Fletcher and the Connecticut government, explaining the new arrangements. Fletcher was specifically forbidden (except when threatened by invasion) to draw more men from Connecticut than he proportionately drew from the other colony quotas. In compensation, he got 200 regular soldiers from England. Connecticut was meanwhile

[29] C.H.S. *Coll.*, xxiv, 78-86; Winthrop Collection, ii, 213-16; *Cal.S.P.Col.*, *1693-1696*, p. 287.
[30] C.H.S. *Coll.*, xxiv, 87-94; *Cal.S.P.Col.*, *1693-1696*, pp. 246-47, 277, 282.

assured that her just rights and privileges would be protected by the crown.

As Fitz well knew, the new quota system was unworkable, what with Massachusetts' concern over her own exposed frontier, Pennsylvania's pacifism, and Virginia's and Maryland's remoteness from New York. Fitz, despite his apparent readiness to promote a unified colonial defense against Canada, had given Connecticut an excuse for denying Fletcher even her 120-man quota. The New York Governor was effectively prohibited from interfering in Connecticut's internal affairs. Most important, the colony's charter government was at last graciously recognized by William and Mary. "I know not what can more reestablish & confirme the charter," Fitz wrote Governor Treat, "& I may let you know the Lords of the Councill are well satisfied with your present administrations, & you stand faire at court. . . . I hope their Majesties letter will . . . settle the minds of the people, in all respects."[31]

Fitz now supposed he was free to go home, but his work had only just begun. A series of unforeseen new threats to Connecticut's chartered privileges kept him in England three more years trying to preserve the terms he had initially secured. Fletcher and the Connecticut government continued to wrangle over the defense of Albany. Both colonies behaved badly. Fletcher made no attempt to draw proportionately from his other neighbors. Every year he demanded Connecticut's full 120 men, on one occasion, as Governor Treat told Fitz, upon an idle report of a canoe seen on Lake Champlain. Connecticut sent 60 men and £600 in 1694; this was her total contribution in four years. Fitz was supplied with figures to show that his colony had expended the vast sum of £7,759 on aid to New York and Massachusetts between 1689 and 1696, but of this only £1,050 went to Fletcher. Since New York, with about the same population, claimed to have expended £30,000 in defense since the beginning of the French war, it is unlikely that Connecticut was being persecuted.[32]

[31] *Ibid., 1693-1696*, pp. 217, 235-38, 299; Winthrop Mss., XIV, 10; C.H.S. *Coll.*, XXIV, 88-89, 94-100.

[32] *Ibid.*, XXIV, 102, 106, 109-16, 127-28; *Cal.S.P.Col., 1693-1696*, pp. 277-78, 586-90; *1696-1697*, p. 79; Winthrop Collection, II, 189, 218; Winthrop Mss., XIV, 93.

On April 23, 1696, Fitz petitioned the King for redress against Fletcher's "unkinde demandes" against Connecticut. His petition was taken up by the new Board of Trade. He was called in to explain why Connecticut had sent no troops to New York the previous year, as well as to describe from firsthand experience the Anglo-French battleground north of Albany. Two agents from New York were on hand to give a contrasting picture. The net result was another qualified victory for Connecticut over New York. Fitz was unable to get his colony's quota relaxed. The Board of Trade in February 1697 instructed Connecticut to be particularly careful to send her 120 men to New York when called for. But at least Fitz helped get rid of Fletcher. The Board of Trade invited him to produce accusations against the New York Governor, and in 1697 Fletcher was recalled to England, where he had to face a full scale inquiry into his governorship.[33]

In almost every letter home, Fitz said he was sailing to New England on the next ship. But he discovered that much of the home government's colonial reorganization in these years seriously menaced his colony's independence. The most immediate hazard for Connecticut was the crown's decision to unite Massachusetts with New York under a powerful royal governor. Sir William Phips arrived in London, February 1695, to face charges of gross misconduct as governor of Massachusetts. Sir William caught a cold ("the usual distemper to strangers" in London, as Fitz observed) and shortly expired. Fitz had attended the beleaguered knight frequently in his final illness. "I am extremely concerned for the loss," he wrote Wait, and added that Phips "had not seene the King nor any hearing before the Council, but beleive all would have been well." Fitz was unduly optimistic. For the government decided that Phips' successor must be an impressive representative of the King's authority over New England and accordingly picked a landed Irish nobleman and Whig politician, the Earl of Bellomont. In July 1695 the Lords Justices recommended that New England

[33] C.H.S. *Coll.*, XXIV, 118-21; Winthrop Collection, II, 219; M.H.S. *Coll.*, 5th ser., VIII, 327-32; Winthrop Mss., VI, 87; *Cal.S.P.Col.*, *1696-1697*, pp. 90, 103, 113, 241, 251; C.A., Foreign Correspondence, I, 57.

and New York be joined under Bellomont in the pattern of Andros' Dominion in 1688, to unite the northern colonies against Canada and to provide a tax base for the Governor's large salary.[34] Newly recognized Connecticut was again in danger of being swallowed up.

Fitz was torn between his duty to Connecticut and his long-standing servility to pedigreed Englishmen such as Bellomont; he had a lingering fondness for a grand Dominion which would sweep away the entrenched petty oligarchs of New England and restore the dignity of his family. His conflict was revealed in a letter to John Allyn on July 13, 1695. Bellomont's commission, Fitz said, may "some way or other affect your government; the ocean naturally swallowes up all the rivolets, & I know it would be very acceptable (& they say most for every ones advantage) to make one body of all our wilderness; but I have no care to that projection, nor is it my busines, . . . however tis prudence not to be out of the way at this juncture; that if there be occation I may answer to any thing objected against the government. I make noe doubt but his lordships presence will make all difficultyes easy in [Massachusetts], & yourselves will be very hapy in soe generous a neighbour."[35]

A year and a half passed, and in January 1697, the Board of Trade picked up discussion of Bellomont's appointment. The board had reason to be disgusted with the northern colonies' war effort, and it was unquestionably influenced by several petitions from frightened New England planters who predicted that France would conquer the bickering English colonies unless New England and New York were pulled together by a single general or governor. Fitz gave the board his reasons against the appointment of a single general, rehearsing his argument of 1694 that Connecticut's civil government must be safeguarded from the arbitrary exactions of an outside soldier.[36] Despite Fitz's opposition, the Board of Trade advised the King on February 25, 1697, to appoint a single man as governor of the

[34] C.H.S. *Coll.*, XXIV, 104-106; Winthrop Mss., VI, 78-79; M.H.S. *Coll.*, 5th ser., VIII, 324-26; *Cal.S.P.Col.*, *1693-1696*, pp. 429, 506, 520, 534, 541.

[35] C.H.S. *Coll.*, XXIV, 107-108.

[36] *Cal.S.P.Col.*, *1696-1697*, pp. 318, 338-41, 347, 352, 355; M.H.S. *Coll.*, 5th ser., VIII, 337-38; C.H.S. *Coll.*, XXIV, 133.

three royal provinces of Massachusetts, New York, and New Hampshire, and general of all the forces in the proprietary colonies of Connecticut, Rhode Island, and Jersey. Bellomont was again named to this far-flung job, and his commission drawn up. Fitz protested stoutly to the Board of Trade. "The Collony of Conecticot have been at great charge in this affaire," he said, "and it will seeme strange to every one that after they have obtayned his Majesties Gracious settlement of this affaire, they should be put to New trouble about it." Yet Fitz did not dare to ask that Bellomont's powers over Connecticut be restricted to a 120-man quota. Instead, he asked the board to insert a clause in Bellomont's commission explaining that the Connecticut government still exercised "the ordinary powers of and over" her militia, and had complete control in peacetime, which thus guaranteed the colony's civil authority. Bellomont and the Board of Trade accepted this clause.[37] Connecticut was firmly bound within Bellomont's military system, and Fitz had yielded much of the ground he had won three years before.

In 1696 and 1697 Fitz not only had to cope with Fletcher and Bellomont but with Edward Randolph. Since his exit from Boston jail in 1690, Randolph had been discovering that other colonials were almost as offensive as New Englanders. His tours up and down the Atlantic coast as surveyor-general of the customs convinced him that *all* the mainland plantations were flouting the navigation laws and would continue to do so as long as most colony governments were protected from royal supervision by their charters. Hence, Randolph tried to persuade the King and Parliament to return to the colonial policy of 1675-1688. Back home in 1695, he recommended to his superiors in the Customs House a parliamentary bill for preventing frauds and regulating abuses in the plantation trade. Further, he urged the virtual annihilation of all proprietary and corporate charters by regrouping the colonies into six large provinces, each to be headed by a royal governor. Connecticut he gave to New York. Randolph's first suggestion was readily adopted, with Parlia-

[37] *Cal.S.P.Col.*, *1696-1697*, pp. 384-85, 399, 446, 449; M.H.S. *Coll.*, 6th ser., III, 22-24; Winthrop Mss., VI, 89; VIII, 13; C.A., Foreign Correspondence, I, 61.

ment's passage of the Navigation Act of 1696. Even his second suggestion was considered. In 1697 a committee of the House of Lords listened sympathetically to his arguments for confiscating all private charters and called William Penn, the biggest colonial proprietor, to answer Randolph's charges against him. But the Lord's committee let Penn go after bullying him and did not press the charges against most of the other private colonies (including Connecticut) at all.[38]

The Navigation Act of 1696 which Randolph helped to instigate was purely punitive. The preceding navigation acts had established a rigid and complex system of mercantilist controls covering all aspects of English trade, under which system English commerce had expanded splendidly. Parliament now tried to coerce the two classes of English-speaking persons who had benefited least obviously from this system and had violated it most freely, namely Scotsmen and colonials. The act of 1696 put special pressure on all colony governors to enforce the trade laws by imposing on them a new oath, new bureaucratic procedures, and new penalties for delinquency. It enlarged the number of colonial waterfront guards, naval officers and customs officers who were responsible to the crown. Most important, it authorized a new colonial institution, the vice-admiralty court, a prerogative court without jury, to handle smuggling cases. Edward Randolph pressed hard for the appointment of royal attorney generals in every colony to prosecute for the crown in these vice-admiralty courts. Fitz sent a copy of the Navigation Act to Connecticut in July 1696. By the following February he was complaining how, "owing to Mr Randolph," the new legislation was being particularly applied against the private colonies. Randolph's designs were not "layde onely against the Collony of Connecticut," he said, "but to the hurt & disturbance of the other proprietary governments, viz. Carolina, Pensilvania, the Jersyes, & Rhode Island . . . who are under one intrest of liberty & priviledg with yourselves."[39]

Still, the Act of 1696 probably had slighter effect on Con-

---

[38] *Randolph*, VII, 474-77; Stock, *Proceedings of the British Parliaments*, II, 191-202; Michael G. Hall, "The House of Lords, Edward Randolph, and the Navigation Act of 1696," *W.M.Q.*, 3rd ser., XIV, 494-501, 509-13.

[39] C.H.S. *Coll.*, XXIV, 131-32.

necticut than on any other plantation. There was a clause which required that governors of private colonies be approved by the King before entering office. Fitz sought legal advice on this point, since Connecticut's annual May election could scarcely "have opportunety for his Majestyes approbation, before a new choise be made for the next yeare." In fact, this clause was applied only to proprietors such as Penn, not to the self-governing corporations of Connecticut and Rhode Island. Likewise, Connecticut escaped the new act's chief feature, the admiralty courts. Spokesmen for the chartered colonies sought safety in numbers by clubbing together to protect their private judicial systems. Among Fitz's papers are five notices to attend these proprietary meetings. It must have given him exquisite pleasure to join noblemen like the Earls of Craven and Bath, and Lords Ashley and Berkeley, in petitioning the crown. He became friendly with William Penn, who wrote from his country estate for news of their common affairs, and asked Fitz to "Salute me to our Society."[40] The proprietors' lawyers advised (as Fitz explained to his government) "that the charters gave noe power of admiralty, & that the King might apoint attornyes generall for himself, if he should think fit; soe that it was thought best to submit that matter to the King. . . ." Despite Randolph, the crown did not press for attorney generals in the private colonies, and one private colony—Connecticut—was not even given an admiralty court. The reason was simply the insignificance of her trade. Randolph had dug up only one case of smuggling in New Haven and another in New London. Though he nominated a separate admiralty judge, register, and marshal for Rhode Island, he placed Connecticut within the jurisdiction of New York's admiralty court. In practice, Connecticut continued as before 1696 to handle her own maritime cases, according to the same procedure as all other judicial business, in either the county courts or the court of assistants.[41]

[40] *Ibid.*, XXIV, 121; Andrews, *Colonial Period*, IV, 171; M.H.S. *Coll.*, 5th ser., VIII, 332-37; Winthrop Mss., X, 139; *Cal.S.P.Col., 1696-1697*, pp. 192, 234, 258; M.H.S. *Proc.* (1871-1873), p. 42.

[41] C.H.S. *Coll.*, XXIV, 132; *Randolph*, V, 137, 143, 158, 162-64; VII, 501; Hall, "The House of Lords, Edward Randolph, and the Navigation Act of 1696," *W.M.Q.*, 3rd ser., XIV, 502-509; Andrews, *Colonial Period*, IV, 232, 255.

The home government by no means entirely ignored Connecticut. The Hartford leaders were made well aware of the new navigation act, for the Privy Council sent them a copy in 1696, and the Treasury Commissioners sent a very full digest. On April 22, 1697, royal letters were sent to all the private colonies warning against further abuse of the trade laws. Connecticut was told that continued dereliction would tend to the forfeiture of her charter. When Fitz returned to America, he carried another unpleasant message from Whitehall. The governors of Connecticut and Rhode Island, "having no proprietors here in England, and being become a great Receptacle for Pyrats, and carrying on severall illegall Trades," were henceforth required to give security to the home government for the due execution of the navigation laws.[42] Bellomont took a bond of £3,000 from Fitz when he became governor of Connecticut.

Fitz's style of life during his four-year English visit was much more humdrum than his father's had been in 1661-1663. Not being an intellectual person, he was indifferent to the artistic and scientific richness of London. Indeed, despite his taste for fashion and pedigree, Fitz felt homesick. "I think it very long till I am with you," he wrote Wait one year after arrival; "noething more pleasing than our owne Country." He took lodgings with a grocer named Richard Dakins in St. Clements Lane. His friends ranged from the Roman Catholic Colonel Thomas Dongan, James II's governor of New York, to the unreconstructed Puritan Sir Henry Ashhurst, Massachusetts' resident agent, who delighted in smiting the Philistines. Money was a chronic problem, but Fitz was eventually supplied with about £800 from Hartford while he was in England, and at least he did not have to mortgage the family estate as in 1663.

Fitz performed a variety of private tasks in England. He tried to retrieve his brother's Negro, Kinch, who had been taken by a press-gang onto a royal warship, but found that the poor fellow had died. He got a new bell for New London church to replace the old one, which melted when the meeting house burned down in 1694. He sent a camlet cloak and two wigs to brother Wait and a flageolet and fishing rod to nephew John.

---

[42] C.A., Foreign Correspondence, I, 51, 60, 61; C.H.S. *Coll.*, XXIV, 137-47.

On the eve of departure in 1697 he made a pilgrimage to the old Winthrop estate, "to Groton Hall in Suffolk," he told his cousin Charles Downing, "with greet Duty and affection to visit the tomb of my Ancestors. my great Grandfather who was your great Grandfather lyes there. . . . he had one son who was my grandfather that went into New England." Fitz sent Downing a copy of the inscription which he had found on Adam Winthrop's tomb. He also bade a fond farewell to his young lady friends at Hackney, and to Cousin Reade's dear nieces at Tunbridge Wells, especially his favorite, Madam Rawlins. "I have a passionate love for your person," the gallant colonial confessed to Madam Rawlins. Fitz at sixty was not yet exclusively interested in tombstones.[43]

On November 8, 1697, Fitz finally started home, sailing from Cowes in the same fleet with the Earl of Bellomont and Edward Randolph. Obviously he had achieved far less for Connecticut than had his father a generation before. In 1661-1663 the home government's colonial attitude had been so casual that John Winthrop, Jr., was permitted to enlarge the bounds and privileges of his colony. In 1693-1697 the home government's mercantilist policy and imperial administration were so fully elaborated that Fitz Winthrop had to accept new restrictions on his colony's privileges. Yet despite the concessions to Bellomont, Randolph, and the Board of Trade, Fitz's agency had achieved its purpose of confirming Connecticut's semi-autonomous position within the Empire. He had won for himself the respect and good will of Bellomont and the Board of Trade. The Board officially notified Connecticut "that he has diligently sollicited all things that concerne the Colony of Connecticut," while Secretary William Popple personally gave Fitz his hearty wishes for a prosperous voyage home.[44]

⫷ THE culmination of Fitz Winthrop's curious odyssey in the postrevolutionary decade came not during his English sojourn, but on his return home in 1698. Although an insignificant

[43] Winthrop Mss., VI, 79, 82, 90-91; XI, 55; XII, 87, 137; M.H.S. *Coll.*, 5th ser., VIII, 325, 339, 509-12; 6th ser., V, 32.
[44] *Ibid.*, 5th ser., VIII, 335; C.A., Foreign Correspondence, I, 61, 63.

provincial at Whitehall, he was the pivotal figure in Connecticut.

On December 11, 1697, Fitz's ship, the *Jeremiah*, docked at Boston after a rapid four-week passage. Fitz bore glad tidings. Enclosed in his letter to Governor Treat announcing his arrival was the Board of Trade's orders to publish the Peace of Ryswick between England and France. Connecticut's welcome to her agent was spontaneous and heartwarming. Joyful greetings came from Governor Treat and Samuel Willys in Hartford, from Gurdon Saltonstall and Captain Daniel Wetherell in New London. Your arrival is as life from the dead, Wetherell wrote; "you came upon the wings of prayer, which has incessantly been put up to the Allmighty God in your behalfe in all the congregations of this Collonie." Saltonstall said, "your being once more among us puts a new life & fresh vigour into our affaires, which I think would soon have expired if they had not met with such a revivall." On orders from the governor and council, Captain Whiting of Hartford, who had been waiting two years for Fitz's arrival, immediately left for Boston with Captain Nichols and Captain Wetherell, despite the unusually bitter winter weather, and escorted him home in early January. A General Assembly was quickly convened to receive from its agent the letters he carried from the King and Board of Trade. Fitz was voted another £300 gratuity, which presumably covered the last of his expenses. A special public day was appointed to thank God for the "restoration of peace to the English nation, and the successe and safe return of our agent."[45]

The reason for this jubilance was that most Connecticut people saw Fitz as the only man who could save the colony from disintegration. In addition to the tensions brought by the French war, wretched weather, failing crops, and epidemic sickness, Connecticut was racked by political faction. Ever since 1689 the colony had been split into three rival parties—left, center, and right—and in such a small society the clashing personalities of the factional leaders were as important as the principles they professed. James Fitch still led the democratic left wing. During Winthrop's absence he had dominated more than ever the colony

[45] C.H.S. *Coll.*, XXIV, 148-49; *Conn. Rec.*, IV, 234, 238, 240-41; M.H.S. *Coll.*, 6th ser., III, 29-32, 253; Winthrop Mss., VI, 92.

government, doing everything from repairing fortifications to drawing town boundaries to revising the laws. Fitch was no statesman. His backwoods manner, indulgent to his friends and rough on his enemies, stirred the passions of men from the center faction such as Willys, Woodbridge, and Saltonstall, who wished to elevate Connecticut's churches and charter government above "the mire of popular confusion." Samuel Willys told Fitz that "hardly any gentleman of this Colony [has] . . . received one graine of justice since your departure." As for the right-wing faction, Gershom Bulkeley's appeals to England had been permanently silenced by Fitz's agency. But Edward Palmes had become an implacable enemy of the Connecticut charter. The quarrel between Palmes and Saltonstall over John Liveen's deathbed bequest to the New London ministry had not been settled. By 1698 neither colony taxes nor Saltonstall's salary as minister could be collected in New London.[46]

Fitz Winthrop, for all his limitations, could offer Connecticut fresh leadership. Having been elected to the magistracy *in absentia* for the past five years, Fitz returned as the savior of the charter and something of a popular hero, eclipsing James Fitch in the eyes of the average colonist. Winthrop's political philosophy, however, was much more snobbish than Fitch's. One month after getting home, February 15, 1698, he expressed his sentiments frankly to the Reverend Abraham Pierson. Fitz argued that it was high time for Connecticut to exert her full chartered privileges by enhancing the dignity and authority of the colony's institutions: "A Government Easy and indulgent beyond what is fitting brings a Contempt upon it and makes rude . . . persons bold and unsafe to the Government and late Experience has made us too sensible of it. I have observed in the kings Courts a most Extraordinary reverence payde to the judges and all ministers of justices. . . . but in this wilderness (eyther from principles of too fond familiarity or not remembring the rules abroad) they are wanting to introduce such fitting formes and customes as should support the honor of the

---

[46] *Conn. Rec.*, IV, 182, 189, 213, 219, 229, 241-42; M.H.S. *Coll.*, 6th ser., III, 31-32; V, 38; Winthrop Mss., X, 62. John Allyn had died in 1696; Willys was dropped from the magistracy; his cohorts Wolcott, Chester, and Nichols had lost their seats as deputies.

Courts and give them a reputation and character abroad in other parts of the world."[47]

Fitz's desire to imitate English forms and customs would never satisfy his wormwood brother-in-law Palmes, who wanted Connecticut's chartered privileges destroyed rather than enhanced. But Fitz's standing with the Board of Trade would protect his colony from appeals to England. And no one else could restore the authority of church and state in New London. His very reappearance, Wetherell hoped, would "scatter those clouds of darkness which some persons of evill principles and mortall enimies to our worthy Minister, have been late endeavoring and contriving."

Fitz had selfish reasons for wanting to overthrow James Fitch. The contest over who held title to Quinebaug, the tract northeast of New London where the Winthrop brothers and Fitch were each trying to plant a new town, had grown ugly during his stay in England. When two of the Winthrop tenants refused to pay Fitch rent, Fitch got a warrant from the New London marshal, broke into their houses and took their corn, oxen, and hogs. Wait Winthrop took the case to New London County Court. When the jury found for Fitch, Wait sent a wild and rambling appeal to the Connecticut Court of Assistants and lost again. In revenge, he tried to harry Fitch's tenants and take *his* corn. Fitch threatened to prosecute Wait in the Connecticut courts and tartly recommended that he try surveying the Quinebaug tract before continuing his loose talk about violation of property rights.[48] Thus the matter stood in 1698, with Fitch plainly holding the upper hand. The Winthrop pretensions to Quinebaug could not be retrieved unless Fitch's political dominance in Connecticut was ended.

In the spring of 1698 the Connecticut freemen in their town meetings voted as usual from a list of twenty nominees for governor, deputy-governor, and twelve assistants. The town deputies brought these votes up to the General Assembly at Hartford, May 12, when Fitz Winthrop was away in New York as Connecticut's ambassador to congratulate the Earl of Bello-

[47] *Ibid.*, VI, 93.
[48] M.H.S. *Coll.*, 5th ser., VIII, 504-507, 514-23; *Conn. Rec.*, IV, 170; Winthrop Mss., XIII, 49-50.

mont on his arrival. Fitz's friend Timothy Woodbridge preached the election sermon. The votes were counted, disclosing that the Connecticut freeman had called for the most significant turnover in the colony's sixty-year electoral history. Winthrop was elected governor, and Treat was lowered to deputy-governor, displacing the decrepit William Jones, who was retired from office, having (as Willys told Fitz) "bin only capable of drinkinge flipp & takinge tobacco . . . , yet beinge an old Crumwelian [had been] alowed 20£ per annum for his supply of those needfull commodytys." Furthermore, James Fitch was dropped from and Samuel Willys added to the panel of assistants. Captain Nichols rode to New York with a letter from the council announcing to their new Governor that his election is "very acceptable to our late Honoured Governour and Present Deputy Governour and to the Assembly." Saltonstall, whose alliance with Fitz in Connecticut paralleled Cotton Mather's alliance with Wait in Massachusetts, struck a more triumphant note. "The election of this day," he told Fitz, "hath been concluded with the joyfull acclamations of all people . . . and your presence here is longed for with universall expectation." Fitz soon joined the General Assembly. On May 20, 1698, he took the traditional governor's oath and the new oath pledging enforcement of the navigation acts, in the presence of the whole court.[49] He continued to take both oaths annually until his death in 1707.

It had taken Fitz nearly ten years to make the difficult transition from James II's appointed councilor to the Connecticut people's elected governor. A bystander during the Revolution of 1689, an inglorious general in 1690, he seemed destined to spend his declining years among the sheep and goats on Fisher's Island. Yet when Connecticut became torn between the Fitches, trying to create a completely anomalous backwoods society, and the Bulkeleys, trying to merge themselves entirely into the English empire, Fitz held the colony together. During the 1690's Fitz himself had changed. His visit to the mother country taught him what his grandfather and father had never had to

[49] *Conn. Rec.*, IV, 224, 238, 244, 251, 257-58; M.H.S. *Coll.*, 6th ser., III, 31-32, 34; Winthrop Mss., XIV, 94.

learn, that in England he was an outsider. Fitz's snobbery and awe of the King was counterbalanced by his love of New England real estate and his identity with the local colonial society. He rejected equally the simple rusticity of James Fitch and the simple Toryism of Gershom Bulkeley. Instead, he epitomized the ambivalent nature of postrevolutionary New England, half-provincial and half-independent, half-English and half-American.

14. *His Provinces Pillar*

Being the third of a Renowned line
Which wee Americans deemed next Divine. . . .
His grandsire by direction of a starre
Conducted all our Tribes hither, thus farr. . . .
Winthrop, the second, of renowned fame
Hath filld this climate with his perfumd name. . . .
WINTHROP, the third with palsied hand I write
His Provinces pillar, and this lands delight.
His anncient Patent while hee livd was free
From all intrusions on their libertie.
While all the neighborhood was set on fire
Hee kept his Paradisian hearts desire
Being garrisond with GOD, all fencd about
With living walls, and hearts of Marble stout.[1]

THE palsied hand belonged to Benjamin Tompson, a
Yankee rhymster elegizing Fitz Winthrop in 1708. Times
had changed since the Dominion of New England. Tompson's
verse was crude, but his picture of Fitz as Connecticut's pillar
was accurate enough. Governor of the colony from 1698 to his
death in 1707, Fitz had completed his transformation from
critic to defender of the Connecticut status quo. He accomplished
what his brother Wait was unable to do in Massachusetts: he
stamped the colony government with a new orthodoxy and
parried efforts by internal rivals—Fitch, Palmes, and the
Hallams—to overturn his leadership. He kept Connecticut on
the sidelines during the French and Indian fighting in Queen
Anne's War and stifled attempts by external rivals—Governor
Cornbury of New York, Governor Dudley of Massachusetts,
and the Board of Trade in England—to destroy his colony's
chartered privileges. Fitz's Connecticut Paradise was only a
petty enclave within a world-wide empire, a far cry from the

[1] M.H.S. *Proc.*, 2nd ser., X, 370.

first Governor Winthrop's "Modell of Christian Charity." And Fitz was not a crusader in the style of 1630; he poured his heart into real estate lawsuits rather than religious causes. But he did reassert his grandfather's formula, doing battle against all critics of his New England regime.

In 1698, at the age of sixty, Fitz set out smartly to overhaul Connecticut, acting on the premise that a new executive must strike fast or not at all. He had three initial advantages: a fresh viewpoint on Connecticut politics, good relations with the powerful Governor Bellomont of New York and Massachusetts, and peace with the French and Indians. All three advantages were soon lost. Fitz's bitterest Connecticut enemies— Fitch, Palmes, and the Hallam brothers—were combining against him by 1700, the Earl of Bellomont died in 1701, and the French war reopened in 1702. There were only two halcyon years, 1698-1700, in which to inaugurate domestic reforms and strengthen Connecticut's standing with the home government. Fitz relieved few of the chronic pressures on the colony, but his governorship did much to consolidate Connecticut's eighteenth-century character as a quietly prosperous, narrowly inbred, backwater community—the land of steady habits.

Fitz's recipe for domestic reform was decidedly conservative. He wanted to enlarge the governor's powers, largely nominal when he took office. In 1698 the assembly gave him broad authority to act between court sessions, assisted only by such magistrates and deputies as he "shall think fitt to call to Councill." The assembly also let Fitz appoint the collectors of a new excise on wine, and made him sole supervisor of the forts at Saybrook and New London and personal guardian of the Pequot Indians. His salary was raised from £100 to £140.[2] Fitz also wanted to revamp the assembly itself. Unlike most colonial legislatures, the Connecticut assembly sat as a unicameral body, its sessions plagued by a more than customary disorder and absenteeism. In May 1699, assistants and deputies were separated into two chambers, meaningfully called the Upper and Lower Houses. Samuel Willys was delighted, though Fitz was

[2] *Conn. Rec.*, IV, 262, 280-81, 329-30, 348-49.

dissatisfied with the first bicameral court session. "Our new forme of Government as to the lower house," he told Wait, "has succeded indifferent well, and yet I think busines is not dispatched sooner than formerly in the old way." At least the two-house system gave the governor and assistants a veto over the more numerous deputies, and it provided new ceremonial. The deputies elected a speaker who, in English fashion, sent an address at the beginning of the session to Governor Fitz, desiring harmonious relations with the Upper House. There were also new fines: ten shillings for missing a day's session, and one shilling for speaking without permission from the presiding officer.[3]

Further, Fitz aimed to increase the independence of Connecticut's judiciary. Before 1698 justices were annually elected in each county. After 1698 the assembly commissioned a judge and a panel of justices for each county on tenure of good behavior, freeing the local courts (as Willys put it) from "the arbitrary humors of the people." The jurisdiction over estates (the chief business of the courts) was redefined, and a table of fees prepared.[4] Finally, Fitz's governorship saw a special effort to protect Connecticut's clergy and improve her schools. A new law in 1699 made every inhabitant support the congregational minister in his town. The colony's two grammar schools were considered inadequate, so the assembly in 1700 ordered two more. The next year the assembly incorporated the Collegiate School, later renamed in gratitude for an endowment of £500 by a London merchant, Elihu Yale. Fitz himself willed £100 to the Collegiate School, though as an East Connecticut man he offered his money only on condition that the institution remain in Saybrook rather than move to New Haven.[5] Had he given a little more generously, we might today have Winthrop University and the "Sons of Fitz."

Obviously the new governor was trying to imitate in Connecticut the English system which he had so admired on his

[3] *Ibid.*, IV, 266-69; M.H.S. *Coll.*, 6th ser., III, 41-44; Winthrop Mss., VI, 113.

[4] *Conn. Rec.*, IV, 235-37, 259-61, 306-14; M.H.S. *Coll.*, 6th ser., III, 44.

[5] *Conn. Rec.*, IV, 316, 331-32, 363-65; M.H.S. *Coll.*, 6th ser., III, 416.

recent visit. By curbing the colonists' undisciplined, anarchic behavior, he could meet charges from the Board of Trade that Connecticut's government was inadequate and irregular. The reforms were particularly designed to break James Fitch's democratic faction. But though "the old Philistine" (as Fitz called him) had been downed in the election of May 1698, he was not out. In May 1700 Fitch was returned to the Upper House, whereas Winthrop's ally Samuel Willys was not re-elected. Fitz himself had neither the vigor nor the stature to hold his commanding role of 1698. Since he lived out of the way in New London, much of the colony business had to be done by subordinates in Hartford. He was frequently ill, very seriously so in the summer of 1699. Already by 1700 Fitz's internal reform campaign had pretty well run its course.

Meanwhile, Fitz tried to improve Connecticut's standing with the home government, relying on his reputation with the Board of Trade. He notified the board of his election in 1698 and dilated on his fellow colonists' "deepe sence of your Lordships favoures . . . they depend greatly upon an intrest in your Lordships continued good opinion and favour." He wrote personally to William Blathwayt and William Popple of the Board of Trade, and William Cowper, crown prosecutor, to thank them for courtesies during his English visit and to ask for their continuing good will toward Connecticut. Fitz was genuinely anxious to carry out the Board of Trade's instructions. He told Willys, "we must have fayth for what they suggest to us therein."[6] When the board called for copies of all Connecticut laws (February 1698), Fitz hastened to obey, despite the colony's chartered exemption from royal confirmation and disallowance. "Gentlemen," he wrote the magistrates at Hartford in July, "I hope you have made a good step in reviseing the lawes. . . . It will be hard for me to answere soe great a neglect, therefore must desire you to loose noe tyme about it." Finding that the revision went slowly, he sent to the board unrevised copies of the laws, partly printed and partly in manuscript. Connecticut's prompt obedience was in great contrast to the

[6] C.A., Foreign Correspondence, I, 68; M.H.S. *Coll.*, 5th ser., VIII, 344-50, 353-56.

behavior of the other self-governing New England colony, Rhode Island. Pleading that they were "a plain and mean sort of people," the Rhode Islanders rarely communicated with the Board of Trade. They delayed more than a year before sending a blotched, irregular abstract of their colony laws, and their Quaker Governor refused in 1698 to take an oath pledging enforcement of the navigation acts.[7]

Fitz knew that he was dealing with a highly energetic imperial administration. The Board of Trade was at its peak of creativity. Its dispatches to Hartford were far more frequent, soundly informed, and searching than the communications from any previous colonial board. The Board of Trade was not merely determined to review Connecticut's laws, but to settle her boundary disputes and especially to make her obey the rules of the English mercantilist system. On January 22, 1699, for example, the board sent the Connecticut government copies of the Navigation Acts of 1660, 1662, 1663, 1670, 1671, 1673, and 1696, together with twenty-two large sheets of instructions on how to enforce them.[8] As always, the home government relied too heavily on paper orders. But the King did have a powerful lieutenant on the scene. Richard Coote, Earl of Bellomont, supervised all the northern colonies in his multiple capacity as governor of New York, Massachusetts, and New Hampshire, and commander in chief of New Jersey, Connecticut, and Rhode Island. Like Andros in 1686-1689, Bellomont had the impossible job of welding six widely scattered societies into a military and commercial unit. Unlike Andros, Bellomont grounded his viceroyalty upon existing local customs and institutions.

Fitz did his best to cultivate Bellomont, much as his father had cultivated Nicolls a generation before. When Fitz went to New York to welcome Bellomont, the Earl was particularly pleased with Fitz's companion, Gurdon Saltonstall, whose dignified carriage seemed *almost* like that of a nobleman! Nevertheless, Bellomont quickly raised an embarrassing question: why had two New York border towns, Rye and Bedford, been

---

[7] C.A., Foreign Correspondence, I, 70; M.H.S. *Coll.*, 5th ser., VIII, 352-53, 359; 6th ser., III, 37; Winthrop Mss., VI, 101, 135; *Cal.S.P.Col., 1699*, p. 162; *R.I. Rec.*, III, 329-31, 374-77.

[8] C.A., Foreign Correspondence, I, 76-77.

accepted into Connecticut's jurisdiction in 1697? Fitz and his council sent three commissioners to negotiate the boundary dispute with Bellomont, and he transmitted the Connecticut and New York briefs to the Board of Trade for its decision.[9] At the board's recommendation, the King in March 1700 awarded Rye and Bedford to New York. Fitz expected this verdict. Still, he was most anxious not to lose his personal land claims in New York. He petitioned Bellomont to confirm his title to a parcel of unimproved land on Long Island which Andros had granted, and he even asked to be excused from paying quitrent on it.[10]

Bellomont intervened, at the Board of Trade's direction, in Connecticut's interminable boundary dispute with Rhode Island. Connecticut's pretensions to the Narragansett Country were hardly more defensible than those to Rye and Bedford, but Fitz had support from Rhode Island malcontents, and he also reckoned that Bellomont would dislike the Rhode Island government. Bellomont visited Rhode Island in September 1699 and notified Fitz that he would arbitrate the Narragansett dispute. "Noething," Fitz assured Bellomont, "could be more contentfull to me for the service of this colony than your Excellencyes condescention to hear the controversy betwene this government and that of Rhode Island. . . . wee hope this will be the tyme (in your Excellencyes presence) that wee shall have opportunety to convince them of our right to the government & propriety of the Naroganset country, which will be made yet more acceptable to us by your Excellencyes good opinion concerning it." It was in a hopeful frame of mind that Fitz and three Connecticut commissioners set out to attend Bellomont in Newport.[11]

On September 23, 1699, the Earl of Bellomont spent a weary morning listening to the heated accusations of Rhode Island and Connecticut. He could not make them agree on anything,

[9] Trumbull, *History of Connecticut*, I, 396; *Conn. Rec.*, IV, 192-93, 205, 238; C.A., Foreign Correspondence, I, 65; Winthrop Collection, I, 32-35; M.H.S. *Coll.*, 5th ser., VIII, 340-41, 348.

[10] *Cal.S.P.Col.*, *1697-1698*, pp. 459-61; *1700*, pp. 124-25, 141-43; *Conn. Rec.*, IV, 328, 335; Winthrop Mss., VI, 94, 107, 114, 140; XI, 2; XIII, 119; M.H.S. *Coll.*, 5th ser., VIII, 378-79, 536.

[11] C.A., Foreign Correspondence, I, 68; *Conn. Rec.*, IV, 239, 243, 271; Winthrop Mss., XIV, 63, 94; XX, 61; C.H.S. *Coll.*, XXIV, 150-54; Winthrop Collection, I, 62; M.H.S. *Coll.*, 5th ser., VIII, 342-44, 366-69; 6th ser., III, 38.

and finally instructed both governments to send agents to England. Bellomont himself clearly took Connecticut's side. He was disgusted with Rhode Island's crude government, which (he told the board) kept the miserable inhabitants of the Narragansett Country in a continual state of war. Connecticut certainly contributed to this state of war by urging the people in the disputed area not to pay taxes to Rhode Island. In 1700 Fitz complained bitterly to Bellomont that the Rhode Island sheriff had crossed the Pawcatuck with an armed posse, "frighted our people, and robed them of silver, &c., and snapt a pistoll at one of them"; the sheriff was caught and jailed in New London. At last both sides began to act more moderately. Governor Cranston of Rhode Island called for peace, warning Fitz against trying "to overthrow us and thereby strengthen yourselves; . . . you may assure yourselves that if wee splitt you will sinke; for wee are both upon one bottom. . . ." Cranston was undeniably right. In 1703 commissioners from the two colonies reached a simple agreement: the Pawcatuck River was to be the boundary, a victory for Rhode Island, and all existing Narragansett property grants were to be confirmed by the Rhode Island government, a victory for Connecticut. This agreement did not end the border feud, but it was the first workable compromise in the forty-five-year controversy.[12]

Connecticut's border conflicts bothered the home government far less than her reputedly illicit trade. The New England coast was increasingly cursed by pirates, who seemed to operate out of the little uncontrolled ports of Connecticut and Rhode Island. Between 1698 and 1701, Fitz was continually pressed by Bellomont and the Board of Trade to catch pirates and enforce the navigation acts. The board authorized Bellomont to receive a bond of £5,000 from Fitz as security for Connecticut's good behavior, though when Bellomont found "that a penalty of £5000 was frightfull to him, he telling me he would sooner throw up his Government, I accepted his obligation of £3000." On taking office, Fitz assured the board that wicked rumors

[12] *R.I. Rec.*, III, 391-92, 400, 474-76; *Cal.S.P.Col.*, *1699*, pp. 531-35; *1700*, pp. 715, 738-39, 748-50; M.H.S. *Coll.*, 5th ser., VIII, 372, 377-78; 6th ser., III, 62-63, 70-75; V, 61-63; Winthrop Mss., VIIb, 12; XII, 32.

about Connecticut commerce were baseless: "Our Trade at the most is so very small and inconsiderable, that it would be impossible for such Illegall Trade (if any such their were) to be undiscerned." Bellomont reported, however, that ships commonly unloaded forbidden cargo in Connecticut and sailed empty into New York. One of the Earl's aides unearthed a quantity of East Indian goods in Stamford, which he surmised was brought by Madagascar pirates. The Board of Trade commended Fitz in 1698 on Connecticut's laws against piracy, but observed that "execution is more wanted then Laws. . . . And we should be glad to see some instance of your Diligence in that kinde."[13]

Fitz's execution was diligent enough to prove that he really wanted to stop piracy and contraband. Privately he reminded his port collectors of their duty not to "countenance in the least the bringing into this Government any of those comodityes soe expresly forbiden." Fitz actually caught some pirates in April 1699. It was rather a pathetic case: the crew of a 400-ton English ship, the *Adventure*, having cast off their captain, Thomas Gullock, in the East Indies, eventually sank their stolen ship off Block Island, and scattered along the coast, four of the crew camping on Fisher's Island. Ten men, with £2,000 in booty, were captured in Connecticut, the others in Rhode Island and Massachusetts. Secretary of State Vernon and the London owners of the *Adventure* wrote Fitz in thanks "for your great care" and sent Captain Gullock to retrieve his cargo. Gullock became less grateful when he found that the Connecticut government had sequestered some of his stolen goods to pay for maintaining the prisoners, and Bellomont sternly wrote Fitz, "I am Inform'd that your Tenants on Fisher's Island have got a great sum of money and some goods left there by some of those Pyrats; you would do well in my opinion to examine them upon oath, to find out the truth." Still, Connecticut was given a letter of discharge from the King when the prisoners and most of their loot reached England. Fitz congratulated his council in

[13] Historical Society of Pennsylvania, Board of Trade Transcripts, Proprieties, v, 15, 77; C.A., Foreign Correspondence, I, 68, 72; M.H.S. *Coll.*, 5th ser., VIII, 345, 368; Winthrop Mss., XII, 64; *N.Y.Col.Doc.*, IV, 319.

August 1700 on settling the case "soe agreable to his Majesty's Comandes."[14]

With the death of the Earl of Bellomont (March 5, 1701), his imposing regime too short-lived to have much effect, Fitz's effort at cordial cooperation with the home government came to a close. From 1701 to 1707, Connecticut's relations with England were strained. Bellomont's successors in New York and Massachusetts constantly complained to the Board of Trade against Connecticut; Fitz's enemies within the colony appealed to the Board of Trade against him; the board itself tried to annul Connecticut's charter. Governor Fitz fought tenaciously to preserve Connecticut's freedom from outside control.

◆₹ A TRAVELER through Connecticut in 1704 found that the "Chief Red Letter Day is Saint Election . . . to choose their Governor," and that the incumbent, the Honorable John Winthrop, Esq., "is a very curteous and afable person, much Given to Hospitality, and has by his Good services Gain'd the affection of the people as much as any who had bin before him in that post." This was not the whole story. Fitz was cordially hated by his several personal enemies within the colony. His worst flaw as governor was his inability to separate private quarrels from the public business of Connecticut. Disdaining to settle differences quietly with James Fitch, Edward Palmes, and John and Nicholas Hallam, he used the weight of his office to prosecute and humiliate them. Of course they retaliated. Fitch did his best to frustrate Winthrop's plans from within the Connecticut government. Palmes and the Hallam brothers were more dangerous; they counterattacked from the outside and appealed to the King against him.

Fitz turned his election victory of 1698 into a vendetta against James Fitch. Not satisfied with reforming the colony government so as to curb Fitch's democratic faction, he wanted the Connecticut assembly to confirm his proprietorship of the whole Quinebaug tract northeast of New London, so as to dispossess Fitch and his tenants. The rancor between Fitch and the

---

[14] Winthrop Mss., VI, 101, 132, 135; X, 14; XI, 3; M.H.S. *Coll.*, 5th ser., VIII, 357-63, 370-76, 547-51; *Cal.S.P.Col., 1699*, p. 191; *Conn. Rec.*, IV, 300.

Winthrops was paralyzing the settlement of the area. The Winthrops' tenants paid no rent and told Fitz they would have to "pluck up stakes and be gon" unless he could stop Fitch from fencing their land and burning their hay. In 1698 Fitz got the assembly to authorize the survey of his Quinebaug tract, and he ordered Fitch to demonstrate to the assembly his claim (if any) to the disputed land. But Fitch plied a new tack. At the May 1699 General Assembly, Fitz reported to his brother: "I see a Couple of Blades with a Petition under the handes of a bove half the [Quinebaug] Inhabitants desiring to have the priviliges of a Towneship . . . which was drawne by the old Philistine"—i.e., James Fitch. To keep control, Fitz hastily submitted his own petition for the incorporation of Quinebaug. The assembly dutifully granted Fitz's petition and also asked him to name the new town. Learning that Fitch wanted to call it Kent, he christened it Plainfield.[15]

So far so good, but Fitch was re-elected to the Connecticut council in 1700, and quickly won two lawsuits from the Winthrop brothers, charging him with trespass in Quinebaug. By the spring of 1702 the doughty Major seemed once more to have the upper hand. Fitz was desperately ill with pleurisy and swelling in his legs, so ill that Wait came down from Boston to doctor him, and the arch Tory Gershom Bulkeley sent medicines and two pages of advice from Wethersfield. Samuel Willys, greatly distressed, told Wait that his presence was badly needed in Hartford, for "by reason of the Governors sundry times absence in the time of the Generall Court & Assistants Court, by reason of his indisposition of body, and the Deputy Governor [Treat] beinge superanuated, Mr. Fitch grows the dictator of both those Courts." Though Fitz was still too weak to ride a horse, he sailed up to Hartford in a pinnace with his brother to face Fitch in the May 1702 assembly. Wait presented an arrogant memorial to the assembly, which insisted that Fitch be made to answer his charges of abusing the Winthrops' tenants at Quinebaug. Otherwise, Wait warned that "the only expedient

[15] G. P. Winship, ed., *The Journal of Madam Knight* (New York, 1935), pp. 44-45; Winthrop Collection, I, 115-16; *Conn. Rec.*, IV, 272, 292, 334; Winthrop Mss., VI, 113; XIII, 50-51; M.H.S. *Coll.*, 5th ser., VIII, 359.

left him, is to apply himself to his Majesty in Councill." Awed by the Winthrop brothers, the assembly censured Fitch. His fellow councilors voted his conduct "very erroneous and illegall," and even the Lower House (Fitch's stronghold) told Governor Winthrop that it resented the Major's insolence toward him and agreed with the Upper House that Fitch should make good any damages to the Winthrops' tenants.[16] It was a reproof which Fitch was unlikely to forget or forgive.

Despite the fact that both parties had the vaguest of Indian titles to Quinebaug, the struggle for ownership dragged on seven more years. The settlers split into two towns in 1703, divided by the Quinebaug River. Plainfield, where Winthrop's tenants lived, was east of the river. The second town, Canterbury, was west of the river, adjacent to Norwich and Major Fitch. By 1706 at least one of the rival proprietors began to see the childishness of the contest. "I am tyred with the trouble & charge of it," Fitz wrote his brother, "& if anybody will buy my pretentions there (which may possibly be as good as Major Fitch's) I will take the first opportunity to dispose. To keep great tracts of land to stop bottles with (whilst one is ready to starve) is very idle and does a publick injury to others that would improve them." Besides, how can the Winthrop title ever be made secure in law? "It must be defended by good testemony," Fitz said, "& I am sure I see none hereabout." When a committee, appointed by the Connecticut assembly, mediated between Fitch and the Winthrops, Fitz agreed in October 1706 to resign his Quinebaug claims to the colony government in exchange for two farms of a thousand acres apiece. It was a good bargain, and Wait confirmed it in 1709, after Fitz's death. Major Fitch remained incorrigible. He was up to his old tricks again in 1717, selling lots for a new plantation along the upper Willimantic River on land to which he had no title.[17]

If the Winthrop-Fitch feud was difficult to mend, the Winthrop-Palmes feud was impossible. For years Edward Palmes

[16] *Conn. Rec.*, IV, 351-52, 368, 380, 391-92, 415; Winthrop Mss., VI, 122, 130; VII, 130; XI, 90; M.H.S. *Coll.*, 6th ser., III, 87-90, 92, 94; V, 111-13.

[17] *Conn. Rec.*, IV, 420, 445, 535-36; V, 10, 101-102, 586; Winthrop Mss., VIII, pt. 2, pp. 4-8; XIII, 58; M.H.S. *Coll.*, 6th ser., III, 343, 358, 385.

had been nursing two grievances against his brothers-in-law. He supposed that Fitz and Wait had cheated him out of his wife's share of the Winthrop property, and that Fitz had cheated John Liveen's stepsons, John and Nicholas Hallam, in executing Liveen's will. No sooner was Fitz elected governor than Sir Hude, as the Winthrops nicknamed him, began to agitate both of his grievances. With John Hallam, he sued Fitz for £2,500 in the New London County Court, September 1698, for stealing their ship. The suit was rejected. One month later, he petitioned the Connecticut assembly to make Fitz and Wait inventory their father's estate. The petition was denied, and Palmes billed with costs of £2 10s. In November, he sailed with the Hallam brothers for England.[18]

Since Palmes and the Hallams, unlike Fitch, had no popular following in Connecticut, their only chance of beating Fitz was to apply to the home government for help. In February 1699 they presented themselves to the Board of Trade, protesting that they could get no justice from the Connecticut courts. On April 24, the board forwarded to Hartford the King's directive that the Palmes-Hallam evidence of Liveen's insanity at the time he made his will be heard, and their suit for £2,500 damages against Fitz be reviewed by the Connecticut courts. Should the colony's retrial of the Liveen case fail to satisfy the plaintiffs, they had the further right to appeal to the King in Council. This was just what Palmes and the Hallams wanted. Before coming home, Palmes took the opportunity to open a more general attack on Fitz's government, enumerating for the Board of Trade the irregularities in Connecticut's judicial system. Wait Winthrop saw Palmes when he landed at Boston in July 1699. "I met Sir Hude in the street with his usual bulk," Wait reported to Fitz, "but he keeps his secrets till he comes to you."[19]

Fitz received the King's order to give Palmes and the Hallams justice on July 24, 1699. In effect the Connecticut govern-

[18] C.A., *Miscellaneous*, I, 105, 107; *Conn. Rec.*, IV, 271-72; *Cal.S.P.Col., 1699*, p. 74; M.H.S. *Coll.*, 5th ser., VIII, 540. For the legal intricacies of the Liveen case, see Joseph Henry Smith, *Appeals to the Privy Council from the American Plantations* (New York, 1950), pp. 140-50.

[19] *Cal.S.P.Col., 1699*, pp. 74, 81, 92-94, 208-209; C.A., Foreign Correspondence, I, 78-79; M.H.S. *Coll.*, 5th ser., VIII, 551, 554-57.

ment ignored it. When Palmes reapplied in September 1699 for administration of his wife's Winthrop estate, he was haled before the Governor and Council and asked why he was stirring up trouble for the colony in England. There was a fiery scene. Palmes accused Fitz of calling the King's attorney general, Sir Thomas Trevor, a knave. He was arrested and fined £5 by the assembly for slander and misbehavior—then Fitz magnanimously asked the assembly to remit the fine.[20] When Palmes and the Hallams reopened their Liveen suit, the Connecticut government again gave no satisfaction. According to several eyewitnesses, Fitz Winthrop positively denied the Hallams' appeal to the King, telling the court that if appeals were allowed, he should not give a farthing for the Connecticut charter.[21]

When Fitz saw that Nicholas Hallam was going to appeal the Liveen case in England, he asked Sir Henry Ashurst to defend the colony's chartered exemption from appeals. Since the Connecticut treasury was empty, Wait had to borrow £200 to pay Ashurst. In his letter of June 2, 1700, to Sir Henry, Fitz described the Palmes-Hallam affair as follows: "the *true Reason* of their complaint is a disgust Mr. P Hath at Charter Government. A disgust which hath increased very much since the happy Revolution and is like to continue, so long as that Cause remaines: the Inhabitants of or Colony unanimously conclude themselves happy under the present Constitution. . . ." Writing again in November, Fitz instructed Ashurst to "insist that the allowing of appeales from hence is contrary to the gracious priviliges granted in our charter and will be most grevous to his Majestyes subjects here."[22]

Though no one could really be as good a colonial agent as Sir Henry Ashurst thought he was, he did serve Fitz and Connecticut very well. Ashurst was an experienced agent, having represented Massachusetts for years; he was a personal friend of Fitz Winthrop; indeed a second-generation friend, for his father

[20] *Cal.S.P.Col., 1700*, p. 265; Winthrop Mss., XVI, 67; XIX, 80; *Conn. Rec.,* IV, 298, 305; C.A., Miscellaneous, I, 139.

[21] *Conn. Rec.,* IV, 303-304; *Cal.S.P.Col., 1704-1705*, p. 669; C.A., Miscellaneous, I, 120-22, 124, 126; C.A., Foreign Correspondence, I, 91.

[22] M.H.S. *Coll.,* 5th ser., VIII, 560; 6th ser., V, 71; Winthrop Mss., VI, 132, 144.

had lent money to Fitz's father; he had a knighthood and good connections—or, as he put it to Fitz, Connecticut was privileged to have "a person of my quality to appear for them"; last but not least, he liked the £100 annual salary which Connecticut promised him. Yet even Sir Henry could not prevent the home government from hearing the Palmes-Hallam appeals. When Nicholas Hallam arrived in London and petitioned the King (December 5, 1700) to hear his case for Liveen's insanity, Ashurst objected that such an appeal was without precedent, that it violated Connecticut's charter, that it threatened "a totall subversion of the said Colony." He told Fitz proudly that the Board of Trade found his objections difficult to answer. This is dubious, since the board believed the King had an inherent right to receive and determine appeals from all colonies. The Attorney General and Solicitor General, though Ashurst's friends, likewise upheld the royal prerogative. In June 1701, the King in Council admitted Hallam's appeal, and instructed the Connecticut government to transmit authentic copies of all proceedings in the Liveen case.[23]

Fitz was now really embattled. Having exposed his colony's chartered privileges to English inspection, he had to stake his honor and reputation on the validity of Liveen's will. "I believe," he wrote Ashurst, "the like fraudulent & wicked indevors to make it voide have not been practised in this Age." He was not helped by the Connecticut assembly's refusal to be a party to the English hearing of Hallam's appeal. The assembly viewed the case as an isolated exception to Connecticut's immunity from appeals, and would not pay for Ashurst's defense of the will, "which is the particular Case of the Governor as Executor, & not of the Government." Testimony for the English hearing had to be prepared in Connecticut, and unhappily the King's instructions that witnesses be cross-examined were violated by both appellant and respondent. The Privy Council took up Hallam's appeal in March 1702. Ashurst reported to Fitz: "They opened such things at the Councel that made your cause look very foul, and all the affidavits that you took in your country after the

[23] M.H.S. *Coll.*, 6th ser., III, 61-66, 69, 75-76; *Cal.S.P.Col.*, *1700*, pp. 750-51; *1701*, pp. 243, 263; C.A., Foreign Correspondence, I, 91, 93.

Appeal was granted, they would not allow to be read, because it appear'd to be an examination *ex parte*." Both parties were sent back to Connecticut, with Fitz ordered to pay for the re-examination of all witnesses.[24] The re-examination took place in New London a year later, March 1703. Major James Fitch was the presiding officer, and he barred Fitz and Saltonstall from cross-examining Palmes and the other appellant witnesses on the ground that they might intimidate the court! Winthrop protested furiously to the Connecticut assembly, Fitch was found culpable of maladministration, and the Liveen witnesses were examined yet again. In July 1703, Fitch met with Palmes and Hallam in Rhode Island and swore evidence against Winthrop and the Connecticut government.[25]

Nicholas Hallam made his fourth and final trip to England for help against Fitz in the fall of 1703. Again the council heard his appeal on the Liveen will, and Ashurst's response. The appeal was dismissed on January 9, 1704. After five years of maneuver, the crown had confirmed the validity of the will. Each party was told to pay court costs—£60 for Fitz and £250 or more for Hallam. But having thrown out Hallam's grievance, the Privy Council turned around and agreed to hear two more appeals against Connecticut justice by Edward Palmes. These appeals attacked Fitz even more directly than had the Hallam appeal. Palmes wanted the Queen to make Fitz pay him £2,500 damages for seizing Liveen's ship and to make Fitz disgorge Lucy Palmes' share of the Winthrop estate. The hearing was scheduled for October 1704, postponed till October 1705, and finally took place in February 1706. This time Ashurst's defense was only half-successful. On April 8, 1706, the Privy Council dismissed Palmes' £2,500 suit, but upheld his appeal for administration of his wife's estate, thereby reversing the 1699 judgment of the Connecticut Court of Assistants. When he heard the bad news, Fitz wrote dejectedly to Ashurst, "I find noe compensation for our great charge."[26]

[24] *Ibid.*, Foreign Correspondence, II, 69, 72; Winthrop Mss., VI, 163; *Acts of the Privy Council, Colonial*, II, 329-30; M.H.S. *Coll.*, 6th ser., III, 82-86, 108, 119-21.

[25] *Ibid.*, 6th ser., III, 94, 123-26, 133-36; C.A., Miscellaneous, I, 128, 132, 135; Winthrop Mss., XIII, 56.

[26] *Acts of the Privy Council, Colonial*, II, 330, 453-54; *Cal.S.P.Col.*, *1702-*

Fitz never did accept the Queen's order to reopen the settlement of John Winthrop, Jr.'s estate. Palmes displayed the order to the Connecticut assembly, October 1706, but the assembly gave him no satisfaction. Wait advised Fitz to keep stalling as long as possible. Once more Palmes petitioned the home government, and in April 1707 the Queen's Order in Council was renewed and enlarged. The governments of Connecticut, Massachusetts, Rhode Island, and New York, the four colonies where John Winthrop, Jr.'s property lay, were all strictly required to grant Palmes letters of administration for his wife's estate.[27] Before Sir Hude could exhibit his latest stroke to the Connecticut government in 1708, the combat had lost its savor, for Fitz Winthrop was dead. There is no sign that Fitz ever realized, as he did in the case of his Quinebaug squabble with Fitch, how negative the combat with Palmes had become. It is melancholy to think of the time, energy, and money spent on litigation by the ulcerous brothers-in-law between 1698 and 1707, merely to enrich London lawyers and to convince the home authorities that colonials are unfit to govern themselves.

⟨⟨ THE internal rebellion against Fitz's governorship was particularly alarming because Palmes, Fitch, and the Hallams had the active backing of Connecticut's hostile neighbors, Lord Cornbury, governor of New York, and Joseph Dudley, governor of Massachusetts. Cornbury and Dudley took up their posts in 1702, dividing Bellomont's sprawling dominion between them. This same year saw the opening of Queen Anne's War, the second phase of the Anglo-French duel for empire. Connecticut's volunteer war effort was minimal, as it had been during King William's War. Cornbury and Dudley tried (like Fletcher before them) to get control of the Hartford government. Once more Fitz mounted the barricades.

It would have been nearly impossible for him to escape trouble from Cornbury. This degenerate gentleman was about

1703, p. 856; C.A., Foreign Correspondence, I, 103–104, 115; II, 79, 86, 100; Winthrop Mss., VIII, pt. 1, p. 58; XVI, 68.

[27] M.H.S. *Coll.*, 6th ser., III, 357, 377; V, 144–46, 149–50; Winthrop Mss., XVI, 69; C.A., Foreign Correspondence, I, 119; *Conn. Rec.*, V, 65.

the worst imaginable colonial officer—a weak, arrogant, vicious, cheating wastrel, who got the job because he was Queen Anne's cousin. Fitz now had a family interest in New York politics, for in 1701 his only daughter, Mary, had married the son of Robert Livingston, the Albany merchant who worked with Fitz on the abortive Canadian expedition of 1690. Livingston liked Cornbury at first, and Fitz wrote in June 1702 to congratulate the new Governor on rescuing New York "from ruin and oppression." Fitz visited Cornbury in 1703. He delicately raised a topic never far from his thoughts, namely the Winthrop land on Long Island, which Bellomont had somehow forgotten to confirm.[28]

Fitz's good neighbor policy abruptly snagged on old military issues. Cornbury carried a commission as captain general of the Connecticut militia, which he told Fitz he was going to publish in Connecticut. His visit would be most welcome, Fitz replied, but as for the commission, Connecticut was not going to surrender control of her militia. Less venturesome than Fletcher, Cornbury did not take up the challenge and visit Hartford. He did try to collect £450 from Connecticut, on orders from the home government, for the fortification of Albany. Fitz and his colleagues were again evasive, figuring that none of the other colonies were helping to defend Albany. They wrote the Queen pleading to be excused. This sort of colonial myopia was the curse of the English war effort. Yet Cornbury had little need of Connecticut's militia or Albany fortifications, thanks to his outrageous deal with New York's Iroquois neighbors, the Five Nations. Instead of trying to incite them against the French, he agreed with the Five Nations to keep upper New York neutral, protecting his colony's fur trade and encouraging the enemy to concentrate her whole attack upon New England. When the French were terrorizing the Connecticut Valley in 1704, Fitz proposed to Cornbury that the Five Nations be stirred up, and that his lordship might well organize an overland invasion of Canada. The only reply was a peevish complaint

[28] M.H.S. *Coll.*, 6th ser., III, 67, 76, 91-92, 100, 128, 130, 137; *Conn. Rec.*, IV, 379; Winthrop Mss., VIII, pt. I, p. 10. On Cornbury, see Leder, *Robert Livingston*, pp. 180-85; and H. L. Osgood, *The American Colonies in the Eighteenth Century* (4 vols.; New York, 1924), II, 61-94.

against Connecticut's messengers for preaching in the New York streets and stealing her soldiers.[29]

Lord Cornbury reported Connecticut's military insubordination to the Board of Trade, and he was soon sending home much graver charges against the colony: Connecticut was a nest of thieves, peopled by the spawn of Rebellion. Cornbury sent the Board of Trade some thirty depositions in November 1705 to prove the colony's crimes: smuggling, piracy, arbitrary laws, religious persecution, and defiance of orders from England. The evidence seems to have been collected for him by Edward Palmes, who in one of the depositions revived the hoary charge that Connecticut protected the regicides Goffe and Whalley in 1661. As Wait Winthrop observed, "sir hude maks himselfe the gratest knave in the world by his letters and his evidence but a shilling will make him say any thing."[30]

Coordinate with Cornbury's essentially frivolous attack was Joseph Dudley's more systematic campaign against Fitz Winthrop and the Connecticut charter government. Dudley returned to Boston in 1702 as an English imperialist first and foremost, and only secondarily a New England native son. Even before his appointment as royal governor of Massachusetts, Dudley had lobbied in England for the abolition of the Connecticut and Rhode Island charters. Ashurst advised Fitz how to handle him: "the Cananite is in your land, therefore it requires and concerns you to be exact in the administration of your justice, that your enemies may have nothing to object against you. . . . be very cautious not to make any laws repugnant to the laws of England, or if any such are already made, of executing them."[31]

Dudley wrote his first letter to Fitz in July 1702 to protest that western Massachusetts was being molested by Connecticut invaders. It was a typical boundary dispute: both colonies claimed the villages of Suffield and Enfield, which were then within Massachusetts jurisdiction though today comfortably south of

[29] *Cal.S.P.Col.*, *1701*, pp. 620-21; *1704-1705*, p. 712; C.A., Foreign Correspondence, I, 92, 102, 163; Winthrop Mss., VIII, pt. 1, p. 11; M.H.S. *Coll.*, 6th ser., III, 114-15, 130-33, 192-93, 267-68.

[30] *Cal.S.P.Col.*, *1702-1703*, pp. 523-24; *1704-1705*, pp. 374, 457, 488, 711-17; M.H.S. *Coll.*, 6th ser., III, 302; Winthrop Mss., VII, 121.

[31] M.H.S. *Coll.*, 6th ser., III, 76, 119-21. For Dudley's career, see Kimball, *The Public Life of Joseph Dudley*.

the Connecticut line. Turpentine-gathering parties from Simsbury and Windsor in Connecticut fought rival Massachusetts parties for possession of the forested no man's land below Suffield. A Windsor man was knifed. A Simsbury man was brought prisoner to Suffield. Thirty barrels of Simsbury turpentine were confiscated. In retaliation, the Connecticut assembly authorized the arrest of Suffield's constable, and he was soon lodged in Hartford jail. All this happened at the height of the dreadful French and Indian massacres in the Connecticut Valley. No wonder Dudley demanded in May 1704 that Fitz immediately release the Suffield constable, with Massachusetts invaded by "the Indians on every side destroying the Queen's subjects; that my neighbours also should take the people of this Province captives, is very surprizing, and I beleive will be so accounted at home. . . ."[32]

By 1704 Dudley had something more serious than turpentine raids to complain about. Fitz's colony was shirking her responsibilities in Queen Anne's War; she was not adequately protecting the Connecticut Valley against French and Indian attack. Considering that the upper valley towns of western Massachusetts shielded Connecticut from direct assault, and that Dudley had more than he could do to guard New England's long eastern frontier in Maine and New Hampshire, it was not unreasonable for him to expect Connecticut to guard the western frontier. Empowered by the home government to call out the Connecticut militia when necessary, Dudley repeatedly asked Fitz for soldiers, 1703-1707. Sir Henry Ashurst advised Fitz against sending any—it would only put money in Dudley's pocket! Happily Fitz's attitude was more responsible. As he told the Connecticut assembly in 1703, the two colonies are "brethren, under one Crowne, one Religion, one intrest, and assuredly under one affection," and he pledged Connecticut's assistance to her exposed northern neighbors.[33] But in fact the Connecticut war machine was cumbersome in the extreme. Fitz's orders had to be relayed from New London to the committee of war in Hartford, militia-

[32] M.H.S. *Coll.*, 6th ser., III, 101-103, 106-107, 142-44, 155-56, 198-99; *Conn. Rec.*, IV, 443, 491.
[33] M.H.S. *Coll.*, 6th ser., III, 143, 158; V, 132.

men were rounded up with great difficulty, officers pleaded to be excused from service, and by the time the troops marched fifty miles or more north to Hatfield or Deerfield, the enemy had come and gone.

In August 1703 Connecticut laboriously sent fifty-three dragoons to Deerfield on a false alarm. A second alarm sounded in February 1704. "I am takeing care," Fitz wrote Dudley on February 28, "for a supply of men for the garison of Deerfeild and Brookfeild." It was too late. Before dawn on the very next day the enemy slipped into Deerfield, massacred fifty of the inhabitants and vanished with one hundred captives. Fitz called an emergency session of the General Assembly and dispatched reinforcements to the upper valley. Nonetheless, the enemy soon struck again at Northampton, and the western Massachusetts people called desperately for more Connecticut troops. By June 1704 Connecticut had 700 militia in service, and the strain was telling on everyone. The militiamen hated to serve away from home, their officers refused to accept Massachusetts commissions from Dudley, the magistrates told Fitz that the war cost was insupportable, and Dudley (with 1,800 Massachusetts men in the field) insisted that Connecticut was still not doing her fair share. The Massachusetts Governor sent three agents to New London in December 1704 with the message that Connecticut must bear one-third of the total war cost—"a motion soe very unreasonable," Fitz wrote Dudley, "that I think it not fit to enter upon any long debate with your Commissioners upon that head." Fitz demanded to know how Dudley could be so grossly unjust as to tell the Queen that Connecticut refused to give Massachusetts any assistance. "Sir," Dudley snapped, "I must acquaint you that I have and shall alwayes do your Province justice in informing her Majesty what you do, as well as what in my opinion you ought to do."[34]

Joseph Dudley not only informed the Queen about Connecticut's delinquency, he also teamed with Palmes and Hallam to poison Fitz's personal reputation. The Palmes-Hallam tech-

[34] *Ibid.*, 6th ser., III, 175-76, 278-81. Fitz's 1703-1704 war correspondence with Dudley, the Hartford committee of war, and the western Massachusetts field commanders is very extensive (pp. 137-281).

nique has already been observed: to hurl every possible charge against Fitz on the theory that some mud is bound to stick. In December 1703, Hallam told the Board of Trade that Connecticut had stolen the planting grounds of the Mohegan Indians near New London. To prevent the persecuted Mohegans from defecting to the French, Hallam wanted the board to commission "the Governor of the Massachusets Bay and some other Discreet and Impartial persons" to give them justice. In vain Ashurst protested that Hallam's new charge was as groundless as his old. On July 19, 1704, the Queen issued a commission to twelve men, headed by Dudley and including Palmes, to hear and determine the Mohegan complaint.[35] The truth of the Mohegan case is now obscure, though it is abundantly clear that all parties concerned were behaving shabbily. The Connecticut government claimed to have secured title to the Mohegan land in 1640, but the land was not actually appropriated by the colony until Fitz became governor. Fitz and Saltonstall each obtained a 200-acre Mohegan farm in 1699. On the other hand, the Mohegans (some fifty in number) made no complaints and served loyally as Connecticut warriors against the French until Hallam got hold of their drunken sachem, Owaneco. The Board of Trade deliberately inflamed the situation by letting plaintiff Hallam nominate the commissioners to try the case. When Dudley received his Mohegan commission from England in December 1704, he innocently assured Fitz, "I am a perfect stranger to that affayre," but the Connecticut leaders believed that Owaneco had deeded him several thousand acres of the disputed land.[36]

Dudley used his commission to derange Connecticut's social and political fabric as far as he could. He came to Stonington, Connecticut, in August 1705 and, having refused Fitz's invitation to visit New London, set up court with Palmes and seven other commissioners. Connecticut sent six representatives to

[35] *Cal.S.P.Col.*, *1702-1703*, pp. 856-57; *1704-1705*, pp. 4, 72-73, 82; C.A., Foreign Correspondence, I, 105-107. For a full account of the Mohegan case, see Smith, *Appeals to the Privy Council from the American Plantations*, pp. 422-42.

[36] M.H.S. *Coll.*, 6th ser., III, 139, 152, 214-15, 277, 304-305, 353; *Conn. Rec.*, IV, 379-80, 469-70; Winthrop Collection, II, 134-35.

attend the trial. As soon as they saw that the commission intended not merely to investigate but to determine the case, they walked out, forbidding Connecticut people to answer the court. Dudley's commission summarily confirmed the Mohegan complaint, ordered Connecticut to restore the Indians to their planting grounds, and levied a staggering bill of costs against the colony—£573. Fitz told Ashurst that Dudley was dispossessing scores of long established Connecticut landowners, many miles beyond the Mohegan claims. And when Fitz found that his own Mohegan farm was gone, he sent the following message to Governor Dudley: "This is my privet letter to you without any relation to Government. . . . if you can finde in yor heart to raise a prejudice against soe just a title . . . I will follow it as fast as I can. It may be as easy to frame scruples against yor mannor at Roxbury or any ones elce which put into the handes of Bawling Lawyeares may make a great Noyes tho Noething in it."[37]

Fitz had more to worry about than a 200-acre farm. The repercussions of Dudley's Mohegan commission rocked his hold on the Connecticut government. He had to persuade the General Assembly to appeal to the Queen against Dudley's verdict, at a time when the colony was desperately short of money, sick of answering the Palmes-Hallam attacks, and downcast by Dudley's influence with the Board of Trade. The assembly met in October 1705. James Fitch was absent, but the two deputies from Hartford argued that Fitz had mismanaged Connecticut's case at Stonington, and that no money should be raised for an appeal. In answer, Fitz made a speech rallying the assembly against surrendering to Dudley, Palmes, and Hallam. Connecticut is plagued, he said, not only by external enemies trying to destroy her constitution, but by traitors "among ourselves who have been bred up under the advantages of the Government, whose intrest has been advanced and their persons betrusted with considerable posts in the Government. . . . Such persons are fit to be observed by the Government as snakes in the grass and vipers that gnaw out the bowells of their mother.

[37] *Cal.S.P.Col.*, *1704-1705*, pp. 605-608, 659-60; Winthrop Collection, II, 133, 136; M.H.S. *Coll.*, 6th ser., III, 301-10, 329; Winthrop Mss., VIII, pt. I, p. 61; XII, 33.

But that wee may not omit our duty to save the libertyes of the country, I desire that you will all joyne with me to preserve . . . by all fitting meanes the priviliges [her Majesty] is pleased to continue to us. Let us doe this and wee shall still be happy, and posterity will rejoice in our memory." Fitz won his point. The assembly voted to supply Sir Henry Ashurst with the information necessary to contest Dudley's Mohegan decision in England.[38]

Sir Henry had much difficulty in appealing the Mohegan case. Connecticut's instructions were inadequate and one box of her Mohegan documents was captured by the French, the Board of Trade fully backed Dudley, and Palmes was on hand to justify the commissioners' proceedings. The Privy Council consented in February 1706 to hear the appeal but required the unwilling Connecticut agent to give bond for £400. The hearing took place on May 21. The council refused to admit any Connecticut evidence against the Mohegans which had not been previously introduced at Dudley's Stonington court, and Ashurst had no proof that the Dudley commissioners were personally interested in the Mohegan lands. His case boiled down to a general charge that Dudley's doings at Stonington were a step in a long-range conspiracy against Connecticut's charter privileges. What Ashurst lacked in evidence, however, he made up in money and connections. For £250 he hired three excellent lawyers, "the best councill in England." The Dukes of Devonshire and Somerset showed up at the hearing, "two of the greatest dukes in England that attended your committee at my request, who never used to appear there." The result was an unexpected victory. On June 10, 1706, the Privy Council reversed Dudley's £573 sentence of costs against Connecticut and ordered the case to be tried again by a commission of review. "I must say this," wrote Fitz's cousin Samuel Reade after witnessing the council hearing, "that Sir Henry Ashurst hath maniged your concernes with greate integrity and diligence."[39]

[38] M.H.S. *Coll.*, 6th ser., III, 290, 311; *Conn. Rec.*, IV, 519-21. The copy in the Winthrop Papers of Fitz's assembly speech is undated. Possibly he delivered it to the May 1705 session, but more likely in October.

[39] *Cal.S.P.Col., 1706-1708*, pp. 23, 26, 56, 150; C.A., Foreign Correspondence, II, 100, 137; Winthrop Mss., VIIb, p. 55; M.H.S. *Coll.*, 6th ser., III, 324-28; V, 139.

"I am able," Fitz announced to the October assembly, "to give you an extraordinary instance of her Majestyes justice in yor behalf, her grace and favour to protect you against your enemyes." If Ashurst's bill of £270 seemed high, Fitz reminded the assembly of Dudley's bill of £573, "that monstrous Bill which that jumbling meeting at Stonington have drawne up against you." The assembly expressed suitable gratitude to Sir Henry and paid his bill. The Mohegan controversy was not yet ended. The Privy Council had merely substituted a new royal commission of review for Dudley's commission. The Board of Trade nominated Lord Cornbury and his New York council as the new commissioners, and Ashurst worked to block their appointment. "I have been five months laboring," he told the Connecticut government in April 1707, "to stop a new Commition to my Lord Cornbury, and presented severall memorials and petitions. Tho the Commition hath passed the Privey Seale, it is at present stop'd."[40] Thanks to Ashurst, Cornbury never did receive his commission, and Fitz's government retained possession of the disputed lands. Many years later the Mohegan controversy was revived, and the case was not terminated until 1773, when at last the Privy Council ruled in favor of Connecticut and against the Indians.

After Dudley's visit to Stonington, the Connecticut government gave him only a bare minimum of military assistance against the French and Indians. Fitz was furious on discovering in June 1706 that Dudley had thirty Mohegan volunteers in service on the eastern front. Three years before, Fitz had been much readier than his Hartford committee of war to guard western Massachusetts; now, he was holding the committee back. On August 15, 1706, he told Dudley that unless the Mohegans were immediately sent home, he was withdrawing all Connecticut troops from western Massachusetts. Dudley did not deign to answer, and in October was still keeping the Connecticut Indians in his service. But the Massachusetts Governor belatedly realized the stupidity of his tactics when he tried in 1707 to organize an intercolonial offensive against the French. His plan

---

[40] *Ibid.*, 6th ser., III, 349-54, 376-79, 383-85; *Conn. Rec.*, v, 8; Winthrop Mss., VIII, pt. 1, p. 60; *Cal.S.P.Col.*, *1706-1708*, pp. 164, 170, 174, 401.

was to capture Port Royal, Nova Scotia, with an army of 1,000 men from Massachusetts, Rhode Island, and Connecticut. Rhode Island agreed to join Dudley, but a special April session of the Connecticut assembly voted the project down. "Everybody wishes well to the designe," Fitz wrote unctuously to Dudley, "& I wish I could any way contribute to it." The Port Royal attack was a fiasco. The army retreated to Casco Bay and sent a delegation home to Boston to explain its behavior. Fitz learned from his nephew John how the Boston women greeted their returning heroes: "Is yor piss-pot charg'd neighbor? So-ho, souse the cowards. Salute Port-Royal." Almost humbly, Dudley asked Fitz to help him retrieve the disaster by sending several hundred Connecticut reinforcements. Fitz declined without even bothering to summon another special assembly. "I am very sensible we are unhapy not to share in the honor of that great enterprize," he wrote on August 14, 1707, "but wee can't help it."[41] Assuredly Governor Winthrop did little to help win Queen Anne's War. Yet perhaps he did as much as his Massachusetts and New York neighbors—or the Queen's government, for that matter—deserved.

Fitz's ceaseless quarrels with fellow colonists and fellow governors help explain the turbulence of his administration, but the root cause of trouble was the Board of Trade's active hostility toward Connecticut. While Fitz was trying to strengthen his colony inside and out, the Board of Trade was trying to destroy the chartered privileges of all private colonies. From the inception of the board in 1696, its members worked for an English Empire more profitable to the home state, more umbilical in sentiment, more uniform in law and custom, and more vigorous against the French. Perhaps they sensed that the home government, despite its web of paper orders and its professional colonial bureaucracy, was failing to shape the character and harness the energy of the expanding American plantations. The board members did not want the absolutism of James II, but they did want all colonies directly supervised by the crown. Rather than prose-

[41] M.H.S. *Coll.*, 6th ser., III, 332-33, 337-42, 367-76, 387-95; *Conn. Rec.*, v, 17-18; *Cal.S.P.Col.*, *1706-1708*, pp. 239-40.

cute charter privileges in the courts, the technique unpleasantly associated with Charles II and James II in the 1680's, the board urged colonial proprietors to surrender their powers voluntarily. The New Jersey proprietors did surrender in 1702, and William Penn offered to sell his rights of government. Obviously the two corporate colonies, Connecticut and Rhode Island, were less likely to volunteer. The board encouraged malcontents like Palmes and Hallam to appeal to the crown, and it sponsored Cornbury's and Dudley's accusations.

Between 1701 and 1706 the Board of Trade tried three times to amend or annul the Connecticut charter. Twice it pressed Parliament to strip the private colonies of their governmental rights, and once it pressed the Queen to appoint governors for Connecticut and Rhode Island. All three attempts failed. After 1706 the board abruptly stopped harassing Connecticut and her sister private colonies. The period of Fitz's governorship was decisive. Of all the private colonies, Connecticut was probably considered the least significant, but thanks to the peculiar venom of her enemies and the stoutness of Sir Henry Ashurst's defense, her case was the key to the survival of charter government in English America.

In 1701 the Board of Trade first tried to pass a bill through Parliament reuniting all private colony governments to the crown. The bill was prepared quickly and secretly, and caught its intended victims by surprise. The timing was shrewd. William Penn, the one remaining vigorous lord proprietor, was in America, the New Jersey proprietors were ready to surrender, the Carolina proprietors were comatose, and Rhode Island was poorly represented. Sir Henry Ashurst was on hand for Connecticut, but he reported to Fitz that when he tried in February and March 1701 to do business with the board, "I was told they were busy & could not attend it. I thought then there was something a brewing by your old friends Mr D: & Mr Rand." Randolph was indeed thick in the board's scheme, arraying an encyclopedic catalogue of the crimes perpetrated by the private colonies. His rogue's gallery included Governor Winthrop, accused of operating a smuggler's den on Fisher's Island. Otherwise, Randolph had little information on Connecticut, less than on any other colony. The board in 1701 reckoned Rhode Island, New Jersey, and Carolina to be the most mismanaged plantations. Connecticut also deserved to lose her charter because she had refused the Palmes-Hallam appeals, and because her Governor "did publickly declare, that no appeals should be allowed from thence to his Majesty in Council."[42]

On April 24, 1701, the Board of Trade's bill was offered to the House of Lords, probably because the upper house had so eagerly investigated Randolph's charges against the private colonies in 1697. Spokesmen for the charter colonies were caught off guard. When they did attack the bill, there was little teamwork. William Penn, Jr., immediately petitioned the Lords to be heard against the bill, but it was May 3 before Ashurst and the Carolina and Maryland proprietors likewise petitioned for hearings. Each petitioner wanted his colony exempted from the bill, Ashurst claiming that Connecticut's "case is different from his Majesties other Plantations." Hearings on the bill were held at the bar of the House of Lords. Ashurst's counsel challenged anyone to prove Connecticut's maladministration, whereupon Randolph, as counsel for the bill, nonplussed him by producing witnesses who swore that the colony protected smugglers. Despite Randolph's strong lobbying and the proprietors' feeble response, the bill was killed by the Lords at an early stage. The bill's second reading was long delayed (May 23), and it never even came to debate in a committee of the whole house, let alone to a vote. "I have been hurryed off my legs," Ashurst wrote Fitz in July, after the close of Parliament, but "by an interest I made in the Lords House it was stopped."[43] No doubt Sir Henry's connections were very helpful, but in all probability the bill killed itself. In an age of strong property rights, and of strong jealousy between Parliament and crown, it was hard to get Parliament to take away the privileges of fellow magnates and of long established corporations, in order to feed more political power to the crown.

[42] Louise P. Kellogg, *The American Colonial Charter* (Amer. Hist. Assn. *Annual Report*, 1903, Vol. I), 284-90; M.H.S. *Coll.*, 6th ser., III, 75; Stock, *Proceedings of the British Parliaments*, II, 368, 399; *Randolph*, V, 217, 233, 253, 267.
[43] *Cal.S.P.Col.*, *1701*, pp. 141-43; Stock, *Proceedings of the British Parliaments*, II, 401-18; C.A., Foreign Correspondence, II, 67-68; *Randolph*, V, 273-74; M.H.S. *Coll.*, 6th ser., III, 69, 75-77; Hall, *Edward Randolph*, pp. 202-207.

Every time that Parliament met in the next four years, Ashurst predicted to Fitz that a second bill would be introduced against the charters. The Board of Trade kept collecting fresh evidence for its case, and instructed Cornbury and Dudley to send home authentic proofs of Connecticut misbehavior. Meanwhile, Connecticut received bad publicity from Hallam's appeal against the Liveen will. In July 1703, with Penn trying to sell his charter rights, a new parliamentary bill in the air, and the Liveen appeal coming to a final hearing, Ashurst became panicky. "I thinke itt absolutely necessary you shuld come yor self to be joint Agent with mee," he wrote Fitz. "I pray Sir immediatly thinke of comeing yor self, or send some persons; yor owne & yor countrys affaires require itt to be heer in October at the sitting of the Parliament."[44]

The next year came the Board of Trade's second attack on the Connecticut charter, this time addressed to the crown rather than Parliament. Gathering together Cornbury's and Dudley's accusations that Connecticut and Rhode Island were actively obstructing the war effort, the board obtained the opinion of the Attorney General and Solicitor General that if the two colonies had defaulted as charged, their charters did not exclude the Queen from appointing a royal governor. The board proposed that Cornbury supplant Fitz in Connecticut and that Dudley take over Rhode Island.

Sir Henry Ashurst was in Oxfordshire, negotiating the sale of his country estate, when he received an order to attend a Privy Council hearing on November 30, 1704, and present his objections, if any, against a royal governor for Connecticut. Again Sir Henry was caught off guard. He had only six days to prepare his case. Thanks to the court influence of his brother-in-law Lord Paget, Ashurst got the hearing postponed till February 12, 1705. But he found the Board of Trade much better stocked with evidence against his client than in 1701. The board even had Gershom Bulkeley's 1692 manuscript treatise, *Will and Doom*. "Theres one Mr Buckly," Ashurst told Fitz, "all by Mr D's Contrivance has sent a large ffolio book, which he

[44] M.H.S. *Coll.*, 6th ser., III, 85-86, 136, 161-63, 212-13, 255, 288; V, 119; Winthrop Mss., VI, 159; C.A., Foreign Correspondence, II, 77; *Cal.S.P.Col.*, 1701, p. 353.

calls . . . Will and Doom or a History of the miseries of Connecticott under the Arbitrary power of the present Government wherein he mightily commends Sir Edmund Andrews's Government, and says all the malitious things he possibly can invent with great cunning and Art."[45] Actually, Bulkeley's book had been resurrected by Cornbury, not Dudley. But the damage was the same.

The royal court, as Robert Livingston reported to Fitz, was now thoroughly roused against Connecticut and Rhode Island. The Queen's husband, Prince George of Denmark, attended the Privy Council hearing of February 12, 1705, together with the chief officers of state. It was a most ominous moment for Connecticut. Both Livingston and Penn helped Ashurst prepare his case. Sir Henry secured the best counsel obtainable, two members of Parliament, and instructed them to ask that the colony government be given time to answer specific charges against her. There have been "more appeals and Complaints," the defense told the Council, "against this poor Countrey within this two or three years, since Mr. Dudley resolvd to take away their Charter than has been in forty years before." Reluctantly the Privy Council granted Ashurst's plea for time. Connecticut at least had a reprieve. The Board of Trade drew up (March 26, 1705) a list of thirteen charges against Rhode Island and ten against Connecticut, to be answered by the two colonies within six months.[46]

Fitz received his copy of the charges in August 1705. He thanked Ashurst for his vigilance, but protested bitterly: "We have always acted directly contrary to what We are accused of with Relation, to the harbouring of Pirates, or Deserters, or allowing any of the Acts of Trade, to be violated . . . and our readiness to assist (far beyond our Quota . . .) the neighbouring Provinces of York or Boston." He sent Ashurst copies of his correspondence with Dudley, to prove that the Massachusetts Governor had actually acknowledged Connecticut's help at the very time he was reporting home Connecticut's refusal to

[45] *Ibid.*, *1704-1705*, pp. 72-73, 311, 318, 328, 338; C.A., Foreign Correspondence, II, 88.

[46] M.H.S. *Coll.*, 6th ser., III, 285-86; C.A., Foreign Correspondence, II, 87-89; *Cal.S.P.Col.*, *1704-1705*, pp. 374, 458.

help—"the wickedness of the man," Ashurst shouted, "to complaine to the Queen & Councill, and the same day thank you!" Fitz was not bitter merely at Dudley's double-dealing. His attitude toward the Board of Trade had completely soured since 1698. Fitz did not call the Connecticut assembly till October, and never wrote to the board at all. Of course the board heard promptly enough from Cornbury and Dudley, each of whom sent a big bundle of documents, largely depositions by Hallam, Palmes, and Fitch. These documents certainly demonstrated hatred for Fitz's government, but not much else.[47]

Adding to Fitz's and Ashurst's woes, spokesmen for the Society of Friends petitioned the Queen to disallow a law entitled "Hereticks," printed in *The General Laws and Liberties of Connecticut Colonie* (1673). The law stipulated that Quakers, Ranters, and Adamites were to be imprisoned or expelled from the colony, and anyone who befriended them or read their books was fined. The Quakers were understandably distressed by this law, clearly violating the spirit of the Toleration Act. How had they discovered its existence? "Hereticks" had been reprinted as a pamphlet in Boston in 1702—pretty clearly the work of Joseph Dudley, though he hotly denied it. Ashurst feebly tried to tell the Board of Trade that the Quakers had initially been so incendiary as to justify the law, and that the handful of Quakers living at present in Connecticut were undisturbed. The board was not impressed, and recommended disallowance. Another blow was struck against Connecticut autonomy. When the Privy Council decreed the repeal of the law, October 11, 1705, it intruded for the first time into the colony's legislative sanctity. The Connecticut assembly, however, refused to admit the council's intervention. In May 1706 the assembly voted that the Heresy law, "so farre as it respects Quakers, be repealed." There was still an open season on Ranters and Adamites.[48]

---

[47] M.H.S. *Coll.*, 6th ser., III, 302, 353, 379; C.A., Foreign Correspondence, II, 92-93, 101; *Cal.S.P.Col.*, *1704-1705*, pp. 651, 668-71, 711-17; *1706-1708*, pp. 33-35; *R.I. Rec.*, III, 540-49; *Conn. Rec.*, IV, 520.

[48] *Ibid.*, *1704-1705*, pp. 487, 503, 629-30, 637; *1706-1708*, p. 234; C.A., Foreign Correspondence, II, 91, 94, 96, 102; Winthrop Collection, II, 248; M.H.S. *Coll.*, 6th ser., III, 291, 381-83; *Conn. Rec.*, IV, 546.

"Now I beleeve," canny Robert Livingston wrote Fitz in 1705, assessing the Board of Trade's campaign against Connecticut, "nothing will be able to hurt you but an act of Parlament, or a fair tryall at law in Westminster Hall." The board did not try prosecuting the colony charters in the courts, but in February 1706 it did introduce a new parliamentary bill "for the better regulation of charter and proprietary governments in America." The board's chances of obtaining legislation against the private colonies perhaps looked brighter than in 1701. The new bill was more modest, "regulating" rather than repealing corporate privileges and property rights. It gave the Queen the power to appoint governors, disallow laws, and hear appeals, as in the Massachusetts charter of 1691, and otherwise left the existing charters intact and existing colony laws in force. The bill's sponsors could rely on stronger supporting evidence than in 1701, especially the Cornbury-Dudley testimony against Connecticut and Rhode Island. William Blathwayt presented the board's bill on February 23 to the House of Commons, no doubt calculating that the proprietary sentiment was less formidable here than it had been in the Lords in 1701.

In fact, the board's bill had even less chance of success in 1706 than five years before. Marlborough's campaigns against the French were all too triumphant. One proprietary colony, the Bahamas, had actually been captured by the enemy, but Parliament was considerably more indulgent and indifferent toward the colonial war effort than in the desperate days of the 1690's. Then too, the Board of Trade was losing its earlier drive and influence. It handled less than half as much paper work in 1706 as in 1701; it reported less often to Parliament; its most zealous servant, Edward Randolph, gadfly for the 1697 and 1701 parliamentary investigations into the private colonies, was dead. The board made the crowning mistake of introducing its bill late in the session and found the charter spokesmen prepared, especially Sir Henry Ashurst, himself a member of the Commons. No opportunity was given for staging embarrassing hearings on the delinquencies of the private colonies, as in 1701. Immediately after the first reading on March 2, the bill was voted down, 50-34. It was a signal defeat for the Board of

Trade. Ashurst may be pardoned for crowing to Connecticut: "they brought in a bill last sessions of Parliament to take away your charter; but I made such interest against itt with some of the leading men of the House, so that it was thrown out att the first reading. I have the vanity to say that if you had not employed me, you would have been in a sad condition to this day. . . . There is none of my quality appears before [the Board of Trade] with the name of an agent, tho I am willing to serve the Lord Christ in the meanest station." Sir Henry did not give himself the entire credit for frustrating the schemes of Dudley and the Board of Trade. "You did your buisiness as Governor to admiration," he told Fitz in 1707 and congratulated the colonists on being "blessed with such a Governour." Even better, Connecticut was blessed with the loving protection of Queen Anne. "We have so gratious a Queen," Ashurst wrote in his very last letter to Fitz, "that desires to make use of noe prerogative but for the good of the people."[49]

The failure of the 1706 bill ended the Board of Trade's sustained war against charter colonies in general and against Connecticut in particular. In 1707, four of the board members were replaced, among them William Blathwayt. The reorganized board behaved like a fact-finding rather than a policy-making body. Adopting a file clerk's technique, it circulated detailed questionnaires among all the royal and private colonies alike. Connecticut's reply (January 1709) to the first questionnaire gives a disarming picture of innocent provinciality at the time of Fitz's death. The colony population is estimated at a stationary 15,000, with 2,000 freemen. Almost all the people are farmers, with homespun cloth the only industry. They have few negro slaves or indentured servants. Their nineteen small ships carry grain and meat to Boston and New York, horses and lumber to the West Indies, and a little turpentine, tar, and pitch to Great Britain. Robert Quary, Randolph's successor as surveyor general of American customs, sent home an entirely different picture. He found Connecticut very populous (about

[49] M.H.S. *Coll.*, 6th ser., III, 287, 326-27, 377-80; *Cal.S.P.Col.*, *1704-1705*, p. 734; *1706-1708*, pp. 3-6, 47, 55; Stock, *Proceedings of the British Parliaments*, III, 113-14, 118; Kellogg, *The American Colonial Charter*, pp. 303-304.

40,000 inhabitants) and very turbulent. When Governor Winthrop asked him not to pry too closely into Connecticut's method of customs collecting, the suspicious Quary found that the seaports were busily smuggling Virginia tobacco.[50] Both reports on Connecticut were simply pigeonholed. The home government did continue sporadically to investigate and regulate the colony's chartered privileges. But down to 1763, Fitz's successors never had to meet any challenge comparable to the Board of Trade's systematic campaign of 1696-1706.

◆ℛ Fitz Winthrop had not turned out to be the peacemaker his fellow colonists were craving in 1698; on the contrary, his governorship was the stormiest in Connecticut's colonial history. Yet Fitz did leave his solid impress on the colony, whereas the net effect made by the pack of enemies hunting him relentlessly from 1701 to 1706 was astoundingly slight. James Fitch made Winthrop withdraw his claims to Quinebaug, without securing the tract for himself. Nicholas Hallam lost both of his appeals to the home government, the Liveen case and the Mohegan case. Edward Palmes won his appeal for administration of the Winthrop estate, but lost his £2,500 damage suit. Joseph Dudley had the temporary satisfaction of disrupting Connecticut with his Mohegan commission, but gained nothing except Connecticut's refusal to help him attack Port Royal. The Board of Trade forced the colony to admit appeals to the home government and secured the repeal of the obsolete law persecuting Quakers, but it completely failed to reach its main objective, the destruction of Connecticut's chartered autonomy.

Fitz was gradually worn down by the incessant struggle. He was no more successful than his father at retiring from the colony governorship. In 1703, 1705, and 1706 he tried to step down, but each time the assembly overruled him, pleading that God intended him to continue "the same watchfull eye for our welfare," blasting the intrigues of Connecticut's restless adversaries. Fitz was now an elderly man, nearly seventy years old, and in chronic ill health. When he got home to New London

[50] Stock, *Proceedings of the British Parliaments*, III, 140; C.A., Foreign Correspondence, I, 118, 120, 126; *Cal.S.P.Col., 1706-1708*, pp. 427-31, 636.

from the May 1707 assembly, he was wretched with ague.
"Deare Brother," he wrote Wait, "I am now very sick, & weary
of my life such as it is. I am not able to write what is done, or
not done, at Hartford. I never found them in a worse temper."[51]
Actually, by 1707 most of Fitz's perennial troubles were falling
away. The Board of Trade had stopped trying to remove him
from office, Nicholas Hallam had given up appealing to England, and Lord Cornbury was soon to be recalled in disgrace
from New York. Even Joseph Dudley was changing from foe
to friend. Dudley was shaken by Ashurst's successful appeal
against his Mohegan decision, and he feared that Sir Henry
might be able to persuade the reorganized Board of Trade to
recall him from Massachusetts. He found an unexpected opportunity to make peace with Ashurst's New England allies, Fitz
and Wait Winthrop. In late August 1707, Wait told Fitz that
an extraordinary thing had happened—his son John was in love
with Governor Dudley's daughter Anne.

Fitz was less than enthusiastic about his nephew's marriage
into the Dudley family, but he approved the match. "Tis the
family now most in fashion," he wrote Wait. Since he intended
to bequeath most of his estate to young John (having no sons
himself), he decided to come up to Boston and discuss his plans
personally with Dudley. Nephew John was very excited at the
prospect of having two governors attend his wedding, especially
since Uncle Fitz had missed hearing his Latin speech at Harvard
commencement several years before. There was to be a double
wedding, for Wait Winthrop, a widower for seventeen years,
announced to Fitz that he was himself getting remarried, to
the widow Katherine Brattle. Feeling faint and feverish, Fitz
set out for Boston in late September 1707.

Fitz had not visited Boston since his landing from England,
almost ten years before. On October 1, his new friend Dudley
gave a party in his honor. On November 13, he celebrated his
brother's wedding. Dudley asked him to stay for his nephew's
wedding also. "I am not worthy of him," the Massachusetts
Governor wrote unctuously, "nor of being established in your

[51] M.H.S. *Coll.*, 6th ser., III, 130, 323, 385; Winthrop Mss., VIII, pt. 1, pp.
46, 48.

freindship, but I will deserve it by all the methods in my power."
However, before the second wedding took place, Fitz had become violently sick again. After a ten-day illness, he died on
November 27. His funeral was very elaborate, costing Wait
the enormous sum of £611. The procession was escorted by the
Boston militia; Governor Dudley and other dignitaries were
the bearers. "Father, Son, and Grandson ly together in one
Tomb in the old burying place," Sewall recorded in his *Diary*.
"Was a vast concurse of People." Sewall particularly liked the
funeral sermon preached by Dudley's implacable enemy, Cotton
Mather. Indeed, Mather himself admitted that the sermon was
worth publishing, and Sir Henry Ashurst did print it in London
at his own expense. In a dedicatory epistle to Lady Russell,
Ashurst explained that Fitz had served Connecticut "with great
reputation to himself, and honour to his country, and loyalty to
our most gracious Queen . . . at a time when a design was formed
by a neighbour Governour, with great art and cunning, to destroy their most valuable priviledges. . . ."[52] Sir Henry was one
man who could not be lightly reconciled to the Canaanite.

The best memorial to Governor Fitz Winthrop was neither
the state funeral in Boston, nor the eulogies of Mather and
Ashurst, but the conduct of his people in Connecticut. When
Deputy-Governor Treat sorrowfully convened a special session
of the assembly on December 17, 1707, to choose Fitz's successor, the majority voted for the dead man's dearest friend and
chief advisor, Gurdon Saltonstall—an unusual choice, since he
was minister of New London church and held no public office.
Saltonstall had, however, done much of Fitz's administrative
work. Now he opened a long and popular administration as
governor in his own right. Among the first fruits of his governorship was the famous Saybrook Platform in 1708, which organized the Connecticut churches into a Presbyterian system so as
to tighten discipline and uniformity. Saltonstall's Saybrook Platform completed the conservative reform program launched by
Fitz Winthrop. It anchored Connecticut's rather undeserved

[52] M.H.S. *Coll.*, 4th ser., VIII, 405-406; 5th ser., VI, 195, 199, 204-205; 6th
ser., III, 396-402, 408-13; V, 191-92.

eighteenth-century reputation as the land of steady habits.[53]

The election of Gurdon Saltonstall emphasized the point to Fitz's whole career—the discovery of his true native identity. In every generation of the Winthrop dynasty there had been a recurrent pattern of youthful protest dissolving into middle-aged conformity. John Winthrop began by challenging Stuart England and ended by protecting Puritan Massachusetts. John Winthrop, Jr., chafed at the limitations of a wilderness environment, yet settled down in frontier Connecticut. Fitz Winthrop went through the same experience. He grew up baffled by the loss of his grandfather's Puritan convictions, and impatient with his provincial life. He looked beyond America to the English aristocracy and London fashions and entered public life as the King's servant, not his fellow colonists'. But the experience as councilor in the Dominion of New England and as London agent for Connecticut shook his faith in this role of Englishman. The pressures of 1698-1707, in particular, forced him to stand against the home government, and to uphold New England's ancient chartered liberties. He always honored his family and loved his Fisher's Island farm, and late in life he developed a more positive, comprehensive pride in the values of the little society he lived in. Fitz did not recover his grandfather's Puritan identity, but found his own. If he began an ersatz Cavalier, he ended a genuine Yankee.

[53] *Conn. Rec.*, v, 38-39, 51-52, 87. For a slightly exaggerated picture of Connecticut's stagnant steadiness in the early eighteenth century, see Oscar Zeichner, *Connecticut's Years of Controversy, 1750-1776* (Chapel Hill, 1949); chapter I.

ABBREVIATIONS

A.A.S. *Proc.*	American Antiquarian Society *Proceedings.*
A.H.R.	*American Historical Review.*
C.A.	Connecticut Archives, Connecticut State Library.
Cal.S.P.Col.	Great Britain, *Calendar of State Papers, Colonial Series, America and West Indies.*
Cal.S.P.Dom.	Great Britain, *Calendar of State Papers, Domestic Series.*
C.H.S. *Coll.*	Connecticut Historical Society *Collections.*
Conn. Rec.	*Public Records of the Colony of Connecticut,* ed. J. Hammond Trumbull. 10 vols. Hartford, 1850-1877.
C.S.M. *Publ.*	Colonial Society of Massachusetts *Publications.*
E.H.R.	*English Historical Review.*
Journal	John Winthrop, *The History of New England from 1630 to 1649,* ed. James Savage. 2 vols. Boston, 1853.
M.A.	Massachusetts Archives, Boston State House.
Mass.Rec.	*Records of the Governor and Company of the Massachusetts Bay in New England, 1628-1686,* ed. Nathaniel B. Shurtleff. 5 vols. in 6. Boston, 1853-1854.
M.H.S. *Coll.*	Massachusetts Historical Society *Collections.*
M.H.S. *Proc.*	Massachusetts Historical Society *Proceedings.*
N.E.Q.	*New England Quarterly.*
N.Y.Col. Doc.	*Documents Relative to the Colonial History of the State of New York,* ed. E. B. O'Callaghan. 14 vols. Albany, 1856-1883.
N.Y.H.S. *Coll.*	New-York Historical Society *Collections.*
Randolph	*Edward Randolph,* ed. Robert N. Toppan & Thomas S. Goodrick. 7 vols. The Prince Society. Boston, 1898-1909.
R.I.H.S. *Coll.*	Rhode Island Historical Society *Collections.*
R.I.Rec.	*Records of the Colony of Rhode Island,* ed. J. R. Bartlett. 10 vols. Providence, 1856-1865.
Winthrop Collection	R. C. Winthrop Collection, Connecticut State Library.
Winthrop Mss.	Winthrop Papers, Massachusetts Historical Society Library.
Winthrop Papers	*Winthrop Papers, 1498-1649,* ed. Allyn B. Forbes. 5 vols. Boston, 1929-1947.
W.M.Q.	*The William and Mary Quarterly.*

At the head of the central staircase in the Massachusetts Historical Society of Boston stands a large and imposing double case crammed full of volumes of Winthrop Papers. This celebrated collection, partly published and partly unpublished, is the backbone of the present study. All four members of the seventeenth-century dynasty carefully collected their papers for posterity. John Winthrop kept his *Journal* and numerous shorter manuscript treatises; his son kept scientific notebooks; his grandsons kept deeds of real estate; all of them kept files of correspondence, not merely incoming letters but copies or drafts of outgoing letters. Unfortunately for the historian, they kept few business records—hence the difficulty in reconstructing John, Sr.'s farming at Ten Hills, John, Jr.'s industrial and commercial speculations, Fitz's stock raising on Fisher's Island, or Wait's career as a Boston merchant. Otherwise, the Winthrop Papers probably constitute the largest, most variegated and most interesting series of private papers in pre-revolutionary America.

During the nineteenth century the Winthrops' descendants gave the great bulk of these manuscripts to the Massachusetts Historical Society. Generations of scholars have mined the elder Winthrop's papers, but the later seventeenth-century material has been largely ignored and the collection as a whole never systematically surveyed. In piecemeal fashion, the Society printed many of the choicest documents in nine volumes of its *Collections* and additional scattered selections in its *Proceedings*. More recently, the Society launched an excellent complete edition (*Winthrop Papers, 1498-1649* [5 vols. Boston, 1929-1947]), so that all the elder Winthrop's papers are now in print. But there is much unpublished material of great value, particularly among the writings of John Winthrop, Jr. (Winthrop Mss., v), shedding light on his charter negotiations and his Connecticut governorship. Surprisingly, a larger percentage of Fitz's and Wait's letters (Winthrop Mss., vi-viii) have been printed. The copious papers of Wait's eccentric son John Winthrop, IV (Winthrop Mss., ix), of marginal interest for the present study, remain unexploited. In the eleven volumes of incoming correspondence, alphabetically arranged by author (Winthrop Mss., x-xx), there are thousands of letters to the second- and third-generation Winthrops, mostly unpublished, among which the following correspondents are particularly enlightening: John Allyn, Sir Edmund Andros, Sir Henry Ashurst, Gershom Bulkeley, John Clarke, James Fitch, John Harwood, Edward Hutchinson, Richard Nicolls, Edward Palmes, John Richards, Amos Richardson, Richard Wharton, and Samuel Willys. Finally, a small section of

Winthrop manuscripts has been detached from the main collection and deposited in the Connecticut State Library at Hartford. This Robert C. Winthrop Collection contains documents of value for post-1689 Connecticut history.

Aside from the Winthrop Papers, this study rests upon a general canvass of seventeenth- and early eighteenth-century New England politics and English colonial policy. The primary sources are mostly familiar to students of the period, and are cited in the footnotes. For the years 1630-1689, the chief sources have long been in print: the assembly records, town records, and documentary collections of Massachusetts, Connecticut, Rhode Island, and New York; the calendars and collections of English colonial documents; the pamphlets, correspondence and diaries of persons connected with the Winthrops. For the years 1689-1717 the documentation is much bulkier, and many of the chief sources are still in manuscript. In the Connecticut Archives (Connecticut State Library), there is a great deal of material in the Foreign Correspondence, Colonial Boundaries, and Miscellaneous Series on Fitz Winthrop's agency to England and his Connecticut governorship. Likewise, for Wait Winthrop's post-1689 career one must read the unpublished Massachusetts General Court and Council Records, and the documents on Foreign Relations, in the Massachusetts Archives (Boston State House).

The student of early New England is extraordinarily fortunate in being able to call upon a long and distinguished local tradition of historical scholarship, from Thomas Hutchinson through John G. Palfrey to Samuel Eliot Morison. Naturally some aspects of the subject have attracted more attention than others. The number of good books on the founding of the Puritan colonies remains out of all proportion to the number of good books on New England at the close of the seventeenth century, and preoccupation with the central colony of Massachusetts has resulted in the almost total neglect of Connecticut and Rhode Island, especially in the late seventeenth and early eighteenth centuries. Nevertheless, many secondary works, cited in the footnotes, have helped to shape the argument of this book, and it is a pleasure to acknowledge a particular indebtedness to four of them: Charles M. Andrews' *Colonial Period of American History*, still the best framework for the study of the seventeenth-century colonies and colonial administration; Edmund S. Morgan's *The Puritan Dilemma*, a model portrait of John Winthrop; Perry Miller's *The New England Mind: From Colony to Province* and Bernard Bailyn's *New England Merchants in the Seventeenth Century* for their parallel and penetrating analyses of late seventeenth-century colonial society in flux.

Bibliographical Note

In transcribing seventeenth century quotations, abbreviations have been expanded, and *v* substituted for *u* and *j* for *i* and vice versa, wherever appropriate. Otherwise the original spelling is preserved. The illustrative sketches are based (rather freely) on seventeenth century portraits of the four Winthrops. Much of the material for chapters 5-8 has been drawn from two articles which I published in 1956: "John Winthrop, Jr., and the Narragansett Country," *William and Mary Quarterly*, 3rd ser., XIII, 68-86, and "John Winthrop, Jr., Connecticut Expansionist," *New England Quarterly*, XXIX, 3-26. Permission for the use of these articles has been granted by the Institute of Early American History and Culture, Williamsburg, Virginia, and by the *New England Quarterly*.

Index

Index

Index

Index

Index

Index

York, 155-56, 162, 165-66, 186, 209-10; and the royal commission, 157-58, 160; and the Winthrops, 153, 164, 167-68, 174, 205
Nipmuck Country, 249n
Northampton, Mass., 339
Northumberland, Earl of, *see* Percy, Algernon
Norwalk, Conn., 82, 105
Norwich, Conn., 330
Nova Scotia, 263. *See also* Acadia
Nurse, Rebecca, 266

Oates, Titus, 216
Oldenburg, Henry, 169-71
Osborne, Thomas, Earl of Danby, 213
Owaneco, Mohegan sachem, 340
Oxenstierna, Count Axel, 71
Oyster Bay, L.I., 122

Page, Nicholas, 260
Paget, Lord William, 347
Paine, John, 95
Paine, William, 86-87, 93-95
Palfrey, John G., 217
Palmer, John, 246, 254
Palmes, Edward, 180, 202-03, 208, 222, 287; advocate of the Dominion of New England, 235, 243, 249; agitates against restoration of the Connecticut charter, 286, 289, 296-97, 302, 316-17; appeals to England against Fitz Winthrop, 331-32, 334, 337, 340, 349; feud with Winthrop, 295, 321, 328, 330-32, 335, 352
Palmes, Lucy, wife of Edward, 202-03, 334
Parliament, attack on colonial charters: bill of 1701, 277, 345-46; bill of 1706, 350-51. *See also* Convention Parliament; Long Parliament; Navigation Acts
Pawcatuck River, 108-09, 141, 147, 326
Pawtuxet, R.I., 21
Pejepscot, Me., 245
Pemaquid, Me., 238
Penn, William, 311-12, 345, 347-48
Penn, William, Jr., 346
Pennington, Isaac, 47
Pennsylvania, 238, 307, 311
Penny, Captain, 113-14
The People's Right to Election Argued by Gershom Bulkeley, 287, 289n

Pequot, *see* New London, Conn.
Pequot Indians, 69, 72, 206, 208; and the Winthrops, 74-75, 321
Percy, Algernon, Earl of Northumberland, 47
Peter, Hugh, agent for Massachusetts, 39, 70; career in Puritan England, 71, 74, 91, 98, 112; and the Winthrops, 54, 66-68, 195; execution, 126
Peter, Thomas, 92
Phips, Constantine, 277
Phips, Lady, 267
Phips, Sir William, 259, 270, 304; attacks Quebec in 1690, 262, 292-93; conduct as governor of Massachusetts, 263-68, 297; death, 269, 308
Pierson, Abraham, 153, 316
Pilgrims, *see* Plymouth colony
piracy in Connecticut, 313, 326-27; in Massachusetts, 274; in Rhode Island, 313, 326. *See also* smuggling
"A Plaine Short Discourse" by James Fitch, 295
Plainfield, Conn., 329-30
Plymouth colony, 11, 42, 50, 183, 290; and the English government, 27, 103, 119, 124; joined to the Dominion of New England, 238-39; joined to Massachusetts in 1691, 263, 270
political philosophy of Fitz Winthrop, 316-17; of John Winthrop, 23-25; of John Winthrop, Jr., 106; of Wait Winthrop, 270-71, 276
Popish Plot, 216
Popple, William, 314, 323
Port Royal, Acadia, 64, 103, 262, 282, 344, 352
Porter, James, 296
Portsmouth, R.I., 46
Povey, Thomas, 278
Presbyterianism in Massachusetts, 50-52
Prince, Thomas, 124
Providence Island, 38
Providence, R.I., 18, 46, 137
Prudence Island, 18
Prynne, William, 128
Purchas, Samuel, 9
Puritanism in 1630, 9; in 1640, 36; in 1644, 46-47; developing conflict between English and American Puritans, 29, 40, 50-51, 54-55, 68, 102; final bankruptcy in England, 112-13,

Index

Index

Index